TRANSFORMING HIGHER EDUCATION

Views from Leaders Around the World

Edited by
Madeleine F. Green

D0081739

AMERICAN COUNCIL ON EDUCATION ★
ORYX PRESS ★
Series on Higher Education
1997

The rare Arabian oryx is believed to have inspired the myth of the unicorn. This desert antelope became virtually extinct in the early 1960s. At that time several groups of international conservationists arranged to have 9 animals sent to the Phoenix Zoo to be the nucleus of a captive breeding herd. Today the oryx population is over 1,000 and over 500 have been returned to the Middle East.

© 1997 by the American Council on Education and The Oryx Press
Published by The Oryx Press
4041 North Central at Indian School Road
Phoenix, Arizona 85012-3397

Published simultaneously in Canada
Printed and bound in the United States of America

∞ The paper used in this publication meets the minimum requirements of the American National Standard for Information Sciences—Permanence of Paper for Printed Library Materials, ANSI Z39.48-1984.

Library of Congress Cataloging-in-Publication Data

Transforming higher education : views from leaders around the world / edited by Madeleine F. Green.
    p. cm. — (American Council on Education/Oryx Press series on higher education)
    Includes bibliographical references and index.
    ISBN 0-89774-891-3 (cloth : alk. paper)
    1. Education, Higher—Aims and objectives—Cross-cultural studies. 2. Universities and colleges—Administration—Cross-cultural studies. 3. Educational change—Cross-cultural studies. I. Green, Madeleine F. II. Series.
LB2322.2.T73 1997
378—dc21
                                          96-51510
                                            CIP

CONTENTS

PREFACE

One of the ironies of higher education today is that although faculty members are a highly internationalized group, policy makers and institutional administrators tend to be focused on their local and national circumstances. When the American Council on Education sponsors meetings of U.S. college and university presidents and their counterparts from other countries, it is quickly apparent that most of those presidents, rectors, and vice-chancellors have little opportunity to think about their roles as institutional leaders in a global context. In past positions as faculty members, these same leaders were in all likelihood part of a worldwide academic network linked by international journals and conferences, and for some, electronic communications. Yet, as policy makers or institutional administrators, their range of vision seems to narrow spontaneously. Daily "fire fighting" and the continual press of business make it difficult to see beyond the current crises, let alone to view one's work as part of a worldwide enterprise.

Thus, this book is especially directed to those who are shaping the future of higher education around the world—to policy makers, institutional heads, governing boards, administrators, and faculty leaders, who we hope will use it to see their own endeavors in a wider national context and to benefit from the remarkable similarities in this global undertaking. I say this knowing that few practitioners have the time or the inclination to take the literature of higher education very seriously. For many, their disciplines are far more meaningful. In fact, higher education in most countries is not a field of study; higher education administration is something one *does* as an academic (if called) but not something one *studies*. However, if higher education is indeed a global enterprise, and if we expect our national institutions of higher education to become increasingly internationally oriented, it is important for academic leaders to see their roles and their national situations in a larger context.

Institutional leaders and policy makers around the world have much to learn from one another. In the United States, state and national education policy is rarely formulated with an eye to learning from the experiences of other countries. Yet, as the chapters in this book amply demonstrate, there are national circumstances, institutional histories, and personal perspectives that are highly relevant for educational leaders worldwide. Although many institutional leaders may have experience with universities outside their own national borders in the specific context of study-abroad programs or institutional agreements for teaching and research, they have few opportunities to understand the larger environment in which these institutions exist or their internal processes and structures. This volume provides a different lens through which to view higher education in one's own country and in other nations.

Although this book is aimed at an international audience, it is likely that a sizable proportion of our readers will be from the United States; a self-selected group of individuals who are not inclined, as are many of our fellow Americans, to dismiss the experience of other countries as irrelevant to our own. This is an attitude that no American can afford in the late twentieth century, least of all educators.

Much of the comparative literature of higher education is concerned with policy and is read by scholars, policy analysts, and those policy makers who value the study of other national models and approaches. In an attempt to reach a wider audience of educators, this volume focuses instead on the experiences of institutional leaders "on the ground," addressing both national and regional contexts. We hope that the more personal views of the authors about the current transformation of higher education—and the roles of academic leaders in guiding that change—will add a valuable dimension to the policy-oriented literature that dominates the field. It is the intersection of external forces, national policy, and life at the institutional level, where teaching, learning, and research actually happen, that forms the focus of this book. Thus, we hope that *Transforming Higher Education* will be read by both scholars as well as practitioners: policy makers, administrators, and faculty members who are curious about educational issues beyond their national borders.

In creating this volume, I suggested an outline to the authors to establish some comparability among the chapters. Nevertheless, there are significant differences among the contributions, reflecting personal styles, different ways of thinking and framing issues, and varied cultural approaches to higher education. Furthermore, many were by authors for whom English is not a first language, and for whom the thought patterns determined by their native language shaped their narrative. The differences among the chapters are as revealing as their similarities.

All the chapters in Part Three are authored or coauthored by current or former institutional heads. These contributors were asked to describe the larger forces of change in their respective nations and to reflect on their experiences as academic leaders and on the behaviors of their countries' higher education institutions in that context. The latter assignment was clearly a difficult one for many; the first-person narrative does not come easily to all. Most authors dwell resolutely on the external forces that are transforming higher education, in part, no doubt, because they perceive them as the essential factors shaping institutional direction and consider the role of the internal institutional actors to be less important. Others may have a certain delicacy about writing about themselves, to avoid appearing self-serving in an academic culture that frowns on too-conspicuous leadership. As I discuss in Chapter 2, Americans are fascinated by leadership; to analyze and reflect— within limits—on one's own leadership role is not considered unseemly, though it is in some other national cultures. Thus, the chapters have different flavors and emphases, but in each, the reader has an opportunity to peer into an institution in a different context and culture and to listen to the voices of those who have had an opportunity to make a difference.

Madeleine F. Green
Washington, D.C.

CONTRIBUTORS

Bai Tongshuo was appointed vice president of Shanghai Jiaotong University in 1986, in charge of undergraduate education. He is a graduate of the Department of Electrical Engineering of the Shanghai Jiaotong University and has taught at the university since he completed his studies.

Kenneth J. R. Edwards has served as vice-chancellor of the University of Leicester in the United Kingdom since 1987. He spent the previous 21 years at the University of Cambridge, where he taught genetics, headed the Genetics Department, and served as secretary of the College Council and as chairman of the Council of the School of Biological Sciences. In 1984, he was appointed to the post of secretary-general of the Faculties, which is one of the three principal administrative offices of the University of Cambridge.

Dr. Edwards was chairman of the Committee of Vice-Chancellors and Principals from 1993 to 1995. He is also a member of the Marshall Aid Commemoration Commission, chairman of the Governing Body of the Institute of Grassland and Environmental Research, member of the Council of the Association of Commonwealth Universities, member of the board of USS Ltd. (Universities Superannuation Scheme Ltd.), and member of the board of CRE: the Association of European Universities.

Brian De Lacy Figaji was named rector of Peninsula Technikon in South Africa in 1995. He began his career teaching mathematics at a secondary school, and in 1980 joined the Peninsula Technikon as head of the Department of Engineering. He later assumed the position of senior vice-rector responsible for student affairs, international programs, financial aid, and institutional strategic planning. He earned his undergraduate degree and a graduate diploma in engineering at the University of the Western Cape. He also holds a diploma in tertiary education (with distinction) from the University of South Africa (UNISA) and a master of education in administration, planning, and social policy from Harvard University. Mr. Figaji serves on the boards of a number of national and community organizations, and in 1995 was appointed to South Africa's National Commission on Higher Education.

Claudius Gellert has served as professor of education at the University of Reading, in the United Kingdom, since 1995. He studied sociology, psychology, and philosophy at the universities of Munich, Frankfurt, and Sussex. He earned his M.A. at Munich University and his Ph.D. at the University of Cambridge. He also obtained a Habilitation (higher doctorate) at the Humboldt University, Berlin. Dr. Gellert taught sociology and conducted research at the University of Munich, Harvard University, the European University Institute (Florence), Klagenfurt University (Austria), and Humboldt University.

Madeleine F. Green is vice president for international initiatives and director of the Center for Leadership Development, American Council on Education. Dr. Green has served on the ACE staff since 1974, as director of the ACE Fellows Program from 1978 to 1990, and as vice president since 1987. During the 1990–91 academic year, she served as interim president of Mount Vernon College in Washington, DC. She has also served as a member of the board of trustees of Wilson College, in Pennsylvania, and of Sweetbriar College, in Virginia. Dr. Green has written widely on topics related to leadership and management. Her recent publications include *Investing in Higher Education: A Handbook of Leadership Development* (1992); *The American College President: A 1993 Edition* (1993); *Minorities on Campus: A Handbook for Education* (1989); and *Leaders for a New Era: Strategies for Higher Education* (1988). She earned a B.A. degree from Harvard University and a Ph.D. from Columbia University, both in French literature.

Suzy Halimi is president of the Université de Paris III–Sorbonne Nouvelle. Prior to her appointment as president, she served for five years as vice president. She earned her license, maitrîse, and agrégation degrees at the Sorbonne in English literature, and has taught in that field at the Sorbonne for her entire career. Her field of research is the literature and civilization of nineteenth-century Britain. She served as chair of the COREX, the Committee of External Relations of the Conference of French University Presidents.

Fred M. Hayward has been a senior associate for international initiatives, American Council on Education, since 1993. A specialist on Africa with more than 25 years of experience as an educator, scholar, and senior administrator, Dr. Hayward holds a Ph.D. from Princeton University and a B.A. from the University of California. He has taught at the University of Ghana, Fourah Bay College, and the University of Wisconsin–Madison, and he has been research associate at the Institut Fondamental d'Afrique Noire in Dakar, Senegal. His higher education administrative experience includes chair of the African Studies Program and the Political Science Department, associate dean of Social Sciences, and acting dean of International Studies and Programs at the University of Wisconsin–Madison. He has written extensively on both African development and higher education. Among his publications is *Elections in Independent Africa*. He has worked on African initiatives for ACE since January 1991.

Tadao Ishikawa served as president of Keio University, a private university in Japan, from 1977 to 1993. Before becoming president, he served as vice president and dean of the law faculty at Keio, where he earned his bachelor's and doctoral degrees. He is a scholar of Asian history and the author of seven books and numerous articles on China, Sino-Japanese relations, and Japanese diplomacy. Dr. Ishikawa has been a visiting scholar at both Harvard University and the University of California at Berkeley. He also has served as chairman of the Tokyo Metropolitan Board of Education, president of the National Council of Prefectural Boards of Education, and leader of the Japanese delegation to the Japan-China Friendship Committee for the 21st Century. He was president of the Japan Association of Private Colleges and Universities, and of the Private Universities Association of Japan.

B. Dalin Jameson came to administration at the University of Western Ontario, Canada, from the Department of English, where he has taught modern British and American literature since 1975. He holds a bachelor's degree from Oberlin College, a master's degree from the University of Utah, and a Ph.D. from Bryn Mawr College. Since 1987, he has coordinated the university's academic planning activities and, more recently, served as executive assistant to the president.

Josef Jarab was elected rector of Palacky University in Olomouc, the Czech Republic, in 1989, in the aftermath of the revolutionary changes in Czechoslovakia. A graduate from Palacky University in English and Russian philology, Dr. Jarab holds a Ph.D. and C.Sc. from Charles University, Prague. He is currently professor of American literature in the Department of English and American Studies at Palacky. Dr. Jarab has published and lectured widely on American literature both in his country and abroad. Among his special fields of interest are African American culture, issues of ethnicity, cultural pluralism, modern poetry, and literary theory. He has edited and cotranslated two representative anthologies, *Masks and Faces of Black America* (1985) and *A Child on Top of a Greenhouse: Contemporary American Poetry* (1989). As a visiting scholar, Dr. Jarab has been associated with New York University, Brandeis University, the University of California at Berkeley, and Harvard University. He is the first chairman of the Czech and Slovak Association for American Studies, chair of the Czech Fulbright Commission, founding member of the Collegium for African American Research, and member of the Czech Council for UNESCO and of the International PEN Club.

D. Bruce Johnstone is professor of higher and comparative education at the State University of New York at Buffalo. He is former president of Buffalo State College and former chancellor of the State University of New York system, which includes 64 campuses, almost 400,000 students, and budget authority of more than $8 billion. He has written and lectured extensively on the economics, finance, and governance of higher education, both in the United States and from an international comparative perspective.

Daniel C. Levy is professor of education, Latin American studies, and political science at the State University of New York at Albany. He has published and lectured on five continents, and his work is highlighted by six books in print and in progress. While most of the work concentrates on political issues related to higher education, Dr. Levy also studies and writes about Mexican politics in general. He has been a consultant for a variety of international and U.S. policy agencies and for universities.

K. George Pedersen served two terms as president of the University of Western Ontario, Canada, from 1985 to 1994. Since his retirement from the University of Western Ontario, Dr. Pedersen has served as acting president of the University of Northern British Columbia and is currently president of Royal Roads University in Victoria, British Columbia. He also served as president of the University of British Columbia from 1983 to 1985. Dr. Pedersen began his teaching career in 1952. He was, successively, teacher and principal in the elementary and secondary educational system of North Vancouver, while earning baccalaureate and master's degrees at the University of British Columbia and the University of Washington. He earned a Ph.D. in education from the University of Chicago. He is an officer of the Order of Canada and the Order of Ontario and has served as chair of the Association of Universities and Colleges of Canada and the Council of Ontario Universities, vice president for Canada of the Inter-American Organization for Higher Education, and a member of the executive board of the Association of Commonwealth Universities.

Gerard A. Postiglione is associate professor in sociology of education at the University of Hong Kong and director of advanced studies in education and national development. He is the general series editor of *Hong Kong Becoming China: The Transition to 1997* (New York: M.E. Sharpe), and associate editor of the journal *Chinese Education and Society*. His most recent works are *Social Change and Educational Development: Mainland China, Taiwan, and Hong Kong*, coeditor with Lee Wing On (Hong Kong: Center of Asian Studies, 1995); *Education and Society in Hong Kong: Toward One Country and Two Systems* (New York: M.E. Sharpe, 1991); and *Asian Higher Education: An International Handbook and Reference Guide*, coeditor with G. C. L. Mak (Westport, CT: Greenwood, in press). He wrote the Hong Kong chapter for *The International Academic Profession: Portraits from Fourteen Countries*, edited by Philip Altbach (Princeton, NJ: The Carnegie Foundation for the Advancement of Teaching, in press).

Sylvia Ortega Salazar was elected rector of the Universidad Autónoma Metropolitana in Mexico in 1989. The first woman rector of a public university in Mexico, she served until 1993. She assumed the position of director for international affairs of the National Council for Science and Technology (CONACYT) in Mexico in 1995. A sociologist by training, she did her graduate work at the University of Wisconsin–Madison and the University of Texas–Austin. Dr. Ortega has been associated with the Universidad Autónoma Metropolitana over the past 20 years, where she has also served as chair of the Department of Sociology and as dean of the Division of Social Science and the Humanities. She has published extensively in specialized journals and has coauthored four books. More recently she has developed a special interest in the areas of international education, quality assessment of higher education, and models of scientific and academic international cooperation. She is founding president of AMPEI, the Mexican Association of International Education, executive director of PROFMEX, and acts as principal investigator of its U.S.-Mexico program of research in the social sciences. She is a member of the executive committee of the Fundación SNTE para la Cultura del Maestro Mexicano, and of the board of the Institute for International Education. She is also a member of the editorial committees of *Universidad Futura* and *El Cotidiano*, national journals that specialize in higher education.

Brian G. Wilson served as vice-chancellor of the University of Queensland, Australia, from 1979 to 1995. From 1970 to 1978, he was academic vice president and professor of astronomy at Simon Fraser University in British Columbia. Dr. Wilson taught physics at the University of Calgary and served as the dean of the faculty of arts and science at that university. He holds a Ph.D. in astrophysics from the National University of Ireland in Dublin. Professor Wilson was deputy chairman of the Australian Vice-Chancellor's Committee, 1987–88, and chairman, 1989–90. He served as president of the International Development Program of Australian Universities and Colleges, 1991–92. He is a member of the Council of the University of the South Pacific and a member of the board of the Business–Higher Education Round Table. He chaired the Australian government's Committee for Quality Assurance in Higher Education from its inception in 1993 until his retirement.

PART ONE

• • • • • • • • • • •

The Context

In a book of this scope, defining a common frame of reference is essential to its coherence. Thus, before plunging into the particulars of what changes are occurring in which regions or countries, we attempt to set the stage by reflecting on the degree to which change has occurred in higher education, by sketching out the forces that are driving change, and by outlining the primary actors. Not every chapter deals with all of the themes developed in Chapter 1, "Forces for Change," but they are leitmotifs that reappear throughout the book. Issues of expanding higher education or "massification," financing, technology, internationalization, accountability, and quality are dealt with by nearly every author. Readers will be struck by the similarities in higher education around the globe and by the degree to which the responses to the challenges and the strategies for the development of higher education are alike. But the chapters also point up sharp differences in cultural context, history, and capacity for institutional development.

In Chapters 1 and 2, we also identify the major actors engaged in transforming higher education and explore their roles. Higher education is unlike any other organization. Its "employees"—the faculty—are more devoted to their disciplines than to their institutions, yet they expect to have a major voice in managing the enterprise. Its "consumers"—the students and other publics—have expectations that may conflict with those of other stakeholders and of the faculty. Its "leaders" are caught between government edicts and policies, pressures from external groups, and the needs of faculty and students. They do not necessarily even see themselves as leaders. Thus, change in higher education is not a straightforward process that results from edicts by government or institutional administrators (though these can be powerful forces). Change occurs from the bottom up, as well as from the top down. Universities do not "restructure" or "reengineer" the way that corporations do; their habits and processes are simply different.

Worldwide trends in higher education toward increased institutional autonomy, decentralization, and more extensive entrepreneurialism will undoubtedly make the leadership and management tasks of institutional leaders more important and more difficult. For institutions to be vital, and responsive to the challenges of a rapidly changing society, they will need vigorous leadership, not only from the top, but from all quarters of the institution. In the final analysis, change is about people—their ideas, their fears, their capacity to imagine and work together toward a different future. Some of these players are change agents, frequently called leaders. Other actors block change; they, too, can be leaders.

Thus, this first section of the book sets the stage for thinking about what and who causes change in higher education. It provides a frame of reference for interpreting the chapters that follow and for highlighting points of convergence and difference.

CHAPTER 1

Forces for Change

Madeleine F. Green and Fred M. Hayward

Executive Summary. Although higher education is often seen as slow to change or downright resistant, it has undergone rapid transformation throughout the world in the last 25 years and may be in a period of unprecedented change. Today, in spite of differences in traditions and structures, higher education institutions worldwide share remarkably similar problems and are shaped by forces that transcend national boundaries.

The authors explore the following forces for change: the effects of the expansion of higher education and the push for greater access, the problems of declining resources and the challenge of diversifying funding sources, the expectation that higher education will make a greater contribution to economic and social development, the pressures to be accountable to an increasingly skeptical and demanding public, the conflicts surrounding institutional autonomy, the growth of technology, and the drive for internationalization. Another perspective on the change process is supplied by an examination of the actors involved: government, faculty members, governing boards, students, and institutional leaders. The role of institutional leaders depends in large measure on the relative importance and clout of the other actors in the change process. The authors suggest that as governments grant more autonomy to institutions—enabling them to pursue differentiated missions, to compete, and to be entrepreneurial—institutional leadership will be increasingly important in charting an institution's course.

• • • • • • • • • • •

As a social institution, higher education is a paradox. On the one hand, its mission is to conserve; to embody the timeless values of scholarly inquiry and the transmission of knowledge from one generation to the next. As Clark Kerr has reminded us, universities are among a very small number of institutions still in existence today doing much the same as in the 1500s (Kerr 1994, 45–46). Some would attribute their endurance to their resistance to change; certainly, much conventional wisdom and academic humor support this view.

On the other hand, higher education institutions are dynamic organizations that have the capacity to adapt to changing conditions and demands. Some of those adaptations have been accomplished quickly, contrary to the stereotype. The face of higher education has changed considerably in the last 25 years. Mass higher education, distance learning, lifelong learning, redefining the relationship of teaching and learning, and developing partnerships with primary and secondary education and with community and business groups are but a few of the dominant themes for universities around the globe that were barely on the horizon in the early 1970s.

Although the pace and manner of change in academe may be unsatisfactory to some (especially to politicians and policy makers), to describe higher education institutions as immutable or unchanging is not borne out by history or by current realities. Universities have changed substantially since their inception in medieval Europe, and the rate of change in higher education— and in society in general—is widely perceived as accelerating. Although we will know only in retrospect, the late twentieth century may prove to be the period of the most rapid change in society and in higher education of all time.

While higher education has proved itself to be remarkably adaptable, not everything about it should or will change. The tendency of individuals and groups to resist change provides stability and continuity, a counterweight to expedient or faddish change. Making good judgments and decisions about what needs to be preserved, what might be altered, and what should be totally redesigned are the difficult issues that institutions face. Because debate, discussion, and disagreement are enduring features of democracies—and of higher education in democratic societies—there is often little consensus in any given country or any institution about what should constitute the agenda for change. One policy maker's or academic's idea of innovation may represent the demise of academic standards to another. For some, technology represents an exciting new frontier for improving pedagogy; for others, it embodies a depersonalized form of teaching that undermines the true value of higher education. Some in the academy view closer working relationships with business as a means to gain social relevance and public legitimacy, not to mention as a source of needed additional revenues. Others are wary, if not hostile, emphasizing the dangers to free inquiry and the potential for subordinating the academic agenda to a commercial one. The balancing act between conservation and adaptation is a delicate one, and it produces a constant level of tension that societies, institutions, and their leaders must manage.

Today, in spite of differences in their traditions and structures, higher education institutions worldwide share remarkably similar problems, as well as common purposes, as they face a future that is increasingly complex, uncertain, and demanding. To be sure, the nature and the severity of the problems they face differ. Increasing demands and expectations combined with declining resources are nearly universal problems, but it is difficult to draw qualitative comparisons among nations. The impact of budget cuts in Western Europe or the United States and Canada, though severe by the countries' own expectations and histories, pale in comparison to the problems of developing economies: in Russia and Africa, for instance, economic crises are crippling their entire higher education systems.

Economic forces are not the only ones that have shaped the course of higher education. Universities have always been susceptible to the dominant ideologies of their societies and to the political and bureaucratic systems that govern them. Communism shaped universities in Central Europe for decades and continues to be a key force in China, in spite of economic liberalization. The Nigerian and Kenyan governments have recently dismissed or imprisoned academics, and in the recent past, Latin American academics were similarly at risk. Political interference is an age-old problem, and higher education is severely threatened when governments decide what is acceptable to teach and utter. Although most institutions have proven remarkably resilient over time, not all have been able to preserve their fundamental goals or modes of operation.

Additionally, higher education institutions in many countries are faced with public doubt about their social usefulness, skepticism about the effectiveness and efficiency of their operations, and increasing unwillingness by governments to pour resources into what seems to be a bottomless pit. In most nations, the move to shift costs to students, as the users and beneficiaries of higher education, is growing. The public mood is distrustful and critical: costs of higher education are rising too fast, classes are too crowded, professors are more absorbed in their highly specialized domains than interested in teaching students, and facilities and laboratories need endless infusions of resources. And perhaps most importantly, universities have lost their monopoly on both teaching and research. Corporations spend billions of dollars on training and educational programs; for-profit postsecondary institutions are thriving worldwide; and libraries, museums, and civic organizations are important resources for lifelong learning. The *Economist*, in a recent critique of higher education, summarized such doubts succinctly: "Today, knowledge is too important to be left to academics" (Universities 1993, 73).

Thus, it is not surprising that higher education reform is on the agenda in a large number of countries. In many parts of the world, the dialogue is no longer about incremental change but about transforming higher education altogether. Transformation implies rethinking rather than tinkering—reexamining the ways of conducting the business of higher education and altering fundamental aspects of its structure and operation. Nations are confronting core questions about higher education. Are the current configurations of institutions adequate? Some countries have created or are considering creating new postsecondary institutions with clearly differentiated missions, rather than having the research university as the sole form of higher education. Should studies be shorter? To address this issue, some countries have created short-cycle programs within existing institutions (France), or are considering shortening the time to obtain a degree (the Netherlands and Germany). Are students really being taught effectively? At the institutional level, the timeless model of the professor imparting information to passive students is being challenged as institutions think about not simply filling young heads with facts but teaching students of all ages how to learn in an information-rich world. Does an institution of higher education need to have a physical location, or has technology made that concept a dated one? The development of the "virtual university" by the Western Governors Association in the United States, the growth of programs that rely on the Internet, and other forms of distance learning suggest that teaching and learning will increasingly ignore constraints of time and place.

FORCES FOR CHANGE

We begin this discussion by reiterating that change is not always desirable; embracing fads and the pursuit of change for its own sake are potentially as harmful as resisting it. Yet stasis is simply not possible. Even if institutions would wish to do so, they cannot insulate themselves from the forces that bear down powerfully on them—changing national political winds, unprecedented expectations of students and families, straitened national economies, and the dizzying pace of technological advancement. While the pressures and demands for change take on different shapes in each country, they are not bounded by national borders or geography.

In this overview, we look first at seven issues that drive change: access, funding, economic and social development, accountability, autonomy, technology, and internationalization. Each of these affects higher education differently in different settings, but that seems more a function of point in time than a difference in kind. In Parts Two and Three of this volume, the authors point to the influence of these issues with remarkable consistency in their analyses of change. In the following section in this chapter, we analyze the role of the various actors in promoting or resisting change.

Access

Throughout the world, there is pressure for greater access to higher education. This pressure comes from many sources—from young people and their families who see higher education as key to a better social and economic future; from employers who see the need for a better educated workforce; and, sometimes, from politicians in response to public pressure. In industrialized countries, increasing access to higher education may mean raising participation rates or including underserved groups (usually women, members of minority groups, and the children of the poor). In developing nations, where participation rates are generally very low, bringing greater numbers of students into higher education—especially women and others who have been excluded historically—and providing them with employment skills are high-priority agenda items.[1]

Even in countries like the United States, with relatively high rates of participation in higher education, access remains one of the most divisive challenges because of the financial and educational hurdles faced by disadvantaged students. Throughout the world, the children of the middle and upper classes are far likelier to attend universities than children of the poor. In Canada and Australia, bringing native populations into higher education has become the focus of special outreach efforts. In South Africa, the legacy of apartheid means that access is an issue for the majority population, rather than for minority groups. The challenge in developing countries (and some industrialized ones) is equal access for women.

Yet expanded access to higher education creates new problems to solve. The high dropout rate that occurs in many countries after access is increased is neither helpful to the students who find themselves with a few years of university training but no employable skills, nor rewarding to governments that have made "wasted" investments on students who are no better off from an economic point of view than when they started. In the United States, for instance, the disproportionate dropout rate of minority students takes a psychological toll on those who "fail" (or who are failed by the system) and incurs economic costs to the taxpayers.[2]

Another potential problem associated with expanded access is that of "oversupply" of higher education graduates, the proverbial university-educated taxi drivers. This is a sticky question in a democratic society, for to define how much education is "too much" for the good of a nation is one task that few policy makers want to tackle head on. In most countries, access is regulated de facto by funding; the amount of support provided by the state and the expected contributions of students function as a regulator of enrollment in the absence of specific enrollment targets. In the United Kingdom, after nearly doubling enrollments from the mid-1980s to the mid-1990s, the government began to regulate access by penalizing institutions for exceeding their designated maximum enrollments. Overcrowding in French universities due to recent access expansion may force the consideration of maximum enrollments there, too. Without increased government spending in France, the introduction of politically volatile measures such as charging tuition or limiting enrollments may once again bring protesting students into the streets. In the Netherlands, there has also been discussion of capping enrollments. In the United States, enrollments in public higher education have fallen in some states, such as California, because of steep and sudden rises in tuition to make up for the falloff in state subsidies. In many instances, political rhetoric about widening access is tempered (or contradicted) by financial policies that either create higher costs to students (or greater loan burdens) or disincentives to institutions, such as reduced funding per student.

Finally, the issue of access raises the question of the division of labor among the various types of higher education institutions. The major growth in enrollments in higher education have been in the "non-university sector" of tertiary education, often as a result of government decisions to shift funds (or add them) to institutions with a lower cost per student. "Non-university education" refers to a very diverse set of postsecondary education opportunities, including non-degree programs, degree programs offered by technical institutions or institutions other than universities, or corporate-sponsored programs at the postsecondary level. As van Vught (1994) notes, the non-university sector means different things in different countries—short-cycle education in the United States and Japan, professional higher education in the Netherlands, or a combination of both in France. It is very likely that the role of the traditional university will be diminished in the future as other kinds of tertiary education institutions provide lower cost education that is more directly useful in the job market.

Funding

Even the richer industrialized countries of the world are increasingly unable (or unwilling) to maintain their previous levels of expenditure on higher education. The very existence of some institutions is imperiled in poorer countries. The World Bank reports declines in average public expenditures per student in real terms in the 1980s in the developing regions: from $6,300 to $1,500 in sub-Saharan Africa, and from $3,200 to $1,900 in the Middle East and North Africa (World Bank 1994, 17). In the former socialist countries of Europe, precipitous drops occurred in the 1990s; Hungary's per-student allocation fell approximately 20 percent.

Diversification of sources of funding seems to be the popular answer to this problem worldwide, though such diversification is easier said than done and brings with it certain costs and risks to the institution. The report of the World Bank suggests that 30 percent of institutional revenues should come from nongovernmental sources (World Bank 1994, 17). In almost every nation, various efforts are being made by higher education institutions to diversify their funding sources, including entrepreneurial ventures; forming relationships with the private sector; and soliciting gifts from individuals, foundations, and corporations. Many countries are seeking ways to have students and their families share more of the financial burden and make higher education more market driven.

On the expense side, questions of economies and efficiency are dominant themes in the discussion of financing postsecondary education. A number of factors contribute to internal inefficiencies. The proliferation of small institutions and low student-faculty ratios are important factors. Since teaching and research are labor-intensive, and to compound matters, universities have in some countries been deliberately over-staffed to create employment, high labor costs decrease economic efficiency. The organization of instruction, which leaves the physical plant unused nights, weekends, and summers, is another contributor. Prolonged studies and high dropout rates make higher education's "output" rate low (relative to its "input" rate). And finally, large support budgets for student living costs also add to overall costs. In francophone Africa, 55 percent of the entire higher education budget is spent on allowances for noneducational expenses. In anglophone Africa, the figure is 15 percent, in Asia 6 percent, in OECD[3] countries 14 percent, and in the Middle East, North Africa, and Latin America, approximately 20 percent (World Bank 1994, 20).

Governments have seized upon the notion of more private monies with an enthusiasm that alarms institutional leaders. In the United Kingdom in late 1995, the secretary of state for education and employment announced that institutions are expected to make up for budget cuts amounting to £500 million (Tysome 1995, 1). Chinese universities now earn approximately 18 percent of their revenues (Hertling 1995, A40). In the United States, federal, state, and local governments provide slightly more than half of all revenues to public institutions; the rest of their support comes from tuition (NCES 1995b, 173). The difficulties of seeking private funding should not be underestimated. In many countries, the corporate sector and higher education have a legacy of mutual mistrust. Few countries have traditions of charitable giving to education or the tax structure to encourage such gifts. Furthermore, only some parts of the university can be privatized; instructional costs can only be passed on to the consumers, and corporate funders are unlikely to support basic research. The consequences of overzealous efforts to privatize pose real dangers. Van Vught (1994, 5) concludes:

> . . . the teaching function will bear the full burden of future reductions in public higher education funding, as it has done in the recent past. Combined with the trend to increased participation, this will lead to catastrophic effects in the foreseeable future: institutions will no longer be able to provide adequate education as available funds, under unchanged circumstances, will be absolutely insufficient to provide the necessary infrastructure of staff, support services, and teacher-related developmental research.

Who pays for higher education reflects a policy answer to the question of whether education is largely a public or a private good. If higher education is seen primarily as a private good, and the individual student as the primary beneficiary, it follows that the potential beneficiary pays some or even most of the cost. Whether the rationale for passing costs on to students and their families is the latter argument, or simply the pragmatic one of diminished public resources available to support higher education, fees for public higher education are a fact of life in many countries. Tuition fees account for more than 10 percent of recurrent expenditures in only 20 countries. In the United States, approximately 22 percent of all revenues in public institutions comes from student tuition and fees (NCES 1995a, 409). Comparable figures for other countries are 36 percent in Chile, 46 percent in Korea, and 22 percent in Vietnam (World Bank 1994, 41).

Student fees in New Zealand are projected to rise to 25 percent of costs from the current 20 percent by the end of the decade (Rivers 1995, 10). In Nigeria, where students pay less then two percent of the cost (Omoregie and Hartnett 1995, 15), failure to confront the issue of student fees is part of the reason for the decline in the quality of Nigerian higher education. Increasing the charges to students has social costs, since the likely effect is to limit access. In the United States, enrollments have grown fastest in the community colleges, which generally charge lower tuition than four-year institutions. In addition, career choices are affected; students who graduate with significant debt are less likely to select low-paying public service jobs or academic careers. In South Africa, student fees have been raised to about 18 percent of costs— roughly the same as public institutions in the United States (South African Ministry of Education 1995, 47). This situation has created a serious crisis for both the historically disadvantaged institutions that are saddled with unpaid fees, and for the new government as it seeks to develop funding mechanisms that will not exclude poor students from higher education.

In many countries, the tradition of full state support for higher education makes tuition a politically explosive topic, and higher education leaders fear that the introduction of fees opens the door to reducing state subsidies rather than enhancing total resources. However, though the discussion period may be long and the controversy heated, some speculate that user fees for higher education are inevitable. In the Czech Republic, the government has been forced to abandon a plan to charge students tuition fees: a law passed in February 1994 authorizing tuition proved impossible to implement because of intense opposition (Navarrete 1995). In Germany, a student fee between DM500 and DM1,000 was proposed in 1994 (Brookman 1994). China plans to have its colleges charge an annual fee to all students by the end of the decade, and in fall 1995, 37 of China's 1,000 colleges began requiring students to pay tuition fees ranging from $117 to $176, based on entrance exam scores (China's students 1994). In Central Europe, Hungary introduced a fee of 2,000 forint in fall 1995 (International notes 1995, A45)—and the subject will undoubtedly be put back on the table in the Czech Republic.

As higher education becomes more expensive to the "consumer," the economic benefit to the individual diminishes. Thus, it is likely that as students consider the costs and benefits of the investment in higher education, they will seek alternatives to universities (van Vught 1994). Short-cycle programs and vocational training may become increasingly attractive alternatives to the longer programs of university study. On the one hand, the development of this non-university sector of higher education can make a major contribution to increasing access and providing students with employment skills. The danger, however, is that such diversification can result in an intensified stratification of institutions according to prestige, with poor students in short and applied programs and richer ones in the university sector. Moreover, such a hierarchy of prestige generally leads to "academic drift," in which institutions with applied programs strive to be more research oriented and to obtain authorization to grant more advanced and prestigious degrees—thereby erasing the advantages of their differences.

Funding and access are central questions to the future of higher education. Nations are making critical choices that will affect successive generations. In some countries, higher education may virtually collapse from underfunding; in others, it may be weakened. The resulting shortage of well-trained personnel—especially in science and technology—will hamper economic development in developing countries. In the stronger and richer nations, continued underfunding is also bound to take its toll. However, the ability of higher education institutions to innovate and survive may produce some transformations that ultimately will make them stronger. The jury is still out.

Economic and Social Development

Pressures for higher education to contribute to economic and social development, both in highly industrialized and in less developed nations, constitute a third important force for change in higher education. Increasingly, governments, the public, and students are calling on higher education to make a greater contribution to development, economic growth, job training, competitiveness, and research that will help build and sustain economically productive activities. These pressures are fueled by the beliefs that well-educated graduates will be contributors to society rather than dependent on it, that the work of scholars can contribute to social progress and economic growth, and that institutions of higher education can form partnerships with other sectors of society such as business, primary and secondary education, and government— partnerships that can contribute to their effectiveness. The demand for highly trained personnel in science, the professions, government, and business is growing, as is the push for higher education to become "more relevant" to society.

Thus, the questions facing both institutions and policy makers are: What can colleges and universities be expected to contribute to the process of economic and social development? How can they help nations become or remain competitive in a highly technological and competitive arena? How can they produce well-trained graduates who are prepared for the jobs of the modern age? How can they contribute to democratization? What are the risks to higher education of the pressures to focus on curricula and research that are economically useful?

To respond to the needs of society, higher education institutions worldwide are developing connections with their communities, with primary and secondary schools, and with businesses. These partnerships provide opportunities for collaborative research and projects that meet community needs, and they reach out to new groups of students in formal study or job-related training. A commitment to providing opportunities for lifelong learning will require that institutions develop more flexible means of delivery of education and varied programmatic offerings, and that they do so in partnership with various groups.

The challenges for developing countries in linking higher education to development are particularly acute, and here comparisons with developed countries are difficult because of the enormous economic differences. Less than 25 percent of all engineers and scientists in the world are employed in developing countries. Seventy percent of research and development funding is in North America and Europe (Verspoor 1994). The "brain drain" in Russia and Central Europe is threatening their scientific and technological capacity. In Nigeria, the system of higher education has deteriorated to the extent that it makes little, if any, contribution to development;[4] the situation is so bad that many businesses look for new employees among those who were educated *outside* Nigeria. In South Africa, the postapartheid government is looking to institutions of higher education to provide the majority population, long restricted from educational opportunities, the tools for national development and economic success. This has to be accomplished in the face of very poor academic preparation of black South Africans in primary and secondary schools and a continuing maldistribution of resources.

The role of higher education in contributing to national economic well-being is not limited to the less modernized nations of the world. Industrialized nations feel the pressure of international competition, and higher education plays a major role in producing the human resources and research that fuel the economy. Indeed, the stakes are so high in industrialized countries that secrecy, restricted access, and espionage are now facts of life on many college and university campuses.[5]

Addressing social problems is another important contribution universities can make to national development. Through outreach programs and research, higher education institutions are uniquely positioned to help solve the difficult problems of disease, hunger, poverty, and crime. Higher education partnerships for economic and social development are nonexistent or in their infancy in many countries, especially in developing nations where they are arguably the most needed. Where they are highly developed, there are potential and existing conflicts between the more focused utilitarian view of the purposes of education and the classic academic mission of the search for knowledge and its dissemination. The search for knowledge without a specific goal is a distinguishing hallmark of universities, which is jeopardized when only "useful" or applied quests are deemed worthy of funding and pursuit. In periods of budgetary constraint, in particular, clashes over the appropriate focus and emphasis of both research and instruction can become major forces for change.

Accountability

The call for higher education to be publically accountable is becoming increasingly strident, even in countries like the United States and the United Kingdom, in which colleges and universities historically have enjoyed relatively little public oversight. However, because they are publicly financed, there is little debate that public higher education institutions are accountable to taxpayers, who are usually represented by government officials. The concept of *autonomy* is never far from any discussion of *accountability*, for it is the potential conflict between the two that makes this such a difficult issue (see also the next section). Indeed, the growing level of control by governments over institutional decisions—in the name of accountability—is creating crises and conflict. Even private institutions of higher education usually receive some public money, whether for research or as subsidies for students, and they, too, are coming under increased scrutiny. Unlike most other publicly funded organizations, universities have argued that the academic freedom needed to create the conditions necessary for high quality research and teaching requires that they retain a high level of independence. Government interference in matters of teaching, learning, and research is seen as a threat to institutional autonomy and to academic freedom. The line between accountability and interference in educational policy and academic freedom is a thin one.

The United Kingdom and Australia provide examples of countries with strong governmental measures of accountability. In both countries, research and teaching are subject to assessments, with the results of the former tied to funding. The two assessment exercises conducted in the United Kingdom have drawn a firestorm of criticism from academics, who cite the unlevel playing field, the excessive paperwork, and the pressures for conformity among diverse institutions. They claim that the exercises have created a new form of "gamesmanship" to produce good results for the assessment exercise. Defenders point to the discipline provided by the processes of self-assessment and peer review, and the potential for improvement based upon these reviews. In Australia, institutional funding is partially tied to the results of an institutional review, which critics claim has enabled the stronger and richer institutions to get even stronger and richer. While the governments develop systems to measure and rank, academics decry the application of undifferentiated criteria for excellence. In the United States, government oversight takes place at the state level, and measures vary from program approval, to statewide tests for admission to upper level study, to legislative reviews of faculty workloads. Institutional reviews are conducted by voluntary accrediting associations, which are voluntary in the sense that they are nongovernmental, but accreditation is a prerequisite for receiving federal funds.

Nongovernmental groups—students, faculty, staff, parents, citizens' groups, businesses, donors, and professional associations—are also increasingly demanding accountability. They argue that they, too, are stakeholders who have a legitimate concern with the performance of educational institutions. However, they often have different agendas from those of government and of higher education, and from one another. Their interests in accountability (and sometimes demands for it) are becoming an increasing part of the national higher education debate in many parts of the world. The discussion about how to provide such accountability, as well as the access and participation in governance it may require, is increasingly contentious in many countries. In South Africa, the process of transformation, for example, involves "broad transformation committees" at each institution (recently required by the Ministry of Education) as a way of insuring the involvement of students, staff, alumni, the community, and government in the process. Representation of students and members of the community are a feature of governing and advisory councils and boards in many countries.

The issue of accountability presents a host of knotty questions: Who defines the measures of performance? Are they the same for different types of institutions? Is it possible to have a system that serves the double purpose of accountability and quality improvement, or must these be separate endeavors?

Autonomy

The issue of university autonomy has been a powerful arena of contestation in most of the world. Part of this debate focuses on the meaning of the term. Autonomy in what areas of higher education? How much? Who is the arbitrator? As noted in the previous section, accountability often comes into conflict with autonomy. To what extent should higher education institutions be allowed to determine their own destiny, and to what extent must they be called to account by the society that supports them? At one end of the spectrum is a 1973 statement from a workshop at the Association of African Universities in Accra: "the university in Africa occupies too critical a position of importance to be left alone to determine its own priorities . . .", and thus it must be subject to the control of the state (AAU 1973, 45). While no government would take the completely opposite view about publicly funded education, few would put it that starkly.

Conflicts surrounding autonomy bring in other pivotal issues. As public confidence in higher education declines, autonomy is viewed merely as a cover for self-interest, arrogance, indifference, and inefficiency. A spate of recent publications in the United States and reports in the popular media have fueled the public perception (not restricted to the United States) that "the universities have been hijacked by 1960s radicals" (Universities 1993, 72), and that professors work too little and protest incursions on their academic freedom too much. Critics argue that demands for autonomy are designed to thwart change and protect privileged elites; that the linkage to academic freedom is spurious—with few, if any, demonstrated results. In this sense, the argument for autonomy becomes a tool both of the advocates and the critics of change. A high degree of institutional autonomy, such as existed under the old system in South Africa or under the new laws of higher education in several Central European countries, provides institutions with the freedom not to change or to pursue directions that are not useful or productive in a larger national context. Yet change decreed by governments brings the risks of interference and insensitivity to differences among institutions; it can be as unproductive as unregulated institutional autonomy.

Technology

In recent years, the impact of new technologies has become a major force for change in colleges and universities; it is clear that this impact has only just begun and that it will potentially have a profound effect on the structure of higher education. Computers and information technology have enhanced our ability to carry out research, and we have begun to harness the potential of technology to deliver high quality, more cost-effective education to students. The revolution in information technology provides the possibility of extending the classroom to any part of the world, which has great potential for increasing access to higher education. It could also determine the continued existence of many colleges and universities as we know them and, in some cases, it could affect their very survival as institutions. The professor at the blackboard in the lecture hall is currently still the predominant mode of teaching. Yet technology exists that has in many ways made the physical location of a university irrelevant for teaching and research purposes. Distance learning, instruction by interactive video, and computer networks are among the many technological tools at our disposal to revolutionize higher education.

The potential for using new technologies to increase access to higher education is formidable. Television, satellite communication, and interactive computer links provide major opportunities to expand access, to be more effective in meeting the needs of individual students, and to link higher education institution around the world. That potential, however, requires major investments, both in equipment and in training professors to use technology in the redesign of instruction. These costs may be out of the reach of institutions in the poorer nations of the world. Declining resources, even in richer countries, makes it all the more difficult to find the additional funds (or to make the necessary reallocations) needed to invest in technology. There may be some surprising twists associated with technology, too. In one scenario, technology may provide alternatives to costly expansion of campus facilities and may provide higher education access to previously unserved individuals. In this scenario, technology becomes the medium of choice for the "poor person's education," much like the correspondence courses of the past few decades, and traditional universities become the province of the elites. Another scenario shows technology as such a powerful force that only those institutions that make the required investment and can incorporate it effectively into their research and teaching will survive or be important centers of learning. In this scenario, the "haves" will be the users of technology at all levels of schooling, while the "have-nots" will be those institutions that are too poor to invest in it.

It is abundantly clear already that technology requires a considerable investment, which even the richer nations find difficult. Will higher education, unable to make a sufficient investment in technology, become a secondary provider of teaching and research, yielding primacy to for-profit educational institutions, to industries with greater technological capacity to conduct research, or to other new providers in both arenas? Technology may reshape higher education in ways that it cannot control or anticipate.

Internationalization

What does it mean for higher education institutions to be truly international? Why is it important? What changes in curriculum, in faculty and staff development, and in government policies, are required for institutions to become full participants in the global academic community? Does it really matter if they do not?

In the contemporary world, knowledge is truly international, available to those with the capacity to communicate with the rest of the world. That fact has significant implications for competitiveness, economic development, scientific discovery, and the exploration of the limits of human knowledge. For higher education, knowledge of the rest of the world is now a fundamental imperative for success; it holds the promise of discovery, the seeds of competitiveness, and a challenge for leadership.

Part of the challenge is awareness of the rest of the world. Part is understanding what the rest of the world has to offer—from the importance (or unimportance) of discoveries to the implications of new ideas and approaches. Higher education institutions in some countries do better than others on that score: facilitating contacts among staff; providing their university communities with access to the vast network of information available elsewhere in the world; and insisting that students learn about other societies, cultures, and ideas and that they study foreign languages and experience other cultures. That focus is not necessarily a function of wealth, though there is certainly a relationship between the two.

Some nations—like the United States—even with great wealth, highly developed economies, and global responsibilities (if not aspirations), are remarkably isolated and parochial. Federal funding for international education at colleges and universities is a low priority. In contrast, the European Union has focused major resources on internationalization, through programs to promote student and faculty mobility, collaborative research, and the inclusion of a "European dimension" in curricula. China, until very recently, sought to remain insulated from the outside world as a conscious strategy of the government; however, there are costs to that isolation that go far beyond the utility of knowledge about other cultures and societies. They include ignorance of new developments in science and technology, economic stagnation, public policy gaffs, and missed development opportunities. Those who do not have some mechanisms to monitor and understand the internationalization of knowledge are likely to be left out of important spheres of discovery, and they may find themselves less competitive in ways that have major economic and political consequences.

MAJOR ACTORS

In addition to the more general forces that drive change in higher education worldwide, what groups are demanding or creating change? Whom do they represent? Are they largely from outside or inside institutions of higher education? How important or effective are these various groups in effecting transformations? The following section discusses some of the major actors in the process of change.

Government

Among the most powerful and persistent forces for change described in the chapters that follow is government itself. Even private higher education institutions in countries such as Japan and the United States are regularly challenged by political leaders with a wide range of demands for change—to be accountable, increase access, lower costs, meet national defense needs, and respond to technological challenges. The process is often posed as cooperative, with incentives designed to encourage compliance. It matters very much to institutions if these are requests from "friends" or are attacks from "foes." The one brings higher education into partnerships, the other sees higher education institutions as part of a vast array of problems to be dealt with—as unresponsive, wasteful, elitist, irrelevant, ineffective, or some combination of these failings—or as part of the opposition to government, to progress, or to desired change. In some countries, government officials see political profit in such attacks (such as during the McCarthy hearings in the United States). Or, higher education can be viewed by government as a problem—a constant source of criticism, tension, and subversion. In that context, higher education (or parts of it) is to be watched, feared, controlled, manipulated, and repressed. Yet even from this perspective there is recognition that higher education institutions perform vital functions. They may be closed for a time, as in China during the Cultural Revolution or today in various African nations, but ultimately they are a necessary part of society. How effectively institutions of higher education respond to government during times of both cooperation and attack are major tests of institutional leadership.

Governments also have been powerful forces in encouraging fundamental changes in higher education: affirmative action in the United States, greater financial efficiency in Great Britain, and adaptation to market forces in China. In Japan, the government's desire for industrial modernization paved the way for grants to selected institutions and initiated a powerful drive to bring the higher education system to the cutting edge of technology. Governments have been powerful adversaries of higher education, too—limiting autonomy, asserting the primacy of political ideology over academic freedom, preventing experimentation through highly centralized rules, and weakening institutions through budget cuts.

Maassen and van Vught (1994, 34–63) have identified two primary models of government steering. One is the *state control model*, characterized by strong centralized control by a ministry and high dependency on government funding, with the objective often being standardization among institutions. Typical of continental European systems and many Latin American countries, the government generally shares authority with the senior chaired professors. In this model, institutional administration is relatively weak, and the leadership role of rectors and deans is limited by the power of the strong top (central state authority) and bottom (senior professors).

The *state supervising model*, with its roots in the American and pre-Thatcher British systems, provides limited direct government regulation. Institutions decide on their own curriculum and admissions policies. In the U.S. system, boards of trustees and administrators have traditionally played an important role in institutional decision making, since relatively little is centrally determined. However, growing pressures for accountability have brought greater state intrusion in institutional autonomy; also, the increase in the number of multicampus state systems of higher education has created a new layer of control in U.S. higher education. Similarly, state-mandated assessments in the United Kingdom have strengthened direct governmental steering. Other nations, however, are attempting to loosen the state control. As Halimi describes in Chapter 12, France, with a highly centralized system, has launched an approach whereby each institution negotiates a four-year contract with the Ministry of Education for its activities and budget, setting its own goals and measures of accountability. Similarly, the former socialist countries have granted nearly total autonomy to universities.

National governments—and in some countries, state governments—are the key actors in shaping higher education. Through policy decisions that affect the amount and distribution of resources, participation, academic programs, and personnel, governments have the first and last word in determining the fate of public higher education.

The Public

At the local level, those who speak in the name of the public are increasingly important actors in higher education debates. Local communities can be a major force for change in higher education through funding (or denial of it), administrative control, local legislation, or pressures for conformity. At the national level, the public also presses its needs, demands, and desires. While the general public does not "act" in the ways government leaders can (who often wrap themselves in the name of "society"), there are striking examples of societal forces at work expressing demands for change. Calls by politicians and policy makers for greater public access to higher education in South Africa, China, and in Nigeria in recent years are made on behalf of the public. Growing public hostility to student unrest in France in the 1960s and in Nigeria in the 1980s gave government an opening to act against the universities on behalf of society. In Japan, public demands for quality education have created a general "culture of education" that has sparked tremendous growth in high quality higher education opportunities—as well as questions about the negative effects of the pressures on some children (Hayward 1995, 129–32). While amorphous in many respects, there is a very real sense in which "society" or the public becomes an actor, with leaders speaking on its behalf.

Within the general community are specific groups with links to higher education. These include business leaders, the donor community, and local officials. These groups, too, provide pressures for change in higher education. Their status in society, the force of their concerns, and their ties to and investment in the success of higher education institutions make them disproportionately influential as actors calling for changes in higher education on behalf of the larger society.

Faculty Members

In many parts of the world, it is assumed that the faculty[6]—especially senior faculty and chair holders—are the primary actors, along with government, in the governance of the universities, and hence the most important institutional players in the change process. They also expect to be the final arbiters of external demands for change. In countries where administrators are relatively powerful, they may hold somewhat different views about how much power the faculty has. But most would acknowledge that the faculty are major actors and participate with administrators and others in the process of shared governance.

Faculty members have played major roles in the process of change in many parts of the world. Sometimes they are encouraged by students (as they were in France in 1968 and in Czechoslovakia during the Velvet Revolution of 1989); often the initiative is their own. They are most easily mobilized by threats to core values of the institution, especially issues related to academic freedom. To be sure, these values are sometimes defined in ways that also reflect self-interest in job security or quality of life.

Faculty members are important actors in bringing about changes that grow out of their work as teachers and scholars. In that context, they are acutely aware of changes in their fields, of technological advancement, and of new approaches that require restructuring of their fields or even their institutions. Certainly, faculty sometimes serve to block change, motivated by a conviction that a particular change is either unhelpful or downright harmful, or by human resistance and fear, or by self-interest. Their focus on their disciplines often prevents them from taking the larger institutional view. Yet, a remarkable amount of fundamental change in the structure of higher education has resulted from faculty initiatives to change curriculum and pedagogy, and from the imperative that most teachers feel to be on the cutting edge of their discipline.

As the ensuing chapters illustrate, even in societies in which there are no expectations about faculty roles in the instigation of large-scale institutional change, few changes succeed without their agreement and support. Those who lead the forces for change, from whatever quarter, are more likely to succeed where they have willing cooperation from the faculty and staff, rather than passive acquiescence or begrudging compliance.

Governing Boards

In many countries, the major responsibility for universities and colleges rests with governing boards—called councils, boards of regents, or boards of trust-ees—comprising some combination of faculty, students, and members of the community.

These bodies may have a political or personal agenda in either promoting or preventing change. If their members are largely external to the institution, their role may be seen as representing the public interest as much as serving as stewards for the institution, with the attendant dangers of being "lay persons" who do not understand the enterprise for which they are responsible, or who bring other agendas to the deliberation. The United States has a highly developed system of governing boards or boards of trustees, whose members are overwhelmingly drawn from outside the institution. This composition makes U.S. boards quite different from those of most other countries, where a heavy representation of insiders on governing boards encourages them to function more as institutional decision-making groups than as oversight boards. The advantages of the latter model lie in the mixture of knowledgeable insiders and, ideally, objective outsiders. The disadvantage lies in the dual function of the insiders who make decisions both as members of the academic community and as members of an oversight group.

Students

Historically, students have been major actors in the process of change in both higher education and society. Under repressive regimes, they have served as the conscience and protectors of ordinary citizens against capricious authority. In France, students have been consistent advocates of change, even bringing down governments in the process. Students' strength has been in their num-bers, volatility, anonymity, energy, and idealism—their belief that change is possible. The same qualities have also been their weakness, coupled with a limited sense of history and an even shorter institutional memory. But those weaknesses have not lessened the ability of students to be primary actors in initiating or preventing change.

In the chapters on France, the Czech Republic, and South Africa, in particular, we will see the hand of students in many of the changes that have taken place. In Africa, parts of Asia, and Latin America, students are also particularly powerful actors in the change process. In South Africa, students have become remarkably astute politically—not surprisingly, since they were major actors in the struggle against apartheid. In the postapartheid era, however, students have been better at accepting their new freedoms than acknowledging responsibilities, thus weakening their effectiveness and creating conditions that threaten the very institutions they would strengthen. In Central Europe, institutional leaders report that although students have up to one-third of the seats of various decision-making bodies, they often fail to attend meetings. The student activism that helped bring down the Communist state has not been sustained for the difficult tasks of reform and renewal. In the United States, once an arena of flourishing student movements, students are not important actors on the contemporary stage.

A look back at the American experience suggests the important impact students can have at particular moments in history. Student leadership in U.S. higher education was acknowledged begrudgingly in the 1960s and 1970s. It was threatening, troublesome, illegitimate. Students questioned the privileged status of higher education, the aims of instruction, the underlying values of many courses, the stodginess of some of the thinking, and the assumptions underlying particular disciplines. They pointed out social and institutional failures—racism, secret research, the failure of some faculty to take teaching seriously, and conflicts of interest—moving the process of change forward through their actions.

Reactions of administrators and governing boards to student activism were mixed. Some were hostile, confrontational, or punitive. These events brought on a series of crises for leaders. Boards blamed the college and university presidents for not having their houses in order—for not controlling the troublemakers: the faculty, the staff, students, minorities, the left, the right, and "outside agitators." Student activism, whether it concerned civil rights or the Vietnam war, "intruded" on the norms and expectations of some university presidents and boards, who saw their role, in part, as ensuring that the products of higher education reflected the traditional values of the academy. The myth of community was being shattered and, like it or not, universities became much more a part of the real world.

Although in other countries, military and police force was routinely applied to student activists, it was a new and disturbing occurrence in the United States in the 1960s and 1970s. In Nigeria, France, China (Tiananmen Square),

Ghana, and Latin America—to name only a few regions—students were expelled, killed, raped, beaten, and jailed. But student activism continued. Its leadership went underground, it was hard to identify, and there seemed to be a never-ending supply of replacements. In important ways, the commitment and sometimes the anonymity of the student leadership gave their efforts a force to bring about changes that could not have occurred otherwise. The role of students as leaders is generally limited to particular kinds of situations, but the impact can be decisive.

Just as student activism can promote change, it can also block it. In France, "since 1986, student unrest has sunk one [higher education] reform plan after another" (Hughes 1995, 9). Students took to the streets again in December 1995 to protest any reform that would block open access, in spite of the fact that French universities cannot accommodate the masses of students they accept, and large numbers will drop out anyway. Absent the institutional flexibility to respond to the crisis of overcrowding and underfunding, the students continue to take their case to the streets. Similarly, in late 1995, violent clashes with police occurred when Greek students protested proposed "reforms," including charging tuition for graduate programs, allowing private institutions to operate, and ending the provision of free textbooks (Doder 1996, A35).

Institutional Leadership

How have higher education institutions responded to pressures for change? Under what conditions have they been forces for change or forces for continuity? What is the role of institutional leadership in change? Can individual leaders provide the impetus for change? Can individuals alter the course of institutions that have remained stable for so very many centuries? Can institutional leaders be more than caretakers or implementers of government policies? How are traditions of shared governance and academic freedom balanced against a need for vigorous leadership to promote and implement change? How do college and university leaders deal with the conflicting demands for change?

The role of formally designated administrative leaders—institutional heads, deans, and department heads—is highly dependent on the structure of the system. We have already noted that the government and faculty are powerful actors, sometimes leaving administrative leadership caught between these two forces. The role of administrative leadership has changed also over the years in many countries, and in some cases it is much more central to both governance and change than in the past. Where institutions become more connected to the publics they serve and undertake change, and when governments move from the model of *state control* to *state supervision*, the role of leaders as links to these constituencies becomes more central, even crucial.

As Green demonstrates in Chapter 2, concepts of leadership in a democratic society are changing. Although societies may have strong cultural traditions of obedience to authority and of paternalistic leadership, the complexity of higher education and the clamor for different voices to be heard make it difficult for any person to lead alone. There are often multiple leaders—students, faculty, and unions internally; politicians, business figures, and community members externally. Conflicting demands and signals shape the leader's role. On the one hand are demands for better management, tighter controls, and greater centralization; on the other are cries for greater freedom and autonomy. Leaders may serve as umpires, peacemakers, advocates for their institutions, or as villains in the eyes of the discontented. The last few decades have been periods of great pressure and tension for college and university leadership. In many parts of the world, to be a university head is to be attacked from all sides—by one's colleagues and students at home, and by the public and government leaders outside.

The nature of individuals in higher education leadership positions has also changed dramatically in some countries, especially in new democracies. Many have moved to leadership from underground teaching, protest marches, prisons, and exile. The champions of democracy must now lead the difficult, slow, and frustrating work of reform.

One of the striking things about contemporary leadership in the larger society is that some of the most effective leaders are not the traditional ones. Rather, they are those with the skills and drive to detect and mobilize a new consensus in a context with many more, and very different, actors than we have seen before. Such leaders are often people who do not fit the usual profile of "potential power brokers." They are citizen-activists, teachers, union leaders, and middle managers; individuals who capture the moment and help mold changes in the system. In higher education, leaders may be in formally designated roles, or they may lead by moral or intellectual authority. Although academic leaders often come from the ranks of senior professors, the successful ones today also exhibit an impressive array of skills as entrepreneurs, politicians, and managers. The contributors to this volume reveal how leaders adapt and respond to the opportunities and problems created by changing external conditions, new demands placed on their institutions, and new modes of discourse that often replace reflection and civility with demands for immediate action on the "change" agenda.

CONCLUSION

We would not want to leave the reader with the impression that the forces for change are so pervasive and powerful that higher education is speeding rapidly and without interruption toward a new future. The need to preserve core values and what is working should not be overlooked. Also, the obstacles to change are real and pervasive. The human response to external pressures is often to hunker down and to resist; fear of the unknown may be more powerful than discomfort with an unsatisfactory status quo. The inability of many of the actors—including government, the faculty, and the public—to imagine a different future preserves traditional ways of thinking when new approaches are needed.

In spite of these and other obstacles noted throughout the book, institutions cannot help but change. Whether they do so purposefully is a different issue, and in reality, institutions constantly undergo some combination of planned and unplanned change. The relative importance of various external forces at any moment in time and the roles of the various actors will vary, to produce an unpredictable combination of ingredients and unexpected outcomes. For institutional leaders, the challenge is to shape the future, not simply to let it happen. No institution or its leader can do this completely, but it is the effort to be purposeful about direction that distinguishes leaders from functionaries or caretakers. In the next chapter, we explore the role of leaders more fully in charting the course of an institution.

NOTES

1. The policy emphasis in developing countries has shifted from turning out unemployable university graduates to providing students with technical and job-related skills. In some countries, limiting enrollments is seen as a measure to restore quality. As part of a World Bank–funded program, Dakar University planned in 1994 to cut enrollments from 24,000 to 15,000 (Hughes 1994, 9).

2. In the United States, with its highly mobile student population of learners who drop in and out of higher education studies, the definition of a "dropout" is more elusive than in other countries, where students are more likely to enter directly after completing their secondary studies and to continue full time until they obtain a degree. The argument about "wasted public resources" is a more complex one when many students are not actively pursuing degrees or are doing so over an extended period.

3. The Organization for Economic Cooperation and Development (OECD) is the international organization of the industrialized, market-economy countries. Its members include Australia, Austria, Belgium, Canada, the Czech Republic, Denmark, Finland, France, Germany, Greece, Hungary, Iceland, Ireland, Italy, Japan, Luxembourg, Mexico, the Netherlands, New Zealand, Norway, Portugal, Spain, Sweden, Turkey, the United Kingdom, and the United States.

4. See World Bank 1994.

5. Louis Branscomb (1995, 76–85) argues that the demands for significant contributions to national competitiveness from university research also pose a dilemma for the free flow of ideas in light of growing demands to protect the findings of scholars by establishing a kind of "intellectual protectionism."

6. We remind the reader of the U.S. usage of "faculty" to denote "teaching staff."

REFERENCES

Association of African Universities (AAU). 1973. Creating the African university. In *Creating the African university: Emerging issues in the 1970s*, edited by T. Yesufu. Ibadan, Nigeria: Oxford University Press.

Branscomb, L. 1995. Technological change and the university: Impacts and opportunities from global change. In *International challenges to American colleges and universities*, edited by K. H. Hanson and J. W. Meyerson. Phoenix, AZ: Oryx Press.

Brookman, J. 1994. German taboo breaks on fees. *Times Higher Education Supplement*, October 28: 10.

China's students to pay tuition by 1997. 1994. *Executive News Service*, November 13.

Doder, D. 1996. Violent reactions: Proposed reforms to Greece's higher education system triggers student unrest. *The Chronicle of Higher Education*, January 19: A35.

Hayward, F. 1995. International opportunities and challenges for American higher education in Africa, Asia and Latin America. In *International challenges to American colleges and universities*, edited by K. H. Hanson and J. W. Meyerson. Phoenix, AZ: Oryx Press.

Hertling, J. 1995. The costs of autonomy at China's universities. *The Chronicle of Higher Education*, February 10: A38, A40.

Hughes, S. 1994. Violent protests roused by tough cuts. *Times Higher Education Supplement*, November 4: 9.

———. 1995. French trapped by their centralism. *Times Higher Education Supplement*, December 1: 9.

International notes. 1995. *The Chronicle of Higher Education*, March 24: A45.

Kerr, C. 1994. *Higher education cannot escape history: Issues for the twenty-first century*. Albany, NY: SUNY Press.

Maassen, P., and F. van Vught. 1994. Alternative models of governmental steering in higher education. In *Comparative policy studies in higher education*, edited by L. Goedegebuure and F. van Vught. Utrecht: Center for Higher Education Policy Studies.

Navarrete, N. 1995. Czechmate for Klaus tuition fee charges. *Times Higher Education Supplement*, October 6: 8.

Omoregie, P. O., and T. Hartnett. 1995. *Financing trends and expenditure patterns in Nigerian universities*. Washington, DC: World Bank, April. Unpublished document.

Rivers, J. 1995. Students to pay 25% of course. *Times Higher Education Supplement*, January 20: 10.

South African Ministry of Education. 1995. *Higher education financing*. Pretoria: Ministry of Education.

Tysome, T. 1995. Budget blight on universities. *Times Higher Education Supplement*, December 1: 1.

Universities: Towers of babble. 1993. *The Economist*, December 25–January 7: 72–74.

U.S. Department of Education National Center for Education Statistics (NCES). 1995a. *The condition of education 1995*. Washington, DC: Government Printing Office.

———. 1995b. *Digest of educational statistics 1995*. Washington, DC: Government Printing Office.

van Vught, F. 1994. Bigger but not better. *Times Higher Education Supplement*, October 7: 5.

Verspoor, A. 1994. Financing higher education: A world view. Presentation at the annual meeting of the American Council of Education, February 21, Washington, DC.

World Bank. 1994. *Development in practice: The lessons of experience*. Washington, DC: The World Bank.

CHAPTER 2

Institutional Leadership in the Change Process

Madeleine F. Green

Executive Summary. Although there are many actors in the change process, institutional leaders, whether or not they are formally designated, can play a significant role. As colleges and universities strive for and obtain more autonomy, institutional leadership is likely to be of increasing importance in the change process. The author begins with definitions of leadership, and then examines three different kinds of institutional heads—U.S.-style presidents ("academic CEOs"), elected rectors, and ministry-appointed heads—comparing opportunities for and constraints on leadership. In spite of the differences among the three types of institutional leaders, they share certain tasks: clarifying direction, managing change, setting the tone, overseeing education and research, and relating the institution to its external constituencies. The ability to perform these tasks, and the way in which they are carried out, are shaped by national as well as academic culture. The latter has some universal characteristics, such as shared governance, amateur leaders and managers, fragmentation, and multiple stakeholders, which make the exercise of leadership a complicated and delicate task. As institutions grow more complex and more accountable to society and to multiple stakeholders, ideas about leadership and the nature of organizations are undergoing significant change. Questions about values, dealing with ambiguity and complexity, and shared leadership and accountability are increasingly central to leadership as institutions try to cope with the rapid rate of change and the attendant stress and confusion.

• • • • • • • • • • •

As we have seen in Chapter 1, there are many different actors in the change process. Institutional leaders—whether in formally designated roles of administrative or academic leadership such as president or rector, vice-chancellor, registrar, dean, or department head—often find themselves responding to change more than initiating it. They may see themselves as guardians of tradition or of the status quo more than as change agents. Yet, as institutions claim greater autonomy and freedom to determine their own futures, the role of institutional leadership will undoubtedly grow in importance. This chapter examines the role of leaders in initiating and managing change, acknowledging the constraints on leadership that are embedded in the culture, traditions, and structures of the academy, as well as the opportunities offered by the current environment.

LEADERSHIP AND MANAGEMENT: AN AMERICAN ROMANCE?

The struggle to capture, define, and measure leadership is ongoing among scholars, popular authors, and practitioners. Definitions of terms are particularly important in a volume that spans many cultures. Even in a single culture, there is always the danger of ascribing different definitions to the same word. Our very selection of the issues we consider important and the way we frame them are uniquely rooted in our cultural patterns of thinking. Thus, it is no accident that the editor of this volume is from the United States, a country fascinated by leadership.

The American romance with leadership has given rise to a vast literature, both scholarly (Bass 1990) and popular. Commercial bookstores are brimming with books on these topics, and new best-sellers appear frequently. Most of the popular literature pertains to the corporate sector, and indeed, many of the concepts of management and leadership that have swept higher education in the United States originated in corporate America. That, too, forms a framing perspective that has influenced the U.S. dialogue in higher education. The considerable body of scholarly literature on leadership is drawn principally from the disciplines of psychology, political theory, and history. Indeed, the fascination with leadership is so great that it is emerging as an academic field in some U.S. institutions. Dozens of programs in "leadership studies" exist in U.S. colleges and universities (Freeman 1994).

In other countries, leadership for higher education has not received such attention, and there has been relatively little literature on the subject produced outside the United States.[1] Several possible explanations for this difference can be cited. An important factor is the tradition of institutional autonomy in the United States, in which institutional leaders at every level play a role in charting the course of the college or university. Another is the existence of a discipline of higher education, which has spawned master's and doctoral programs in the field throughout the United States and has produced considerable research and commentary. A third is cultural: American individualism prizes exceptional people—leaders—in politics, business, and other walks of life. Ideals of heroic leadership have been dominant for many decades, and they are still a powerful presence. In political life, Americans lament the absence of the "giants of yesteryear"—Abraham Lincoln, Franklin D. Roosevelt, John F. Kennedy—those who led the nation with courage and conviction. In the corporate world, the "turnaround artists," such as Lee Iacocca of the Chrysler Corporation, are cited as examples of leaders who can take charge and get things done. In the world of higher education, the United Kingdom, Australia, and Canada seem to share the American preoccupation with both leadership and management, reflecting perhaps similar cultural and political climates. This "managerialism," with all its negative connotations (Trow 1985), produces a greater emphasis on the idea that higher education institutions are not simply communities of scholars and students, they are enterprises that place a high value on effectiveness, efficiency, and public accountability.

In addition, the United States has a well-established group of professional administrators, both academic and nonacademic, who see themselves as part of a profession and for whom leadership is a legitimate part of their work. These administrators constitute the reading public, although they tend not to be consumers of the research by faculty members in the field.

The first section of this chapter, which outlines definitions of leadership and provides an overview of contemporary thinking on the topic, is rooted in the U.S. experience and the U.S. literature. Undoubtedly, American values and cultural assumptions—such as the value of the individual, the forces of the market as a determinant of behavior, and the tradition of democracy—shape the thinking in profound and unseen ways.[2]

From time to time, I will comment on the cultural implications of the concepts presented, but it is each reader's task, viewing these ideas through a different cultural lens, to determine which of these concepts are applicable to a particular country and in what ways.

Toward a Definition of Leadership

To study leadership is to transcend disciplinary and cultural boundaries. Leaders are products of different times and of different cultures. They can be studied through political, psychological, and historical lenses; no single interpretation provides a complete understanding. Their cultures shape who they are and what they can and cannot do, yet there are also similarities to be discovered and parallels to be drawn. The task of defining leadership is an important first step in understanding how it works in different settings.

Most scholars tread cautiously when providing definitions and approaching the topic of leadership. Birnbaum (1992, 3) opens his study with the following warning: "There is a constant temptation to say more than we know about leadership in higher education." British scholar Robin Middlehurst is similarly wary of generalizations:

> The idea of leadership is complex, difficult to capture and open to numerous definitions and interpretations. Neither in common parlance nor in the literature on the subject is there consensus about the essence of leadership, or the means by which it can be identified, achieved, or measured. (Middlehurst 1993, 7)

In spite of the murkiness of the territory, scholars have persisted in their attempts to clarify and define leadership. Views of leadership have evolved over the twentieth century. Until the late 1940s, writers and researchers concentrated on the traits and personality of the individual leader; the underlying premise was that individual characteristics determined success-ful leadership. For the following 20 years, the emphasis shifted to behavioral theories: studying leaders' actions and behaviors, rather than their person-alities. In recent decades, the research has emphasized the importance of context and situation ("contingency theories"). The latest scholarship stresses the cultural and symbolic aspects of leadership.[3]

Contemporary scholars emphasize that leadership is an *activity* or a *pro-cess*, not a *trait*. The "great man" theory, which predominated in discussions in the first half of this century, attempted to locate all leadership in the personality of the leader, and thus to identify the personality traits of suc-cessful leaders. The list of the specific characteristics associated with suc-cessful leaders will vary according to who is compiling it. The legacy of this approach is strong today; its appeal is powerful to leaders—who often find it difficult to give up control—and to followers—who are often tempted by quick fixes. Searching for the "right" leader who will "fix" things, or blaming the current one for not doing so, is to take the path of least resistance. It is far more difficult and painful for an organization to take collective responsibil-ity for its future, or for leaders to "mobilize people to tackle tough problems," which is actually the essential work of leadership, according to Heifetz (1994, 15). "Heroes" and "fixers" absolve others of responsibility.

Contemporary scholars deemphasize the traits of the individual leader, however, focusing more on the *process* and the *results* of leadership. Leader-ship implies *producing change* and *setting the direction of that change* (Kotter 1990, 104). Gardner defines leadership as "the process of persuasion or example by which an individual (or leadership team) induces a group to pursue objectives held by the leader or shared by the leader and his or her followers" (1990, 1). Leaders shape the goals of followers, producing a com-mon vision and shared goals; they accomplish this not by coercion, but through a relationship with their followers. Contemporary definitions of leadership go beyond the one-way effect of leadership on followers; the central concepts are *mutuality* and *followership* (Gardner 1990; Wills 1994; and O'Toole 1995). Followership is as important as leadership; leaders cannot lead without followers. Wills (1994, 9, 15) maintains that the notion of a leader as someone who simply affects another is inadequate. "The leader does not just vaguely affect others. He or she takes others toward the object of their joint quest . . . A leader whose qualities do not match those of potential followers is simply irrelevant."

THE LEADERSHIP ROLE OF PRESIDENT, VICE-CHANCELLOR OR RECTOR

The most conspicuous institutional leader in higher education, at least from a symbolic point of view, is the institutional head. This person carries different titles in different countries—*president* in the United States and several other countries (among them anglophone Canada, France, some places in Germany, and Japan), *vice-chancellor* in the United Kingdom and some British Commonwealth countries, and *rector* in most other countries. While many others exercise leadership in academic institutions (not all in formally designated leadership roles), the institutional head is a visible and important symbolic leader. Three different types of university heads can be outlined, although the distinctions are blurry.[4]

The Academic Chief Executive Officer (CEO)

This model predominates in the United States, Canada, and to a slightly lesser extent, in the United Kingdom and Australia. The academic CEO is most entrenched in the United States, with a long history of presidents as managers, external figures, and fund-raisers. Academic CEOs are experienced academic managers—generally academics by training—who often begin their careers as faculty members and progress through the administrative ranks, typically as dean, vice president, and then president. In 1990, 18 percent of U.S. presidents had already served as president in one or more institutions (Ross, Green, and Henderson 1993).[5] U.S. presidents are selected by governing boards, which in the public sector are popularly elected or named by the state's governor, and in private institutions are named by the board itself ("a self-perpetuating board"). A study of the career paths of Australian vice-chancellors shows a similar career progression: 75 percent of vice-chancellors held the position of vice-chancellor or deputy vice-chancellor prior to their current position (DEET 1994, 28).

As Clark Kerr points out, the U.S. president has multiple masters, and is answerable to governing boards (and in the public sector, sometimes also to the legislature), community groups, donors, and multiple campus constituencies (Kerr 1995, 22). Institutional heads who are elected by their peers or named by the government may also find themselves mediating among institutional constituencies or between the ministry and campus groups, but the range of relationships and their centrality to the institution's future is generally greater for the academic CEO. In his now classic description, Kerr describes the U.S. university president as follows (1995, 22):

> The university president in the United States is expected to be a friend of the students, a colleague of the faculty, a good fellow with the alumni, a sound administrator with the trustees, a good speaker with the public, an astute bargainer with the foundations and the federal agencies, a politician with the state legislature, a friend of industry, labor, and agriculture, a persuasive diplomat with donors, a champion of education generally, a supporter of the professions (particularly law and medicine), a spokesman to the press, a scholar in his own right, a public servant at the state and national levels, a devotee of opera and football equally.

Academic CEOs generally have more power and authority than elected rectors (Trow 1985). They usually have control over the budget, and multiple funding sources that enable their institutions not to depend on any single one. Untenured administrative staff allow flexibility in staffing decisions and provide academic CEOs greater control over the appointment of the internal senior management team and the designation of their responsibilities.

Nonetheless, most academic CEOs assert that their formal powers are relatively limited and that they lead mostly by persuasion, as do elected rectors. Few academic CEOs function like their corporate counterparts; they are answerable to multiple constituencies, and there are greater limits to their formal authority. In the United States, boards of trustees, system heads, and legislatures add additional crucial variables to the leadership equation. Vice-chancellors in the United Kingdom and Australia are answerable to councils, whose members are both external to the institution and internal; many other countries have similar structures. Students, faculty members, staff, and often community members and other external groups expect to participate in important decisions, and they may have real power to block the president's initiatives. Wise presidents rarely seek to impose their vision or will; they are more likely to rely on persuasion, conciliation, and consensus building. Labor unions pose a special challenge for academic leaders: many areas of academic as well as organizational life may be subject to formal labor negotiations, thus defining the leadership role in a very particular way.

The academic CEO is squarely in the middle of external and internal pressure groups. Lawmakers and funding agencies demand "greater productivity," but faculty members guard their right to teach as they deem educationally sound; students need courses to be offered frequently enough to allow them to move through the curriculum in a timely way, but budget cutters require that course offerings be reduced.

In the growing non-university sector of postsecondary education (in the case of the United Kingdom, the former polytechnics), the academic CEO may indeed function more like a corporate executive. Without the tradition of faculty self-governance and the autonomy of schools and faculties within the university, such institutions are freer to make top-down decisions and to base their actions on purely financial considerations; in short, to behave more like businesses.

In spite of the constraints, academic CEOs have more points of leverage than other types of institutional heads to act as change agents—through allocation of resources, contacts with external constituencies, or flexibility in staffing. They are often appointed with the expectation that they will initiate change—even if it consists only of doing things differently from their predecessors! The pressures for change from external constituencies and the expectation that the academic CEO can "make it happen" are great. Thus, academic CEOs are often in the position of explaining the academic enterprise to skeptical or hostile outsiders, educating those who equate hours in the classroom with total hours spent on the job, defending academic freedom even when it offends, and arguing for stability and preservation as a counterweight to political, financial, or ideological pressures. Academic CEOs find themselves in multiple binds. When acting as change agents, they will often encounter resistance within the institution, while at the same time they must defend and interpret the very institution they would want to change.

As academic institutions become more complex and the demands of society more insistent, the academic CEO model seems to be gaining appeal, but certainly not without real trepidation on the part of many. The corporate model does not sit well with most academics, who see the core values and purposes of the academy as fundamentally at odds with corporate-style management. Yet, as pressures mount for institutions to be more relevant to economic development, to be more accountable to the public, to find alternate sources of funds, and to take a more active role in developing linkages with external groups of all sorts, it will be difficult for academic leaders to be simply first among equals. And as the dialogue at many international meetings of U.S. presidents and rectors from other countries reveals, strengthening the role of leaders through changes in governance structures and policies appeals to many elected rectors who perceive that they have insufficient authority to discharge their responsibilities. As institutions shed their special status as protected, well-financed communities of scholars, the kind of leadership required seems to be changing. This shift to stronger managerial leadership is a trend that bears watching.

The Elected Rector

The most prevalent model of university head, worldwide, is that of the rector who is elected directly by senior faculty members or by a broadly representative senate. The rector is usually from the ranks of the senior professors; an insider to the institution.[6] Unlike the academic CEO, the rector frequently "campaigns" for the office in a competitive election. The base of support built by an election can be much broader than that of an appointed academic CEO. If the voters are solely senior professors, the rector's constituents represent an "electoral oligarchy." A "multiple constituent" model, in which electors include administrative staff, students, and perhaps others, would presumably require an even broader base of support (Neave 1988, 107).

The elected rector plays both an internal and external role, presiding over institutional decision-making groups, as well as representing the institution externally. In many respects, the elected rector combines the responsibilities of the U.S. chief academic officer and the president. The result of this heightened internal role is generally that the rector, unlike the U.S. president, is not perceived as a distant manager who is no longer personally connected to the academic enterprise, and whose chief concerns are public relations, fund-raising, and representation. Rectors are "real" academics who, after their term or terms expire, return to the classroom. Most continue to teach while they serve as rectors and consequently do not lose touch with their disciplines (which the academic CEO most often does).

As Trow (1985) points out, the ability of rectors to exercise leadership is limited not only by their method of selection, but also by the complicated structures within the university, in which representatives to decision-making councils are expected to act as representatives of their constituencies. These individuals are answerable to the groups they represent, and they come to the table primarily to negotiate on behalf of their constituencies. (This can also happen in universities where the head is an academic CEO; for example, on unionized campuses in the United States.) Constituent politics can take on a life of their own; newly developed mechanisms to democratize the universities of Central Europe and South Africa have resulted in the creation of processes and bodies that have the potential of paralyzing an institution. At one institution in South Africa, various groups took the better part of a year to negotiate the composition of the search committee for the new vice-chancellor.

To the American observer, the system of electing the rector seems to guarantee that vigorous leadership will be thwarted. But academic leaders in countries where this model prevails find having "real academics" as leaders to be a tremendous advantage because of their stature and credibility. Another critical view of the role of the rector is that the "best and the brightest" are not attracted to the job, since it is not a position of much importance. A civil servant or other professional administrator often serves as chief administrative and financial officer, thus "freeing" the rector to tend to academic business, but possibly wielding a great deal of power through budgetary knowledge and control. The rector may not have any say in who occupies that position.

The limited terms of elected rectors can also hamper their effectiveness. Typically, the term of an elected rector is between three and five years. Most institutional heads agree that it takes at least two years to learn the job, so that a term of only three years is generally insufficient to actually accomplish any ambitious agenda. The academic CEO theoretically can serve indefinitely, and thus stay in office long enough to have a much greater impact than the short-term rector. In practice, however, the differences in the length of service may not be so great. Many rectors are elected for a second term, and the length of service of U.S. presidents is decreasing. The average terms of presidents of public U.S. research universities is 4.8 years (Ross, Green, and Henderson 1993, 38). Intense pressures—especially in public institutions—make U.S. presidents highly vulnerable to being fired by their boards or resigning before their terms are up, either under pressure or out of frustration.[7] Thus, in spite of the potential for elected rectors to serve much shorter terms than U.S. presidents, the terms of both are likely to range between three and five years. Those rectors who serve two or more terms might actually serve longer than their typical U.S. counterparts.

The Ministerial Model

In many countries, the Ministry of Education or the head of state has the final say in the appointment of a rector. The "approval" role is generally a rather benign one, though the potential for using this power to exert control always exists. This type of approval for the appointment of a rector is prevalent in continental Western Europe (Neave 1988), where universities are subject to constitutional and administrative law, and the heads have civil service status, as do tenured staff. The Japanese Ministry of Education also approves the elected rector of public universities.

In less democratic nations, the ministerial role is more direct, with the education ministry sometimes appointing and firing the rector at will. Recent government crackdowns in Nigeria and Kenya have included the removal of the heads of higher education institutions. Until recently, rectors were named directly by the ministries of education in Central Europe and South Africa, and for some institutions in Mexico, by the state authorities. However, reforms granting institutional autonomy in Central European nations have now eliminated any role for the government in approving the appointment of rectors in that region. The ministry, or its equivalent, also plays an important role in Korea, Singapore, and China.

Clearly, the potential for government interference and ideological control is high when the institutional head functions more as an extension of the government than as an intermediary between campus constituencies and government. However, there are important gradations of the ministry role. A strong ministry, such as in Japan or France, can have a profound effect in terms of highly centralized direction of policy and programs, but without the motive of ideological control that is found in repressive political regimes.

THE TASKS OF LEADERS

While systems, structures, and national norms vary, it is possible to identify a set of leadership tasks that are common to all university heads. Leading an academic enterprise involves a core group of functions: responding to external pressures, managing financial and human resources, juggling multiple and conflicting constituencies, and promoting change. The leadership tasks outlined below[8] suggest a common framework for considering the tasks of institutional leaders.

Clarifying and Determining Direction

Conventional wisdom holds that leaders have "visions" for their countries, organizations, or institutions. As noted earlier, vision is a necessary but insufficient ingredient for leadership, which requires the ability to engage followers in formulating and implementing a shared agenda. Thus, the process of clarifying and determining direction is an arduous and continuous interactive process. Shaped by external realities and pressures, it draws on the institutional head's unique capacity to see the whole of the institution (in contrast to others, who operate from the vantage point of a particular function or department) and the aspirations and visions of various constituents. The task of clarifying and determining direction will be carried out differently by the academic CEO, who may have more license than the elected rector to assert a leadership role in developing a vision. In the case of the ministerial head, the institution's direction is most likely determined by the government, leaving less freedom for the head to shape the institution's course.

Managing Change

While the phrase "managing change" overstates the case, suggesting that the change process can be controlled by an adept leader, it is not inaccurate as a descriptor of a major leadership task. As higher education around the world undergoes profound change, leaders must shape the process to the extent feasible, monitoring and interpreting the external environment and providing a forum for change to be discussed, understood, debated, and implemented. Societies and organizations cannot change if they cannot clarify the values that underlie conflicts or see dissonant points of view that permit collective learning. The role of the leader is to facilitate the process of "adaptive change" (Heifetz 1994), engaging people in the hard work of facing tough issues and closing the gap between aspirations and reality, with all the pain, anxiety, and conflict that this effort entails. It is no wonder that institutions (and societies) are so often ungrateful to those who take on these difficult tasks. It is always tempting to avoid the work involved and to look for easy solutions in the form of scapegoats, or to seek omniscient leaders who will take the burdens of change off the shoulders of others. The search for charismatic leaders is the opposite of the struggle to face change. As Heifetz points out, "the source of their charisma is our own yearning" (1994, 66).

Setting the Tone

As the chief spokesperson for the institution, internally and externally, the president, vice-chancellor, or rector is constantly articulating institutional values and aspirations. However, leaders set the tone not simply through rhetoric (which, if it does not match actions, is quickly seen as hollow). The leader's own behaviors, the policies and procedures that are instituted, and the way decisions are deliberated and made, are important determinants of institutional climate. That is not to say that leaders can single-handedly control institutional climate—nothing could be more unrealistic, given how complex its determinants are. But through the moral force of their words and actions, they can set an example for the community.

Overseeing Education and Research

Teaching, learning, and research—the core functions of higher education— must be the driving concern of academic leaders. Sometimes, the attention paid to these issues will be quite direct; for example, through deliberations about curriculum, approval of academic appointments, or development of student policies. In other instances, the attention paid to academic matters will be through resource issues, questions pertaining to the use of facilities, or by explaining and defending the institution to external publics. Even though the academic CEO is more likely to spend time providing a context and support structure for teaching, learning, and research through external relations and fund-raising, the ultimate objective is still to enhance the core functions of the institution. Broader educational policy issues such as academic freedom or affirmative action pose special challenges for academic leaders, and they often find themselves called upon to defend the rights of individuals to express unpopular and offensive views on their campuses.

Relating the Institution to Its External Constituencies

Academic leaders speak for the institution to the many publics that it serves and that support it. These publics include students, parents, faculty members, staff, alumni, donors, government officials, employers and the business community, and the general public. Increasingly, presidents, vice-chancellors, and rectors also represent their institutions internationally. As traditional universities have tried to become more relevant to social and economic development and to seek alternative sources of funding, they have worked harder to foster ties with various external groups. In the growing non-university sector of postsecondary education, and in the community college sector in the United States and Canada, such ties are part of the institution's mission and are less novel to their leaders.

Increasingly, academic leaders are called upon to defend the institutions they lead to a skeptical public and to make the case for funding to government agencies and ministries. The competition for resources in many countries has required institutional leaders to be advocates, defenders, and lobbyists for the whole of higher education. As the imperative to become more international has seized higher education, leaders have taken a more active role in promoting and finding the resources to fund collaboration. The push for a "European dimension" has sharply accelerated the international activities of most European universities and their rectors.

Securing Resources and Overseeing Their Use

While many systems of higher education are largely dependent on government funding, the trend worldwide is to diversify funding through contracts for research and services with private industry, summer programs and other events that provide revenue, and, increasingly, through fund-raising. The role of the president or rector ranges from actually seeking funds to fostering a climate and developing policies that will enable institutional units and individuals to be entrepreneurial themselves. The task of overseeing the use of resources, like that of overseeing the academic function, is subject to considerable variation. In some countries, a chief administrative officer has primary responsibility for managing the budget, and the rector has relatively little involvement. In the United States, while there is a chief financial officer, that person works under the broad policy direction of the president. Increasingly, leaders are recognizing the importance of the link between the deployment of resources and strategic planning and change. Given the growing constraints of most institutional budgets, leaders can ill afford to ignore this dimension, whatever the structural arrangements and traditions of the particular country.

Overseeing Operations

In some countries, rectors concentrate their efforts on academic matters, leaving issues of administration, budget, and physical plant to others. The academic CEO, however, has overall responsibility for such issues, which are usually led by senior administrators with a high level of experience and expertise. These senior administrators, usually vice presidents, form the president's "management team" and keep the president informed on routine matters, seeking policy guidance in general and consulting on problem areas as needed.

THE ROLE OF CULTURE:
OPPORTUNITIES AND CONSTRAINTS FOR LEADERSHIP

National Cultures

Academic leaders operate within their national cultures, as well as in the academic culture. Cultural values underlie a society's assumptions about the role of higher education in that society—for example, whether higher education provides greater benefit to the society or to the individual. The norms regarding individual and collective behaviors in an academic community are cultural creations. In some societies, leadership is equated with forcefulness and authoritarian behaviors; "servant leadership" would be inconceivable. In others, as Ishikawa illustrates in his chapter on Japan (Chapter 15), it is unseemly for the rector to appear to lead too vigorously. But social norms can change, or at least give way to external pressures.

Societies also differ in their conception of how higher education serves society. Who attends and who pays are fundamental issues, reflecting the changing nature of many societies. Although there is a worldwide effort to develop mass systems of higher education, in most countries higher education historically served a small proportion of the university-aged population. Canada and the United States have extensive systems of community colleges—a strategy for mass education that is barely 30 years old but has been highly successful in opening access to postsecondary education. Also, ideas about higher education's relationship to the larger society are influenced by different cultural norms and traditions. How directly involved in the problems of society should an institution of higher education be? To what extent will partnerships with business distort the basic mission of a university, directing it to opportunities to produce revenue rather than to teach and conduct research? While the recognition is growing worldwide that higher education must be more connected to national and international development, traditions of conserving the distance and the autonomy of the academic enterprise are powerful.

It is important to note that external realities can change quickly and often profoundly. Environmental shifts may clash with prevailing norms and practices, or they may reflect cultural shifts already underway. Democratic elections in South Africa and the transition to democracy in Central Europe and many Latin American nations illustrate dramatic and rapid social transformations that have affected higher education. The former Communist countries are rethinking basic issues such as the structural separation of teaching and research. Emerging Latin American democracies are examining the relationship of universities to national economic development. Postapartheid South Africa must restructure its entire education system to meet the needs of the previously excluded and drastically undereducated majority and of the nation as a whole. Government policies such as those introduced by the Thatcher government changed the face of British higher education in less than a decade. Australia seems to be headed for similar financial cutbacks. Institutions all over the world are under pressure from their governments and from international donors to be more entrepreneurial and to generate income from nongovernmental sources, using such means as auxiliary enterprises, research contracts, and fundraising.

Academic Culture

In spite of the notable differences of traditions and cultural norms in different countries, academic institutions seem to have more cultural similarities that derive from their academic mission than differences that can be attributed to the country in which they are located. To speak of a "universal academic culture" is not an overstatement. The values of unfettered inquiry, the pursuit of knowledge for its own sake, the quest for freedom from external interference, and the dedication to preparing the next generation of leaders, professionals, and citizens are transcendent academic values. Several common characteristics of higher education institutions are especially important to enhancing or reducing their capacity to change.

Shared Governance

Teaching staff expect to play an important role in making academic and institutional decisions. Nearly every institution has multiple committees and a faculty senate or similar body that deliberates and makes decisions about curriculum, academic and research policies, and budgetary matters. The power of these bodies varies from one country to another. In the new democracies of Central Europe, the faculty senates have substantial formal power, whereas the rectors have relatively little. In the United States, presidents and other administrators have comparatively greater authority, but as Johnstone asserts in the chapter on the United States (Chapter 7), they still feel relatively powerless.

The exercise of power by an institutional head in ways that suggest lack of consultation, arbitrariness, or high-handedness is likely to meet with disapproval, anger, or resistance. Collegial governance, with its prevailing norms of consultation and building consensus, makes change a slow and laborious process. Industries seeking to restructure, reengineer, or simply cut costs have far greater ability to move swiftly and decisively. A pivotal question in the change process is whether it is possible (or desirable, some would say) to preserve collegial shared governance in light of the need for constant and rapid change.

But not all decision making is internal to institutions. Individuals and groups vested with decision-making powers are generally answerable to a governing body or to the government, or both. In many countries, institutions are governed by a council or board that is the supreme institutional authority. In the United States, the governing board or board of trustees (known as a "lay board") is composed mainly or entirely of individuals external to the institution. Students or faculty members may have seats on the board—sometimes as voting members, other times without voting privileges. Many other countries have councils whose members are largely (or exclusively) members of the academic community—students, faculty members, administrators, and technical staff. Councils in the United Kingdom, South Africa, and France, for example, are mixtures of insiders and outsiders. Who decides? is a central question in any academic governance system; countries vary in the structures they use to balance the rights and responsibilities of various decision-making groups. Where a governing board or council does not exist, the ministry of education may have a freer hand to dominate institutional decision making.

Amateur Leaders and Managers

Academic culture also creates expectations about leadership and management. On the one hand, universities are recognized to be complex entities, involving tens of thousands of students, thousands of academic staff members and other employees, and large budgets. Although there continues to be resistance to the growing "managerialism" in higher education, it is increasingly difficult to ignore the fact that complex enterprises must be expertly managed, especially because the public demands efficiency in return for its financial support. But the coexistence of academic and managerial values is an uneasy one, and academics continue to bemoan the intrusions on their autonomy created by external evaluations, efficiency measures, and efforts to "rationalize" an enterprise that is fundamentally difficult to quantify and measure.

The compromise is that academic administrators—presidents, rectors, or vice-chancellors; vice presidents or vice-rectors; deans; and department heads—are generally "insiders" to the academy; academics themselves. This academic legitimacy is an important source of power and of the leader's ability to garner support. The obvious disadvantage to this traditional selection process is that good researchers or teachers do not necessarily make good managers or leaders. The prerequisites to be selected for the job are not related to the requirements for performing it, and most academic leaders have no preparation for their managerial responsibilities; they simply learn on the job through trial and error.

In contrast to most other countries, where rectors, vice-rectors, or deans are elected for fixed terms and then rotate back into their old jobs as faculty members, the United States has developed a "managerial class"; people who pursue careers in academic administration. Typically, these individuals may spend the first part of their careers as teachers and scholars, and when they have attained the rank of full professor, they begin a new career phase as deans, vice presidents, and sometimes presidents. The advantage is the existence of a pool of experienced individuals who may have attended a few workshops here and there, but who have learned their jobs primarily by doing them over a period of years. Each step up the administrative ladder builds on the previous position. U.S. administrators are highly mobile, bringing fresh perspectives and different experiences to a variety of institutions. The price, however, is considerable. The tensions between faculty members and administrators run high at many institutions. Administrators often perceive faculty members as refusing to recognize the external realities that are driving institutions and as unwilling to change. In turn, faculty members accuse academic administrators of being insensitive to the academic enterprise (even though they come from the ranks of the faculty) and more preoccupied with money and efficiency than with academic excellence. Distrust, too, frequently permeates the relationship between faculty and administration; the resulting struggle is a serious impediment to positive change.[9]

The tradition of the amateur manager/leader is a double-edged sword; that leaders are generally insiders, that is, cultural products of the institutions that they seek to shape, is a source of both strength and weakness. On the one hand, their heritage gives these leaders the understanding of the culture and the enterprise, some shared values, and the credibility that are central to their ability to lead. On the other hand, it may fail to give them the critical distance or the willingness to violate the cultural norms sufficiently to function as change agents. To be both a product of the environment and a change agent is not an easy combination, but it can also be a powerful recipe for leadership.

Fragmentation

Contemporary university leaders are dealing with institutions composed of nearly autonomous schools and faculties. To further complicate matters, in democracies, individual professors decide what to teach and how, and departments and schools decide whom to hire, what curriculum to teach, and frequently, how to allocate its resources. Faculty members' loyalties are more often to their discipline than to their institution; the search for truth, as defined by each professor, is far more important than the search for institutional cohesion. The lack of cohesion in a complex university makes it very difficult to steer; the department and the school or faculty are usually the most important units of decision making. Thus, devolution of authority is a mixed blessing. The advantages are increased flexibility and greater opportunity to hold individual units accountable. The disadvantages are that decentralization can contribute to incoherence and balkanization. How, then, does an institution develop a common agenda or the sense that the whole is greater than the sum of its parts? How can institutions develop a concept of the common good that transcends the interests of a single department or school?

Multiple Stakeholders

Higher education has many different and often conflicting stakeholders, including students, faculty members, staff, the public, and governments. Meeting the needs of multiple groups presents difficult policy dilemmas. While students who have enjoyed free postsecondary education will resist giving up this benefit, competing demands for national resources are pushing governments to pass at least some of the costs to students and their families. While teaching staff cherish their academic freedom and the structure of academic life that gives them time out of the classroom to conduct research and stay current in their fields, governments are seeking to expand higher education with little or no additional resources. These conflicting interests pose similar dilemmas for institutional leaders. American presidents who run afoul of their governing boards are fired; elected rectors who make enemies among their voters are not reelected. Discontented faculty members, workers, and students strike, and they have the capacity to close an institution indefinitely, as has frequently been the case in Africa and was formerly so in Latin America. Keeping all these groups equally satisfied is clearly an impossible task; a more modest leadership challenge (which is sometimes beyond the control of an institutional leader) is to prevent any one group from bringing the institution to a halt.

John Coleman, former president of Haverford College, describes the position of the leader among conflicting stakeholders:

> Organization charts show the president of a college on top, just a step below the financial angels. In actuality, a president is at the center of a web of conflicting interest groups, none of which can ever be fully satisfied. He is, by definition, almost always wrong. (Coleman 1974, 6, cited by Strauss 1995, 109)

THE FUTURE OF ACADEMIC LEADERSHIP

As institutions around the world become more entrepreneurial, more relevant to society, and more accountable to funders and "consumers," the role of institutional leaders at all levels is likely to become more important. What, then, might be the context for academic leadership in the next century? Will the tasks of leaders be the same or different than they are today? An examination of current thinking on leadership and on the nature of organizations is instructive in considering the future.

Contemporary writing about leadership is distinguished by several predominant themes, reflecting changing ideas about political systems and social structures, the nature of work and organizations, and the rapidly accelerating rate of change. Images of static organizations have given way to fluid ones that must forever reinvent themselves. Leadership in today's terms is less about power and control than about understanding ambiguity, developing other leaders, accepting that change is a permanent state, and creating a shared vision and meaning. In this more ambiguous world of contemporary organizations and structures, leaders' strategies are shaped by the moment in time, the situation at hand, and the larger culture. However, strategies are not ends unto themselves; they must be rooted in a moral vision that anchors leaders and followers, a value system that transcends the needs of the moment or the fad of the day. Group effort and teamwork have supplanted competitive individualism—so dominant in Western thought, especially in the United States—as the predominant way of getting work done; collaboration is valued over competition. The salient themes of current thinking about leadership are discussed in following five sections.

The Role of Values

As contemporary society searches for moral anchors, leadership is increasingly seen as values-driven (Bennis and Nanus 1985; Burns 1978; De Pree 1992; Gardner 1990; Greenleaf 1977; Heifetz 1994; O'Toole 1995; Senge 1990). Leaders have moral obligations to their organizations and to society—to treat people decently, to encourage good citizenship, to promote collaboration, and to develop organizations that are humane and socially responsible. Leadership can serve as an ennobling force to followers, by being morally elevating or "transformational" (Burns 1978). Leaders help organizations or societies revitalize shared beliefs and values. For many scholars of leadership, the values dimension is what distinguishes leadership from management.

O'Toole (1995, 11) asserts that leadership is not situational or "contingent"; it stems from a moral imperative. Universal values of trust, respecting and listening to followers, and inclusion must guide all leaders. "In this realm of morality," he asserts, "there are no contingencies." While leadership by inclusion, respect for followers, and becoming a leader of leaders may be "unnatural behavior" to those who would command change through heroic leadership, O'Toole insists that such "command and control" behaviors are both morally wrong, and in the long run, ineffective. But the latter is the less important point for him. Some have rushed to adopt values-driven leadership and espouse the principles of respect and inclusion because they are expedient and because they fit with the expectations and conventional wisdom of the 1990s. To be fashionable in management theory and practice is far less important than to be fundamentally moral, maintains O'Toole.

Greenleaf's (1977, 13) servant leader is a dreamer, but one who listens first and is acutely attuned to the needs of others. Those who are served by the servant leaders are "healthier, wiser, freer, more autonomous." Senge's (1990) learning organization is based on the concept of "personal mastery," in which leaders are continually examining the spiritual and moral aspects of their lives and their work, what matters to them, and how they can help others grow.

While the concern with values is not always explicit, higher education is always dealing with these questions. Who teaches, what is taught and how, and who decides are all values-laden issues. Similarly, societal values come into play in deciding who attends higher education institutions, how society pays for higher education, and what the public expects from these institutions.

Higher education leaders are in the center of these crucial issues. They must have a consistent framework of values that guide their own actions and that focus the campus's attention on the institution's values and purpose. A strong sense of values is essential to temper the managerial concerns that can easily predominate as institutions grapple with an unending series of budget, regulatory, and operational issues.

Certainly, not all leaders are noble; many have been responsible for terrible destruction and evil. Because leadership is a reciprocal activity, followers are not innocent of the evil seemingly wrought by their leaders. Evil leaders elicit the collaboration of their followers, perhaps exploiting their weaknesses and hatreds, but nonetheless leading either with outright permission or tacit complicity. The ability of leaders to tap into the values and aspirations of their followers, be they noble or base, is the source of their power and legitimacy. Burns (1978, 20) asserts that leadership derives its strength from the congruence of the goals of leader and followers. Such congruence does not necessarily take leader or follower to a higher moral ground, but it has the potential to do so. "Transforming" leaders bring a moral dimension to leadership; they "*engage* with others in such a way that leaders and followers raise one another to higher levels of motivation and morality."

Complexity and Ambiguity

New metaphors to depict organizations abound. Today's theorists no longer view organizations as tidy hierarchical structures. Organizations are not Newtonian machines—closed systems organized into clearly delineated parts, functions, and roles, with clear boundaries and lines of authority (Wheatley 1992). Because organizations are complex webs of seemingly chaotic inter-relationships, patterns and connections can be discerned only over long periods of time. Organizations are networks of people and problems; webs of culture, habits, myths, and formal and informal authority. The predominant image is one of overlapping circles rather than a pyramid. Furthermore, organizations (including institutions of higher education) are part of a complex network of other institutions and entities; depending on the country, they may include ministries, other government agencies, intermediary bodies, and voluntary organizations.

Organizations are also capable of regeneration and renewal. Healthy and adaptive organizations are "learning organizations, organizations where people continually expand their capacity to create the results they truly desire, where new and expansive patterns of thinking are nurtured, where collective aspiration is set free, and where people are continually learning how to learn together" (Senge 1990, 3). A key skill for leaders of such organizations is the ability to engage in "systems" thinking; that is, to see the connections rather than the discrete parts, "to see patterns of change rather than 'snapshots'" (Senge 1990, 68). Organizations are organisms in constant movement, where the whole is different than the sum of its parts. In such organizations, leaders are stewards, designers of processes, leaders of leaders, rather than omniscient decision makers or crusaders. They orchestrate a process of discovery and learning; they do not hand down solutions.

Such thinking has come a long way from the management theories that predominated in the United States for the better part of this century and that still underlie much of American thinking about organizations and political life. Beginning with the assembly line in the Ford Motor Company, management has been concerned with creating systems that can be controlled in an environment presumed to be stable. Leaders who know what is best for the organization and its workers sit atop a hierarchy. The need to rely on a wise few to lead society and to preserve stability and order is a fundamental concept of Plato's meritocracy, as well as of Confucian thought (O'Toole 1995). It is so deeply rooted that new paradigms such as those described above are often met with skepticism or outright hostility.

As the environment gets more turbulent and the pressures mount, some react by calling for stronger leadership at the helm; the heroic leaders and "tough guys" who will navigate the stormy seas and keep the ship afloat. Others maintain that it will never be "smooth sailing again" (Champy 1995) and that we now live in a time of "perpetual whitewater" (Vaill 1989). New times call for a new model of leadership.

Sharing Leadership and Accountability

The corporate sector has discovered shared leadership and embraced it with great enthusiasm. While higher education often adapts innovations in management from the corporate sector, academe has practiced shared governance since medieval times, when the European university was a community of scholars. But the trend in many countries has been to move away from the collegial model and to take a more managerial approach to institutional processes. The result has been a growing tension between the teaching staff and academic and other administrators, or between institutions and external bodies. The question of who decides is often contentious. As noted earlier, some argue that the more institutions are stressed with financial pressures or government directives, the greater the need for swift and decisive action by powerful leaders who have freedom to act without cumbersome consultations (Fisher 1984; Kerr and Gade 1986).

This corporate model of decision making does not fit readily into academe, which is more fluid as an organization and more difficult to control than a corporation. Universities have multiple centers of power and multiple leaders. Some leaders have formally designated roles; others are highly respected members of the institutional community who have no formal leadership positions. The challenge for the designated leaders is to mobilize the energy of informal leaders in service of a shared agenda, in many ways a more complex undertaking than in a corporation. (In the absence of effective leadership from the top, others in the institution may play the same role, albeit with greater difficulty since their formal authority may be limited or nonexistent.) Without such overall direction, dispersed leadership can worsen fragmentation and political conflict on campus, but at its best, it can provide energy, creativity, and new ideas.

Dispersing leadership is not synonymous with having everyone participate in every decision.[10] Sharing leadership and accountability means making decisions at lower levels in the institution and having those groups or individuals also be accountable for those decisions. Shared leadership rejects the "command and control" model of managing organizations. New-style organizations are flat, giving people autonomy over their own work and removing layers of people whose jobs were to look over other people's shoulders. The Total Quality Management (TQM) and Continuous Quality Improvement (CQI) movements emphasize the importance of simplifying procedures and the participation of those who will do the work in the design of systems that they will use. Participation in addressing the larger questions of institutional direction, as well as in shaping one's own work, are important factors in enabling higher education institutions to adapt to an uncertain and changing environment.

Leadership by Teams

Groups are an important mechanism to accomplish the work of organizations and higher education institutions. The choice of the word "team"—derived from the world of competitive sports—undoubtedly reflects a U.S. cultural value of competition. Teams are distinguished from other kinds of working groups by their sense of shared purpose, by having real work to accomplish as a group, and by sharing accountability for the outcome (Katzenbach and Smith 1993). Teams are not the same as traditional academic committees, which often deliberate and advise rather than make decisions, and whose composition is more likely to be determined according to political representation than by the skills of the individual members. Many presidents and rectors have a senior management team. Some are advisory to the institutional head, others make decisions as a group. Teams have the advantage of bringing multiple perspectives to bear on issues and of promoting thinking that goes beyond the confines of a single department, unit, or discipline. As institutions strive to be more cross-functional and interdisciplinary, teamwork will be key.

Creating Meaning

A final theme in the current scholarship on leadership concerns the role of leaders in creating meaning (Middlehurst 1993; Bensimon, Neumann, and Birnbaum 1989; Bolman and Deal 1991). This interpretive role of leaders involves fostering shared perceptions and beliefs, drawing on the institution's values, culture, and traditions. The symbolic dimension of leadership implies that perceptions of reality count more than "objective" reality, and that language, rituals, and stories help create shared meaning in an organization. In so doing, leaders help people make sense out of confusing events.

To the extent that shaping culture is an important task for leaders in the change process, the symbolic dimension of leadership is a preeminent one. Influencing culture is a complex and subtle task, for institutions have multiple cultures that are firmly entrenched. Thus, a leader's work—whether it be a speech, a management decision, or a casual conversation—always has a symbolic and interpretive dimension. Leaders create meaning, shape reality, and articulate values at the same time that they engage in a variety of the seemingly pedestrian tasks of administering, convening, and decision making.

CONCLUSION: THE LEADERSHIP CHALLENGE

Despite constraints imposed by human nature, structures, and traditions, higher education leaders can and do make a difference. While some scholars assert that leaders have a minimal impact in the ambiguous and anarchic culture of higher education (Cohen and March 1974), this view is not universally shared by U.S. scholars of academic leadership. At one end of the spectrum, Cohen and March view educational institutions as "organized anarchies" characterized by unclear goals and decisions that are often unplanned. It is extremely difficult to exercise leadership in an organization that is so confused about its purposes. Bennis (1976, 26) agrees with this characterization, contending that the university "is society's closest realization of the pure model of *anarchy*, that is, the locus of decision making is the individual." Trow (1985, 145), among others, disagrees, claiming that the ability of institutions to adapt and respond "must be attributed to the ability of institutional leaders to innovate, to motivate, and above all, to lead." The realities of leadership may lie between the two extremes, as is so often the case. Higher education leaders are neither omnipotent nor powerless; the art of leadership is to recognize the constraints while seizing the initiative. Similarly, leaders must balance the need to initiate change and to preserve what is central to the long-term well-being of the institution. The latter task still requires leadership, for its absence produces incoherent or inappropriate changes in terms of the overall institutional and social needs. As the authors of the following chapters illustrate, although national and institutional norms provide different concepts of the role of president, vice-chancellor, or rector with varying limitations on that individual's ability to create and implement an agenda for change, the fact remains that the role always has the potential for leadership, no matter how subtly or indirectly it is exercised.

It is also worth stressing that not all academic leaders are change agents, and that higher education will change even without strong leadership at the helm of an institution. Some leaders are appointed or elected *not* to move the institution forward, but rather to preserve the status quo. This mandate may be explicit or covert. Institutions will undergo change as a natural process, even if there is no conspicuous leadership. These changes will represent the sum of the efforts of enterprising individuals, or the effect of pressures that could not be resisted. Absent leadership, *reactive change* will fill the void. And indeed, should there be a leadership void at the top, many different individuals throughout the institution can still provide leadership, causing considerable forward motion in some areas. In fact, it is highly likely that leadership will emerge somewhere else in the institution.

Change is not always traumatic or highly visible, and leaders who are managing that process are not necessarily doing so with great fanfare. "Leaving one's thumbprint" on events (Gardner 1990, 53) may be a quiet act. Changing the culture of an institution in order to effect deep and lasting change is a long-term effort, and one that requires working within the framework of the existing culture, rather than going to war with it (Birnbaum

1992). Resistance to change is pervasive in individuals and in groups; the leader's task is not to impose change (for it will surely be resisted), but to provide ways for people to see the need for change, embrace it, and to share the vision of the rightness of the change. Therein lies an enormous and frustrating task.

Change is also unpredictable, jumbled, and messy. Even leaders who are change agents are not changing things all the time. Nor is change a linear process; it stops and starts, goes sideways, shifts emphasis, and loses intensity and momentum. Not only is its path uneven, but the role of leadership is not necessarily clear at the time.

A major challenge for institutional leaders is managing the impact of the external forces that are either demanding or imposing change. External mandates from government agencies or accrediting bodies and public opinion undoubtedly can force changes in curricula, hiring practices, or rewards. But if leaders do not engage the people who must live by these different rules, it is entirely possible, as van Vught (1994) argues, that the result will be a "culture of compliance" rather than any real shift in attitude or values. Absent the pressures, the behaviors revert. Enduring fundamental change requires that those who are affected undergo a change in their beliefs and values so that they become the implementers of change, not the passive victims of changing policies and pressures.

The challenges for higher education leaders are enormous and the stakes are high. Higher education has much to preserve, but without forward movement, colleges and universities will deteriorate. Society needs institutions that will stand apart and criticize it; that will produce knowledge and prepare professionals, workers, and good citizens; and that will contribute to the social and economic development of the nation that created it, while participating in an international community of academics. Institutions and their leaders have their work cut out for them.

NOTES

1. The United Kingdom has produced a number of important works in this area. For example, see Middlehurst 1993 and Weil 1994.

2. Hofstede (1993), for example, maintains that American concepts of management do not necessarily apply in other countries. In Germany, highly skilled workers, a historical product of the guild system, are more important than managers, and certainly do not need managers to motivate them to excellence. In Japan, worker groups are central, and individualistic theories of leadership do not apply to a culture where the group is expected to exercise control. He cites five important cultural variables that locate management in a culture: *power distance* (the degrees of inequality that are considered relatively normal within the society; *individualism/collectivism* (the value placed on individual as opposed to the group); *masculinity/femininity* (the degree to which such "masculine" behaviors such as assertiveness and competition are prized, as opposed to the more "feminine" ones of

collaboration and caring); *uncertainty avoidance* (the degree to which people prefer structured over unstructured situations); and *long term vs. short term* (particularly important to
Asian cultures, describing a value oriented to the future such as thrift and persistence).
Managers from different countries, he found, placed different values on the five dimensions, resulting in a different cultural profile for each country.

3. See Middlehurst 1993, 12–27, and Bensimon, Neumann, and Birnbaum 1989, 7–
33, for useful historical summaries.

4. I am grateful to D. Bruce Johnstone for this typology.

5. There are notable differences in the career paths of presidents of different
institutional types. The profiles of presidents of U.S. research universities—the U.S.
counterpart to classical universities in other parts of the world—are more like those of
their colleagues in other countries. They tend to come from the ranks of tenured
professors, but unlike their counterparts in other countries, are more likely to be humanists
or social scientists than natural scientists. The presidents of community colleges are more
likely than other U.S. college and university presidents to have a doctorate in the field of
education and to have spent fewer years teaching.

6. An effect of this method of selection is the low probability of naming women to
this position. In 1995 in the United States, approximately 16 percent of colleges and
universities were headed by women (ACE: Office of Women in Higher Education,
unpublished document, 1995). Data collected by ACE's Office of Women in Higher
Education indicate that there are only a handful of women who are university presidents or
rectors in other countries.

7. Typically, U.S. presidents have contracts that specify a term, often five years.
These contracts are nearly always renewable. It is only during the past decade that
contracts have become the norm; previously, most presidents served under informal
agreements established with the board. In the United Kingdom, some vice-chancellors
have lifetime appointments, others, appointed more recently, have contracts for a specified
term, also renewable.

8. Several of the tasks listed are drawn or adapted from Middlehurst 1993; Green
and McDade 1994; and Green 1989.

9. It should be noted, however, that distrust between faculty members and administrators is not unique to the United States, although it may be exacerbated by our structure.
See Boyer, Altbach, and Whitelaw 1994 for international perspectives on faculty-adminis-
trator relationships.

10. In the Netherlands, a three-person executive board, appointed by the Minister of
Education and Science and consisting of the chairman of the board, the rector (who also
serves as chairman of the council of deans), and a chief financial officer, makes administrative decisions jointly, replacing a single institutional head.

REFERENCES

Bass, M. M. 1990. *Bass and Stogdill's handbook of leadership: A survey of theory, research, and
    managerial applications.* 3rd ed. New York: Free Press.
Bennis, W. G. 1976. *The unconscious conspiracy: Why leaders can't lead.* New York:
    AMACOM.
Bennis, W. G., and B. Nanus. 1985. *Leaders: The strategies for taking charge.* New York:
    Harper and Row.

Bensimon, E.; A. Neumann; and R. Birnbaum. 1989. *Making sense of administrative leadership: The "L" word in higher education.* ASHE-ERIC Higher Education Report, no. 1. Washington, DC: School of Education and Human Development, George Washington University.

Birnbaum, R. 1992. *How academic leadership works: Understanding success and failure in the college presidency.* San Francisco: Jossey-Bass.

Bolman, L., and T. Deal. 1991. *Reframing organizations: Artistry, choice, and leadership.* San Francisco: Jossey-Bass.

Boyer, E.; P. Altbach; and M. J. Whitelaw. 1994. *The academic profession in international perspective.* Princeton, NJ: The Carnegie Foundation for the Advancement of Teaching.

Burns, J. M. 1978. *Leadership.* New York: Harper and Row.

Champy, J. 1995. *Reengineering management: The mandate for new leadership.* New York: Harper Collins.

Cohen, M., and J. G. March. 1974. *Leadership and ambiguity: The American college president.* New York: McGraw Hill.

Coleman, J. R. 1974. *Blue collar journal.* Philadelphia and New York: B. Lippincott & Co.

De Pree, M. 1992. *Leadership jazz.* New York: Doubleday.

Department of Employment, Education, and Training (DEET). 1994. *The modern vice-chancellor: Proceedings of a national conference initiated by the centre for continuing education, the Australian National University.* Canberra: Australian Government Publishing Service.

Fisher, J. 1984. *The power of the presidency.* New York: American Council on Education and Macmillan Publishing Company.

Freeman, F., ed. 1994. *Leadership education: A source book.* Greensboro: Center for Creative Leadership.

Gardner, John W. 1990. *On leadership.* New York: Free Press.

Green, M. 1989. *Leaders for a new era.: Strategies for higher education.* New York: Macmillian Publishing Co.

Green, M., and S. McDade. 1994. *Investing in higher education: A handbook of leadership development.* Phoenix, AZ: American Council on Education and Oryx Press.

Greenleaf, R. 1977. *Servant leadership: A journey into the nature of legitimate power and greatness.* New York: Paulist Press.

Heifetz, R. 1994. *Leadership wtihout easy answers.* Cambridge, MA: The Belknap Press of Harvard University Press.

Hofstede G. 1993. Cultural constraints in management theories. *Academy of Management Executive* 7 (1): 81–94.

Katzenbach, J., and D. Smith. 1993. *The wisdom of teams: Creating the high performance organization.* Boston: Harvard Business School Press.

Kerr, C. 1995. *The uses of the university.* 4th ed. Cambridge: Harvard University Press.

Kerr, C., and M. L. Gade. 1986.*The many lives of academic presidents: Time, place, and character.* Washington, DC: Association of Governing Boards of Universities and Colleges.

Kotter, J. P. 1990. What leaders really do. *Harvard Business Review* 68 (3) (May–June): 103–11.

Middlehurst, R. 1993. *Leading academics.* Buckingham, England: Society for Research in Higher Education and the Open University Press.

Neave, G. 1988. The making of the executive head: The process of defining institutional leaders in certain western European countries. *International Journal of Institutional Management in Higher Education.* 12 (1): 104–13.

O'Toole, J. 1995. *Leading change: Overcoming the ideology of comfort and the tyranny of custom*. San Francisco: Jossey-Bass.

Ross, M.; M. Green; and C. Henderson. 1993.*The American college president: A 1993 edition*. Washington, DC: American Council on Education.

Senge, P. 1990. *The fifth discipline: The art and practice of learning organizations*. New York: Doubleday.

Strauss, J. 1995. *Lessons learned*. Unpublished manuscript.

Trow, M. 1985. Comparative reflections on leadership in higher education. *European Journal of Education* 20: 2–3, 143–61.

Vaill, P. 1989. *Leadership as a performing art: New ideas for a world of chaotic change*. San Francisco: Jossey-Bass.

van Vught, F. 1994. Western Europe and North America. In *International developments in assuring quality in higher education*, edited by Alma Craft. London: The Falner Press.

Weil, S., ed. 1994. *Introducing change "from the top" in universities and colleges: Ten personal accounts*. London: Kogan Page.

Wheatley, M. J. 1992. *Leadership and the new science: Learning about organizations from an orderly universe*. San Francisco: Berrett-Koehler.

Wills, G. 1994. *Certain trumpets: The call of leaders*. New York: Simon and Schuster.

PART TWO

• • • • • • • • • • •

Regional Views

As nations attempt to remove trade barriers and form new economic alliances, regional groupings are taking on greater significance. The European Union stands out in its ambitious agenda, embracing mutual recognition of professional credentials, uniform standards for products, free flow of goods, and ultimately, a unified currency. Its educational programs have been equally ambitious, aiming to have 10 percent of its higher education students study in another country under the SOCRATES program. Asia has undertaken similar measures of economic cooperation and a new program to encourage mobility of students, faculty, and researchers—the University Mobility in Asia and the Pacific (UMAP). The North American Free Trade Agreement (NAFTA) is in its infancy, and efforts to promote trilateral collaboration among Mexico, the United States, and Canada are proceeding with very little government support.

Regionalization will, we believe, become an important force in the development of higher education. Therefore, in this section of the volume, we preface the national chapters, characterizing four larger regions. Clearly, there are dangers here. We would be unwise to overstate the commonalities within regions, caused by mere geographic proximity. As Postiglione indicates, the 30 countries in Asia are vastly different from one another. Africa has two distinct traditions from its colonial past—French and British—and other differences of size, political situation, and history. And South Africa certainly quite unlike its neighbors to the north. The delicate balancing act underway in European higher education, where the question of the day is how to provide a "European dimension" to postsecondary studies while preserving the unique cultural differences and strengths of national systems, is no easy task.

Thus, we turn first to a broad sweep of higher education as it unfolds in large regions of the world. The chapters on Asia, Africa, Western Europe, and Latin America are broad in scope and different in their approaches. They represent important ways of thinking about the future of higher education.

CHAPTER

3

Asian Higher Education

Growth, Diversity, and Change

Gerard A. Postiglione

Executive Summary. Asian economic growth has been the fastest in the world during recent decades. As many Asian nations have experienced strong economic growth and transitions to market economies, higher education has also undergone considerable expansion. With 30 countries, Asia is large and diverse, which makes concise descriptions and generalizations difficult. Among the similar challenges faced by higher education in Asian nations are: determining its role in economic development, funding, and responding to demands from the public and the expectations of the faculty. Although contributing to economic development is seen as valuable, that goal is balanced by competing demands that grow out of the social, cultural, and political contexts of the different countries—including religious goals, adherence to ideology, and equal access to higher education by minority ethnic groups and women. Participation rates are still relatively low in Asia (with the exception of Japan, the Philippines, South Korea, Taiwan, Hong Kong, and Singapore), and investment per student and as a percentage of total education expenditures are very modest. There are important distinctions among Asian nations according to levels of national income.

The author provides an overview of higher education in East Asia—Japan, Taiwan, China, South Korea, Singapore, and Hong Kong. Private higher education is flourishing in Japan, Taiwan, and South Korea, while in Singapore, Hong Kong, and China, only government-sponsored institutions can award degrees. Japan, with a participation rate of approximately 60 percent, is facing a declining population of college-age students, which may have severe consequences for private higher education, especially. At the other end of the spectrum is China, where about three percent of the college-age group attends universities; its challenge is both to expand and to improve quality.

In South Korea, Japan, Taiwan, and China, there is movement toward decentralization and greater institutional autonomy. Universities in Singapore enjoy some autonomy over internal administration, and administrative control and contribution to modernization are not seen as incompatible. Similarly, in China, institutions are called on to serve economic modernization while the Communist party maintains political control. As institutions become more independent and faculty members more professionalized, they are likely to seek greater voice in decision making and the selection of administrators.

• • • • • • • • • • • •

The pace of change in Asian higher education is as much a function of rapid economic development as it is of sociopolitical transition. Asian economic growth, the fastest in the world, was 8.6 percent in 1994 (IMF 1995), and much of the region is experiencing a transition in emphasis from Marxism to markets. The preference of many Asian nations for stability has not hindered major changes in higher education. Aside from expansion of enrollments, the relationship between universities and the state is changing, with increased calls for institutional autonomy, financial diversification, and quality control in higher education. Meanwhile, more traditional concerns—on the one hand, demands of different social groups for access, and on the other hand, the state's priority for strengthening its position in the world economy—have also contributed to the transformation.

GROWTH, DIVERSITY, AND CHANGE IN ASIAN HIGHER EDUCATION

Asian higher education will continue to be distinguished by its size and diversity. Four Asian countries, Japan, South Korea, China (including Taiwan and Hong Kong), and India represent close to 45 percent of the world's population and over 77 percent of the population of the whole of Asia. Their universities produced more than twice as many natural science and engineering bachelor's degrees as the United States in 1990 (Johnson 1993). Asia has over 30 other countries, most with expanding higher education systems.

Marked diversity makes it virtually impossible to offer a concise overview of Asian higher education. Long entrenched but differing cultural traditions interweave with colonial heritage, multiethnic and religious states, socialist regimes, and divided states, as well as some genuinely democratic systems. The giants, China and India, have struggled to maintain their unique intellectual traditions in the face of Western interventions. Higher education systems in Hong Kong, Malaysia, and Singapore have preserved aspects of their British colonial heritage, just as the Philippine universities have preserved American styles. Indonesian universities have completely discarded Dutch colonial influence, as South Korean universities have shed the Japanese colonial influence. Although Thailand and Japan have never been colonized, the latter has borrowed many innovations in higher education from Germany and the United States (Altbach and Selvaratnam 1989).

Challenges Differ According to Context

Despite much diversity, growth, and change, Asian leaders in higher education face strikingly similar challenges. All have budgets to balance, standards to maintain, faculties to satisfy, and demands from the public to meet. However, the contexts within which they face such challenges differ greatly and inevitably influence the ways in which they deal with their common problems.

There is little argument in Asia over the role that higher education must play in economic development. However, that priority is compromised to a greater or lesser extent by social, political, and cultural contexts. Malaysia seeks to balance economic development with ethnic equity in higher education. Iran is hesitant to diminish the priority given by its universities to the religious goals of the revolution that overthrew the secular regime of the shah. China's universities have set a high priority on promoting economic development, but they are not permitted to challenge the authority of the Communist Party. The new states of Central Asia born out of the collapse of the Soviet Union view higher education as a way of strengthening national identities. Transition societies such as Laos and Cambodia aspire to having good universities as an indication to international investors of their potential for technological progress. In the Philippines, university leaders get well-deserved credit for having achieved great progress in giving women access to higher education, yet they must continue to be sensitive to issues of access by different regional groups and social classes. Japanese universities have long been viewed as a model for supporting economic development, but the impending crisis caused by a shrinking student-age group has pushed it to consider broadening access to women and mature students.

As literacy rates continue to increase and basic education becomes universal, expanding populations will inflate university enrollments, inevitably making Asia the largest higher education system in the world. Participation rates
of the college-age cohort in higher education are still generally low, however,
but they will not remain so for long. With the exception of Japan, the four
tigers (South Korea, Taiwan, Hong Kong, and Singapore), and the Philippines, most participation rates are under 10 percent (Tan and Mingat 1992,
130–31). This will change, however, as economies continue to prosper in
other Asian countries. China, with its massive population, has already decided
to increase the percentage of the relevant age group in higher education from
three to eight percent between 1994 and 2000.

Nevertheless, even as these rates increase, Asia will continue to depend on
North America and Europe for advanced degrees for some time to come; this,
in turn, will further global academic integration and internationalization of
the academic profession. In some specializations, Asia might even take the
lead, as professors of Asian origin in Western universities are attracted back to
Asia with high salaries (Nash 1994; Webster 1994).

Financing the Expansion

The anticipated rapid and massive expansion in higher education participation rates will not be accompanied with proportionally increased budgets.
Asian governments are notorious for their conservative levels of funding for
educational institutions.

> [T]he achievement of Asian education becomes all the more remarkable
> when levels of government spending on education are compared across
> regions. Expressed as a percentage of GNP, governments in Asia spend
> less on education than governments in all other regions. This apparent
> paradox—high coverage despite relatively little financial effort—gives a
> first indication that as a determinant of education development, public
> policies in the sector are at least as important as the size of public
> spending. (Tan and Mingat 1992, 11)

Most Asian governments will only support a small group of national universities, leaving the rest to the private sector. Even national universities are
increasingly expected to raise more of their own funds.

In a 1990 sample of low- and middle-income countries in six world regions
(plus the OECD countries),[1] the World Bank noted that the two Asian
regions—South Asia, and East Asia and the Pacific—had the lowest percentages of public recurrent expenditures on higher education, 14.8 percent and
13.9 percent, respectively, compared with 18.4 percent in Latin America and
the Caribbean, 19.7 percent in sub-Saharan Africa, and 20.6 percent in the
OECD countries. Between 1980 and 1990, public recurrent expenditures on
higher education in the sampled low- and middle-income countries of South

Asia actually dropped by over 10 percent. East Asia had only a nominal increase, and its public spending per student in higher education from 1980 to 1990, as a multiple of primary education, declined from 30.8 percent to 14.1 percent (World Bank 1995, 56–57).

The figures above highlight the importance of viewing the challenges facing higher education in Asia according to levels of national income. For example, the governments of Singapore and Hong Kong spent 31 and 25 percent, respectively, of their education budgets on higher education in 1985, while Malaysia, Thailand, and Indonesia spent only 15, 12, and 9 percent, respectively (World Bank 1995, 57). This is so despite the fact that the proportion of the relevant age group in universities in 1985 in Hong Kong and Singapore was below 10 percent, and private universities were (and still are) prohibited from conferring degrees. Higher education in South Korea received only 10 percent of the government education budget at that time, even though it was heading toward mass higher education. The more higher education costs are financed by student fees, the higher the participation rates (World Bank 1995, 71). East Asian countries have taken note. Taiwan and South Korea have relied heavily on private higher education for their expansions.

Many Asian governments are placing more of the financial responsibility on leaders of institutions of higher education by providing policy frameworks that permit more autonomy from the state. In exchange, university leaders in Asia—as in other parts of the world—must begin to generate more of their own funds, and must justify themselves on the basis of the quality of their programs and the quantity of the human resources they produce to support national development. However, as responsibilities shift from government to the institution, the autonomy of institutional leadership becomes more complex. Culpability for poor performance rests more with institutional leaders than before. Nevertheless, while some Asian systems are moving in this direction, others still cling to old ways, despite inefficiencies. Moreover, while some profess to be moving in this direction, there is evidence to the contrary.

Social Perspectives: A Market of Demands

Institutions of higher education in Asia are reacting to a variety of demands. There are demands by individuals for high level scientific and professional skills, demands by social groups (including elites, social classes, ethnic groups, and women) for status and prestige, and the demands of the state for social order, as well as legitimacy in the global order. The three types of demands change often and overlap within specific contexts; they operate much like a market that shapes the form and content of higher education in Asian societies.

In the functionalist view, enrollment increase is cited as evidence of development and is correlated with economic productivity and per-capita gross national product. In short, higher education expands to meet the increasing need for science and technology that will contribute to economic development. This view has been influential in Japan and the four tigers, where it appeared to work. However, using research that includes Asian data, Ramirez and Lee (1995, 33) have cast doubt on the functionalist view:

> There is apparently a considerable degree of loose coupling between both what takes place within the science sector of tertiary education and scientific and infrastructural formation and between the latter and economic development.

The conflict perspective sees access to higher education as part of a mechanism of domination and social class reproduction. While this perspective has much relevance, its focus on economic struggle causes it to pay less attention to cultural aspects. For example, despite high underemployment rates among university graduates from the Philippines, the demand of the population for university credentials has not decreased, as higher education is still a key resource for status group competition, as well as a better job.

Without a full consideration of the role of the state, these perspectives provide an incomplete picture. Universities play an indirect role in maintaining social order through support of an ideology, preparation of civil servants, and legitimacy of the state and the credentials it confers (Carnoy and Levin 1985; Collins 1979). The state in China and Singapore is still very important in this respect, and while Hong Kong is considered a laissez-faire system, it joins Singapore and China in giving the state a virtual monopoly over higher education.

The future challenges facing higher education leaders in Asia are many, and are not easily generalized. On a whole, the main challenges are tied to the expansion of the student enrollments, including financial viability, support for economic development, and the social integration of an increasingly diverse population (women, minorities, rural and adult students, and the expanding middle class). Moreover, there are increasing demands placed on institutional leaders by academic staff, who have a crucial role to play in a context of rapid change (Altbach in press). Cultural traditions will continue to play an important role within higher education as part of status group competition, but they will also be essential tools of academic staff in helping their institutions to cope with rapid change. In fact, it could be argued that change is occurring faster in Asia than anywhere else, and that as a result, a future crisis in Asian higher education should not be unexpected. Wang Gungwu (1992, 17–27), vice-chancellor of the University of Hong Kong, places a heavy emphasis on the role of cultural tradition as the solution to such a crisis: "Where [Asian universities] have failed most notably has been their inability to provide this area of their work with the vitality to cope with the conditions of rapid change." The next section will further reexamine forces that are contributing to the transformation of Asian higher education, and the challenges they provide for leaders in higher educational institutions.

CHALLENGES IN EAST ASIAN HIGHER EDUCATION

The East Asian region is the most dynamic area in Asia, both economically and sociopolitically, and this is reflected in its rates of enrollment in higher education. If we put aside reformist Mongolia and isolationist North Korea, we find that Japan, South Korea, and Taiwan (all with close post–World War II ties to the United States) have well-established systems of mass higher education. Singapore and Hong Kong, which have colonial ties to the United Kingdom, moved more slowly but rapidly expanded enrollments in the early 1990s. In Singapore, Hong Kong, and China, only government-sponsored institutions can award university degrees. Japan, Taiwan, and South Korea support a number of high prestige national institutions, but most students attend private institutions. The challenges facing each also differ. Japan's mass higher education system is experiencing demographic challenges, while Taiwan and South Korea are struggling financially to support their greatly expanded systems and at the same time to incorporate sociopolitical changes into their institutions of higher education to meet the growing demands of their academic staff for more autonomy. China's major challenge is also economic; increased autonomy is viewed as a way of not only generating more financial resources, but also of increasing efficiency. While little is known about North Korea, Mongolia's higher education is probably the most rapidly expanding sector of its education system (Weidman and Bat-Erdene 1995).

Enrollments

In 1992, Japan had 523 universities (73 percent private), 591 junior colleges (84 percent private), and 62 technical colleges (5 percent private), along with a variety of other institutions (over 90 percent private) that provided postsecondary education. Twenty-five percent of all female university students are enrolled in one of the 91 women's universities. Forty percent of all high school graduates are pursuing higher education (60 percent, if all institutions offering some kind of postsecondary education are included). South Korea has the highest proportion of the age cohort in higher education of the four tigers of Asia (Fujimura-Fanselow in press). The South Korean system had 295 institutions of higher education (over 80 percent private) with 1.8 million students in 1994, a 15-fold increase in institutions and a 228-fold increase in students since liberation from the Japanese in 1945. Enrollment in higher education per 1,000 of the population was 47.7 in 1993 (Lee in press).

Taiwan had 124 institutions of higher learning in 1993 (50 universities and independent colleges and 74 junior colleges). There were twice as many private as public institutions of higher education, and they enroll 70 percent of the students. In 1991, 37.9 percent of the 18- to 21-year-old age group attended higher education institutions (Chen in press). Singapore has two major universities, as well as a system of polytechnics and colleges. Access to higher education has remained selective until recently. Only 15 percent and 20 percent of each age cohort were enrolled in local universities and polytechnics, respectively, in 1991. There were about 11,500 Singaporeans pursuing undergraduate and postgraduate courses in overseas universities in 1990, about half the total enrollment in local universities that year (Tan in press). In Hong Kong, a government decision to nearly double the number of students admitted to university degree studies by 1994 was taken in October of 1989. The mean percentage of the relevant age group admitted to degree study increased to 18 percent in 1994–95, when total enrollment reached about 58,000 (University Grants Committee 1995). An estimated 30,000 or more attend universities overseas (excluding mainland China and Taiwan).

Mainland China, with 1,074 regular higher educational institutions and an almost equal number of adult higher educational institutions, has a great potential for further expansion. Yet most of its current institutions are small; 668 (63 percent of all) institutions have under 2,000 students and 864 (81 percent of all) institutions have under 3,000 students. The number of full-time undergraduate students in regular institutions in 1993 was only about 2.25 million (Educational statistics 1993, 28–29). Although only about three percent of the age group attended universities in 1994, the figure will reach about eight percent by the year 2000. Only 36 institutions are administered by the central government through the state education commission. Another 316 are administered by various ministries of government, and the remaining 722 are administered by provincial education commissions or local governments. All the above are state-run institutions. Private colleges and universities administered by local communities, associations, and individuals have grown in number. While reliable data on North Korea is difficult to obtain, Mongolian figures reveal a small but rapidly expanding system, with over 5,000 students in national universities and over 10,000 in its other public universities. Its gender ratios are unsurpassed in Asia, as the proportion of women in the national and other public universities is 58.9 percent and 65.9 percent, respectively (Weidman and Bat-Erdene 1995).

Japan's Challenges

In Japan, the most serious challenge is demographic. As Ishikawa notes in Chapter 15, there will soon be a sharp decline in the population of 18- to 22-year olds, the group that makes up more than 90 percent of the college enrollment in Japan. The very survival of many institutions will be at stake, since 70 percent of all institutions are private. Another challenge is to change the rigidity and uniformity that mark structure, curricula, and teaching methods and to replace them with a system that encourages creativity, diversity of talent, and a broad international outlook, which is necessary for Japan to face an increasingly complex and competitive world. Finally, women (as well as older and foreign students) are demanding greater access to the system.

Proposed changes have been aimed at improving the quality of higher education and promoting greater diversity and flexibility in order to respond better to existing student needs and to attract a wider clientele of nontraditional students (Fujimura-Fanselow in press). The greater freedom to set up faculties, departments, and programs has led to the establishment of several new faculties and departments, as Ishikawa illustrates in the case of Keio University (see Chapter 15). Leaders at Japanese institutions of higher education face the task of redefining, diversifying, and expanding their functions to meet the needs of new clientele at a time when budgets are tightening and Japan wants to reposition itself in the world economy via internationalization. An incremental approach may not be enough. To Kitamura (1990, 315), "[w]hat is really needed is a basic structural change which will include significant innovations for strengthening the functions of education." However, it is not yet clear how much initiative and autonomy the country's Ministry of Education is prepared to grant over the actual direction and content of change.

Finally, administrators in Japan have the mandate from the academic profession to make changes. In a recent study (Boyer, Altbach, and Whitelaw 1994), the Japanese faculty ranked themselves highly in their ability to shape key academic policies at the department, faculty, and institutional levels. They also viewed institutional decision making as highly decentralized, as compared with other countries, in decisions regarding the selection of key administrators. Moreover, 58.2 percent of Japanese faculty respondents agreed that top-level administrators were providing competent leadership, the highest percentage of the 14 other participants included in the international study, including its neighbors in South Korea and Hong Kong. When asked if their institutional administration supports academic freedom, 67 percent of Japanese faculty agreed, which was also higher than its East Asian neighbors.

Korea's Challenges

In South Korea, the dual challenge is to generate alternative sources of income for private universities, which make up the bulk of the system, and to deal with increased calls for autonomy. Over three-quarters of all of the institutions of higher education in South Korea are private. In 1992, the national government provided 71.7 percent of the income of public institutions and only 1.7 percent of the income of private institutions (Lee in press). Student tuition accounted for 28.3 percent of the income of public institutions and 80.3

percent of the private institutions. Still, the public institutions spend more money on educating students than the private institutions. Autonomy is controversial. According to Lee, "Korean higher education is undergoing a paradigmatic shift from government hegemony to university autonomy, and from autocratic external governance to democratic internal governance."

A key factor affecting autonomy available to institutional leaders is the nature and views of the academic profession in South Korea. The ability of institutional leaders to affect change may be tempered by the outcome of current struggles within institutions over decentralization of authority, including the appointment of institutional leaders. For example, only 10 percent of South Korean faculty believe they have been influential in shaping key academic policies at the institutional level, and only 1 percent characterized the relationship between faculty and administration as excellent. Lee (in press) notes: "Professors in many institutions have begun to organize their own councils and to raise their voices against their government boards." Related results from the survey conducted by Lee show that only 24 percent of South Korean faculty believe that top-level administrators are providing competent leadership. And while 66 percent believe that academic freedom is strongly protected in their country, only 34 percent believe that their institutional administration supports academic freedom.

Taiwan's Challenges

As in Korea, funding and autonomy are key challenges in Taiwan. The Ministry of Education still has a major influence over educational reform. It approves the establishment of new institutions and departments, and it controls the size of enrollment, tuition rates, and required courses at both public and private institutions (Chen in press). However, the promulgation of the University Act in 1994 has established a legal basis for decentralization and depoliticization. Government control will be loosened somewhat, and universities will play a decisive role in choosing their presidents.

Sociopolitical transitions in Taiwan have led to major changes in its higher education system. A noted scholar on the subject explains:

> The institutionalization of political pluralism in Taiwan facilitates the shift of university administration from a highly centralized bureaucratic model to a participatory one. The ministry of education has devolved some institutional powers to individual universities and colleges. University teachers and students become new actors in the formulation and implementation of higher education policy. Collegial leadership is increasingly common. . . . Mechanisms are established to protect academics' rights to nominate their university presidents and participate in university administration. Students can have their representatives in university councils. Appeal courts are also stipulated to be established for students and teachers on campuses. (Law 1995)

There have already been indications of faculty struggle for autonomy in presidential selection (Chen in press). In Liu's survey of a sample of university faculty in Taiwan, over 80 percent of the faculty members sampled approved of open selection procedures for the selection of university presidents (Liu 1993, 232). Over 80 percent also believed that administrative procedures in universities are not in keeping with the spirit of professors governing the universities. Finally, only about one-third of academic staff, mostly full professors, said they had a chance to participate in administrative decisions.

Singapore's Challenges

In Singapore, the government has a monopoly on higher education. Tan (in press) states,

> The main control mechanisms of government are finance and the appointment of senior academic and administrative staff . . . The government clearly pays a dominant interventionist role in controlling and directing major policy decisions concerning higher educational institutions.

The former prime minister, Lee Kuan Yew, has personally intervened in policy decisions affecting institutions of higher education: he forbade the formation of an academic staff union in the National University of Singapore in 1980. Singapore's development strategy seems to go against the international trend moving institutions from state control to state supervision. Nevertheless, there is a certain amount of autonomy internal to the institution in such areas as student recruitment, development of courses, determining examination, and internal financial management. This self-administration, however, is conditional upon meeting the needs defined by government agencies. Meeting the needs of the market economy is not viewed as incompatible with the great extent of administrative control. The Singapore case raises fundamental questions about government control and institutional autonomy. The university is pressed into the service of the market economy, and everything becomes subordinate to economic modernization. Finally, there is little indication that this situation will change: it has delivered the second highest living standard in Asia, as well as social stability, to its population.

Hong Kong's Challenges

For Hong Kong, 1997 is the year that it will become a Special Administrative Region of the People's Republic of China. Under the "one country, two systems" arrangement, the current education system may be maintained. Within the context of decolonization, higher education is confronting at least three issues. First, rapid expansion means increased competition among the seven major institutions of higher education for funding, students, and faculty.

Second, higher education must continue to work toward serving the goals of modernization in China. Third, higher education must balance a localization of administration, a nationalization of the university mission, and a regionalization of academic leadership with the internationalization of knowledge. This issue is complicated by the large number of overseas appointees; moreover, about 90 percent of all doctorates of Hong Kong faculty were earned overseas, usually in Australia, Canada, the United Kingdom, and the United States. Within a period of less than 10 years, Hong Kong has moved from a colonial society with two universities serving a small elite to a transitional society with six universities serving a larger population, as well as the modernization of mainland China.

The rapid expansion has not occurred without difficulty. The resulting decrease in student ability levels, especially language ability, has created a need for more effective teaching, as well as the addition of a foundation year at the start of the three-year university degree program. Also, the diversity that has accompanied the expansion has led to increased demands on university administrators to operate more transparently in order to contribute to improved morale and institutional loyalty among the faculty. Channels of communication between faculty and administration have to be improved continually (Boyer, Altbach, and Whitelaw 1994; Postiglione in press). Finally, whether or not they accept the challenge, Hong Kong's universities will continue to be viewed as key institutions for the development of democratic institutions in Hong Kong's future.

China's Challenges

Probably no other nation in Asia has greater potential for a massive transformation of higher education in the coming decades than China. As the central government looks more toward the localities and individual universities to raise funds for resources, it is promising more autonomy. The government has increased its allocation to higher education in absolute terms and relative to government expenditure and GNP. Calls for efficiency, equity, and transparency are increasingly heard. Willingness to grant autonomy is conditional upon a guarantee of stability. Universities are called on to serve economic modernization while accepting political control (Hayhoe 1989). China is facing a major transition to a socialist market economy and it prefers a slow pace. Private universities, self-paying students, professors supplementing their incomes, and an open labor market for graduates are quite novel for a society which, not long ago, saw capitalism and free markets as enemies of the state. Min (in press) notes some of the more important changes:

> Graduates were trained as elements of the planned economy. They were locked into very narrow fields of specialization. When the central planning economy was transformed into a more dynamic market economy,

these graduates became less flexible and less adaptive to the rapidly changing labor market needs and technologically induced changes in the workplace. Thus since the mid-1980s, the state education commission has made great efforts to broaden each field of study and reduce the number of specialties. Some narrow specialties were combined with others. By the end of the 1980s, the total number of specialities was reduced from 1,419 to 832. Universities were given more autonomy to adjust their curricula according to the local needs.

Institutional leaders are faced with a number of challenges. These include raising funds through university enterprises and through tuition fees, increasing enrollments, offering specializations that will attract students, stemming the flow of academic staff leaving the university, and developing economies of scale by consolidating with other universities when necessary. On top of this, university leaders must still deal with the remnants of the socialist system, including the allocation of housing, medical coverage, and other benefits. Despite the fact that student-teacher ratios average seven to one, it is virtually impossible to dismiss staff. Institutional leaders are also responsible for the moral and political development of students, a difficult task at a time when ideology has lost its appeal.

To respond to developmental needs, more initiative is encouraged, including sources of funding. The training of human resources in a market economy is emphasized. There has been a broadening of the curriculum in order to make graduates more flexible and adaptive to the labor market. The procedures by which graduates locate occupational positions is becoming more open and transparent than before. The salary system for professors within universities has the effect of encouraging practices to supplement income through employment outside the university. The number of private universities will be permitted to continue to grow along with the demand, though it will be a minor sector. The future will bring a need for a better legal system as well as an accreditation system for universities. With the expansion of enrollments, quality and efficiency will have to be proficiently monitored (Min in press).

Among the internal demands facing the system and institutional leaders is to increase female and national minority participation, and the implementation of tuition fees will make it necessary for university leaders to see to it that those of peasant background find sufficient funds to attend their institutions, as well as ways to repay their loans to the university. There are other challenges, too, including the necessity to give time to professors to upgrade their education. In 1991–92, only 1.4 percent of faculty in Chinese universities had a doctoral degree, 20.7 percent had a master's degree, and 42.3 percent had a bachelor's degree or equivalent. The rest had no academic degree (Educational statistics 1993, 28–29). Also, faculty salaries are low, and international links have to be steadily improved.

CONCLUSION

Asian higher education is characterized by expansion, production of a large number of the world's scientists, and the export of students and highly educated personnel. Despite colonial legacies, there is widespread agreement among leaders of Asian higher educational institutions that the Western academic model (especially the American version) has made, and can continue to make, a significant contribution. Aside from being increasingly research oriented, Asian higher education has become increasingly integrated into the global academy, ensured by continued student and faculty flows and the use of English as a regional medium. Nevertheless, while these trends are seen in many Asian nations, it should not be unexpected that Asia's diversity often seems to overshadow the traits held in common.

Throughout many parts of East Asia, leaders of higher education institutions are gaining autonomy. As the state tightens its purse strings and loosens its grip, however, the locus of influence follows new sources of funding. Support from industry, enterprises, and students calls for a different type of leadership. Support from business, commerce, and industry will demand practical scientific skills and quantifiable outcomes that institutions of higher education are not always disposed or able to provide.

Although the state will loosen control, it will still place more traditional demands on higher education. This includes the demand for social order, support for a state ideology, and continued service to the state bureaucracy, as well as the preparation of civil servants by national universities.

Until student fees and student numbers increase, their demands and those of their families will be less felt, though not less important. Moreover, as institutional leaders get more autonomy in the selection of students, they may lose some of the insulation from social groups that call for more access, including women in Japan, rural students in China, workers in South Korea, and ethnic minorities in other countries. Nevertheless, the expansion of the middle class in Asia will continue to become a major force in many places. Though higher education is still an institution mostly serving a small elite in many places, this situation will gradually change.

Many East Asian higher educational leaders will find their institutions with more professionalized faculty. As the level of qualification rises, faculty will demand more participation in decision making, as well as more guarantees of academic freedom and autonomy. While the Philippines, Malaysia, Indonesia, Vietnam, and most Southeast Asian nations, as well as China, face a daunting challenge to upgrade the qualifications of their faculties, other countries in East Asia have already reached an important threshold. Faculty members in Taiwan, Hong Kong, and South Korea are beginning to expect more transparency in institutional decision making.

NOTE

1. The Organization for Economic Cooperation and Development (OECD) is the international organization of the industrialized, market-economy countries. Its members include Australia, Austria, Belgium, Canada, the Czech Republic, Denmark, Finland, France, Germany, Greece, Hungary, Iceland, Ireland, Italy, Japan, Luxembourg, Mexico, the Netherlands, New Zealand, Norway, Portugal, Spain, Sweden, Turkey, the United Kingdom, and the United States.

REFERENCES

Altbach, P. In press. *The international academic profession: A portrait of 14 countries*. Princeton: The Carnegie Foundation for the Advancement of Teaching.

Altbach, P., and V. Selvaratnam. 1989. *From dependence to autonomy: The development of Asian universities*. Amsterdam: Kluwer Academic.

Boyer, E.; P. Altbach; and M. J. Whitelaw. 1994. *The academic profession in international perspective*. Princeton, NJ: The Carnegie Foundation for the Advancement of Teaching.

Carnoy, M., and H. Levin. 1985. *Schooling and work in the democratic state*. Stanford, CA: Stanford University Press.

Chen, S. In press. Taiwan. In *Asian higher education: An international handbook and reference guide*, edited by G. A. Postiglione and G. C. L. Mak. Westport, CT: Greenwood Press.

Collins, R. 1979. *The credential society: An historical sociology of education and stratification*. New York: Academic Press.

Educational statistics yearbook of China. 1993. Beijing: People's Education Press.

Fujimura-Fanselow, K. In press. Japan. In *Asian higher education: An international handbook and reference guide*, edited by G. A. Postiglione and G. C. L. Mak. Westport, CT: Greenwood Press.

Hayhoe, R. 1989. *China's universities and the open door*. New York: M.E. Sharpe.

International Monetary Fund (IMF). 1995. *World economic outlook*. Washington, DC: IMF.

Johnson, J. M. 1993. *Human resources for science and technology: The Asian region*. Surveys of Science Resources Series, Special Report, 93–303. Washington, DC: National Science Foundation.

Kitamura, K. 1990. The future of Japanese higher education. In *Windows on Japanese higher education*, edited by E. R. Beauchamp. Westport, CT: Greenwood Press.

Law, W. 1995. The impact of socio-political transition on higher education: Taiwan. Paper presented at the International Symposium on Education and Socio-Political Transition in Asia, 29–31 May, at the University of Hong Kong.

Lee, S. In press. South Korea. In *Asian higher education: An international handbook and reference guide*, edited by G. A. Postiglione and G. C. L. Mak. Westport, CT: Greenwood Press.

Liu, X. 1993. *Woguo Taiwandiqu daxuejiashi zuanye zizhuquan zhi yanjiu* (*Research on the autonomy of the academic profession in Taiwan's universities*). Taipei: Taiwan Shudian.

Nash, M. J. 1994. Tigers in the lab: Asian born, U.S. trained researchers are headed home to challenge the technological supremacy of the West. *Time* (International Edition) November 21: 48–49.

Postiglione, G. A. In press. Hong Kong's academic profession in a period of profound change. *The international academic profession: A portrait of 14 countries*, edited by P. Altbach. Princeton: The Carnegie Foundation for the Advancement of Teaching.

Ramirez, F. O., and M. N. N. Lee. 1995. Education, science and development. In *Social change and educational development: Mainland China, Taiwan and Hong Kong*, edited by G. A. Postiglione and W. O. Lee. Hong Kong: Center of Asian Studies, University of Hong Kong.

Tan, J. In press. Singapore. In *Asian higher education: An international handbook and reference guide*, edited by G. A. Postiglione and G. C. L. Mak. Westport, CT: Greenwood Press.

Tan, J., and A. Mingat. 1992. *Education in Asia: A comparative perspective of cost and financing*. World Bank Regional and Sectoral Studies. Washington, DC: World Bank.

University Grants Committee. 1995. *University grants committee of Hong Kong: Facts and figures*. Hong Kong: University Grants Committee Secretariat.

Wang Gungwu. 1992. Universities in transition. *Oxford Review of Education* vol. 24. London: Oxford University Press.

Webster, J. 1994. Success in Hong Kong: Universities attract top international scholars despite concern about colony's future after 1997. *The Chronicle of Higher Education* October 19: A60–61.

Weidman, J. C. and R. Bat-Erdene. 1995. Higher education in Mongolia. Working paper, University of Pittsburgh.

World Bank. 1995. *Priorities and strategies for education: A World Bank review*. Washington, DC: The World Bank.

CHAPTER 4

Latin America and the Change in Change

Daniel C. Levy

Executive Summary. Perception of change—or lack of it—in Latin American higher education is colored by myths and stereotypes. Contrary to the stereotype, the most important transformation of higher education in Latin America—the dramatic expansion of participation since 1960—was not the result of planned policy initiatives. The growth of private higher education, where much of this expansion took place, did not stem from a centralized reform. Where policy initiatives to stimulate change and reform have been undertaken, they often have had uneven and unintended consequences.

The author presents several views of how change occurs in Latin American higher education, citing Marxist and neo-Marxist theories that attribute substantial power to forces outside the country; the forces of modernization directed by some leadership from national government; the statist approach, assigning the most important role to centralized national policy initiatives; the model of the feudal university that invests most of the power in the various schools and deans; the concept of institutions as competing interest groups; and the bureaucratic model, in which the prime motivation of the players is self-interest. None of these perspectives leaves significant room for institutional leadership.

However, with major change on the higher education agenda in Latin America today, a new and different model is gaining ground. This modernization model combines shaping change through good (and different) policy, stressing differentiation among institutions, and accountability. With shrinking state funding, the drive toward privatization, and internationalization, new conditions are being created that could enhance the role of institutional leadership. In a competitive and democratic market, institutional leadership is needed to formulate coherent institutional responses and processes to design and implement academic change.

• • • • • • • • • • • •

C hange is nothing new for Latin American higher education. Notwithstanding stereotypes about immovable universities or about the newness of today's rage for change, change has occurred repeatedly since the region established its own nations and educational systems in the first half of the nineteenth century. In particular, the last few decades have brought transformations in higher education's goals, clientele, structures, policies, and outcomes.

Change changes, however. Today's powerful agenda for change differs in important respects from earlier agendas, even as it largely parallels the contemporary agenda in much of the world. Key features include reduction of state subsidies, ties to the productive sector, and increased evaluation and accountability for elevated quality and efficiency (Neave and van Vught 1994; Task Force 1994), and this new agenda could increase institutional leadership's role as an engine for change.

This chapter presents its argument in three main sections. First, it contrasts perceptions of the lack of change with realities of ample change, sketching a few key features of today's Latin American higher education. Second, it explores how views (and sometimes realities) of change in Latin American higher education have historically diminished the role of institutional leadership. Third, it analyzes the enhanced role for such leadership that could accompany the regionally dominant contemporary model of modernizing reform. Just as much of the argument in all three sections could be adapted to apply beyond Latin America itself, so it varies in detail and applicability among Latin American nations.

CHANGE: PERCEPTION VERSUS REALITY

One stereotype of change in Latin American higher education is that it is excessive. Bred of incessant conflict, instability, incompetence, and other maladies that also plague the region's politics and economics, this change is supposedly frequent and revolutionary. Much more prevalent, however, is the stereotype that little change occurs, a characterization that invokes most of the same "explanations," but emphasizes that Latin American higher education serves elites and the status quo.

Why the huge gap between perceptions of little change and realities of significant change? The main answer holds for higher education generally, but for Latin America and most of the world more than for the United States. It is that the reigning paradigm of change fails to identify where much change really occurs. It does not direct our attention there. The paradigm—which operates for scholars and policy makers alike—focuses on change prescribed by central plans explicitly aimed at altering extant policy, often at the systems level.[1]

As a long trail of studies on policy implementation in many fields and many parts of the world now makes painfully evident, the results of such grand plans for reform are usually disappointing.[2] Certainly this is the finding from most studies of reforms for Latin American higher education. But much more change occurs outside the paradigm. Our first and broadest example is growth in enrollments. Growth in enrollments resulted less from planned reforms calculating its extent, pace, and contours than from a variety of forces mostly unplanned and unguided, if not unforeseen; indeed, the growth often overwhelmed and frustrated planners. Heading the forces was a powerful social demand, itself fueled by an array of economic, cultural, social, political, and psychological factors.

And so Latin American higher education changed from a rather elite to a comparatively massive enterprise between 1950 and today. From a cohort enrollment of only 2 percent in 1950, encompassing just over 270,000 students, we arrive at an estimate of 18 percent today, encompassing about 7 million students (Brunner, et al. 1995, 11–14, 85). Brazil, Mexico, and Argentina each have over a million students, while Argentina, Uruguay, and Ecuador have more than 30 percent of their cohort enrolled. Similar transformations have emerged regarding institutions, expenditures, the distribution of enrollments by field of study, graduate enrollments, and the professoriate (to roughly 0.6 million), and proliferating fields of study beyond the traditional "big three" of law, medicine, and engineering. The number of institutions grew during those 4 decades from 75 to 690 universities and 3,000 other postsecondary institutions.

The proliferation of institutions (and fields of study) illustrates another point about how change eludes conventional perspectives. Observers often train their eye on where explicit policy aims to turn an existing structure or system into something else. As much literature in both organizational sociology and policy implementation properly observes, however, it is usually difficult to achieve such change. Instead, change within a system often occurs as new institutions emerge to challenge old ones by doing something different or by doing something differently. Even if change is not their prime purpose, they may achieve it because they are less encumbered by existing norms and interests or simply because they realize they cannot compete on the same turf with venerable institutions.

Of course, some new and distinctive institutions do result largely from centrally planned reforms. Technical institutes and certain leading public universities and freestanding public research centers are examples in Latin American higher education. But such planning does not account for most of the shift away from the old system of just one national university or just a restricted number of mostly public universities. The proliferation of private institutions best illustrates the point (Levy 1986). Their 15 percent of enrollments in 1960 already represented a major increase from historically marginal shares, and by 1975 it increased to about 34 percent, subsequently consolidating and slightly growing. Thus, the big jump in the prominence of private institutions preceded inclusion of privatization as a key feature of broad projects for political-economic reform.[3]

The rise of private research centers outside universities was even less planned. They grew mostly in reaction to repressive military rule or to the failures of public universities (Levy 1996). Almost nobody expected either their initial surge or their continued growth in the late stages of military regimes and the early stages of ensuing democratic rule. Yet they have brought enormous change, making revolutionary breakthroughs in the amount, quality, and relevance of social science and policy research, often presaging key items on the modern agenda for university reform (e.g., heavy private funding, and funding based largely on performance). Similarly, private universities have brought fundamental changes in finance, governance, and output, not just a new juridical labeling for traditional practice. And all this proliferation of private institutions makes attempts at centralized reform of the higher education "system" much more complicated.

Even change that emerged from conscious, planned reform efforts has escaped the eye of many grim observers. Study of grand reform projects launched jointly by foreign donors and their domestic partners suggests why this is so (Levy forthcoming). For one thing, results that fall far short of what was projected generate commentary on the failure and the difficulty of reform. Generally overlooked or underplayed is the emergence of unanticipated forms of change that are hybrids between projected and traditional forms. Moreover, considerable successes achieved at particular institutions or units within them often get obscured in system-wide assessments, especially when numerical growth mostly apes old forms.[4] Thus, for example, while heady and naive expectations that the U.S. norm of a full-time professoriate could be established collapsed, many fine enclaves were established, as were unorthodox or hybrid ones (e.g., full-time work through the simultaneous holding of appointments in different institutions).

Finally, most observers do not count "bad" change. This is another manifestation of counting only the change detected under the lamp installed at the spot of projected policy impact. Depending on one's beliefs, bad changes could include the repressive elimination of personnel and their fields of study, greatly expanded participation in governance, suddenly open or restricted admissions, proliferation of poor institutions, and so forth. Such changes may even sustain some critics' perception that revolutionary instability is common. But a balanced view of change would also have to weigh the largely positive and often sustained changes involving matters from social mobility to democratization to solid professional training to pockets of enviable academic quality. Stereotypes of bad change are as falsely prejudicial as stereotypes of no change when it comes to Latin American higher education.

CHANGE WITHOUT INSTITUTIONAL LEADERS?

A U.S. propensity to see leadership at higher educational institutions as a key instigator of change is not widely shared in Latin America. Overall, there is perhaps a cultural tendency in Latin America to view institutions more as ongoing realities of life than as actors for change. The degree of change is minimized, and whatever change does occur is attributed to dynamics other than institutional leadership. A number of these alternative dynamics credited with causing or preventing change are discussed below. An analysis of how much effect they really have is beyond the scope of this chapter, but each has some validity; even perceptions of their force are important, because they devalue institutional leadership.

1. Marxist Perspective

One powerful perception emphasizes the lack of latitude for leadership: Marxist, neo-Marxist, and "dependency" theories stress that developing regions suffer from a lack of change or from change that reinforces the status quo. Economic factors and the needs of foreign powers, not local leadership, determine this change.[5] Revolution, if possible, is the only route to real change. Progressives who try to invent higher education reforms are tinkering rather pointlessly. In fact, such pessimistic interpretations were wildly exaggerated for Latin America and have recently lost some influence.

2. Liberal Determinist Perspective

The liberal determinist perception was consistently and profoundly optimistic: Natural forces of modernization would make Latin America like the First World in higher education, just as it would in the interconnected areas of political, economic, and social development. This perception also marginalizes institutional leadership and has also lost some of its luster (though not as much). It never gathered much force in actual policy making except as crucially modified to allow for leadership that would accelerate and improve the natural process. The modified version became the dominant one in reformist circles of policy makers and certainly among international donors, at least until the mid-1970s. It sometimes pointed to institutional leadership but usually pointed more to leadership from national government to make better policy, better funded.

3. Statist Perspective

Indeed, one influential perspective on change stresses national policy in pointed supremacy over institutional policy. We may call it a statist or at least national perspective, and it is a key manifestation of a European orientation in Latin American higher education. The U.S.-style alternative involves much more by way of initiatives at lower levels, decentralized experimentation, incrementalism, small-scale successes and failures, markets, and voluntary accords and diffusion (Clark 1986).

The statist perspective holds that, even in democracies, centralized processes should identify the public interest and the best policy for the system. That usually means either the predominance of a "national university" as the state's arm in higher education or standardized policies across institutions. Those policies concern hirings, salaries, access, structural configurations, curriculum, and degree requirements. Differentiation across institutions is also possible, but it must be designed by central authorities. Institutional heads, therefore, administer policy made elsewhere much more than they make policy. Institutional autonomy is minimal.

In practice, twentieth-century Latin American higher education did not usually go as far as Europe with such statist approaches, but it did assume something of a middle position between European and U.S. practice (Levy 1994). And the strong normative attachment to the European view has had great influence in orienting attention toward proposals for major reform of the system—and limiting the role for individual institutions and their heads. This orientation even insinuates itself into reform processes that might otherwise draw off U.S. pluralist-market models; contemporary movements for evaluation and accreditation are prime examples. And as with Argentina and several other nations in 1995, concern to improve higher education leads to a huge national debate and forum aimed at comprehensive new legislation.

4. Feudal Perspective

Even where institutions have autonomy, the role for leadership may be severely limited by a feudal dispersion of power among oligarchs or units. Again following European example (though not going as far), the idea is that rectors and other university authorities sit above professional faculties and their deans less than they sit among them. They are selected neither for their managerial prowess, nor to impose institution-wide changes. The politics of their role involves balancing the interests of various units more than authoritative leadership. University administration is weakened as the institution is decentralized. Feudalism often means a lack of change, but if change occurs it does not originate with institutional leaders.

Although one view of leadership is that it brings diverse groups together, Latin American public universities have often suffered from excessive accommodation and an extreme diffusion of authority. What might at first glance appear to be institutional action, because it occurs somewhere at the institutional site, is usually action by groups or units within the institution. The relative autonomy and even isolation of faculties of the university epitomizes the point. Rectors of national universities may be simultaneously powerful politically, based on their constituency and the political importance of the university, and yet impotent regarding academic change.

5. Interest Group Perspective

Overlapping the "feudal" diffusion of power, in which central administrators are overwhelmed by others within the university, is an interest group perspective. Here, however, the focus switches to conflict and diverse groups. Rather than understandings among gentlemen, different interest groups antagonistically alter what institutional heads would otherwise do. Again, this means either blocked change or change not directed by institutional leaders.

Advocates point to the democratic participation involved, but critics emphasize the anarchic triumph of haphazard change, or the cold triumph of selfish political power over change based on academic and other desirable criteria.[6] Student politics, which have lost much of their high profile regarding great national issues, retain force as obstacles to academic change. Professors and blue-collar university workers have gained strength. And too often underestimated are professional associations (e.g., in the field of engineering) keenly interested in what pertinent university faculties do. The role of interest groups in electing the university's highest officials is especially critical.

6. Bureaucratic Perspective

Another perspective considers the behavior of bureaucrats. High officials neither comfortably fit with those from whom they emerge, nor do they uncomfortably find themselves constrained by them, as much as they naturally and rationally pursue their own interests. If those interests are shaped by constituent forces or, instead, by forces outside the institution, so be it. Prominent in contemporary political-economic theory is the idea that officials operate to preserve or enhance their own positions. Even where that allows for initiatives aimed at important change—and it usually does not—the motive is less a leadership vision of what change is good for higher education than a calculation of what is good for oneself.

Societal Demands

All six perspectives discussed above appear to run against what the volume's editor perceives or prescribes for healthy higher education;[7] all undermine a major positive role for institutional leadership. So would a possible seventh perspective, which could be included under liberal determinism. It would emphasize changes that stem from interest groups and other demands emanating outside both the institution and the state, in society. This perspective fits much of the real change (e.g., growth) sketched earlier in the chapter, in which institutional officials find themselves responding to societal demands more than shaping policy.

A NEW MODEL OF MODERNIZATION

For institutional leadership to play a vigorous role in higher education, two basic conditions must obviously be met. First, major change must be on the agenda. Second, among the various possible instigators and leaders for that change, institutional leadership must step forward.

The first condition is increasingly being met. Major change is integral to what has become the predominant policy model among government reformers, international agencies, and a core of consultant scholars—though not among students, professors, and other actors.[8] This modernization model emphasizes both the ongoing failures of higher education and the changing environments that require positive response from higher education. Towering above democratization and social mobilization are political-economic considerations centered around neoliberal policy; this policy emphasizes shrinking state funding, various forms of privatization, and internationalization.

The modernization agenda has made its earliest and heftiest progress in Chile (Brunner and Briones 1992). Mexico exemplifies countries where some important progress has also been made and the agenda has a strong wind at its back. Brazil (the clear leader in graduate education) represents countries where the modernization measures are more stymied by opposition, with Argentina and others still further behind. Almost everywhere, however, the modernization model is at least under more serious consideration than a decade ago (Wolff and Albrecht 1992).

Whatever its degree of implementation to date, or the motivations for it, or the variations according to proponent, the modernization model has certain key features. The clearest specific ones involve finance. These are intertwined with the basic rationales and purposes of prescribed change (Neave and van Vught 1994; Levy 1994). Funding must be diversified beyond state subsidies, and there must be greater self-financing, tuition, contract funding, and "cost-recovery." Additionally, even state money must come increasingly on the basis of evaluated performance rather than traditional criteria of student numbers, "sunk" costs of salaries, or political pressures. Rewards must therefore be differential among both institutions and personnel. To escape unconscionably low efficiency and to allow for greater equity as well, much more and better output must flow from fewer resources. Surrendering traditional assumptions that money for higher education is inherently justified, the new model stresses accountability through evaluation. And the accountability stresses contributions to the changing economy over myriad other university functions.

The new model obviously contemplates major change. As far as the role it designates to institutional leadership in effecting that change, one point is that it strongly rejects most of the alternative dynamics for change identified above. It is decidedly more positive on the possibilities of shaping good change through good policy, but it insists that good policy must be changed policy. It sees improved prospects for such change as the sorry overall state of higher education becomes plain and especially as changes occur in the broader political economy.

Privatization exemplifies how increased change may emphasize institutional leadership.[9] At least the last four of the six dynamics that work against institutional leadership apply much more powerfully to most public than most private universities. Thus, top administrators at private universities usually have far more leeway for vigorous, coherent, leadership. This private-public contrast is greater in Latin America than in the United States (Levy 1986, 229–51). That does not mean, however, that the majority of private institutions see academically oriented leadership, and of course much depends on the external funders and authorities tied to the particular private institution.

Taken to an extreme, a market model could become another scenario in which leadership disappears. Actors would simply respond naturally to market forces. But this extreme rarely finds either proponents or precedent in Latin American higher education. Reforms pushed around 1980 by Chile's "Chicago boys"—academic economists who were adherent to the University of Chicago economic model and who were architects of Chile's free market reforms—came closest.

Instead, market rationales usually couple with a directive role for various actors to make policy within a decentralized, competitive system. Institutions would operate then in what could be called a pluralist-market system, emulating the U.S. model in certain crucial respects. They would set many of their own policies, freed from standard policies set centrally, their autonomy from government enhanced. But they would be accountable for their policies as students, professors, and donors would be able to choose other institutions. So would the state, which could actually increase in influence while shrinking in size, as it could give more where it judged performance superior. This is one reason for the region-wide (indeed worldwide) preoccupation with formal evaluation, a pointless if not destructive undertaking under other circumstances.[10]

But to make policy in a competitive environment, institutions probably need strong leadership (Neave 1988). Otherwise, policies suit the interests of individual actors and units. They handicap institutions by not allowing them to formulate coherent responses to the external forces that determine their fate. For example, who will gamble on institutions whose policies are continually up for grabs among contending parties, or subject to abrupt changes in leadership? What seems in order then, to use Burton Clark's now famous phrase, is a "strong middle" of institutional leadership facing down the units or groups below and the state above. The requirement of hierarchy and centralization of authority within institutions competing within a democratic and decentralized system is at once highly controversial and yet essential to pluralist market models.

A brief comparison of the present model of change and the last one enthusiastically pushed throughout the region by domestic officials and international agencies is instructive. Reaching its zenith in the 1960s, the earlier model placed greater faith in the almost inherent blessings of higher education and its expansion. Today's model insists more soberly that there are both good and bad higher education policies and effects; the right policies must be chosen. The old model also emphasized state funding and state planning, providing fuel and direction for expansion. The strategic reversal with respect to the role of the state opens space for other actors. And it implies a major role for institutional leaders.

Another difference between the two models of change further suggests an enhanced role for institutional leaders. The old model concentrated much more than the present one on substantive academic matters. These included curriculum, creation of departments, new fields of study, professionalization of the professoriate, research, and so forth. The old model thus tended to prescribe the "what" and almost assume there would be a "who" to bring it about. The new model, by prescribing such academic initiatives much less, appears to place greater emphasis on leadership to design and implement sound academic change.

On the other hand, the old model sometimes depended on institutional leaders. International assistance invested heavily in particular projects at chosen institutions. These projects included many aimed specifically at institutional development. And they featured administrative as well as academic centralization that would move power from individual faculties to institutional leaders. Examples included construction of campus-wide facilities (e.g., libraries), general studies programs, departments, common credit systems, and electives. Philanthropic foundations, in particular, chose institutions largely for the soundness of their leadership and the trust they could place in it. They also sponsored travel and conferences to bolster leaders' sense of their important roles (as the American Council on Education does on a smaller scale today). For its part, the Inter-American Development Bank invested in infrastructure for enlarged central administration. (A criticism is that central administration grew much more in size than in effective leadership.)

Whatever the postulates of the old reform model, the new model does not stake out a strong, explicit position on either academic substance or the motors needed for change. Its position is skimpy and rather vague on most aspects other than financial ones. Regarding governance, it does not get much beyond its prescriptions for a smaller yet more influential "evaluation state" and its denunciation of the power perniciously wielded by most actors and units within universities.

Thus, while the logic of the new model suggests a strong role for institutional leadership, little is specified in that regard. Our points about how such leadership may be necessary for the good performance that brings financial success are implicit more than explicit in the new model. Where the new model mentions management, it does so in terms of sound financial management or seems to assume that good management will flow from a new insistence on evaluation, accountability, and differential rewards.[11]

Accordingly, we still see only isolated efforts to train higher education administration as managers and leaders. Programs such as IGLU (Instituto de Gestión y Liderazgo Universitarios/Institute for Higher Education Management and Leadership) sponsored by the Interamerican Organization for Higher Education, as well as by institutions like IESA (Instituto de Estudeos Superiores Administrativos/Institute for Advanced Administrative Studies) in Venezuela and the University of the Andes in Colombia, are exceptions. The new model also gives scant attention to the question of how to select institutional leaders most capable of effecting desired change. Again, the pluralist-market logic might appear to suggest something akin to common U.S. practice, trusting to institutional boards and avoiding either direct state appointment or selection from democratically represented units within the institution. In practice, Latin America has varieties of all these possibilities: private universities and research centers feature the strongest boards, while public technical institutes most often have direct government appointment and public universities most often select from wide democratic participation. Nor is there a clear trend toward selection by U.S.-style boards; just as military rule often meant increased state control over leadership selection, redemocratization has boosted direct elections.[12]

CONCLUSION

The problem with change in Latin American higher education over recent decades lies much less in the lack of it than in the qualitative shape of it. Stereotypes about continuity stem from tendencies to dismiss many kinds of change. These changes include important ones that are normatively negative, unplanned, inferior to anticipated amounts, or hybrid between prior forms and projected ones. Furthermore, several perspectives on change (Marxist, liberal determinist, statist, feudal, interest group, and bureaucratic) emphasize forces other than institutional leadership. These forces block change or effect it without institutional leadership, for better or worse. In contrast, the increasingly dominant modernization model takes an antagonist stance toward most of these other forces. It is much more compatible with the idea of institutional leadership, though that is too often left implicit and some contradictory points arise.

Observers should take a fairer, fuller, and more realistic look at the truly ample change achieved in Latin America to date. Much of this change has occurred at innovative institutions that escape the generalizations that remain accurate for the bulk of the system. Appropriate lessons must help guide present and future policy. Then, too, the six perspectives outlined above must decline some in influence. This is partly because they are factually exaggerated, partly because belief in them saps energy needed for institutional leadership for change. Mostly, the hope is that a decline in these beliefs would base itself on a real decline in the forces they emphasize, and this sort of decline seems to be happening.

Much of the challenge for change emanates from outside higher education itself. The two crucial and interrelated factors are the broad transformations in the political economy (in both ideology and practice) and the international movement toward a similar modernization agenda for higher education. Indeed, both factors are already having a big impact on Latin American higher education. So far, however, the impact is much stronger on proposals than on practice. Nor has the modernization agenda sufficiently clarified or promoted the role for institutional leadership. Finally, even if that agenda gathers momentum and specifies a pivotal role for institutional leadership, it remains to be seen how much and how well institutional leaders will assume that role.

NOTES

1. Participants in a Ford Foundation–sponsored fellows program at Harvard University for spring 1995 came to note a common pattern in their discussions: Morning sessions on prescribed topics often lamented the lack of change, whereas in more fluid afternoon sessions, numerous examples of change were cited. Much of the difference concerned the assessment of big reforms aimed explicitly at change for the system versus citation of examples of particular changes at particular places. The contrast has been noted for the situation in Mexico, for example: Almost all analysts have found that repeated efforts at big reform have failed; but while some on the Marxist left have also blasted the lack of change in general, other analysts have pointed to massive changes quite outside big, designed, national plans (Kent 1993; Levy 1994).

2. One dissenting approach finds the conventional wisdom too negative and instead seeks to identify the key ingredients where large-scale reform does not work (Grindle and Thomas 1991). More than the dissent offered in the present chapter, the dissent stresses the role of central government. In any case, most literature on policy implementation focuses on

why policies are not successfully put into effect, though that may be changing. The most extensive work on policy implementation of higher education reform is Cerych and Sabatier 1986.

3. As with other mostly unplanned changes, official policy affected developments. Thus, by maintaining a stiff access policy for its public universities, Brazil became the region's first nation to push a majority of its enrollments into the largely uncontrolled private sector. But few officials elsewhere realized that their more open public access would, in its own way, stimulate private growth in response to perceived deterioration on the public side.

4. Titles such as *Transforming Higher Education* run the risk of focusing attention overly much on the system's mainstream norms, whereas a major rationale for this volume was that important change often comes from initiatives at the institutional level. Evaluation of attempts at change should focus somewhat less on the limited amount of change effected on the average in the system and more on the stratification that builds as some places change a great deal.

5. A related perspective is "world systems theory." This emphasizes the decisive impact of reigning models and ideas, transferred to the developing world and largely conditioning what it does (though some authors allow that domestic policy makers have latitude to affect how the transfers play out).

6. Neither the interest group perspective nor the feudal perspective is similar to voguish notions of shared decision making or total quality management, because these notions stress working together with a strong sense of institutional purpose and identity.

7. The political accommodation that arguably triumphs over directional academic leadership casts management in less flattering tones than the editor would want. Further, using Green's terms, the extreme diffusion of authority undermines academic culture as well as the penetration of international academic culture. On the other hand, this chapter does not attempt to specify the real weight of the six dynamics just cited, and it argues that the increasingly dominant model of reform can increase the role of institutional leadership.

8. The persistence of alternatives to the dominant model limits its appeal and certainly its prevalence. Aside from those who focus on blocking change (or on blocking change in the way change is made), some want to bolster the democratic participation most closely related to the fifth alternative identified above. For Brazil, for example, see Klein and Schwartzman 1993, 28–32.

9. Yet the statist perspective may well be the one perspective on change (among the six cited above) that retains great attractiveness for many pushing the new modernization model. This is paradoxical given the model's generally neoliberal thrust, but it relates to our points about the evaluation state.

10. These circumstances include where states provide resources on criteria other than performance, where institutions lack the possibilities of self-improvement, and perhaps where a pure market model reigns. A parallel exists with the primary and secondary levels where there is decentralization to states or provinces, which then seek enhanced policy influence through evaluation and specific funding for specific activities or performance.

11. The relative inattention to politics or governance, except as obstacles to change, is a sad hallmark of much technocratic advice from international agencies. In fairness, such matters are tricky and sometimes too sensitive and detailed for outside meddling. But even some matters that are not so sensitive fail to gain attention. For example, the great push in earlier decades towards professionalizing the professoriate contemplated an enhanced role for this group in decision making; today's push for modernization basically ignores such vital questions.

12. Redemocratization also brought interesting dilemmas for believers in pluralist-market systems, as seen in Chile. Should they favor mandatory persistence of boards (introduced repressively by the military) or allow individual institutions to abolish boards and return to their more traditional selection patterns? This is an example of the wider dilemma of how much the state should push standardized, mandatory policy measures aimed at insuring available plural systems.

REFERENCES

The references are largely limited to sources in English, although the bulk of the relevant literature is in Spanish. For additional sources in English see two special issues of *Higher Education*: volume 21 (1991) and volume 25 (1993).

Brunner, J., et al. 1995. *Educación superior en America Latina*. Bogotá: Universidad Nacional.

Brunner, J., and G. Briones. 1992. Higher education in Chile: Effects of the 1980 reform. In *Higher education reform in Chile, Brazil, and Venezuela*, edited by L.Wolff and D. Albrecht, II, 1–44. Washington, DC: World Bank.

Cerych, L., and P. Sabatier, eds. 1986. *Great expectations and mixed performance: The implementation of higher education reforms in Europe*. Trentham, Stoke-on-Trent, Great Britain: Bemrose Press.

Clark, B. 1986. Implementation in the United States: A comparison with European higher education reforms. In *Great expectations and mixed performance*, edited by L. Cerych and P. Sabtier, 259–67. Trentham, Stoke-on-Trent, Great Britain: Bemrose Press.

Grindle, M., and J. Thomas. 1991. *Public choices and policy change: The political economy of reform in developing countries*. Baltimore: Johns Hopkins University Press.

Kent, R. 1993. Higher education in Mexico: From unregulated expansion to evaluation. *Higher Education* 25: 73–83.

Klein, L., and S. Schwartzman. 1993. Higher education policies in Brazil: 1970–90. *Higher Education* 25: 21–34.

Levy, D. 1986. *Higher education and the state in Latin America*. Chicago: University of Chicago Press.

———. 1994. Mexico: Towards state supervision? In *Government and higher education relationships across three continents*, edited by G. Neave and F. van Vught, 241–63. Oxford: Pergamon Press.

———. 1996. *Building the third sector: Latin America's private research centers and nonprofit development*. Pittsburgh: University of Pittsburgh Press.

———. Forthcoming. *To export progress: U.S. assistance to Latin American universities*. Manuscript in progress.

Neave, G. 1988. The making of the executive head: The process of defining institutional leaders in certain Western European countries. *International Journal of Institutional Management in Higher Education* 12: 104–14.

Neave, G., and F. van Vught, eds. 1994. *Government and higher education relationships across three continents: The winds of change*. Oxford: Pergamon Press.

Task Force on Higher Education of the Latin American Studies Association. 1994. Higher education amid the political-economic changes of the 1990s. *LASA Forum* 25: 3–16.

Wolff, L., and D. Albrecht, eds. 1992. *Higher education reform in Chile, Brazil, and Venezuela: Toward a redefinition of the role of the state*. Washington, DC: World Bank.

CHAPTER 5

Higher Education in Africa

Crisis and Transformation

Fred M. Hayward

Executive Summary. Independence brought great hope that higher education could provide a key to the economic development and well-being of African nations, but the political instability of the 1970s brought with it increasing politicization of higher education and dampened expectations. The 1980s saw an economic decline in Africa. Fueled by government expectations that university education would provide the base for national economic development, expansion continued in spite of the economic decline, and the resulting underfunding and overcrowding weakened higher education throughout the continent. Per-student expenditures declined from $6,300 in 1970 to an average of $1,500 in 1988, as university enrollments grew from 20,000 at the time of independence in the early 1960s to almost one million by 1990 (excluding South Africa). Yet participation rates remain low, with only seven percent of the college-age population attending higher education in sub-Saharan Africa, and men nearly twice as likely to attend as women.

Political turmoil has further weakened higher education in many African states, with a series of wars and political crises creating general instability, and military dictatorships cracking down on universities who dared to be critical. Since the 1970s there have been numerous student demonstrations, civil strife, and university closings by governments. Higher education leadership in this highly politicized environment is a nearly impossible task. Some institutional heads are extensions of the government; those who seek to promote academic freedom and institutional autonomy are often forced to resign. Almost all are caught in the conflicts among students, faculty, and government and are faced with the monumental problems of deteriorating quality and funding.

Quality is a central issue, given the lack of resources, the brain drain, and the reality that those faculty members who do stay need to hold several jobs in order to survive economically. There are signs of hope, however, in such countries as South Africa, Namibia, Mozambique, and Ghana, where governments are reexamining issues of financing higher education, especially by charging tuition. A re-evaluation of the relationship between government and higher educa-tion is also underway in some countries, an essential step to restoring institutional autonomy to demoralized and passive institutions. African states will confront difficult choices to improve efficiency and to maximize quality and revenue while preserving access. For some nations, solving political problems will be an essential first step. The positive transformation of African higher education could serve as a model for the rest of the world.

· · · · · · · · · · · ·

Higher education in sub-Saharan Africa has been under siege for the last two decades as a consequence of economic decline, political crises, social demands, and a variety of external factors. With a few notable exceptions, higher education systems today are weaker than they were two decades ago, their infrastructures deteriorating, their staff and curricula less internationally competitive, and their ability to respond to national needs impaired.[1] There are exceptions in southern Africa and in a few other en-claves; however, most of Africa's once outstanding institutions like the Uni-versity of Ibadan, Fourah Bay College, Makerere University, and Cheikh Anta Diop University are but pale reflections of their former excellence.

Even though university enrollments alone increased from about 21,000 at the time of independence to almost one million by 1990, only about 7 percent (9.7 percent male, 4.9 percent female) of the college-age population in sub-Saharan Africa attend some kind of tertiary institution, and only 2 percent of that number are in universities (UNESCO 1995, 36).[2] After a period of rapid growth in the 1970s, spending on education in sub-Saharan Africa fell from $10 billion in 1980 to $8.9 billion by 1983 (World Bank 1988, 1–5). Average expenditures per student were $6,300 in 1970, dropping to an average of $1,500 in 1988 (World Bank 1994, 3).

CRISES IN AFRICAN HIGHER EDUCATION

In the following section, we focus on four factors contributing to the crises in African higher education: the economy, social demands and expectations, political crises, and the external environment.

Economic Crisis

Real GDP per capita in sub-Saharan Africa fell between 1980 and 1995, dropping almost one percent a year until 1985 and about one-half of one percent per year thereafter (IMF 1995, 98). The terms of trade deteriorated for almost all African countries, especially after 1985, with the price of basic export commodities (with the exception of oil) falling throughout the period. This had a devastating effect on countries that were dependent on the export of primary products. Inflation has ranged from 14 to 36 percent for the last 5 years (IMF 1995, 102).[3] Overall budget deficits widened sharply, while the inflow of direct foreign investment was minuscule: 1.5 percent of the total going to all developing countries (IMF 1995, 103). The aggregate performance of African states is skewed somewhat by the very poor economic performance of Nigeria, Zaire, and Cameroon, however. Since 1986, some real growth in GDP has taken place in about a dozen African states,[4] which have grown at a rate of about four percent during this period. The South African economy has also grown since elections in 1994, which should help stimulate growth in the whole southern African region, and recently improved prices for metals will help a number of African economies.

The financial crisis throughout Africa limited the ability of governments to fund higher education at previous levels, curtailed the development of its infrastructure, and prevented significant additional funding for expansion in the size and number of institutions of higher education. The impact of the economic crisis has been exacerbated by the fact that universities and other teritary institutions, which are nearly all dependent on foreign exchange, have been unable to find alternative sources of income or to institute economies.

Social Demands and Expectations

Part of the crisis in African higher education grows out of the rapid expansion of postsecondary education—an expansion that continued after the economies began to decline. Growth in the number and size of tertiary institutions was fueled by government expectation that university education would provide the base for national economic development and the public's expectation that a university degree would guarantee economic and social success for their children.

In the process of expanding higher education, little attention was given to concerns expressed about the areas in which expansion took place, even though there were numerous warnings about potentially excessive numbers of students in the humanities. By the 1980s, there were far too many unemployed humanities graduates; by 1987–88, business enrollments had increased markedly, although humanities remained the largest area of focus (Saint 1992, 20–21). Continued university expansion in the midst of economic decline resulted in an ever increasing proportion of costs dedicated to staff salaries and services for students (accommodations, food service, and health care), rather than to instruction, research, and infrastructure expenses.

Many universities were located in rural areas or away from major population centers. They were expected to be responsible for the development and maintenance of infrastructure services usually provided by the local community. As less and less funding was available, the quality of these services declined, as did instruction, research, and public service.

Political Crises and Instability

The last 20 years has also seen a veritable epidemic of political crises that have affected higher education adversely. Since the late 1960s, military dictatorships have become common, and with them a level of authoritarianism increasingly incompatible with free inquiry. Long a bastion of critical thinking, higher education soon became a focal point for criticism of governments and public policy. In most cases, governments reacted to this criticism with repressive measures. During the 1970s and 1980s, most colleges and universities experienced numerous student demonstrations, civil strife, and closings by the government. In this context, governments were even less willing to fund higher education adequately.

Civil wars closed colleges and universities for long periods of time in Angola, Mozambique, Liberia, Ethiopia, Rwanda, Sierra Leone, Zaire, Burundi, and Togo, among others. Already eroding facilities deteriorated further, faculty fled or were killed, and opportunities for education were lost to future generations of young people. Even without civil strife, the level of political repression in many countries was so high that many students and staff fled the university and often the country. The loss of talent in countries like Nigeria, Kenya, and Ghana posed significant problems for higher education. In the 1990s, the World Bank estimates that 23,000 qualified academic staff a year were leaving Africa, with 10,000 Nigerians alone employed in the United States (Blair and Jordan 1994, 3). Many more worked in other African countries. In Nigeria, it is estimated that half the faculty left the university over the last few years—half going abroad, the others taking nonacademic jobs in Nigeria. This is a different kind of brain drain, one of push rather than pull. It has benefited higher education in other countries, especially Europe and the Americas, where many of Africa's best and brightest scholars were hired.

External Developments

A number of external factors have also impinged on higher education during the last decades, undermining earlier achievements. There were prolonged droughts in the Sahel, east Africa, and southern Africa; economic problems in the industrialized world that had devastating consequences (including a sharp fall in commodity prices) for almost every nation in Africa; a decline in development assistance (11 percent or $1.3 billion from 1990 to 1991 alone); and a deterioration in terms of trade averaging 7 percent a year for the last 5 years (Carter 1993, 34, 100). Against this background, let us look at major forces for change in Africa.

FORCES FOR CHANGE

There is substantial commonality in the forces for change in Africa, although the relative importance of each varies from one country to the next and over time. In many respects, the pressures and demands for change in Africa are not unlike those in the rest of the world, but there are important differences of history as well as economic, social, and political conditions.

Development

Colonial conquest and occupation of Africa increased the demand for educated Africans. Colleges and universities such as Fourah Bay College (founded in 1827), the University of Fort Hare (established in 1916), Makerere University (1921), the University of Dakar (1957), the University of Ghana (1948), and Ibadan University (1948) were established to meet this demand, but it quickly became clear that these new institutions were not sufficient. As early as 1945, the Elliot Commission on Higher Education in West Africa was recommending further expansion of higher education.

The link between higher education and development is widely accepted in Africa. However, the failure to realize the potential of this connection, and the inability of higher education to make the expected contributions, concerns many educators and political leaders. Abiola Irele underscores the profound political and economic consequences of the failure—the technological stratification of people in the contemporary world in ways that leave Africa underdeveloped. He suggests: "Education in the modern context, for us in the underdeveloped world, especially in Africa, means nothing less than the development of a new mental universe" (Irele 1989, 129). He argues that in responding to social and political pressures for education as a symbol of modernization, there has been more appearance than substance, and he posits that education in Africa needs to be rethought ". . . so that it cultivates a frame of mind that is attuned to the scientific model" (ibid., 135).

Access

The demand for greater access to higher education has been an almost constant theme in Africa from the time of the establishment of Fourah Bay College in 1827. In the colonial plan, mass higher education for Africans was not anticipated—indeed, it was not a tradition at home. France and Britain, too, saw education as a privilege of the elite; Portugal was even more restrictive. From the mid-1940s, Africans criticized the elitist focus of colonial education.

While the colonial authorities were largely unresponsive to populist appeals for broader access to higher education, and the early period saw very slow growth in higher education (or none at all in the Portuguese colonies), that changed quickly after independence. A combination of pressures resulted in rapid expansion of higher education. Among the most important pressures was the need of the new governments for trained personnel to replace colonial officials. The new political leadership had great faith in education as the key to development, and responded quickly to public demands for education. The result was a substantial increase in the total numbers of university students in higher education in sub-Saharan Africa. The totals (excluding South Africa) grew quickly from a mere 20,000 in the 1960s to about 400,000 by the 1980s (World Bank 1988, 5). During this period, the growth in enrollments in Africa was the highest in the world. From 1970 to 1986, it grew by 14.2 percent a year, slowing somewhat after that to 8.2 percent in 1990, but remaining substantial (UNESCO 1991, 4).

In the Africa of the 1960s and 1970s, it seemed as if everyone should, and would, have access to higher education if they wished it. The first hints of economic problems were downplayed in the expectation that they would be short lived. By the 1980s, it was clear that was not the case, and most institutions of higher education were in such serious financial crises that major surgery was need. They suffered from overcrowding, inadequate infrastructure, rapidly decreasing standards of living for staff and for students, and growing problems of morale on campus. The issue of access was an especially difficult problem for governments. Limitations on access, for whatever reasons, flew in the face of public demands for more opportunities. Higher tuition (in some cases, *any* tuition) and fees provoked strong opposition on economic grounds from students and families. The low economic status of the majority of students laid those suggesting increases open to charges of elitism, even though for most institutions, student contributions were less than two percent of costs.[5]

Few countries were successful in managing the consequences of the economic crisis for higher education. Cutting student intakes, reducing the number of degrees offered, eliminating staff positions, closing some institutions, raising tuition, and other economies, were not seen as politically acceptable or socially responsible. Although the crisis continued to grow worse, there were few attempts by either higher education officials or governments to solve the problem.

Cost and Financing

The growth of higher education in the colonial and immediate postcolonial era was largely unfettered by economic restraints. Building and expanding higher education had enthusiastic public support. Universities symbolized a commitment to modernization and were held in high esteem.

Tuition and fees for tertiary education (where they existed at all) were low, covering a very small percentage of total costs. Most of the cost of higher education was borne by the state. Some universities attracted gifts, grants, and donor funding, but these sources seldom exceeded five percent of total costs and were usually much lower. As tertiary education expanded, higher education consumed an increasing percentage of government funds.

Most African colleges and universities were established as residential campuses. These institutions needed water, electricity, fire protection, and roads and transportation systems. Building and maintaining this infrastructure was part of the cost of education, at some institutions as high as 15 percent of total recurrent expenditures (Omoregie and Hartnett 1995, 1), and in all cases a significant part of the total budget.

Government subsidies for food services and accommodations for students and staff have been significant costs in most African states, ranging from 16 to 55 percent of costs. Often because of their remote locations, but partly as a consequence of the idea of the importance of residential colleges as a way to mold leaders, students had to live on campus. Fees for food and accommodations were seldom raised in proportion to increased costs, creating additional expenses for the state each year. In Ghana, the cost of student maintenance alone was recently estimated to be 17 percent of the total cost of education (Adu and Gaye 1995, 25–26). In many countries, subsidized staff housing is also provided at colleges and universities.

The funding crisis that had set in by the 1980s focused attention on a number of policy issues. Should the state be the primary source of financing for higher education? Should access be open, or limited only to those who meet certain standards or who can be accommodated by existing facilities? Who benefits from higher education—the state, the individual, or both? Should the individual student (or family) pay for these benefits? Was higher education living up to its expectations? Did it make a contribution to development? Could Africa afford higher education consonant with international standards? Should highly specialized training be done abroad? Should students make a greater contribution to their education through loans, a graduate tax, or public service?

The debate about financing higher education has been contentious. Universities have been criticized for their failure to provide training in critical areas, for the growing number of unemployed graduates, and for low quality. The expected development potential of higher education has not been realized. The relatively comfortable lifestyle of students and staff has been resented by an impoverished citizenry. Only a small number of people directly benefited (in Rwanda, for example, 15 percent of the national education budget benefited 0.2 percent of the student population; World Bank 1994, 23). The large number of graduates sent abroad by African governments to study (especially in science and the health professions), but who failed to return to Africa, were a direct financial loss to the country and led to growth in Africa of high-cost programs in areas such as medicine and engineering.

In spite of spirited debates, very few concrete decisions were made to resolve these problems. Government responses to the financial crisis were compounded by the often critical attitude of students and staff toward government, making governments less willing to tackle the economic issues and so reward their critics.

Financial support for students through various loan schemes has not proven to be a long-term economic success. Almost all of the programs ran into repayment problems, saddling governments with growing debts. In Ghana, for example, the low rate of recovery on student loans (50 percent) has increased government costs to the point that subsidizing the debt cost 15 percent of the total budget in 1995 (Omoregie and Hartnett 1995, i).

Faculty and staff salary levels fell significantly in the 1980s and 1990s. This remains a major unresolved problem, both for the cost of higher education and the retention of staff. By the 1990s, real staff salaries had fallen in most institutions, in some cases to levels at which faculty could not survive. In Uganda, the monthly salary for a lecturer was estimated at $19 in 1992, in Nigeria about $60, in Kenya $250. While these figures are difficult to compare, given a variety of subsidies, annual salaries at a large number of universities do not begin to cover expenses and represent a quantum decline in purchasing power from the 1960s. Faculty and staff have increasingly had to take second jobs during the 1980s and 1990s.[6] The consequence is that large numbers of faculty have become part-timers, affecting their performance in the classroom and almost totally eliminating time for research and service. The faculty exodus continues as morale falls in many countries.

The overall decline in the infrastructure of African universities in the 1980s and 1990s continued. Repairs and upkeep were put off in the hope that the economic situation would improve. Expenditures on books as a percentage of the budget were about 3 percent (about half that allocated in the United States). A study by the Association of African Universities (AAU 1991, 36) notes that "... libraries in African universities have been allowed to decline to a pitiable state. Most libraries do not have current issues of books and journals."

The economic news for higher education in Africa is not all grim. Ghana has made major strides after more than a decade of decline. Namibia and Botswana have made progress in building and maintaining quality institutions. South Africa is dismantling the shackles of apartheid education.

Autonomy

Most African universities had relatively high levels of autonomy in their early years. They were highly favored by colonial and postindependence political structures, the faculty were held in high esteem (often playing major roles in social and political life), and their leaders enjoyed ready access to the power structure. Private institutions, like the University of Fort Hare, were run by their own governing councils with little interference from outside.

With growing conflict over national political life beginning in the 1970s, higher education, too, became embroiled in conflicts. The conflicts of the nation were usually mirrored in its universities. Where regimes became repressive, opposition was often centered in the colleges and universities. Government expected administrators to control student and staff protests and opposition. When they could not, they were replaced. The state increasingly moved to limit the freedom of higher education, increasingly politicizing governing boards and councils, exerting control over administrators, and passing legislation that intruded on the autonomy of higher education.

Since the 1970s, the previous autonomy of higher education has been progressively weakened. Because most institutions of higher education are primarily funded by the state, its increasing intrusion in governance has not been seriously challenged. Indeed, the right of government to control higher education has been generally accepted in Africa. In many cases, government control became so pervasive that it included appointments of the vice-chancellor or rector. Governments regularly exerted pressure on institutional heads to insure that government positions were supported (or at least not opposed). In Zimbabwe, Senegal, Kenya, Sierra Leone, Nigeria, and many other countries, higher education became subservient to the wishes of those in power. As a consequence, colleges and universities were increasingly politicized, as in Nigeria, where the office of vice-chancellor has become a victim of national politics. In cases of conflict with staff and students, the vice-chancellors are increasingly dependent on government, and sometimes have called on national authorities to back up their authority—occasionally resulting in police and army intervention on campus.

The loss of autonomy created another kind of crisis for higher education as economic conditions worsened. If the state was not able to provide adequate funding, what other avenues were there to revitalize and rebuild higher education? To create alternative sources of power was to risk treason. Criticism of government's inaction was dangerous. Yet, if the government did not act, who would? Under such conditions, growing alienation and loss of morale became endemic to higher education in many African states. Large numbers of scholars, teachers, and administrators left higher education—and often the country. People felt they were powerless to bring about change.

There were a few exceptions to this pattern, notably South Africa. At one level, even the apartheid higher education system allowed individual institutions a remarkable degree of autonomy. Tuition fees differed from one university or technikon to the other, the course structure was different (except at the technikons that had a centralized syllabus), and campus administration was left primarily to the councils, rectors, vice-chancellors, and senates. As the transition to majority rule became increasingly possible in the 1990s, that very autonomy became contentious because it also created the potential to continue the apartheid structure in the name of autonomy.

The transition process has provided an opportunity for a major debate about higher education autonomy. Some viewed autonomy as providing the force for change, others saw it as creating a bastion of opposition to it. Indeed, the vice-chancellors and rectors of the 15 historically disadvantaged universities and technikons in South Africa urged the National Commission on Higher Education to examine the concept of institutional autonomy, suggesting:

> The way in which the term is used in South Africa needs to be redefined in ways that accept that such autonomy is not absolute and that it needs to be balanced with public accountability. We believe that the term should not be invoked in ways to obstruct institutional transformation and to maintain the old order. (NCHE 1996, 5)

Related to autonomy, though not synonymous with it, is academic freedom. A high proportion of African universities are under such external pressure and control that there is little academic freedom. As higher education has expanded in Africa, issues of academic freedom and artistic expression have become increasingly important and contentious. For example, academic freedom has been a major issue in Ghana over the years, with attacks on a university publication, *The Legon Observer*, and other newspapers and journals, because of their criticism of nondemocratic actions. Academic freedom, in the long run, is essential to creativity and discovery. As African states seek to become more competitive in economic spheres, higher education must have the freedom to explore, test, and challenge ideas if they are to give African states the competitive base essential for development and flexibility in the modern age.

Accountability

With the rapid growth of higher education and its increased cost as a percentage of government expenditures, demands for accountability have increased across Africa since the 1970s, reflecting concerns about focus, duplication, rationalization, and standards.

Government efforts to control costs and quality have increasingly involved national coordinating bodies, many called "national commissions." Nigeria's National Universities Commission (NUC) was set up in 1974 to provide oversight of universities in cooperation with the Ministry of Education; Kenya established a National Commission for Higher Education, which has responsibility for planning and accrediting all higher education including private education (about five percent of the total student population); and South Africa appointed a National Commission on Higher Education in 1995 to recommend a framework for transformation of the national system (though it is not clear whether it will have an ongoing governance function).

In recent years, a number of new actors have focused on accountability. They include students, businesses, professionals, unions, alumni, and the community, who argue that they, too, have a stake in higher education and will hold it accountable. These stakeholders have been especially vocal in South Africa over the last few years, demanding a voice in the transformation of higher education and demonstrating their strength both on and off campuses.

Technology

For African higher education, technology is the key to reversing the crisis in higher education, meeting demands for access, and providing the quality education necessary for competition in the modern world. One of the biggest gaps for higher education in Africa is its lack of technological capacity compared with the most advanced nations. The deficiencies include: information technology, science labs, computerization, and budget and management systems. There is an associated lack of skilled faculty and technicians in these areas.

The advent of new information technologies provides an opportunity to minimize some of the deficiencies in infrastructure, especially for libraries and science facilities. For example, the Internet enables African students and staff—long isolated from the rest of the world because of lack of travel funds, journals, and other means of communication—to have almost instant access to the international intellectual community and its scholarly resources.

Yet, this technology is expensive, and only a few African nations currently have the capacity to take advantage of it. Nigeria, the second largest higher education system in Africa, is almost completely devoid of information technology. South Africa, one of the few with access to the Internet, had limited that technology primarily to the historically White institutions. In 1996, it is struggling to provide similar technology to historically Black institutions.

Internationalization

Most sub-Saharan African universities were, in at least a limited sense, products of internationalization due to their origins either as colonial institutions or products of external initiatives such as the missionary societies that established the University of Fort Hare and Fourah Bay College. They were modeled after European institutions, their degrees were originally awarded by universities in France and Great Britain, their staffs were largely international, and so was the curriculum (in the sense that it reflected European views of what was appropriate for higher education). The student population, too, was diverse. Most early institutions were designed to accommodate whole regions of Africa. The tradition of higher education in Africa's leading institutions approximated Kerr's internationalization of learning in all four of its components: the flow of new knowledge, scholars, and students, as well as the content of the curriculum (Kerr 1994, 12–13).

One consequence of the external impetus for the establishment of African higher education was a widespread reaction against internationalization in many parts of Africa. Part of this was a demand for Africanization of the staff and administration, since the majority of faculty and administration were non-African at the time of independence. For some institutions, like the University of Dakar in the 1960s, the number of African staff was pitifully small, including only a handful of faculty and one administrator. There was also a reaction against the exclusion of African subject matter in most African universities, including African politics, history, and even African languages. At Fourah Bay College, those subjects were added only in the 1960s; in South Africa, Africans were prohibited from teaching African subjects, including languages, until the 1990s.

The nationalization of African higher education during the early independence period weakened both the universalism and internationalization process in Africa, but it was very important to asserting African control of higher education. Over the years, the international character of most colleges and universities has declined. However, these trends are being countered by other realities. One of these is information technology, which is a powerful tool for helping African universities counter their isolation and parochial tendencies. By facilitating external contacts, technology is also a vehicle for internationalization. The fact that a large proportion of African academics were trained in Europe or the United States fuels universalism. Any nation with aspirations to be internationally competitive must, in the long run, internationalize higher education. Those that fail to do so may survive, but will not be able to make the contributions to the national economy necessary to build modern and competitive political and economic systems. Such transformation is taking place in South Africa, Ghana, Namibia, Senegal, Botswana, and Mozambique. All see themselves as part of a system of global higher education. This does not diminish the tensions between local demands and open institutions, between access for the local population and limitations on non-nationals, or between those who would eliminate external influences and those who see them as essential to intellectual growth and national development.

Quality

One of the most difficult and subtle debates taking place in African higher education today is that of institutional quality. It is not the stuff of public speeches or political pronouncements. Indeed, because of its sensitive and potentially explosive consequences, it is one of the quietest debates currently underway. It touches on a number of other major issues: access, massification, elitism, cost, competitiveness, self-interest—all capable of inflaming raw nerves. Nonetheless, these are critical issues for the future of Africa.

The bottom line for the institutions and the nations involved is their ability to establish and maintain institutions of higher education that meet international standards of scholarship and research. In the long run, this is not just a question of pride; it is a test of how well a nation's institutions of higher education perform in training their students, providing the skills needed for the modern age, giving citizens access to state-of-the-art knowledge, and providing a base for economic competitiveness.

The question of establishing and maintaining higher education institutions of international quality becomes a difficult one for many African states because of their financial crises. Can they afford the technology? Is the open research university a model that is right for Africa? Is it necessary for every country to have such higher education institutions? Can't they send their specialists elsewhere for technical and highly specialized training? Will the expenditures on higher education really produce the desired outcomes? These are not easy questions in any country. In the world's poorest continent, they are even more difficult to answer. Yet, they can not be ignored unless one is willing to permanently relegate Africa to second-class status not only economically, but in social and political life as well. Some aspects of the quality question were addressed in October 1995 during a meeting of the Caucus of African Ministers of Education; in particular, the possibility of sharing facilities in specialized areas to limit costs. There was a general recognition that Africa is falling further behind the rest of the world, and that a combination of growing population and failure to be competitive is hurting economic prospects.

The issue of improving the quality of education is a complex one.[7] The economic decline in Africa has, as we noted earlier, sparked a huge brain drain of many of Africa's finest scholars. Part of the issue is salaries, which have declined in much of Africa to the point that faculty can not survive. Another part of the problem is the decline of the institutions themselves, their libraries, laboratories, and working conditions. That, too, drives people away, leading to large numbers of vacancies at universities including the University of Zimbabwe, which had a vacancy level of 35 percent in 1992 (Blair and Jordan 1994, 3). Even South Africa, which does not have the salary problems of many African states, suffers from large numbers of faculty vacancies.

The issues involved in providing high quality higher education are not easy to resolve in any society. They require measures of institutional performance, quality assessment, institutional and program reviews, and performance of graduates. Improving quality may entail setting up differentiated systems of institutions with admission based on different preparations and demonstrated academic success, or it may mean limiting enrollment only to the number of people a country can afford to educate at standards that meet international qualifications. It will certainly mean redefining priorities (for most of Africa) in ways that focus some funding to high quality institutions of higher education, whether public or private.[8]

MAJOR ACTORS IN THE CHANGE PROCESS

Governments

In the 1950s and 1960s, African universities were a source of great pride and high expectations, with commensurate financial investment. In Africa, education, independence, and development went hand in hand. Education was seen as the key to development: education *was* development.

During this early period, universities were largely left to run themselves, but the honeymoon was short-lived. As economic crises loomed, politics became increasingly contentious and political repression began to be a major factor in African life and in the academy. Universities encouraged people to think and to challenge; in Hannah Arendt's words, "thinking is dangerous" in that it often leads to dissent (Arendt 1977, 176, 199). As a consequence, governments began to assert their authority over university administration and governance. Vice-chancellors were often more political than academic appointments, sometimes more dependent on government than on faculty and students for power and support. Major policy making fell increasingly to the politicians and bureaucrats rather than to the faculty or administration. And when tensions spilled over, it was government that intervened—further weakening autonomy.

A number of vice-chancellors were dismissed because of conflicts between the university and government, and others found their powers severely limited. Some distinguished higher education leaders resigned in protest as a result of political intrusions and lack of government support. In 1991, Professor Walter J. Kamba, then vice-chancellor of the University of Zimbabwe, stepped down in protest over increasing political interference by government. In his final address to the university community and the president of Zimbabwe, he noted that "there are too many fingers in the affairs of the university—nonprofessional fingers with a wide range of agendas" (Kamba 1991, 4).

In Kenya, by 1996, the universities were seen as "silently dying." Government was suffocating them by means of limited funds and political pressure. Those who criticized government or called for improved conditions were fired or imprisoned. Elections of deans and other officials were no longer held, with vice-chancellors and other senior administrators appointed by Kenya's President Moi, and others appointed by those administrators. Kenyan universities have been closed much of the time in recent years, and when open, they operate in a climate of fear and repression (Kenyan universities 1996).

Loss of autonomy has left institutions at the mercy of the interest, attention, and priorities of the government—and in many cases, the head of state alone. Where the interest has been minimal or hostile, nothing happens. There is no one making decisions, setting priorities, giving direction (or changing it), or making hard choices in a difficult economic and political climate. Many administrators, academic staff, and students are torn by these crises. While they are increasingly unhappy about the state of affairs at the colleges and universities, some acknowledge government's right to control the institutions. Some have come to feel that the situation is no longer their problem, since power, authority, and responsibility have been taken from them. Others feel helpless, cynical, and discouraged. As the situation has deteriorated on many campuses, people have become overwhelmed by the tasks of surviving. For many, the human and political costs of fighting one losing battle after another for funds, autonomy, and freedom no longer seems worth it.

There is a small sector of private higher education in Sudan, Madagascar, Kenya, Niger, Rwanda, Zimbabwe, and Zaire. The most established and successful are in Kenya, where about a dozen private institutions encompass about five percent of the student population. Even if private higher education succeeds at some level, and it has in Kenya and Sudan, it is likely to be limited to a small group of middle- and upper-income individuals. Nonetheless, private colleges and universities do offer an alternative. Those institutions perceived to have special benefits to offer, like a religious environment[9] or high quality courses in specific subject areas, may draw students from families or communities able to pay and thus ease pressure on public institutions.

Faculty and Staff

During the 1980s, in most of Africa, faculty and staff became increasingly less important actors in the governance of higher education. Their traditional role was eroded by increasing politicization. Many staff organizations were outlawed (such as the Kenya University Academic Staff Union in 1994) or became moribund. A few of the staff associations, including the Nigerian Academic Staff Union of Universities (ASUU), were able to have some impact, but neither they nor others were able to stem the deterioration of higher education. In the 1990s, this situation changed slightly in Nigeria with the ASUU success at the end of a strike in 1992. A renewed faculty strike in 1996 and government crackdown paralyzed Nigerian higher education once again.

In contrast to much of the rest of Africa, staff associations in southern Africa have played an important role, sparking major changes in higher education. In South Africa in particular, the Union of Democratic University Staff Associations (UDUSA) has been a major actor in planning fundamental change for the postapartheid period since 1990. Faculty and staff played a major role in the National Education Co-ordinating Committee (NECC). They have been working to bring about changes, organize broadly based policy forums, and help establish new structures. With the coming into power of the ANC following the first democratic elections in 1994, this work has had a major impact on restructuring higher education.

The Public

In general, the role of the public in higher education in Africa is small. However, there have been public pressures for more open access, to which governments have responded. In that sense, the public has played an important role in the massification of higher education. It continues to play that role today, and when quality is pitted against access, it has opted for access. Part of the problem of public participation remains, as Ajayi noted in 1973, ". . . the mass of Africans do not understand what our universities are about" (Ajayi 1973, 12). He remarks that universities have done little to inform people about their role in society or to answer the questions that bother people most. "And when they do look up to the universities on these problems, they rarely get answers that they can understand or find relevant to their predicament." Reiterating that position in 1995, Ajayi states: "On the whole, the universities have generally failed to give adequate information about themselves to the general public. The absence of an effective commitment, by governments, to the universities should also be seen as the failure of the universities to generate and sustain such commitment" (Ajayi, Goma, and Johnson 1995, 143). The failure to inform and involve the general public has made them weak allies of higher education. They are eager for opportunities for their children, impressed by what these opportunities imply for the future, but little able to assess need, demand quality, or assist in insuring that higher education has adequate support and working conditions.

Governing Councils

Although most African universities are nominally governed by councils (or similar bodies), many have lost their traditional roles with the expansion of government power over higher education. Their members are frequently appointed by the government, taking their cues from the political sector. Councils seldom protect the university, its autonomy, or academic freedom. In some places, as in Nigeria and South Africa under apartheid, they serve to support government positions. Where they are more autonomous and powerful, as in South Africa in the 1990s, they suffer from a far too limited understanding of their own role—and in many cases, a lack of vision for the future of higher education. Councils have a potentially vital role to play in Africa, as buffers and protectors but also as a source of thinking and long-term planning for the future. This has been an area of significant reform in Uganda, Zambia, and Tanzania.

Students

The role of students in higher education in Africa has been an important and often pivotal one. Students were frequently at the forefront of the struggle against colonialism, or in South Africa and Namibia, against apartheid. They have played major roles as critics of repression and defenders of democratic values. To be sure, they have also been used by dictators and tyrants for other political ends. But on the whole, students have been important to higher education in keeping the pressure on those who would repress society and its colleges and universities.

The Mobutu regime in Zaire has had a long-term running battle with students. In the 1960s, Mobutu became so exasperated with students that he drafted them into military service. Nigerian, Cameroonian, Senegalese, Ghanaian, and Kenyan universities, among others, have had periodic confrontations with government that have led to military and police action against students and closure of the institutions for long periods of time. While some of these conflicts have grown out of desires to protect or improve institutions of higher education, on the whole, the conflicts have reflected national political issues. In that sense, the campus has mirrored the national political arena.

Students have not always been helpful to the cause of higher education, and some of their self-serving demands have hurt student causes. Nonetheless, students are an important force whose independence, relative freedom, and anonymity make them powerful influences. Furthermore, their criticisms of higher education have frequently focused new energy on changing the institutions. Their role in the transformation of higher education in South Africa has been very important, and their contributions often more thoughtful and well organized than those of their teachers and administrators. Like student groups everywhere, they also suffer from rapid turnover within their organizations, a lack of continuity, and limited historical perspective. Nonetheless, we will continue to see them as powerful actors in many African states.

University Leadership

The role of university leadership in the change process in higher education in Africa is a very mixed one. As noted earlier, it has been severely eroded in most of Africa by government intervention and repression. Some college and university leaders have not always served their countries well, nor stood up for autonomy, freedom, and justice. They have sometimes failed (as have university leaders in other parts of the world) to make the case for the needs of higher education. As Ajayi observes:

> The inability of the university communities themselves to prevent the massive deterioration of the universities cannot be blamed entirely on factors external to the institutions themselves. If the state collapses, it is inevitable that the university should also collapse. Many academics have been part of governments that prey on their people to the point of total collapse. African university people have not always stood up on the side of democracy, or of imposing limitations on the exercise of state power. (Ajayi, Goma, and Johnson 1995, 142)

A number of university leaders have played major roles in the process of change. The willingness of some university leaders in South Africa to stand up against the apartheid regime helped bring it down. The courage of people in leadership positions, where they are visible and more vulnerable than others, to fight for the rights and dignity of the majority population in South Africa will be remembered as one of the finest hours of higher education. In South Africa, Zimbabwe, Ghana, and a few other states, higher education leaders continue to play a central role in the change process.

In periods of transition, the position of leaders is particularly difficult. They are usually attacked from all sides. They are expected to support the government position, but they are also criticized for it. They are to be advocates for campus groups, and they are to be responsive to the community. They are to support creativity and questioning, and they are to control it. These tasks are usually incompatible. In the highly charged and politicized environment that prevails, it is difficult to stand up for the values and principles essential for quality higher education and to maintain public, university, and government support. Yet, where policy debates have been possible, the confrontations and debates over policies have brought important changes—as in Namibia, South Africa, and Mozambique.

In many African states, the higher education policy arena has developed into a stalemate. There is an underlying level of unhappiness, sometimes punctuated by student and staff strikes and protest, but little change. Life on campus becomes a series of struggles to function and confrontations over conditions. These situations put tremendous pressure on those leaders who try to keep their institutions functioning and seek to bring about changes in the deteriorating conditions of the universities. The debilitating and stultifying nature of the situation is well described by Vice-Chancellor Akilagpa Sawyerr, of the University of Ghana, in a speech given shortly before he stepped down from office. He discusses his concerns about the difficulty of promoting the mission of the university, defending its integrity, and making sure it made a real contribution to national development. He concludes:

> It is, therefore, a matter of very deep regret that, because of their pre-occupation with matters that would normally be considered secondary, very few Vice-Chancellors in Africa today are in any position to devote adequate time and attention to these responsibilities. The seemingly interminable student crises; the constant battle to restrain undue govern-mental intervention in university affairs; the often desperate struggle to ensure the adequacy and timeliness of subventions from government; and the maintenance of the municipal services in these times of inadequate finance—these are matters very few Vice-Chancellors can afford to ig-nore. They constitute a major diversion of attention and talent from the leadership of the university in its quest for academic excellence and innovation in its academic and organizational arrangements. (Sawyerr 1991)

Even where progress is being made, the personal price paid by leaders is high. They are under tremendous pressure from all sides. Government, eager to please the majority population, often puts pressure on them for quick decisions or actions that will avert crises. Sometimes, working through a crisis is important to making progress; external pressure can be counterproductive and confusing. The crisis in 1996 in South Africa regarding the admission of students who have accumulated tuition debts from previous years is such an example. Statements by government officials have encouraged students to think they can register without paying back debts. That, in turn, has put pressure on universities and technikons to admit such students. Many did so during 1995, accumulating debts of millions of rand in the process. The brunt of the conflict falls on the institutional administrators. The toll has been heavy, including violence, intimidation, hostage taking, and demonstrations. All this puts higher education leadership under extreme pressure. Its conse-quences are reflected in rapid turnover (creating new instabilities), a life of crisis management, and a lack of time for long-term planning.

MAJOR THEMES IN CONTEMPORARY AFRICAN HIGHER EDUCATION

The postindependence period saw major changes in the direction and fortunes of higher education in Africa. The period of the 1960s was one of euphoria, hope, and romanticism. Higher education was the future, the key to development and well-being. By the 1970s, expectations were somewhat dampened, stung by the wave of military coups starting in Ghana in 1966 and spreading to almost every other country in Africa by the 1970s, and confronted by the growing politicization of higher education. By the 1980s, disillusionment and decline were the norm. Higher education was besieged by a seemingly endless economic crisis coupled with widespread political instability and repression. The decay of many of Africa's campuses continued, overcrowding became an increasingly vexing problem, and the quality of colleges and universities in most parts of Africa continued to fall. The first half of the 1990s was a period of growing pessimism in higher education, although there were also some signs of hope (in Ghana, Mozambique, and South Africa, for example). The successes were eagerly examined as potential models for change.

During the postindependence era, a number of themes dominated African higher education. Four that help define the current situation in Africa are examined here: living with economic crisis, politicization and marginalization, searching for allies and funding, and seeking new models for higher education transformation.

Living with Economic Crisis

The economic crisis in Africa, especially since 1980, has been the single most important factor affecting higher education. Most institutions have fared very badly, ruled by the downward economic spiral but unable to respond to it. The successes have most often been in nations with more resources, countries like Ghana and South Africa. Yet, national wealth is not necessarily a key to success as we have seen in both Nigeria and Kenya. They, like many other systems in Africa, are victims of political crises much more than of economic decline.

The ability of nations to manage economic decline is a critical determinant of the conditions of higher education in Africa today. To date, their success rate in managing the crisis has been low.

On the other hand, there have also been creative responses to the financial crisis at the institutional level. The ingenuity involved in trying to keep a University of Sierra Leone (Fourah Bay College and Njala) or a University of Ghana going during periods of major economic collapse provides striking examples of what can be done. When water and electricity were on only two hours a day at Njala College,[10] labs were doubled and tripled, with student teams alternating days to experiment and days to watch. In Legon, major sections of the campus (lawns and all) were turned into vegetable gardens so that people could eat at least one meal a day. Everyone became a trader. External examiners traded their services for lab chemicals, books, and supplies. Lecturers made their own equipment, students scrounged supplies. Finance officers also carried out remarkable accounting exercises when no money was available to pay staff. That the university was a community made this possible. But even for the best and most creative managers, faculty, and students, the cost of economic decay was very high. The fact is that experiments and creativity could not replicate better days. That many of these universities have survived at all—and still provide the base for renewal and development—is remarkable. In spite of losses, there is a remarkable corps of people who remain to rebuild these institutions.

Politicization and Marginalization

The politicization of higher education in the 1970s and 1980s fostered a deep sense of powerlessness and despair in many parts of Africa, manifested by the failure of higher education to tackle the difficult tasks that needed to be addressed. Governments were held responsible for both the decline and for the failure to resolve current problems. Government hostility to political activism on campus and the failure of colleges and universities to deliver the promised development contributions made governments less concerned about the condition of higher education, further contributing to its marginalization.

The politicization of higher education and the fight for survival have resulted in growing instability on campus and an often paralyzing struggle for institutional power and control. This struggle reflects growing frustration and cynicism about higher education leadership on many campuses. The mood is exemplified by more frequent confrontations with both campus administration and with government. No longer are strikes and demonstrations a part of just student life. Increasingly, faculty and staff, and in some cases even administrators, have been involved in protest, strikes, and violence. In recent years, these disruptions have led to the closure of institutions in most African countries, with some having been closed for large parts of the academic year, as was the case in Senegal, Kenya, Côte d'Ivoire, Zaire, and Nigeria.

One of the most serious long-term costs of the political repression and violence that has afflicted much of Africa is individual withdrawal from active participation in efforts to change the institutions and the loss of a sense of responsibility among much of the higher education community. For some, the withdrawal is a consequence of the high cost paid by individuals who tried to foster change. The examples of people who tried and failed (some paying with their lives) are powerful deterrents to others who would try to spark change under current circumstances. Withdrawal is not limited to repressive situations. Many institutions subject to decades of deterioration have lost their most able and determined advocates of change. Passivity in the face of repression and economic decline has become the major reaction to years of deteriorating conditions.

Searching for Allies and Funding

With the decline of state support, both economic and political, colleges and universities are searching for new bases of support—in the community, among alumni, foundations, external donors, and in the business sector. A few institutions have had remarkable successes, such as the technikons in South Africa, which are receiving funding, state-of-the-art equipment, grants, internships, and job placement from business. Several institutions have been successful in efforts to build links with alumni, but it is slow and time consuming. There are initiatives, such as those underway in Ghana and the Côte d'Ivoire, to rebuild a healthy relationship between higher education and government.

Recognizing the need for new sources of income for higher education, some institutions have focused on tuition and fees. While only a handful of countries have instituted significant fees, the debate has been opened almost everywhere. Among those who have increased tuition and fees are Ghana (6 percent of the cost), Sierra Leone (100 percent of the cost of education for the first year only), and South Africa (where students now pay about 18 percent of the cost of education); (see Adu and Gaye 1995, 27; Ministry of Education 1995, 47). Other countries are exploring tuition increases. Cameroon has been considering a tuition increase from 0.8 percent of the cost to 11 percent (Assié-Lumumba 1993, 34). Most African countries with significant tuition levels have student grants, but the number available is usually small. The business community is also being asked for financial support for both students and the institutions.

The long-term effect of shifting the burden increasingly to students will not be clear for a number of years. Where unemployment of graduates is high, as in Ghana, it is already having a serious negative effect on the government budget, requiring major shifts of funds to cover the cost of the interest subsidy and student loan defaults. The current cost is 15 percent of total expenses on higher education (Adu and Gaye 1995, i). Loan schemes place a significant debt burden on a large number of young people at graduation. Depending on their ability to find employment, these debts can have significant negative political implications of their own. The long-term burden on students may help shape their choices of field (away from those without job prospects), higher education decisions about priority fields, as well as considerations about admissions and support in general. Nonetheless, it is hard to see that there are alternatives to a significant level of student contributions to the cost of education if quality is to be achieved.

Redefining the Relationship with Government

In spite of the mood of pessimism of the early 1990s, the mid-1990s have seen new hope for successful change and transformation of higher education. The kinds of change occurring in the bright spots in Africa—in South Africa, Namibia, and Mozambique—shine like a beacon to many who have lost hope. The recent changes in South Africa in particular, have sparked optimism for the future of African higher education in 1996 that did not exist in 1994.

Part of the process of change in South Africa involves rethinking the role of the state. Some of the most innovative work has occurred as part of efforts to explore new models of the relationship between government and higher education. One of the major concerns of the National Commission on Higher Education (NCHE) during 1995–96 has been to formulate a new structure of higher education based on a very different relationship between higher educa-tion and the state. The current thinking on this subject in the Ministry of Education, the NCHE, and policy circles, was outlined by Teboho Moja at the meetings of the Association of African Universities (AAU) in Lesotho:

> A new approach should depart from the assumption that we should strive toward a strong democratic state; strong in the sense of an assertive government with a professional bureaucracy. . . . This new approach accepts that governance in modern societies can no longer be conceived in terms of external government control of society, nor of a reflexively oppositional stance between state and civil society, but as a co-production of complementary and competing interests. (Moja 1995, 19)

The response of other African education leaders to the South African efforts has been striking. After initial skepticism about change in South Africa, the early successes there have stimulated a reappraisal of prospects for change.

The old assumptions about government control of all aspects of higher education, best articulated by the Association of African Universities in 1973, are suddenly open to question. For the first time in two decades, the views that the national government was in the best position "to determine the priorities for the university" and that "the university in Africa occupied too critical a position of importance to be left alone to determine its own priorities" (Yesufu 1973, 44) were being reexamined. Although most African institutions are not currently moving toward autonomy, as South Asian institutions are doing (see Chapter 3), the discussion and policy choices being made in several African states suggest that the issue of autonomy is once more a focus of attention and that efforts are being made to define major areas in which higher education should become autonomous.

CONCLUSION

Although the crises besetting higher education in Africa and the difficulties involved in responding to them are neither an indictment of African higher education nor a prediction that Africa is relegated to a second- or third-class fate, the problems are all too real. The responses, in general, have been too weak to be effective, and both the economic and political crises, where most severe, are major impediments to significant changes in the near future. In many cases, needed reform and transformation will have to await a solution to national political problems, as occurred in South Africa. In others, however, solutions seem possible but are inhibited by cynicism, passivity, and the unwillingness of educators to take responsibility. While government may have a monopoly on power over higher education, the options for action within institutions are much greater than seems to be acknowledged. Indeed, there are successes and responses underway in parts of Africa that, in the view of this writer, are some of the most interesting currently taking place anywhere. The successes in South Africa, Mozambique, and Ghana, for example, can serve as a powerful model to others.

In most parts of Africa, major impediments to effective change remain, which could derail the process of transformation. The continued economic uncertainties remain the biggest stumbling block. All African economies remain far too dependent on the export of primary commodities and thus they are especially susceptible to fluctuations in the international economy. Nonetheless, for the first time since 1980, the overall economic picture for Africa is looking better. According to an International Monetary Fund study, the prospects for 1996 have improved with an expected five percent growth in real GDP with a real per capita growth of two percent. Inflation is also expected to fall to about 12 percent overall during 1996 (IMF 1995, 106–07). Furthermore, reductions in protectionist trade policies by industrialized nations, which hurt African export growth, are expected. Added to this, the improvement of the South African economic situation and the resolution of its political problems following democratic elections in 1994 promise economic growth for the whole southern Africa region and its education transformation process.

Political instability, civil wars, repression, and other local conflicts continue to plague a large number of African states. The prospects for any significant improvement in the conditions of higher education in countries like Nigeria, Sierra Leone, Kenya, Rwanda, and Liberia remain small until political problems have been resolved. The political settlements in Namibia and South Africa have demonstrated what can be done and have resulted in major changes in higher education. The settlement of a long, cruel civil war in Angola and of an insurgency in Mozambique also create conditions for change—already marked by successes in Mozambique.

The extreme inequalities in income in most African states pose special problems for African higher education since they affect the ability of students to pay. This brings higher education into the middle of the larger debate over the redistribution of wealth in African nations. That problem will not go away and makes it more difficult to establish public policy about access, tuition, fees, and optimal size of higher education enrollments since such decisions, in the end, will be political.

Higher education is not immune from struggles for power. Indeed, in most of Africa, higher education is intimately involved in politics. Students play a powerful role where participation is tolerated, and they have a long history of activism in politics throughout Africa. Higher education institutions are very likely to become embroiled in political conflicts nationally, even if they try to remain neutral. Given the extent of politicization of higher education at the present time, it is likely to continue to be a serious detriment to change. To the extent that higher education in Africa succeeds in reasserting some degree of autonomy and in diversifying its base of funding, it may be able to provide at least a degree of protection from political conflicts and control.

Massification remains another potential stumbling block for higher education. While the expansion of educational opportunities (especially in science and technology) is a long-term condition for economic growth in Africa, it must be carried out in a way that does not compromise quality or the economic viability of higher education. Similarly, the tradeoffs between the need for substantial tuition increases and the goal of open access to higher education must be weighed carefully to insure that educational resources are not over-stretched, in the name of equality, to the point of collapse.

Finally, the issue of quality will continue to be a thorny one. Not every institution can match the flagship institutions of Europe or the United States, but for economic success in Africa, some of them must do so; they must provide students with state-of-the-art instruction, carry out first-rate research, and provide a wide variety of high quality services to their governments and communities. This will be costly, and with a few exceptions such as South Africa (and perhaps Nigeria, Kenya, and Zaire in the distant future), few nations have the resources to do it alone. For the majority, those who succeed will need to build on some of the cooperative efforts begun in the 1990s in areas such as economics. This allows for pooling of resources, economies of scale, and maximizing available African talent.

Where is African higher education headed in the near future? For most systems, it seems likely that the stagnation will continue for the next several years. However, both the economic prospects and the will to change seem to be improving. There is also a growing respect for the world of ideas coupled with new demands for development.

Successful transformation of higher education in Africa can be instructive to the rest of the world. Among the lessons might be new models of transformation, more effective integration of cultures, more task-oriented and less wasteful systems, greater focus on what one can do (rather than who one is), more openness to individual worth, more effective citizens of the world, and distinct African cultural contributions to academic life universally.

My guess is that part of the vision for the future will grow out of the survival skills and the realism born of the last two decades. Africa's higher education leaders, and some of its political leaders, will come to realize that the world is divided between those with technical skills and an open environment, and those without them. The resulting stratification can only be bridged with quality higher education systems founded on state-of-the-art science and technology. Part of that recognition will include a long-term commitment to establishing high quality institutions and a new focus on students, research, and service. It will also include a rethinking of the role of research and technology in African societies, something already underway in several Africa states.

NOTES

1. Trevor Coombe (1991) presents an excellent review of higher education in the English-speaking African states. A similarly useful work on francophone Africa is offered by N'Dri Thérèse Assié-Lumumba (1993).

2. William Saint (1992) estimated 542,700 for 1990. If one adds the 323,000 university students in South Africa at that time, the total is 865,000.

3. This figure excludes Zaire, which had an inflation rate of 23,900 percent in 1994 (IMF 1995, 102).

4. The World Bank listed 14 such countries: Benin, Burundi, Gambia, Ghana, Kenya, Lesotho, Malawi, Mali, Mozambique, Niger, Senegal, Tanzania, Togo, and Uganda. To that list should be added South Africa.

5. In Nigeria, the contribution was 1.6 percent in 1995 (Omoregie and Hartnett 1995, 15).

6. At Fourah Bay College, in Sierra Leone, one official estimated that 75 percent of the faculty had second jobs. Those who did not had difficulty making ends meet.

7. For an excellent discussion of the issue of quality and suggested strategies that might be pursued to reverse the decline, see Saint 1992, Chapter 9.

8. A number of scholars are thinking and writing about these issues in Africa. It is the theme of Abiola Irele's piece (1989), discussed earlier. It has been a regular theme of the work of Jacob Ajayi, going back as far as 1973 (Ajayi 1973).

9. Eisemon gives an excellent assessment of the attractions of private higher education institutions associated with religious organizations, especially their "character building function," in his thoughtful study of Kenyan higher education (Eisemon 1992, 21).

10. Before the civil war totally destroyed Njala University College in 1995.

REFERENCES

Adu, K., and M. Gaye. 1995. Ghana tertiary education project: Mid-term review. Unpublished internal document. Washington, DC: World Bank. November.

Ajayi, J. F. 1973. Towards an African academic community. In *Creating the African university: Emerging issues of the 1970s*, edited by T. M. Yesufu. Ibadan, Nigeria: Oxford University Press.

Ajayi, J. F.; L. K. H. Goma; and G. Ampah Johnson. 1995. *The African experience with higher education*. Accra, Ghana: Association of African Universities.

Arendt, H. 1977. *Thinking*. New York: Harcourt Brace Jovanovich.

Assié-Lumumba, N. T. 1993. *Higher education in francophone Africa: Assessment of the potential of the traditional universities and alternatives for development*. Washington: World Bank.

Association of African Universities (AAU). 1991. *Study on cost effectiveness and efficiency in African universities*. Accra, Ghana: AAU.

———. 1995. *The university in Africa in the 1990s and beyond: A summary report*. Accra, Ghana: AAU.

Blair, R., and J. Jordan. 1994. *Staff loss and retention at selected African universities: A synthesis report*. Washington, DC: World Bank Technical Department.

Carter, J. 1993. Global development: Cooperation for development can prevent Somalias. In *Carnegie Commission: Science, technology, and government for a changing world*. New York: Carnegie.

Coombe, T. 1991. A consultation on higher education in Africa: A report to the Ford Foundation and the Rockefeller Foundation. January.

Eisemon, T. 1992. *Private initiatives and traditions of state control in higher education in sub-Saharan Africa*. Washington, DC: World Bank.

International Monetary Fund (IMF). 1995. *World economic outlook: May 1995*. Washington, DC: IMF.

Irele, A. 1989. Education and access to modern knowledge. *Daedelus* 118 (1): 128–35.

Kamba, W. J. 1991. Address of welcome: Graduation Day. University of Zimbabwe, 13 July.

Kenyan universities are "silently dying." 1996. *Telegraph* February.

Kerr, C. 1994. *Higher education cannot escape history: Issues for the twenty-first century*. Albany: SUNY Press.

Ministry of Education. 1995. *Financing higher education*. Pretoria, South Africa.

Moja, T. 1995. *Public policy perspectives on the future of the university in Africa: Towards a new relationship between government and higher education*. Pretoria, South Africa: Ministry of Education.

National Commission on Higher Education (NCHE). 1996. Submission to the NCHE by historically disadvantaged tertiary institutions. Johannesburg. South Africa. January 16.

Omoregie, P. O., and T. Hartnett. 1995. *Financing trends and expenditure patterns in Nigerian universities*. Washington, DC: World Bank.

Saint, William S. 1992. *Universities in Africa: Strategies for stabilization and revitalization*. Washington, DC: World Bank.

Sawyerr, A. 1991. Leadership and organisation of African universities. Paper prepared for the UNESCO/AAU Higher Education Governance and Management Seminar, November, at the University of Ghana.

UNESCO. 1995. *World education report*. Paris and Oxford: UNESCO.

———. 1991. *Priority Africa*. Accra, Ghana: UNESCO.

World Bank. 1988. *A World Bank policy study, education in sub-Saharan Africa: Policies for adjustment, revitalization and expansion*. Washington, DC: World Bank.

———. 1994. *Higher education: The lessons of experience*. Washington, DC: World Bank.

———. 1995. *World development report*. New York: Oxford University Press.

Yesufu, T. M., ed. 1973. *Creating the African university: Emerging issues of the 1970s*. Ibadan, Nigeria: Oxford University Press.

CHAPTER 6

Higher Education in Western Europe

Claudius Gellert

Executive Summary. As European higher education has sought to expand during the last 20 to 30 years, new forms of postsecondary education have been created to meet the needs of increased participation and new populations of students. The expansion of higher education has provided access to previously underserved groups, such as women, students of lower socioeconomic groups, and "second chance students" returning to postsecondary education. New institutions have been created—usually in the non-university sector (NUS)—with more practical and structured curricula, shorter study programs, less basic research, and generally a more limited range of programs. In addition, a "third sector" of private programs is now growing—"corporate classrooms," or programs created through partnerships with government and industry. The author reviews the major differences between the university and non-university sectors, and points to some problems, especially "academic drift." Although the NUS institutions were intended to emphasize instruction and career preparation, the research paradigm of traditional universities has a powerful impact on them, tempting NUS institutions to undertake research activities similar to those of the universities. At the same time, however, NUS institutions have established an identity and niche in conducting practically oriented research, and traditional universities have sought to become more relevant to the needs of society caused by rapid technological and economic changes. The author concludes that both types of institutions serve important roles, and when measured in terms of their distinctive goals and missions, each can achieve excellence in its own way. In order for higher education to garner continued political support, it needs diversified systems—institutions with clearly differentiated missions and that meet different societal needs.

• • • • • • • • • • • •

T here is likely to be little disagreement that in most countries, educational structures are becoming more differentiated. This institutional differentiation has produced much greater institutional diversity, a wider range of qualification opportunities, and substantially greater participation rates than existed 30 years ago. These increases are especially prevalent in the higher education sector.

The terms "institutions of higher education" and "higher education systems" refer to broad sectors of tertiary education for which a secondary school qualification (earned at about age 18) is normally a prerequisite; such a qualification (like A-levels in the United Kingdom or the *Abitur* in Germany) entitles the secondary school graduate to study at a university or comparable institution. This definition comprises all university as well as non-university institutions. The latter are new forms of tertiary education that came about in most industrial societies in the late 1960s or early 1970s and which, as will be shown in more detail later, are usually characterized by a more strongly practical course of study than the curriculum offered by universities, more responsiveness to the requirements of industry, shorter study programs, less fundamental research involvement, and a more limited range of disciplines, to include such fields as engineering, social work, and business studies.

In Germany, the primary group of such institutions are the *Fachhochschulen*, which are also being established in Austria and in Switzerland.[1] In the Netherlands, the corresponding sector is the HBO (*hoger beroepsonderwijs* or higher vocational training) sector, which already has more students than the country's universities. In France, the sector comprises the *Instituts Universitaires de Technologie* (IUTs) and the *Instituts Universitaires Professionalisés* (IUPs) which, although housed within universities, offer shorter, more practically oriented courses of study than universities. In Norway, the sector includes an entire group of institutions, including the "regional colleges" and the colleges of teacher training, engineering, and social work (OECD 1991, table 13, 32). Spain and Italy have a somewhat special situation; these countries are attempting to revive the old French short-cycle study concept of the 1970s. In those countries, short-study programs are being offered within the universities as alternatives to the traditional study courses.[2] Several of the Central and Eastern European countries are showing strong interest in developments at

Fachhochschul-type institutions, but discussion of these reform efforts is beyond the scope of this chapter. Finally, we should note the largest exception within Europe—the United Kingdom. That country's large alternative higher education sector, the polytechnics system, was recently integrated into the university system; all former polytechnics are now universities.

This chapter describes and analyses the current higher education situation in Western Europe, with particular attention to the institutional and functional differences between university and non-university institutions. Quantitative trends and the relevant institutional differentiation processes are outlined, and several specific features of the trends and their current effects are described: social characteristics of student bodies; contents and structures of studies; curricular changes; the changing role of research in higher education and the problem of blurring of boundaries between higher education sectors; financing; aspects of internal and external administration and autonomy; and differences between the employment opportunities afforded by the different higher education sectors. Finally, some aspects of higher education policy and change in the context of European integration are highlighted.

GROWTH AND DIVERSIFICATION

Expansion

During the last quarter of a century, hardly any other institution within the Western industrial societies has experienced such a comprehensive and rapid transformation as tertiary education. The number of pupils in upper-secondary schools and the entrance rate into the tertiary education system has risen dramatically nearly everywhere; for example, the percentage of the age cohort entering higher education in Germany rose from 7.9 to 35.7 percent between 1960 and 1992 (Federal Ministry of Education and Science 1993, 128; OECD 1989a, 7). However, in most European tertiary education systems, the proportion of those who complete secondary school, as well as the percentages of the age cohort that enter higher education, are considerably smaller than other leading industrial nations. They are still far away from the tertiary participation rates of countries such as Japan, the United States, or Canada.

The trends in the numbers of those who leave secondary school with a higher education qualification are a central factor in the expansion of higher education systems. Until a few years ago, less than 20 percent of the age group in most European countries left secondary school with such a qualification,[3] a figure that was rather low compared with the United States and Japan. This situation is changing. In the Federal Republic of Germany, some 40 percent of the age group are now thought to be working for their *Abitur*, the general higher education qualification (Federal Ministry of Education and Science 1993, 73). In general, the European countries are still only about average in this respect, taking into account that over 90 percent of all young people in the United States and Japan earn a secondary school qualification (OECD 1989b; 1989e).

Nevertheless, the numbers of students at most European tertiary institutions have increased fourfold, if not fivefold or more. Whereas this expansion began in the early 1960s in the United States, Canada, and Japan, it did not commence in Europe until about 10 years later. However, many countries have experienced little growth since the end of the 1970s, for demographic and financial policy reasons.[4] Germany was one of the few exceptions in which the expansion continued without interruption. Since the beginning of the 1990s, nearly all European countries are again experiencing growth in higher education.

Diversification

This strong quantitative increase would not have been possible without a parallel process of institutional differentiation. For the most part, since the late 1960s and early 1970s, alternative types of higher education institutions developed outside the universities.

In general, the growth rates in the nonuniversity sector (NUS) was greater, and continue to be greater, than those in the university sector. In some countries, such as the Netherlands, Norway, and the United Kingdom, the NUS is already larger than the university sector.

These new NUS institutions in Europe and elsewhere all had quite similar political and socioeconomic expectations and aims. They were intended to be more occupationally oriented than the universities, and their teaching personnel were meant to be less focused on research, with a greater teaching load than their university counterparts. In addition, they were expected to respond flexibly to the requirements and needs of the employment market and industry, and in some ways they seemed better suited than the universities to offer socially disadvantaged groups an attractive range of studies. Finally, these alternative sectors were expected to provide higher education more cheaply than universities. The following section describes the extent to which such expectations have been fulfilled, as well as the problems that have arisen in this context.

The "Third Sector"

We call attention first to the most recent developments in institutional differentiation in many Western and European industrial countries. These developments have gone largely unnoticed by the general public and are difficult to quantify, since they are not reflected in public statistics. The "third sector" refers here to mostly private education programs—highly specialized and application-oriented vocational training programs—for graduates of secondary schools who have not earned a higher education qualification. These programs are either conducted within large companies (the "corporate classroom") or are organized in cooperation with regional government authorities. Although this sector is still largely invisible, the OECD speaks of its "significant growth" (OECD 1991, 27). This growth is already quite visible in the United States, where it is estimated that some $40 billion are spent in the "corporate classroom" area alone—approximately as much as for all American four-year higher education institutions (OECD 1989e). In Europe, the growth of the "third sector" is significant but less spectacular. A number of companies already offer accredited study courses with fully recognized higher education qualifications. The United Kingdom's Ministry of Education estimates that the country's private higher education sector numbers some 300,000 students (OECD 1991, 28; OECD 1989d). The situation in Germany is unclear; there are no official German statistics for this sector, and German schools and employers take a restrictive approach to recognizing and certifying higher education qualifications that are not accredited by the government.

There are eight vocational academies in Germany that are institutions of the *Länder* and of industry. Their basic funding comes from the relevant *Land*. The legal status of their teaching personnel is similar to that of teaching personnel at *Fachhochschulen*, and a high percentage are employed on a part-time basis. As a rule, an *Abitur* is required for admission. Students at vocational academies are already employees of the companies that send them; most remain with these employers when they finish their studies. By virtue of their close cooperation with industry and of the qualifications they offer—which are comparable to those offered by *Fachhochschulen*, the vocational academies are the higher education institutions that are most comparable to the third sector in other countries. In 1992, they had a total of some 12,000 students (Federal Ministry of Education and Science 1993, 124).

The emergence of the third sector continues to be spurred by rapidly transforming technology and by economic demands, together with the apparent inability of the traditional university sector to cope with the resulting technological transfer and workforce demands of the economy and employers. This third sector may well turn out to become a strong component within the alternatives to traditional higher education and a major challenge to the formalized, securely established traditional university sectors and the almost equally institutionalized structures of the NUS.

CHANGES IN THE STUDENT BODY

As European higher education has expanded and diversified, the composition of student bodies has changed considerably. In addition to the "traditional" secondary school graduate, there are also two new categories of students:

adults entering higher education for the first time (i.e., following an initial occupational phase) who are seeking a standard higher education qualification, and students pursuing continuing education. In addition, the number of women has grown in nearly all sectors of higher education.

However, there is considerable variation among the different higher education sectors and among disciplines. In some sectors—such as the French IUTs and the *Fachhochschulen* in Germany, which offer a relatively limited engineering or management-oriented education—the participation rates of women students are lower, while in other systems, such as those of the United Kingdom, Canada, and Japan, women account for over half of student bodies (OECD 1991, 34). Such differences are due primarily to specialization, as discussed below.

Students at NUS institutions tend to be older than university students. The reason for this has to do with the NUS's important "second chance" function; that is, creating greater educational participation among segments of the population that were formerly not education oriented. These NUS functions are reflected in some countries in opportunities for part-time study. In nations such as Norway, the opportunities for pursuing studies in the evenings and on weekends have grown rapidly.

In addition to having more older students, the social composition of student bodies at NUS institutions differs from that at universities, since NUS institutions have more poor students. In the Netherlands, the percentage of students from lower socioeconomic classes was twice as high at NUS institutions as that at universities (OECD 1989c).

ORGANIZATION OF STUDIES: STRUCTURES AND CONTENTS

In most countries, another difference between the non-university and the university sectors is that the former organize studies and teaching in a manner rather like secondary school. This difference is more prominent in countries where universities traditionally have loosely organized study and examination regulations, especially the continental European countries. Universities in the United Kingdom (like those in North America) are considerably more regimented than continental European universities; consequently, their non-university sectors differ less sharply from universities in this regard.

Austria's non-university sector has a particularly school-like structure, which offers hardly any elective subjects. Students are organized into class associations: attendance is compulsory and students must attend some 30 hours of classes per week.[5] Even if the NUS in most other countries exhibits greater flexibility than in Austria, in general, curricula in NUS tend to be more clearly structured than those of universities, with more classes and with examinations administered at shorter intervals.

While countries such as the Netherlands accord their NUS a relatively high degree of freedom in determining curricula, most other systems do not permit such a free hand. Most tend to offer a limited number of subjects, primarily in the areas of engineering, business, and social work. Often, they are more willing than the universities to respond to the requirements of the commercial and industrial sectors in times of rapid technological change.

RESEARCH AND "ACADEMIC DRIFT"

The Changing Role of Research

Research in higher education, in contrast to research done in academies and research institutes outside colleges and universities, cannot be separated totally from teaching. The process of disseminating knowledge includes, however, more than teaching students because it also includes all academic activities relating to publication, exchange within the scientific community, and interpretation of research findings.

Without going into a historical account of the changing role of research at higher education institutions,[6] it is evident that, along with the growth and institutional transformations of European higher education, highly significant *functional modifications* have occurred; i.e., the emergence of new tasks and purposes in these systems. To a large extent, this phenomenon was linked to the fact that the non-university sectors in most countries are not characterized simply by their more practical orientation of teaching and learning, and by greater responsiveness to demands from industries and the labor market, but also by a redefinition of higher education as no longer exclusively based on parallel processes of research and research training, but as science-based applied training for the professions. The main difference consists in the notion that students at NUS institutions, unlike those at universities, are not being prepared to become researchers themselves, but that it is sufficient to base development of their practical skills and abilities on science and academic knowledge.

But the universities have not remained totally untouched by this process of functional modification. The successful examples of the non-university sectors, together with growing pressures from the economy, employers, and governments, have also made the traditional academic institutions aware of the need to be more oriented to "useful" professional knowledge or to practical ventures such as science parks and centers for technology transfer.

The training of future researchers has become a focus of European policy measures and institutional changes. There have been clear indications in the recent past of dangers that the funding base for basic research in the university sector was gradually shifting toward outside research organizations. The profitability of investments in pure research institutes seemed to be higher and the returns more promising, since the researchers in such institutes were not burdened with high teaching and administration loads.[7] But this trend, despite the existing overcrowding of institutions of higher education, may recently have come to a halt. New initiatives can be observed in some systems for a more systematic support for graduate training and the implementation of organizational frameworks, like the *Graduiertenkollegs* at some German universities, which provide special support for financing infrastructure as well as intensive counseling and teaching for small groups of doctoral students in specific disciplines. Such initiatives are meant to assure the future supply of highly qualified researchers and academics.

This research-based training of advanced scholars and future academics is in most national systems restricted to the university systems, while the non-university sectors are often not engaged in postgraduate activities. This is one of the major determinants of "academic drift," which we will address in the following section.

Differentiation and "Academic Drift"

As noted earlier, some of the alternative higher education institutions became serious competitors of universities in terms of the quality of teaching and their relevance to the labor market. This was particularly true in Europe. From the beginning, however, there were problems with regard to the definition of their tasks and purposes. Above all, the intended policy of discouraging the teaching faculty in these alternative sectors from engaging in independent research or to limit such activities to applied and immediately useful research for the economy, has led to a permanent process of "academic drift." Faculty members in the non-university sectors have, in many cases, tried to undertake research on a similar level to that of universities. Since the teaching personnel in these institutions is burdened with much higher teaching loads than at universities, and since the infrastructure support in terms of laboratory equipment and research personnel is inferior to that at universities, there occurred a growing tension between the original aims and purposes assigned to these institutions and the intentions of their faculty. The research paradigm of the universities had a powerful impact on related activities in the non-university sectors. Increasingly, the latter institutions adopted research activities that resembled those at universities. And in the most prominent example of that development, in Great Britain, the government decided to abolish the binary line between universities and polytechnics, and the polytechnics are now universities (Department of Education and Science 1991).

Despite the continuing problems of "academic drift," in many European non-university sectors, research has established its distinctive role. In many systems, it is now accepted by all stakeholders—teaching faculty, students, the economy, and the governments—that applied research is of vital importance for the economy and the labor market. There are even indications that the universities themselves have begun to rethink their positions concerning research, insofar as the ability of the non-university sectors to respond successfully to economic and technological needs puts public pressure on the traditional university sectors to be similarly accountable in terms of the relevance and usefulness of research. Thus, we can observe three interrelated processes: the continuing drive of some non-university sectors to become more similar to universities in their research activities; the parallel development of a more self-confident attitude towards its own more practically oriented research; and finally, an increasing willingness of the universities to adapt their own research paradigm, perhaps under the influence of the other higher education institutions, to more practical needs in times of rapid economic and technological change.

ADMINISTRATIVE AND INSTITUTIONAL AUTONOMY

In most European countries, state control of the NUS tends to be closer and more direct than control of universities. NUS institutions usually cannot determine their study programs independently, and their professors have less opportunity to structure curricula than university professors. However, there has been a tendency in recent years for the university and NUS sectors to receive equal administrative treatment. In Germany, the *Fachhochschulen* have long had the same legal status as the universities, and non-university higher education institutions in the Netherlands are also in the process of obtaining greater latitude.

Admission Requirements

The admission requirements of non-university higher education institutions in Europe vary considerably, in contrast with those of the relevant university systems. In Germany, the *Fachhochschul* entrance qualification (*Fachhochschulreife*) is the prerequisite for admission. As a rule, it is awarded for completion of the senior technical school (*Fachoberschule*), or for completion of an equivalent education lasting at least 12 years. If the applicant has the general higher education qualification (*Abitur*), he or she is normally required to have completed a practical course before undertaking studies, or to take such a course during the first four semesters of study. The percentage of holders of the *Abitur* (with which they could also have gone to a university) among *Fachhochschul* students has been increasing for years and has now reached nearly 50 percent (Federal Ministry of Education and Science 1993, 174).

Teaching Personnel

The qualifications required for teachers at NUS institutions also tend to be more occupationally oriented than qualifications required for university teachers. Often, NUS teachers are required to have practical occupational experience. Also, the percentage of part-time teaching personnel at NUS institutions tends to be higher than at universities, but unlike North American community colleges, the proportion of part-time faculty does not approach 50 percent.

The teaching load in almost all NUS systems differs considerably from that found at universities. But in spite of their greater loads, instructors and professors at NUS institutions are not as well paid as their university counterparts. Recently, some systems, such as those of Norway and Sweden, have begun eliminating such discrepancies. In addition, the "tenure" principle—employment for life—which is customary at universities, is found less frequently in the NUS sector. In Germany, professors at *Fachhochschulen* are normally civil servants with employment for life. The prerequisites for obtaining this status are completed higher education studies—normally a doctoral degree and at least five years of occupational experience relevant to the subject being taught. At least three years of this occupational experience must be acquired outside of higher education.

FINANCING

In Europe, most NUS institutions are administered and financed by the state. Outside of Europe, however, there are also many privately financed and organized institutions. This is especially true of North America and Japan. And in these countries, a trend has become apparent that has recently acquired significance in Europe: higher education institutions are becoming more "entrepreneurial." Such trends are apparent in the Dutch *Hogescholen* and in the United Kingdom, where the government has recently been promoting the expansion of the tertiary sector through more private initiative and collaboration with industry. In Germany, all but a few *Fachhochschulen* are state financed; they levy no student tuition. The *Länder*, in charge of tertiary education, are clearly tending to grant higher education institutions greater autonomy, especially in the area of financing through global (lump-sum) budgets. The German federal government supports these efforts.

In many systems, financing also has an important role as a control mechanism—in both the university and non-university sectors. Whereas nearly all higher education institutions are moving toward greater autonomy in regulating their internal affairs, state agencies are exerting more and more control over the goals of higher education. For example, funds are being earmarked for specific subjects in an attempt to achieve expansion or restriction of enrollments in certain subject areas.

EMPLOYMENT OPPORTUNITIES

The employment opportunities for NUS graduates are generally considered good. Due to rapid technological and industrial change, there is increasing

demand—in industry, commerce, service sectors, and public administration—
for graduates with a practically oriented education. And in general, NUS
institutions have responded more flexibly than the universities in almost all
areas to these new expectations. Their response has included introducing new
programs and study courses. However, employers often still choose university
graduates over NUS graduates, in spite of similar qualifications, for reasons of
the prestige carried by universities. But NUS graduates have good employment chances, often because they are employed in midlevel jobs at lower pay.
In Germany, for example, lower starting salaries for *Fachhochschul* graduates
are still the rule in many areas, although such disadvantages are decreasing in
private industry.

In general, comparison of employment opportunities for NUS graduates
with those for university graduates produces a range of different results. For
example, unemployment among polytechnic graduates in the United Kingdom was 10.8 percent—higher than that of university graduates, which was
6.9 percent (OECD 1991, 61). Because unemployment levels vary widely
according to subject, the reason for the higher unemployment of graduates of
polytechnics was the relatively large proportion of humanities graduates of
these institutions. Whereas NUS institution graduates in engineering and
business fields often have better employment chances than university graduates, the opposite is true for graduates in the humanities and social sciences. In
such cases, either the prestige of the institution concerned is more important,
or the NUS institutions are simply assumed to have greater competency in
engineering and business. For example, in the Netherlands, the unemployment rate of NUS graduates is higher than that of university graduates, but the
unemployment rate of graduates in engineering is only one-third that of
graduates in health or education (OECD 1991, table 30, 62). In Germany, the
unemployment rate of *Fachhochschul* graduates is considerably less than that of
university graduates. In September 1993, Germany had 146,000 unemployed
graduates; of these, 45,900 (31 percent) were *Fachhochschul* graduates (Federal Ministry of Education, Science, Research and Technology 1994, 308).

THE EFFECT OF EUROPEAN INTEGRATION

One of the major recent determinants of change in European higher education has been the influence of the integration process of the European nations.
The Maastricht treaties, in particular, have strongly emphasized the importance of training and education in the Community's development in order to
ensure unhindered development and the free exchange of ideas as parallels to
the free movement of people, goods, services, and capital.

The European Union (EU) programs aimed at promoting European integration are an important driving force. The ERASMUS program's student-

exchange opportunities have been of primary importance. The program's success still seems modest in terms of absolute figures; the aim has been to reach 10 percent of all European higher education students, but only half this level has been reached to date. Nonetheless, because higher education institutions involved in the program must deal with the different initial qualifications and expectations of other countries' students, and because program participants wish their studies to be officially recognized, there is considerable pressure on the various participating institutions to coordinate their curricular and exam structures. In the future, if the organizational and informational basis of these exchange programs is to function, study courses will have to be made substantially more stable and transparent (i.e., explained clearly in handbooks) to students, academics, and administrators. While this desirable continuity of curriculum and exam requirements is a common and normal practice at many U.S. universities, thus far, many continental European systems have been characterized by a lack of clarity and consistency in their curricula. The European Credit Transfer System (ECTS) also helps address this issue.

The COMETT program for promoting continuing education in technological areas, as well as cooperation between higher education institutions and industry, is also important. Introduced in 1987, it provides new challenges for many higher education institutions. The ERASMUS and COMETT programs, which in the future will be subsumed into the SOCRATES and LEONARDO programs, both provide an important impetus for adding flexibility and promoting harmonization of national higher education systems. Higher education curricula in EU countries are currently being modified through inclusion of specifically European elements—for example, considerably expanded foreign-language training—and through establishment of departments of "European studies." In addition to these programs, others such as LINGUA and JEAN MONNET have similar aims.

Finally, the TEMPUS program has now incorporated Eastern Europe into this development. This program expands student and instructor exchanges to Eastern European countries. Needless to say, the institutional influences of these exchanges do not flow only in one direction; return effects upon Western European countries can also be expected.

It should be noted in this context that all these developments are not aimed at achieving a general harmonization of European higher education structures. Different institutional requirements for higher education study, and the so-called "subsidiarity principle," as explicitly set forth in the Treaty of Maastricht, are being jealously protected. Within political systems, the "subsidiarity principle" is the guiding policy principle that decisions should be made at the lowest level possible and by those who are most directly affected. This concept is of particular importance in federally organized countries like

Belgium or Germany, but it is also important with regard to the relationship between member states of the European Union and the European Commission in Brussels.[8]

SUMMARY AND CONCLUSIONS

The strong expansion of European higher education during the 1960s and 1970s was possible because these industrial societies developed at a steady rate, with exceptionally high rates of economic growth and simultaneous improvement of their overall standard of living. This economic growth enabled the national governments to support a rapid expansion of the tertiary education sector, thus allowing increasingly larger proportions of the population to participate.

The reasoning underlying such developments rested on two main political considerations. The first, the so-called "manpower approach," consisted of the conviction of employers and policy makers that the national supply of highly qualified manpower had to grow if the respective countries were to compete successfully in the world market in times of rapidly changing technologies. The second consideration related to overall educational and social aims and was thus described as the "social demand approach." Its supporters maintained that, by being highly selective, the traditional education systems primarily served small societal elites, and that large proportions of gifted young people never got a chance to develop their talents. Postcompulsory education, in other words, was regarded as a general civil right.

As a consequence, public authorities developed a series of measures aimed at extending compulsory education and developing a wider range of secondary and postsecondary programs designed to meet the needs and aspirations of new groups and to draw on the "pool of educational talent." They introduced or improved comprehensive systems of means-tested grants for students. At the higher educational level in particular, resources were deployed to diversify a system that was dominated by the university sector.

Thus, recent developments in European higher education can largely be described in terms of its institutional and functional differentiation—new institutions and new missions. Diversification, accomplished mainly through development of new types of institutions and instructional programs, has had many effects. It has brought more equal opportunity to formerly disadvantaged socioeconomic classes and increased the percentages of women students. The NUS institutions, in particular, have played a positive role in this connection by offering "second chances" and by admitting applicants without formal school qualifications.

The argument is often advanced that enhanced access to higher education cannot be reconciled with maintenance of high standards, especially in times of financial difficulties. Such conclusions are hardly appropriate. The key to understanding this issue lies in acceptance of differences in function, which has been recently seen in the internal and external relationships of many NUS institutions. Many NUS students and instructors, along with governments and the general public, now accept that research and teaching have different goals and results; consequently, such diverse higher education systems are not dominated exclusively by university paradigms.

The fact that the NUS institutions frequently have the additional functions of continuing education and "remedial education," which have often been criticized as "secondarization" of the higher education sector, is no sign of lesser quality. Such functions are certainly legitimate functions of the higher education sector, if the principle of functional differentiation is accepted.

While the research function in most of European higher education continues to favor the status and political standing of the universities over the non-university sectors, the latter have in recent years improved their public standing through specific research and development activities in times of rapid economic and technological change. Particularly in export-oriented economies, which most European industrial societies are, investment in conducting research and preparing researchers is considered vitally important. This is one of the reasons that both universities and other institutions of higher education enjoy the continuing provision of vast financial resources by governments and foundations.

But the principal direction of ongoing public expenditure in higher education continues to be professional training. This explains why institutional differentiation ultimately is the measure of the political success of higher education. Public support for the various higher education sectors will be maintained only if higher education continues to be diversified; that is, if it includes institutions with differentiated missions and contributions that meet diverse socioeconomic needs. Thus, governments will need to ensure differentiation of the system if they wish to avoid large-scale trends of "academic drift" or the further expansion of the "third sector." While the latter is not necessarily detrimental to the economy (despite the corresponding decrease of governmental influence), the former probably is, because "academic drift," as was pointed out above, tends to diminish functional differences. The British example of the recent decision to confer university status on the former polytechnics has demonstrated that a totally unified and integrated system does not work in the long run, because it fails to overcome the built-in contradiction of such a model. This contradiction lies in the policy aim for all institutions concerned to have equal standing, coexisting with the need—for budgetary as well as functional reasons—to distinguish between institutions oriented more toward research and those primarily oriented toward teaching. The former institutional differentiation that existed between universities and polytechnics has now been transferred into the unified university system itself. The main difference between the old system and the new unified one—besides a short-term status advance for the former polytechnics—is that functional differentiation is now considerably more difficult. The allocation of diverse tasks that meet different public needs is more difficult to accomplish within this newly integrated system.

NOTES

1. This discussion does not include colleges of art and other special institutions of higher education.

2. For comparison, see Moscati 1993, 72–83; and Lamo de Espinosa 1993, 84–96.

3. For comparison, see Teichler 1990, 78–84.

4. From 1975 to the late 1980s, a number of OECD countries had little growth. Some, such as France and Denmark, even experienced a real decline in numbers of students (for comparison, see OECD 1991, Table 1.B, 18).

5. However, the NUS in Austria existed only on a rudimentary level in the past, in the form of teacher-training colleges and similar institutions. Only recently, the government has begun to create a separate *Fachhochschul* sector.

6. For comparison, see Gellert 1992.

7. For comparison, see Gellert 1993b.

8. For comparison, see Gellert 1993b.

REFERENCES

Department of Education and Science, United Kingdom. 1991. *Higher education: A new framework.* London: Her Majesty's Stationery Office.

Federal Ministry of Education and Science, Republic of Germany. 1993. *Basic and structural data 1993/4.* Bonn.

Federal Ministry of Education, Science, Research, and Technology, Republic of Germany. 1994. *Basic and structural data 1994/5.* Bonn.

Gellert, C. 1992. Faculty research. In *The encyclopedia of higher education,* edited by B. R. Clark and G. Neave, vol. 3, Analytical perspectives, 1634–41. Oxford: Pergamon.

―――. 1993a. The German model of research and advanced education. In *The research foundations of graduate education: Germany, Britain, France, United States, Japan,* edited by B. R. Clark, 5–44. Berkeley: University of California Press.

―――. 1993b. Subsidiaritätsprinzip. In *Handlexikon der Europäischen Union,* edited by J. Monar, et al., 319–22. Stuttgart: Kröner.

Lamo de Espinosa, E. 1993. The Spanish university in transition. In *Higher education in Europe,* edited by C. Gellert, 84–96. London: Jessica Kingsley.

Moscati, R. 1993. Moving towards institutional differentiation: The Italian case. In *Higher education in Europe,* edited by C. Gellert, 72–83. London: Jessica Kingsley.

Organization for Economic Cooperation and Development (OECD). 1989a. *Alternatives to universities in higher education—Country study: Federal Republic of Germany.* Paris: OECD.

―――. 1989b. *Alternatives to universities in higher education—Country study: Japan.* Paris: OECD.

―――. 1989c. *Alternatives to universities in higher education—Country study: The Netherlands.* Paris: OECD.

————. 1989d. *Alternatives to universities in higher education—Country study: United Kingdom.* Paris: OECD.

————. 1989e. *Alternatives to universities in higher education—Country study: The United States of America.* Paris: OECD.

————. 1991. *Alternatives to universities.* Paris: OECD.

Teichler, U. 1990. *Europäische Hochschulsysteme: Die Beharrlichkeit vielfältiger Modelle.* Frankfurt: Campus.

FURTHER READING

Bundesministerium für Bildung und Wissenschaft. 1993. *Die Fachhochschulen in der Bundesrepublik Deutschland, Grundlagen und Perspektiven für Bildung und Wissenschaft.* Nr.: 37, Bonn.

Bundesministerium für Wissenschaft und Forschung 1992. *Fachhochschule als Alternative zur Universität.* Vienna: L & R Sozialforschung.

————. 1993. *Das österreichische Bildungssystem in Veränderung.* Bericht an die OECD über die geplante Diversifikation des Postsekundarsektors. Vienna: Bundesministerium für Wissenschatt und Forschung.

Commission of the European Communities. 1991. *Memorandum on higher education in the European Community.* Brussels: Commission of the European Communities.

Ewert, P. and S. Lullies. 1984. *Das Hochschulwesen in Frankreich—Geschichte, Strukturen und gegenwärtige Probleme im Vergleich.* Munich: Institut für Hochschulforshung.

Furth, D. 1973. Short-cycle higher education: Some basic considerations. In *Short-Cycle Higher Education* 13–42. Paris: OECD.

Gellert, C. 1988. *Vergleich des Studiums an englischen und deutschen Universitäten.* 2nd ed. Frankfurt: Lang.

————. 1991. Andersartig, aber gleichwertig—Anmerkungen zur Funktionsbestimmung der Fachhochschulen. In *Beiträge zur Hochschulforschung* 1, 1–25.

————. 1991. The emergence of three university models. In *Institutional and Functional Modifications in European Higher Education.* European University Institute (EUI) working paper ECS 91/5. Florence: EUI.

————. 1993. Academic drift and blurring of boundaries in systems of higher education. *Higher Education in Europe* 18 (2): 78–84.

————. 1993. The conditions of research training in contemporary German universities. In *The research foundations of graduate education: Germany, Britain, France, United States, Japan,* edited by B. R. Clark, 45–66. Berkeley: University of California Press.

————. 1993. Differenziazione e sviluppo di settori non universitari nella educazione superiore in Europa. In *La "Laurea Breve": Formazione e Figura del Diploma,* 1–4. Florence: Istituto Gramsci Toscana.

————. 1993. Structures and functional differentiation: Remarks on changing paradigms of tertiary education in Europe. In *Higher Education in Europe,* edited by C. Gellert, 234–46. London: Jessica Kingsley.

————. 1993. *Wettbewerb und Leistungsorientierung im amerikanischen Universitätssystem.* Frankfurt: Lang.

Gellert, C.; E. Leitner; and J. Schramm; eds. 1990. *Research and teaching at universities: International and comparative perspectives.* Frankfurt: Lang.

Gellert, C., and D. Izzo. 1993. Il cambiamento di funzioni nelle università tedesche e italiane. *Educazione Comparata* 4: 10–11, 27–39.

Goppel, T., ed. 1991. *Kontinuität und Wandel: Perspektiven Bayerischer Wissenschaftspolitik.* Munich: Oldenbourg.

Gottschal. P. 1992. *Levels and the pluriformity of higher education: On comparing curricula.* The Hague: Nuffic.

von Harnier, L. V. 1990. *Elemente für Szenarios im Hochschulbereich.* Munich: Institut für Hochschulforschung.

Moscati, R. 1988. Editorial: Higher education in Southern Europe: Different speeds or different paths toward modernisation? *European Journal of Education* 23 (3): 189–94.

Organization of Economic Cooperation and Development (OECD). 1987. *Universities under scrutiny.* Paris: OECD.

―――. 1989. *Alternatives to universities in higher education—Country study: Austria.* Paris: OECD.

―――. 1989. *Alternatives to universities in higher education—Country study: Canada.* Paris: OECD.

―――. 1989. *Alternatives to universities in higher education—Country study: New Zealand.* Paris: OECD.

Rau, E. forthcoming. Radical restructuration: The consequences of West German interventionism for the East German system of higher education. In *Innovation and adaptation in higher education: The changing conditions of advanced teaching and learning in Europe,* edited by C. Gellert. London: Jessica Kingsley.

Schweizerischer Wissenschaftsrat. 1993. *Zielvorstellungen für die Ent-wicklung der schweizerischen Hochschulen.* Horizont 2000, FU 8a.

Schmidt, S. H. 1991. *Ausbildung und Arbeitsmarkt für Hochschul-absolventen: USA und Deutschland.* Munich: Institut für Hochschulforschung.

Teichler, U. 1988. *Changing patterns of the higher education system: The experience of three decades.* London: Jessica Kingsley.

Wissenschaftsrat. 1990. Empfehlungen zur Entwicklung der Fachhoch-schulen in den 90er Jahren. Drs. 9992/90, Berlin, 16.11.

―――. 1994. *Zwischenbericht über die Umsetzung der Empfehlungen des Wissenschaftsrates zur Entwicklung der Fachhochschulen vom November 1990.* Drs. 1394/94, Cologne, 10.1.

PART THREE

· · · · · · · · · · ·

National Perspectives

As much as we would like to envision the world as a global village, it is still organized primarily by nation-states. We think of culture and history primarily in national terms (with all the attendant perils) and of higher education as a national effort, influenced by national governments and their changing policies over time, as well as by their distinct histories and traditions. Comparisons of higher education systems and policies are most often made among nations, and the future of most colleges and universities lies largely in the hands of the funders and policy makers at the local, state, or national level.

Thus, the ensuing chapters are organized by country, for it is national politics and traditions that have the most immediate impact on the fate of individual institutions. It is from the national perspective that the institutional leaders see their realities and tell their stories.

CHAPTER 7

The United States

D. Bruce Johnstone

Executive Summary. U.S. higher education is characterized by its enormous scale (nearly 3,600 institutions and some 15 million degree-seeking students), its diversity (including two-year and four-year, public and private institutions), and its accessibility. Sixty-two percent of 1992 high school graduates went on directly to some form of higher education. U.S. higher education is distinctive in several ways. Competition is a hallmark of U.S. higher education, with institutions competing for students, faculty, and prestige. Secondly, interinstitutional permeability results in students transferring freely from one institution to another at the same degree level or to pursue a higher degree. Third, the federal government plays a minor role; policy is made at the state level. Finally, there is the expectation that higher education institutions will contribute to their communities and to the solution of social problems.

The agenda for change takes two major forms. One is the traditional reform agenda that deals largely with undergraduate education, focusing on the need to improve teaching, raise standards, improve the curriculum, and recognize the needs of a changing student population. The second agenda concerns resources—how to cope with diminishing resources and rising costs. Some look to business for a model of restructuring—cutting costs, eliminating functions, flattening the bureaucracy. Colleges and universities have already done a great deal of cutting, and further restructuring could include closing institutions or programs, increasing faculty teaching responsibilities (as well as measuring them differently), and privatizing various institutional functions.

What are the implications for leadership? Although U.S. college and university presidents have more formal power than their counterparts in many other countries, they do not perceive themselves as able to fundamentally alter an institution's course. Indeed, leadership is a balance between holding the institution's course and altering it to meet changing needs. The mix will depend a great deal on the particular history and circumstances of the institution. In many instances, leadership is "the leader's capacity to make a difference, but only in the direction toward which the institution is already heading." In this case, leaders can tilt the direction of the institution and provide guidance about desired directions. Other situations may call for more drastic change in course, but these are difficult to accomplish in light of the traditional modes of decision making.

• • • • • • • • • • •

The U.S. college or university president, by all of our textbook understandings of organizational governance, should be a notably strong leader, at least in comparison with heads of colleges and universities elsewhere.[1] He or she is appointed not by the faculty from within the faculty but by a lay, or voluntary, board, generally from outside the institution, and is usually appointed for a term unspecified but anticipated to be lengthy. The American president is increasingly a career academic administrator, still ideally from within the faculty, but generally having left a career of full-time scholar-teacher for a series of posts such as department chair, dean, and chief academic officer before moving on to a presidency, from which, if the experience is thought to be successful and the incumbent ambitious, he or she may be tapped in 5 to 10 years for a larger and more prestigious presidency elsewhere.

The American tradition of the lay governing board diminishes the potentially countervailing power of the organized faculty. And, by its extension in the public sector to the model of the public corporation with a publicly appointed but nonetheless independent governing board, the concept of lay governance tends to diminish also the authority that state governors and state legislatures typically have over public colleges and universities. (This distancing of university governance from state governmental authority goes even farther in states such as California, Michigan, and Minnesota with their constitutionally autonomous public universities.)

Other conditions would also seem to lend strength to the American academic leader. The appointing lay board is likely to be dominated by corporate executives who, in spite of significant faculty participation in the selection process, have the final appointing authority and will generally insist on certain "executive characteristics" such as decisiveness, corporate "presence," and at least some financial acumen, along with whatever scholarly credentials the faculty is insisting on. (Interestingly, faculty members of search committees generally want the same leadership attributes as the lay board members.)

American college and university presidents also tend to be surrounded by high-ranking executive officers of considerable experience (e.g., chief financial, planning, public relations, and management officers) who serve at the discretion of the president (i.e., not in tenured or civil service capacities), who frequently come out of corporations or public agencies, and who bring not only managerial sophistication, but expectations of strong executive leadership in the president or chancellor whom they serve.

Finally, there is the history of the strong university presidents of the past, such as Tappan of Michigan, White of Cornell, Gillman of Hopkins, Wheeler of California, Eliot of Harvard, and others. However dated and even irrelevant these early figures may be to the needs and issues of present and future leadership for American higher education, such legendary presidents, to some observers, suggest that the current crop of leaders are missing some mettle or vision or backbone, and that a different selection process or a further blunting of the faculty voice in governance might recapture a bygone era of presidential giants.

Against such a rationale for a strong U.S. college and university presidency, we must consider why it is that the American president does not *feel* particularly strong—if "strength" is measured in the president's perception of his or her ability to put a truly personal and lasting stamp on the institution, to make a difference, or to alter the course that the institution would otherwise be traveling. And we must consider, too, why much of the American public believes that something is lacking in higher education's leadership: that an absence of effective leaders, able to make a difference, must be at least a substantial part of the explanation for why the American university seems increasingly to be the object of such criticism. Why, other than for some flaw in its leadership, would the academy persist in permitting faculty to (allegedly) slight the undergraduate, teach half-heartedly, produce volumes of such pedestrian scholarship, and cave in to the forces of "political correctness"?

To better answer such challenging questions, it is first necessary to examine the features that distinguish American higher education from higher education in other countries, and then to look at some of the forces both external and internal to the academy that define the leadership challenge and circumscribe its execution.

CHARACTERISTICS OF AMERICAN HIGHER EDUCATION

Higher education in the United States stands out in contrast to other nations in six major dimensions:

Scale

Higher education in the United States is an enormous enterprise, whether measured in numbers of institutions or students, proportion of age cohorts studying or actually receiving degrees, perceived significance to such nearly universal goals as economic growth and social mobility, or proportion of national wealth devoted to the enterprise. For example, according to 1994 statistics, higher education in the United States

- Consisted of 3,595 institutions (counting branch campuses), including 236 doctorate-granting institutions: 1,166 4-year institutions, almost half of which granted various master's degrees in addition to the dominant baccalaureate degree; 1,471 2-year colleges; and nearly 700 other specialized institutions granting bachelor's and other advanced degrees (Classification 1994, table 4).[2]
- Enrolled just over 15 million degree-seeking students, including more than 8 million full time and almost 6.7 million part time; some 12.8 million at the undergraduate level (pursuing associate or bachelor's degrees), and more than 2.1 million at the graduate and advanced professional levels of master's and doctoral study (Almanac issue 1994, 16).
- Consumed some $200 billion, including institutional expenditures and the costs of student living, or about 3 percent of the nation's annual gross national product (Business Higher Education Forum 1994, 5).

Openness and Egalitarianism

Higher education in the United States, at some level, is available to virtually anyone with a general high school diploma, regardless of academic preparedness, age, or previous records of academic trial and failure. Higher education is also available (although becoming less so) to anyone regardless of family financial circumstances, providing the student is willing to incur some (increasing) debt, hold down a part-time job while studying, and study at a lower-cost institution, perhaps while commuting from home. Sixty-two percent of 1992 high school graduates went directly on to some form of higher education, about 37 percent of these to a community college, many with aspirations to transfer to a four-year college and receive a baccalaureate. In 1993, 51 percent of all Americans between the ages of 25 and 29 had some college education; 24 percent had at least a 4-year degree (NCES 1994, 40, 68).

The Curriculum

Americans generally begin a college or university at age 17 or 18, and require a minimum of 4 years to complete the first, or baccalaureate, degree. Beginning students vary enormously in their preparation, particularly in mathematics, languages, and in general knowledge of history, geography, and literature. Although increasing numbers of American students are beginning higher education with *advanced placement*, or college credit earned in accelerated high school programs, the first two years of college or university are typically spent in *general education*, either sampling the major knowledge domains of humanities, social sciences, and natural sciences, or, less frequently, in a broad study of the Western historical, literary and philosophical canon. Students may also be expected to demonstrate minimal proficiency in elementary mathematics and written English; a few colleges require demonstrated competence in computer skills; and an increasing number, although still a minority, are reinstating foreign language requirements. By the second or third year, the student is expected to have selected a major, or area of specialization, the study of which will eventually occupy between one-third and one-half of the four-year baccalaureate program. The rest of the undergraduate curriculum may be filled with electives, frequently taken far afield of the student's major program, or with courses reflecting major program interests tried and then abandoned.

Diversity of Institutional Types

Institutions of higher education in the United States vary along many dimensions. The most significant are

- **Predominant control:** public, private nonprofit, or proprietary for-profit
- **Selectivity**: on a continuum from open admissions to highly selective
- **Highest degree awarded**: associate degree (granted by two-year colleges), baccalaureate degree only (usually in the liberal arts), baccalaureate and some (mainly professional) master's degrees, or doctorate-granting (almost all doctorate-granting institutions also grant bachelor's and master's degrees, but not associate degrees)

The diversity in selectivity—generally measured by the academic ability or preparedness of the undergraduate entering class—seems to be a function of tradition, institutional wealth (according to per-student endowment), and the size of the applicant pool from which the institution is able to draw its entering class. The most selective institutions are private and heavily endowed (with per-student endowments as high as $300,000), but some of these are undergraduate liberal arts colleges and others are private research universities. However, some public research universities are also highly selective at the undergraduate level, and many private institutions, both universities and colleges, are only minimally selective.

Most four-year colleges and universities are fiercely competitive, striving to enhance their prestige by recruiting and matriculating the ablest possible entering class. Secondary students of high academic ability and other desirable characteristics (e.g., special talent, leadership potential, minority status, or athletic ability) are recruited heavily and have their pick of many desirable college options. Universities also compete for academic status by attracting the most prestigious faculty, as reflected by scholarly reputations and research dollars attracted. Because the United States has excess higher educational capacity, this intensive marketing is carried out by nearly all institutions, with handsome publications, direct mail solicitation, traveling admissions staffs, college fairs, and other sophisticated marketing techniques, all designed to meet enrollment targets to earn the necessary tuition dollars or to meet the enrollment quotas required in the public sector to secure state funding.

What is perhaps most significant about this diversity and institutional marketing from a comparative perspective is the extraordinary interinstitutional permeability of these institutions, with students typically changing institutions, especially between degree levels (e.g., associate to bachelor's, or bachelor's to master's), but even between institutions at the same degree level. The ease of changing colleges, even within the undergraduate baccalaureate program, is facilitated by the American tradition of granting undergraduate degrees mainly on the basis of an accumulation of course credits, which generally transfer among institutions.

The role that in Europe is played by the non-university institutions (e.g., *Fachhochschulen* in Germany, *HBOs* in the Netherlands, *Institute Universitaires de Technologie* in France or, until recently, the *polytechnics* in Britain; see Chapter 6), featuring short-cycle programs, a more vocational or practical orientation, and less rigorous admission standards, is thus played in the United States either by the community colleges or by the lower divisions of the less selective comprehensive colleges and universities themselves.

Role of Government

About 45 percent of the institutions, enrolling about 75 percent of all students, are considered *public*, meaning they are creatures of state government, substantially dependent on state tax revenues, and more-or-less subject to state laws and regulations (NCES 1995, 192, 247). Most public colleges and universities are buffered from direct agency or ministerial control by some form of *public corporation* status, in which a publicly appointed lay governing board appoints the chief executive officer and determines overall policy in a fashion not unlike the lay board of trustees of a private college or university. (The constitutionally autonomous state university is even a step farther removed from direct gubernatorial and legislative control.)

There in no national ministry for higher education, as this is one of the public functions reserved by the U.S. Constitution for the states. The United States Department of Education, although technically "cabinet level," is in no way comparable to ministries of other countries, either for basic or for higher education. The Department has almost no role in higher education apart from the provision and oversight of federally provided student assistance in the forms of loans and grants. It is significant that student financial assistance from the federal government is given without regard to institution attended (i.e., federally provided aid is fully portable), the academic promise or actual performance of the student (other than a minimal requirement for satisfactory academic progress toward the first degree), and without regard to program of study or the presumed "national need" thereof.

At the same time that *private*, tuition-dependent colleges and universities are becoming more dependent upon taxpayer-generated revenues via portable student assistance and full eligibility for government-sponsored research grants, so U.S. *public* institutions are becoming substantially more dependent on nontaxpayer revenues generated by tuition and fees (averaging almost $2,500 a year, but ranging as high as $4,000), as well as by private fund-raising and revenue from privately invested endowments. In short, public institutions are becoming increasingly privatized, both in their growing managerial autonomy and in the proportion of their revenues coming from other-than-taxpayer sources, just as most private institutions are becoming more and more dependent on public revenues, either via portable student assistance (captured through tuition) or publicly supported research.

Community Service and Public Responsibility

All institutions, public or private, research university or undergraduate college, are expected to contribute to their communities and to be responsible institutional citizens. This may take the form of faculty and staff service to local government study commissions, student contributions to local voluntary agencies, or the provision of university facilities to community groups and causes. Colleges and universities are expected to be major players in the reform of health care and the welfare system, and to help solve problems of the economy, the environment, and the schools. Institutions of higher education are also expected to be major institutional players in the social agendas of promoting greater racial, class, and gender equity.

THE CHANGE AGENDA

The forces for change that are pressing on American higher education and determining its leadership agenda are of two types. The first, the traditional reform agenda, is concerned mainly with alleged inadequacies in teaching and with insufficient attention to undergraduate education generally. The second is preoccupied with financial austerity and faces the new challenges of downsizing and restructuring.

The Traditional Reform Agenda: Balancing the Demands of Teaching, Learning, and Scholarship

The traditional reform agenda arises from the inherent difficulty of maintaining professorial accountability in the academy, particularly in the face of rewards that are not necessarily compatible with the stated aims of the institution. The problem, allegedly, is a neglect of students and an imbalance in the university's dual missions of teaching and scholarship. This traditional reform agenda has been around since the turn of the century. The alleged inadequacies are manifested mainly in the behavior of the professoriate, but the core indictment is against leadership—presidents, trustees, government policy makers—for distorting the incentives and the other rules of the game, and for permitting the self-interest of professors to prevail over the larger purposes of the university.

Among these alleged inadequacies, and forming the core of the traditional reform agenda, are the following:

- Insufficient attention to the undergraduate, to the craft of teaching, and to the integrity of the undergraduate curriculum
- Insufficient rigor in standards and expectations, both for entry and for degrees granted
- Insufficient recognition of the changing student population of more adult and part-time students, and less-well-prepared students, requiring different teaching methods, curricula, support services, and academic calendars
- An inadequate undergraduate curriculum, with some critics finding fault with what they believe to be a demise of a traditional core curriculum of largely Western philosophical and literary classics; others finding fault with what they believe to be insufficient attention to newer and more relevant issues, to the non-Western world, and to newer literature and social commentary, especially by women and people of non-European descent; and critics of all stripes generally united in the belief the faculty is insufficiently engaged in these curricular issues
- Scholarship that is time consuming and often expensive, but that is too often trivial, needlessly (but purposefully) arcane, and useful neither to other scholars or to some broader social purpose

For all the hoary venerability and superficial consensus behind this agenda, it is also in some ways strikingly naive. For example, for most of higher education—at least as measured by sheer numbers of undergraduates—the alleged and much-vilified faculty preoccupation with research to the exclusion of teaching is largely a straw man. More than half of all undergraduates begin their college careers in community colleges, where there is neither an expectation, nor a reward, nor even sufficient time, for significant scholarly activity. The same could be said of most of the nation's public comprehensive colleges and the less-selective, regional private colleges. While there are clear expectations even in these colleges for some kind of continuing scholarship, and while the diligent faculty member with research ambitions can fulfill them, albeit at some cost, most faculty at such predominantly undergraduate institutions teach full loads (three or four courses), maintain heavy student advising responsibilities, participate in the work of their department and college, keep up with developments in their fields, and write an occasional article.

Furthermore, in comparison with faculty elsewhere in the world, these faculty (i.e., of predominantly undergraduate institutions) stand out for their dedication to the undergraduate education, both to the craft of teaching and to the integrity of the curriculum. The reason lies not in a more virtuous or talented American professoriate, but in the enormously competitive American higher education market, with tuition dependence, mobile students (aided by portable financial aid and transferable course credits), and a surplus of higher education capacity all placing a premium on the college that can market and deliver a good undergraduate "product"—which includes, in addition to a handsome campus and a good food service, a reputation for quality teaching and a caring faculty.

In other words, that part of the reform agenda having to do with teaching and the undergraduate curriculum may be relevant to those institutions either in, or aspiring to enter, the ranks of top research universities. In their quest for institutional scholarly prestige—the coin of the realm—is maximum faculty discretionary time and clear rewards for research. Leaders of institutions competing for scholarly prestige are rewarded for the research grants and national recognition earned by their faculty. There are unquestionably elements of the traditional reform agenda that could be changed by strong and sustained leadership without necessarily compromising the basic scholarly orientation of these institutions. The difficulty is that no *single* institution can do this and not jeopardize its place in the highly competitive queue for top faculty. And for institutions to band together to declare that they will begin to demand high quality teaching for the minimal teaching demands that they make, and furthermore that they will demand a curriculum that suits the needs of the undergraduates rather than the interests of the professors, all of this to be enforced with rewards and sanctions, would almost certainly bring down upon these institutions the full might of the U.S. Justice Department's Anti-Trust Division for restraint of free competition.[3]

So the president of the research university is caught: either continue the quest for scholarly prestige while fighting a probably ineffective battle for greater attention to undergraduates, or abandon the quest for prestige and risk losing the support not just of the faculty but, perhaps ironically, of the students, parents, public, and trustees as well—who may *say* that they want a caring faculty, but who seem mainly to want the prestige that goes with institutional scholarly reputation. Thus, if "leadership" is to be defined mainly as the ability to *alter fundamentally* the institution's natural trajectory, then a strong university leader might be expected to strive to divert his or her institution away from its natural course of prestige maximization and toward a course of undergraduate student orientation—i.e., toward the traditional reform agenda. However, if "leadership" is to be defined by the leader's capacity to make a difference *but only in the direction toward which the institution is already heading*—i.e., a direction that will be full of compromises and the balancing of multiple missions, including both prestige and undergraduate attractiveness—then a very different picture may emerge of the leadership qualities needed by America's 200 or so research and doctorate-granting universities.

In this light, American colleges and universities may be far less resistant to change than they are commonly thought to be, especially in matters having to do with curriculum and academic programs. In fact, colleges are forever modifying their curricula, generally at great expense, at least in the time demands upon a few faculty. The recent reforms, over the past decade and a half, have even shown some clear themes in precisely the directions favored by the reformers; e.g., introduction of basic skill requirements in mathematics and writing, new computer literacy requirements, and restoration of foreign language requirements, as well as the more familiar attention to the classics of literature and philosophy, albeit with more attention to non-European sources.

Presidents are also forever modifying the organizational structures of their institutions in ways designed to further academic ends, such as the formation of new interdisciplinary centers, or the merger, reorganization, or even elimination of traditional discipline-based departments.

True, administrators and faculty keep on modifying and reforming in spite of the fact that the last change may not really have "taken," and the one being proposed may look a lot like one that was tried back in the early 1970s, and a little like the one from the mid-eighties. There may be some leadership (or management) failure in the seeming inability of so many of these "reforms" to take hold. But the common view that higher education leaders are either resistant to change, or have no purposeful agenda for change, is simply not borne out by history. In fact, it is at least an arguable proposition that colleges and university leaders are unique among American CEOs for their almost constant dissatisfaction with, and reexamination of, the most fundamental assumptions and missions of their organizations, and that most presidents, other academic administrators, and those faculty in leadership positions may generally be "out in front" about as far as they can effectively be, given the natural homeostasis of academic organizations.

In conclusion, what may be most missing from American higher educational leadership, at least with regard to the traditional reform agenda, is less the attribute of vision (the characteristic most commonly associated with leadership), but rather the combination of academic management skills and courage required to actually implement those changes that may run contrary to the self-interest of the faculty. In other words, the academy and its present leadership may lack neither agenda nor vision, but mainly the capacity to *implement* and to *institutionalize* what the leaders—and most of the faculty— know full well needs to be done. But higher education also needs academic leaders who can communicate better to the general public, as well as to government and other civic leaders, just what out of this traditional reform agenda does and does not legitimately apply to their institutions, and to more effectively defend their institutions and the academy generally from much of the generally accepted criticism that is, in fact, incorrect or misplaced.

The Austerity Agenda: Resources and Restructuring

The second set of forces pressing upon American higher education and defining its leadership agenda are fiscal: forces that sum to a serious and worsening divergence between the current trajectory of cost increases and a reasonable projection of increases in revenues. Cost increases for almost all colleges and universities are driven mainly by the costs of faculty and staff labor, which tend to rise, on average, at rates that mirror the rate of increases in wages and salaries in the general economy, or a little in excess of the prevailing rate of inflation. Other costs—e.g., of scientific equipment, books and periodicals, and costs associated with teaching hospitals—also tend to increase at rates above the average price increases for goods and services in the economy as a whole. The costs of increasing enrollments, or new regulations, or the need for increased financial aid, or the increased services needed by a less-well-prepared student population will be *in addition to* this underlying natural inflationary pressure. Similarly, any costs of new services, or new physical amenities, or new academic programs will be *on top of* the underlying per-student costs already rising at rates in excess of prevailing inflation.

Meanwhile, revenue increases in the private sector are constrained by a combination of demographics and price resistance. The result is a static (at best) or declining number of students and parents both willing and able to pay yearly tuitions that are already nearing the U.S. median family income and that will probably rise every year at rates at or above the prevailing rate of inflation.

In the public sector, the core problem is a powerful antigovernment sentiment at both the state and local levels, manifested by a conviction that there is rampant waste throughout government (including public higher education), an impatience with the historic progressive or liberal agendas of "access" and "opportunity," and, of course, a demand for tax cuts. Public higher education is made further vulnerable by making up a significant share of the discretionary portion of most state operating budgets (that is, excluding debt service, Medicaid, corrections, and local school aid), and by having alternative income sources in tuition and private fund-raising, which make public higher education seem better able (than other public agencies) to withstand the new public sector austerity.

This fiscal dilemma poses both similar and different leadership challenges for the public and private sectors, and for selective and less-selective institutions. In all cases, the option of increasing revenues usually seems preferable to program cuts and institutional downsizing, yet this option seems less and less possible. Tuition resistance appears finally to have come to the private sector. And even in the public sector, with total costs to the student and family at about $10,000 for an undergraduate year in residence, the potential for very large tuition increases covering equally large withdrawals of state tax funds, year after year, appears to be limited, both practically and politically.

The major leadership challenge for the less selective institutions, both public and private, is to hold a market niche amid increasing competition, growing price resistance, a nearly saturated higher educational market for adults and other part-time students, and a generally flat supply of high school graduates for the rest of the decade. Most of the remedies on the cost side have been taken: administrative, professional, and clerical staff has been cut; faculty have been nonreplaced, nonrenewed, laid off, and sometimes replaced by low-cost, part-time faculty; maintenance has been deferred; and depreciation reserves depleted.

On the revenue side, most have already done the easy and the obvious: sophisticated (and expensive) marketing campaigns, finely tuned price discrimination, new and trendy academic programs, foreign student recruitment, partnerships with feeder schools, and student-friendly calendars featuring evening colleges, weekend colleges, self-paced distance learning, credit for life experiences, and other alternatives to the traditional full-time, daytime, nine-month academic year. Whether imaginative and courageous leadership can open new student markets remains to be seen. But it seems possible that no amount of "leadership" can overcome what is at the heart a combination of bad demographics, excess capacity, and a softening of demand, partly in reaction to price.

The major leadership challenge for the very selective and affluent colleges and universities is rather simple. They must slow somewhat their rate of tuition increases, and probably will need to make some easy economies— essentially ones that their less affluent and less selective brethren, both private and public, have long since made. But mainly, they will be expected to maintain very high standards, to resist major change, and to hold to the Western scholarly tradition of *Wissenschaft*: the free, rigorous pursuit and dissemination of what is held to be true and important.

The rest of higher education, both public and private, faces a deep challenge on the cost side. Politicians, many trustees, business leaders, and citizens are all looking for something called *restructuring*—and are disappointed that so little of it seems to have occurred in American higher education. Many are looking for something analogous to what has occurred in American business and industry:

- Eliminating employees, especially professional and white collar, with the expectation that production will be maintained by eliminating nonessential procedures and enhancing productivity
- Closing down plants that are inefficient and/or in high-wage areas
- Seeking "give-backs" in labor contracts: cuts in benefits and direct compensation, and changes in work rules
- Contracting out major parts of the production process to firms that may be able to negotiate lower wages and benefits, or turning to subcontractors or new plants in Latin America, Asia, and other low-wage countries
- Abandoning entire product lines that have come to be less profitable than alternative uses of the organization's capital
- Paying more attention to the consumer or client, flattening the bureaucracy, and decentralizing decision making

Business and political leaders seem to be looking at higher education for the same kinds of *painful, wrenching changes* that private corporations have endured in their quest for greater profits or for sheer survival in the face of competition. They are also looking for the same kind of *decisiveness* that corporate leaders typically exhibit, with little of the sharing, deliberation, and delay that is so characteristic of decision making in higher education.

In the public college and university sector, genuine "restructuring" would seem to mean either an alteration of the fundamental higher educational production function—i.e., changing faculty workloads, or even the meaning of *taught courses* as the principal mode of learning and instruction—or a fundamental reorganization of the university itself, yielding a different and leaner array of offices, divisions, departments, and schools. "Restructuring" in reality always means less of something: *fewer* faculty and staff, *fewer* departments or schools, *less* cost.[4] In connection with public higher education, then, "restructuring" suggests one or another of the following:

- The closure of some smaller institutions and/or the elimination of schools, faculties, or programs that are either very small, arguably undistinguished, or not considered by state government to be critical to the future of the state.
- Either an increase in faculty teaching loads, or a differentiation in loads, with the goal of increasing the average teaching loads, measured in teaching clock hours as well as in numbers of students (mainly undergraduates) taught.
- The shedding, or at least the elimination of state tax financing, of any number of functions not considered fundamental to the basic mission of teaching or to the necessary support for the conduct of externally sponsored research. This might include the closure or privatization of campus schools, clinics, teaching hospitals, university presses, dining halls and canteens, bookstores, and residence halls. (Most of these functions at most public colleges and universities are already substantially or totally privatized, frequently as a result of a decade or two of budgetary austerity.)

However, a case can be made that in most states public higher education has already undergone significant downsizing, productivity enhancement, and restructuring—although admittedly falling short of the outright closure of public campuses.[5]

More importantly, public academic leaders may only be acting rationally and responsibly for resisting the closure or radical alterations of their campuses. State elected leaders, after all, are in the business of responding to their perception of the demands of the electorate—which in most American states in the mid-1990s are perceived to be demands mainly for lower taxes and a smaller government, without much regard to the functions performed by the units of "government" that might be so downsized. The only way that governors and legislatures can judge either the importance of a part of the public sector to the long-run health of the state, or the priority of that part to the electorate, is to attempt to cut it, perhaps drastically, and then to see whether there are either clearly damaging consequences, or an unequivocal signal from the electorate that this particular cut is not their wish.

The great dilemma of public college and university leadership in the 1990s is whether to accept as inevitable the loss of public resources and the consequent faculty and staff reductions, increases in faculty workload, and closure of academic units, and thus to get out "in front of the wave" and lead the institution toward this future of more productive, more privatized, and generally smaller public institutions. The alternative is to see this future as not at all inevitable, but only an option, temporarily caught up amid the much larger and more fundamental goals such as lower taxes, less government, less crime, a restoration of family values, and the end of liberal welfare programs. In this latter case, true leadership in the academic community needs more to *resist* these forces and to advocate the continuation of public commitment to the nation's state-supported colleges and universities.

THE CHALLENGE OF LEADERSHIP
IN AMERICAN HIGHER EDUCATION

Leadership in any organization is a balance between holding to the organization's course in the midst of inevitable forces for disruption or distraction, and redefining or even altering that fundamental course in light of equally inevitable changes in preferences, needs, and production possibilities. Particularly in a college or university, where the centrality of the faculty to organizational governance is not a matter of choice or leadership style, but of the very nature of the organization's fundamental production processes, whether of research or teaching, leadership must both *enable* and *alter*. Academic leadership is thus very situational, depending both on the nature and mission of the institution, and on the circumstances (e.g., demographics and economics) prevailing at the time.

Where the faculty march overwhelmingly to the drummer of research and scholarly prestige, the effective leader must tilt the organization to the goals that will not be naturally maximized: e.g., attention to the undergraduate, to the craft of teaching, and to the integrity of the undergraduate curriculum.

Where the faculty and the governing board aspire to an elevation in scholarly prestige beyond that currently "deserved" by the faculty, the leader may have to alter the university's past practices of hiring, promotion, expectations, and support, and tilt toward a more scholarly orientation, even accepting some diminution of attention to undergraduate education.

Where the faculty are concerned mainly with job security and work rules, the leader may need to impart a more professional orientation: more scholarly pride, more attention to teaching, and a greater stake in the goals and successes of the organization as opposed to the welfare of the individual professors.

Where the institution is private and neither greatly endowed nor highly selective, and thus vulnerable to the combination of bad demographics and price resistance, the leader may have to alter the mission and the market niche, even if this strategy means abandoning missions and practices that have served the institution well in the past.

Where the institution is public and vulnerable to the current mood of public sector downsizing, the effective leader may have to resist making the task of the budget cutters any easier and fight to preserve the place of public higher education in the priorities of the state's public sector.

Where the institution is secure in its position, both for students and for scholarly prestige, leadership probably needs to resist the many pressures, internal or external, either from politics or from the market, that would fundamentally change either the scholarship or the education that the faculty seems to be successfully producing.

And for virtually all institutions, leadership needs to reinforce certain commitments made by the institution that most faculty will support intellectually and emotionally, but not necessarily behaviorally—commitments that are not in the natural self-interest of the faculty, such as increased access, the expansion of educational opportunity, the racial and gender diversification of the faculty, community service, and the like.

The essential question for leadership in the coming decade, then, is whether either of these fundamental challenges—the traditional reform agenda of better balancing the demands of teaching and scholarship, or the new austerity agenda of restructuring and cost containment—can be carried out within the traditions of American academic governance and leadership. This tradition has placed a premium on

- The ability to shape the direction of a college or university by encouraging the best inclinations of the faculty, with respect for the principles of shared governance and the primacy of the faculty in the setting of academic policies
- The capacity to inspire trust and convey the centrality of integrity to an organization of professionals
- The ability to communicate and relate to a great range and number of constituencies, both internal and external, all of whom need to feel in some way directly connected to the chief executive officer
- The capacity to manage and lead an organization with multiple goals, uncertain and sometimes disagreeable feedback, and increasing stress

In all likelihood, these attributes will continue to yield the kinds of presidents and chancellors currently in office: extraordinary individuals by most measures, and selected through one of the most meritocratic processes to be found in American society, yet apparently either unwilling or unable to dramatically and fundamentally alter the course of American higher education. The appropriateness of the selection process, then, like the appropriateness of the current leaders of American higher education, depends on whether one believes that American higher education needs "dramatic and fundamental change," or whether it needs mainly stability and defense against the buffeting of demographics, politics, and the inherent challenge of managing so complex an organization serving so many social ends. Arguably, it needs the latter as much or more than the former.

NOTES

1. See Trow 1994.
2. Totals differ slightly from those provided by the National Center for Education Statistics (1994).
3. See Winston 1994.
4. See Slaughter 1993, 250–81.
5. Only four public four-year institutions have closed since 1969–70, three of them branch campuses. Thirty public community colleges have closed in the same time period, including six branch campuses. Comparable numbers for the private sector are 174 four-year and 138 two-year institutions and branches. (NCES 1994, table 233).

REFERENCES

Almanac issue. 1994. *The Chronicle of Higher Education* 41 (16). Data from the U.S. Department of Education.

Business Higher Education Forum. 1994. *Corporate lessons for American higher education.* Washington, DC: American Council on Education.

A classification of institutions of higher education. 1994. Princeton, NJ: The Carnegie Foundation.

National Center for Education Statistics (NCES), U.S. Department of Education. 1994. *The conditions of education.* Washington, DC: Government Printing Office.

————. 1995. *Digest of education statistics.* Washington, DC: Government Printing Office.

Slaughter, S. 1993. Retrenchment in the 1980's. *Journal of Higher Education* 64 (May/June): 250–82.

Trow, M. 1994. Comparative reflections on leadership in higher education. In *Higher education in American society,* edited by P. G. Altbach, R. O. Berdahl, and P. J. Gunport. New York: Prometheus Books.

Winston, G. 1994. The decline in undergraduate teaching: Moral failure or market pressure? *Change* 26 (September/October): 8–15.

CHAPTER  8

Canada

B. Dalin Jameson and K. George Pedersen

Executive Summary. With approximately 100 degree-granting institutions, serving 62 percent of the college-age cohort, Canada is second only to the United States in postsecondary education participation rates. Private postsecondary education is all but nonexistent, and the current system is highly decentralized, under provincial control. Dependency on government funding has left Canadian higher education vulnerable in the competition for scarce resources. While institutions are being pressed to find alternative sources of revenue, each provincial government has set a maximum tuition rate for all institutions in its province. Forces for change include pressures for accountability, the growing diversity of the student body, the internationalization of knowledge, and technology. The latter has particular significance for Canada, in light of the size of the country and the challenge to provide access for remote populations.

The authors point out a number of obstacles to change. The lack of competition has stifled innovation and has led to a degree of complacency and difficulty in undertaking changes that would more sharply differentiate institutional missions. Shared governance inhibits institutional responsiveness, and presidents are increasingly detached from the academic business of the institution as they turn to politics and fundraising. Presidents do, however, play an important leadership role in building external support for the institution in government and the private sector, and in building an internal community that can serve as a counterweight to the fragmentation caused by the primacy of disciplinary loyalties and tensions between faculty and administrators.

• • • • • • • • • • •

I n comparison with many, if not most, national systems of higher education, the university sector in Canada is characterized by its decentralization. This phenomenon is largely the result of geography and settlement patterns: Canada is a vast country, developed in progressive stages, with comparatively recent national confederation. The federal government of Canada generally approaches education indirectly, leaving jurisdiction with the 10 provincial governments. There is thus a conspicuous heterogeneity among the provinces as to the structures and philosophies of higher education. Also, importantly, Canada is unusual among developed countries in having no federal agency or coordinating body responsible for educational issues.

While diversity among the provinces might be seen to manifest itself in the co-presence of English- and French-speaking institutions, reflecting a social context that spans two founding European cultures, it is also indicative of the early founding of universities in Upper and Lower Canada and in the Maritime Provinces patterned on institutions that settlers from Britain, Scotland, France, and the United States believed reflected the values of culture, education, and professional training in their former homelands, which they sought to emulate.

As early as the mid-seventeenth century, institutions for theological instruction had grown following the model of European seminaries and colleges in both New France and English-speaking Canada. In 1635, a Jesuit college was established in Quebec, beginning on an elementary-school level but broadened under Bishop Laval to provide professional theological training. In the course of the next century, this seminary developed a wider curriculum, including rhetoric and philosophy. Toward the end of the eighteenth century, the first royal charter granted to a Canadian university was awarded to the University of King's College in Nova Scotia, founded by United Empire Loyalists who had followed their inclinations to remain British by migrating northward after the American Revolution. During the next half century, charters were granted to English-speaking universities in Nova Scotia, New Brunswick, Quebec, and Ontario. In general, the more ambitious of these followed the Oxbridge examples, believed to be cornerstones of the culture that new Canadians wished to preserve and build in their growing country. Most, however, derived more specifically from religious backgrounds, training aspirants to the clergy and, over time, becoming broader in their secular offerings. From theological programs, they expanded into general arts and humanities study, mathematics and physical sciences, and professional training, including languages, medicine, and engineering.

As the settlement of Canada moved westward, and as society matured, the provincial governments moved to establish regionally focused universities. The acquisition and transmission of knowledge were seen as keys to the future of individual provinces, and it was felt that Manitoba, Saskatchewan, and Alberta would become vigorous participants in the modern age if they could provide universities to educate their citizens. In British Columbia, contention between Vancouver and Victoria as to which would be the appropriate location for a provincial university led to smaller schools in both of those cities becoming "extension" affiliates of McGill near the turn of the century, with the University of British Columbia eventually being established in 1915. Although these institutions answered to what were essentially populist political aspirations, the early colleges and universities throughout the country were in fact smallish and definitely elitist institutions. They reflected the culture of the times, including the individual and class differences in opportunity and the requisite resources to pursue higher education.

As was the case with most Western cultures, and particularly those of North America, university-level education became accessible to a significantly larger segment of the population only following the Second World War. Both social and economic aspirations led an entire generation to look toward university education. This pattern is reflected in vastly increased enrollments—and in participation rates among those who had not, in previous generations, been part of the university population. Women entered the classrooms in record numbers, a trend which has continued, and in many major universities, female undergraduates now outnumber their male counterparts. Students who might in earlier times have remained isolated in rural areas found themselves as potential postsecondary students, perhaps at the newer universities that were created throughout the country in the 1950s and 1960s.

As the base of the university-sector pyramid broadened with entering undergraduates, so did graduate and professional programs at the top. By the 1970s, the Canadian university system had taken on much of the appearance it has today: a widely diverse collection of educational environments of varying size, discipline focus, and institutional character—offering, in general, a very high quality of academic experience. In its range of institutional types—from the medical/doctoral multiversity to the comprehensive graduate and undergraduate university to the college of arts and sciences—Canadian higher education resembles systems found in other advanced Western or westernized countries.

There are just over 100 degree-granting institutions in Canada, which ranks second only to the United States in the proportion of its population enrolled in postsecondary education. The actual number of full-time postsecondary students has increased more than ninefold in the last 40 years, growing from 91,000 in 1951 to nearly 900,000 by 1990. Between 1983 and 1988, postsecondary enrollment as a proportion of the 20- to 24-year-old age group rose from 50.2 percent to 62.2 percent. In 1986, nearly 10 percent of all Canadians 15 years of age or older, and over 15 percent of those between 25 and 44 years, held university degrees, representing a doubling of these figures over 15 years (Department of the Secretary of State of Canada 1992).

This growth attests to the value Canadians place on university education. In the period 1965–1988, total public expenditures for education averaged eight percent of the GNP, placing Canada near the top among developed countries (Department of the Secretary of State of Canada 1992). It should be pointed out, however, that primary emphasis has consistently been placed upon the elementary and secondary sectors, with funding for universities coming in far behind. While university participation expanded tremendously during this time, they have increasingly felt the pressures of inadequate resources.

Importantly, the secularization of Canadian universities gradually brought them into an entirely public system; private universities are all but nonexistent in Canada. The absence of a private postsecondary educational system has shaped Canadian universities in significant ways. While the decentralized national character of the university sector and its particular patterns of evolution have been advantageous in promoting autonomy at the level of individual institutions, dependence on a single major funding source has created some serious problems. Deriving their revenues overwhelmingly from funds administered by the provincial governments, universities are vulnerable to engagement as instruments of public policy at a variety of levels. Further, they must operate within a culture in which support of postsecondary education is seen as a government responsibility—an attitude that makes fund-raising among alumni and in the corporate world extremely challenging.

The most dispiriting aspect of the public-only system in Canada, however, is the tendency toward complacency. The competition afforded by private universities, including the flexibility of market-driven tuition fees, would be an added incentive toward excellence in both teaching and research. Universities would cease to regard themselves as public utilities and would have to become increasingly proactive in securing resources through enhanced research profiles or by way of the educational environment they offer to prospective students. Such an incentive would allow them to redefine their specific institutional missions in ways that would capitalize on identified areas of strength—and to respond much more quickly to opportunities in new disciplines. Some institutions could focus on the highest levels of graduate and professional training, with their correlative intensive research efforts, while others could place their emphasis on a liberal arts–type environment geared to enhancing the quality of the undergraduate experience.

In fact, governments are increasingly yielding to the temptation to manage—largely at the system level. This is having an homogenizing effect because of funding mechanisms that are geared to reward easily measured indices of presumed productivity, such as undergraduate enrollment. There is considerable fear that diverse and vital university communities, including strong graduate and research components, will be pushed toward redefinition as "teaching factories" in response to direct, manipulative fiscal pressure. Both the politicians and the public must be educated in the value of the historical richness and diversity that exists in Canadian higher education.

In general, political and social leaders possess considerable knowledge about the abstract values of universities. This has traditionally been reflected by gratifying esteem and levels of support, particularly in fiscally good times. In the face of increasing preoccupation with deficits and public debt, however, the "ivory tower" is a more frequent object of criticism and attack. The university community finds itself arguing issues of isolation and elitism, productivity, and contributions to society, a pattern that seems to appear on a recurrent and cyclical basis. In Canada, the 1990s have brought the return of such a cycle, with universities on the defensive. We are being challenged to prove our value and to demonstrate our contributions to society in order to ensure its continued support. We are in competition—not in invigorating intellectual challenges among institutions and within disciplines—but in a struggle against other providers of public services for increasingly scarce funding. While Canadian universities are only metaphorically under siege, it seems a time of confrontation, challenge, and redefinition on campuses across the country.

FORCES FOR CHANGE

While Canadian society is essentially stable and evolutionary, rather than given to precipitate shifts in emphasis or direction, the environment of postsecondary education has changed significantly in recent years. As indicated earlier, the postwar expansion of universities reflected a progressive inclusion of segments of the population that had not before been participants in the higher educational system. Correlative with this expansion was, of course, the economic and technological growth on an international scale that placed university-level education—as well as the research activities focussed in universities—in a position of particular importance both in individual lives and in the public direction of the provinces and of the nation.

Public Support

By the mid-1960s, the "massification" of higher education had led to the secure establishment of universities as important social and cultural institutions throughout Canada. In both their teaching and research roles, they were seen to be essential to the future development of the country. This acknowledgment continues to be reflected in overall levels of public support, although not without frequent reminders from the university community of its concerns about progressively declining commitments of increasingly scarce resources. By international standards, Canadian universities enjoy considerable public confidence and respect—and derive from that a reasonably consistent level of support. University education is a broad expectation in Canada. Participation rates are among the world's highest, and the values of postsecondary education are widely embraced.

It is nearly axiomatic among Canadian university leaders that the level of educational experience for our students across the country is uniformly quite high, but that the uniformity of overall quality inhibits efforts by individual institutions to achieve genuine academic excellence and distinction, as might be recognized on an international level. The tendency toward homogenization might seem advantageous if we consider simple instruction and the broad provision of tertiary education to be an absolute good; if we aspire to lead in the international scholarly community, however, we must expand both our horizons and our capacities.

Many of Canada's most outstanding universities have looked toward this goal, and it is here that we find our most pressing challenges. Primary dependence on a single funding source has rendered us particularly vulnerable to the general governmental tendency to see its educational responsibilities in quantitative rather than qualitative terms. While this is most obvious in the area of financial commitment, where the issues are directly quantifiable (cash input), it is troublesome in the correlative performance indicators that are used to measure the universities' effectiveness (student output). These most generally are seen to reside in enrollment figures—easy to count, and perceived as directly correspondent to the public role of tertiary education. This type of focus, however, profoundly distorts the range of contributions we seek to bring to the society that supports us. It all but ignores our essential role in graduate and professional education and in the pure and applied research that will shape the economic, technological, and cultural future. These are the qualities that create eminent universities on an international scale; by these measures, we are comparatively disadvantaged. In many ways, then, universities throughout Canada are constrained by governments-of-the-day, which have built their mechanisms of fiscal support around "measurable" short-term objectives.

Much of the difficulty derives from the fact that, in Canada, the federal role in higher education is somewhat veiled; the provinces have primary jurisdiction over postsecondary education, with little direct involvement at the national level. Direct participation by the federal government in the funding of universities is largely limited to project-based awards through national granting councils, which sponsor research in the arts and humanities, social sciences, science and engineering, and medicine. The government of Canada also underwrites federal student loan programs and, through various agencies, oversees international agreements and academic exchanges. On the whole, however, the federal government presence is that of a "silent partner" in

Canadian higher education, with the bulk of its support coming through transfer payments to the provinces for the funding of colleges and universities, as well as programs in extended health care and other medical services. The provincial governments receiving these funds hold discretionary power as to their apportionment among the designated recipients, and it is quite clear where postsecondary education will rank in competition for public attention with the immediately perceptible needs in health and medical services.

Universities are thus doubly disadvantaged in their attempts to secure a larger share of public resources: first, because the federal government can withdraw support through the rather indirect means of freezing or reducing transfer payments to the provinces, and secondly because of the intense competition with very visible social needs at the provincial level. Throughout Canada, both of these factors have placed universities in positions of acute vulnerability as increasingly difficult fiscal decisions have had to be made at all levels of government. Public debt has become a political obsession that has brought massive spending reductions in federal programs and at the level of every Canadian provincial budget. At the same time, tax increases have provoked strident calls for increased "accountability" in public spending, which have been visited upon universities in the form of pressure to develop appropriate "performance indicators" to justify the expenditure of hard-won public funding.

Fiscal challenges and "the idea of the university" thus come full circle, as scarcity of resources forces universities to define their academic activities according to externally imposed concepts and fiscally based prescriptions. These types of measures, in turn, place a premium on factors that measure instructional capacity and a penalty on those that foster a vigorous scholarly environment for research and graduate education. As many Canadian university presidents have suggested, a prescription for mediocrity resides in this view of our university community—and this is perhaps our greatest cause of concern.

These are broad philosophical difficulties, which are directly exacerbated and brought to the fore by "forces for change." Fiscal constraint and a progressive reduction of resources available to support university education have had very serious effects in Canada. Under current discussion is "The Green Paper," a document produced by the government of Canada (Department of Human Resource Development 1994), which calls for a progressive reduction of transfer payments to the provinces in support of higher education. Over a period of several years, the cash portion of these payments will be eliminated, leaving them only as "tax points" within the jurisdiction of the provinces, with a small amount being reserved to support student loan programs. Should these proposals become policy, the federal government would all but relinquish its role in supporting Canadian universities, doing this only through the granting councils and residual funding of some types of student loans. Such a course would, quite naturally, impose increased burdens on the provinces—themselves struggling with massive public debt and the need to decrease expenditures.

There seem very few options available to sustain Canadian universities at levels that will ensure their international competitiveness. A tradition of dependence on public funding has made it difficult for us to look to alumni, friends, and the general public for significant amounts of support, but that is changing as circumstances force us to seek alternative means of maintaining our academic activities. Major fundraising initiatives in the private and corporate sectors have brought us some success, and we have sought to develop a more vigorous approach to seeking partnerships with business and industry. We have been compelled to look outside our normal sources of funding, and this necessity has brought both success and invigoration of the university community. The new fiscal environment has presented challenges, but Canadian universities have, by and large, responded with ingenuity and resiliency.

Regulation of Tuition Fees

Indeed, the governments' role in establishing fee levels is yet another challenge for most Canadian universities. In Ontario, as in most provinces, maximum tuition fees are set annually by the ministry responsible for postsecondary education. Individual institutions may not exceed those levels without corresponding reductions in provincial operating grants. This policy, while addressing some concerns about accessibility to university education, guarantees that very little differentiation will develop among the various institutions and that genuine excellence in academic programs and scholarship will be increasingly difficult to support. Recently in Ontario, there have been proposals advanced by the universities to deregulate tuition fees, but these have not been well received by a government placing priority on numerical measures of overall enrollment as the index of academic effectiveness. Still, the universities continue to press for differentiation by program, with professional schools such as law, medicine, and dentistry, for example, given the flexibility to set fees more commensurate with actual costs. As a correlative of these proposals, the universities strongly advocate the development on the national level of an income-contingent repayment plan for student loans, placing more of the responsibility for funding professional education on those who will be its direct beneficiaries.

Diversity

Several other evolutionary changes, in our society and in the roles we conceive for higher education, have also worked to reshape Canadian universities. A look at any campus across the country will quickly reveal that the university population has become far less homogenous and more diverse—among students, faculty, and staff. In Canada today, the larger part of our undergraduate student contingent is often female; in our own university, we monitor faculty advertisements, interviews, and appointments very carefully and have found a steadily increasing percentage of female candidates joining our professoriate across the disciplines. We seek and have acted strongly to achieve appropriate representation of those from traditionally disadvantaged groups, broadening the opportunities for the handicapped, visible minorities, and others who may require special accommodation in realizing their potential as members of the university community.

In many of these areas, it would be disingenuous to suggest that institutional resources and the priorities for investing those resources would have produced the diversity we celebrate without specific governmental incentives and encouragement. Indeed, such public policy commitments are often seen as intrusive and politically motivated. It remains true, however, that diversity within the university is a fundamental intellectual value and that the richness of the educational experience is directly affected by the heterogeneity of the academic environment. The breadth of contact with new ideas, beliefs, and cultural values is perhaps unique to the university experience; certainly, universities are places where such encounters are specifically the business of the institution. While many in Canada and elsewhere may resent the seeming heavy-handedness of "equity agendas," the goal of maximum diversity and accessibility is one that universities express by their very nature as academic communities. Achieving these aspirations may present specific challenges, such as recruitment of both students and faculty and the provision for transitional and special assistance programs, and these require specially designated funding—above and beyond that provided for the basic operational responsibilities of the institution. To some extent, this support has been forthcoming in particular areas, but the tension between social commitment and the essential academic mission of the university will always tend to be most apparent in times of severe resource limitations.

Internationalization

"Diversity" as a term takes on added implications when we consider the tremendous internationalization of knowledge and of educational opportunity that has characterized the last three decades. The world has become smaller and more integrated in almost every way, and universities exist as a network of communication and discovery that is truly without borders. Academics conduct their research and exchange ideas along the "information highway" as they once did in the common room or faculty club; desktop workstations link professors, librarians, and students with their counterparts around the world;

administrators share ideas and strategies through electronic mail and videoconferencing. All these technological developments break down the barriers of space and time, creating at least the possibility of a genuinely cosmopolitan intellectual environment in even the most geographically isolated of our universities.

It is not enough, however, to broaden our horizons only electronically. We need to explore our world from an international perspective by more vigorously developing exchanges, cooperative programs, and research projects. In Canada, we have in recent years looked outward and assumed an international political role. As active partners in United Nations and Commonwealth activities for nearly half a century, we have an established presence in many areas of the world; more recent economic participation in the Group of Seven industrialized nations and the North American Free Trade Alliance (NAFTA) has broadened our national perspective as a player on the world stage. Canada's university community has long sought to increase its diversity through wider international participation, and we are actively moving in the direction of multinational associations and exchanges. Through such organizations as the World University Service (and WUSC, its Canadian branch), Canadian Bureau for International Education, and the Inter-American Organization for Higher Education, we look toward closer and mutually enriching associations both within our own region and more broadly. Particularly in the western provinces, there is increasing attention to developing ties to Asia and the Pacific Rim, while universities in central Canada are working to establish links with Mexico and Latin America to complement the economic and political connections established through NAFTA.

Against this background of internationalization, it may appear ironic that some Canadian provinces continue to impose differential tuition fees for foreign students as a revenue-generating mechanism. At Ontario universities, students from outside Canada must pay several times the fee levels established for Canadian citizens and permanent residents. At the University of Western Ontario, current tuition for a basic, full-time undergraduate program in 1995–96 was $2,890 for Canadian students and $9,600 for international students; in professional programs, the respective fees are $3,496 and $14,897.[1] This government-prescribed differentiation is not conducive to the diversity of our campus environment, a diversity otherwise seen as having an intellectual and cultural value to the university community. While it is easy to acknowledge the putative arguments of the Ontario taxpayer as to the education of "outsiders," we can also observe a steady decline in the number of international students, particularly at the graduate level, in recent years. This may, in some senses, be a greater impoverishment to the life of the province than the marginal revenue loss to the government, were differential fees to be abolished.

Technology

Perhaps the greatest force for change in recent years—and one that is certain to grow in importance as we look toward the future—is the pace of technological development. In the last two decades, technology has reshaped the academic landscape and redefined the way we approach our two central roles of teaching and research. This pedagogical revolution began with rather clumsy attempts to capitalize on television to teach large numbers of students economically, but in very traditional ways. Hanging television monitors in large classrooms created a remoteness around the instructional process that still haunts many institutions. Some remain timid in exploring new technological initiatives; others sense a certain apathy toward their university experience from alumni of that period. This should serve as a valuable lesson that technology itself is not a universal panacea and is not invariably effective. The need to develop appropriate techniques for the presentation of course material in mediated formats is essential if the potential of technology is to be realized.

Canada faces particular challenges of geography in the provision of access to colleges and universities. Mediated and distance learning provides us an avenue for making higher education available to a much broader constituency. From the traditional correspondence courses, mediated learning has evolved through video- and audiotapes to interactive, participatory teaching by means of computer linkages and videoconferencing. This is an extremely promising area for development—in part, because it allows universities to respond to accessibility-related issues, increasing enrollments with minimum added stress on physical facilities and the already-overcrowded campus environment.

Expansion through technology, however, also requires the appropriate construction of course materials and the development of faculty teaching skills. We often find that the level of our students' sophistication in these areas exceeds that of faculty (and administrators), who inhabit another era. A substantial rethinking of professors' approach to their academic disciplines is often required in order to make the activity of teaching relevant and accessible from both sides of the lectern or the screen. Often, this type of reassessment becomes a major factor in the evolution of an academic career—and therefore has considerable implications for how the institution will define its expectations for scholarly activity. In many Canadian universities, offices of educational development support faculty in realizing these changes in their approach to teaching and learning, working as well to promote more systematic study of the pedagogical challenges that new technology is bringing into our profession.

Related to developing the ability to use technology effectively is the challenge of acquiring it. As equipment becomes increasingly expensive and the orientation in purchasing shifts toward high tech, interactive teaching facilities, yet another major stress arises to visit itself on shrinking university budgets. Refitting of classrooms and securing the devices that will enable a single campus to broaden into an electronic network with a national constituency become major factors in setting the university's academic policy. Almost all institutions will increasingly look toward the "open" concept of learning, and this is a major shift in emphasis for most.

If the teaching role has been redefined through this revolution in technology, the nature and quality of academic research have undergone changes that are perhaps even more profound. The "information revolution" has altered our approach to knowledge in every discipline, as scholars now have direct and immediate access to a worldwide body of text, experimental data, speculation and work-in-progress, and—most importantly—to their colleagues on other campuses. In addition, the very nature of academic libraries has changed. Access to their catalogues, and in many cases their holdings themselves, is as close as the computer terminal on the student's or professor's desk; on-line searches yield material hitherto inaccessible or only serendipitously discovered; interlibrary access across continents facilitates a much higher level of scholarship.

As with all revolutions, there are significant stresses involved. In Canada, as elsewhere, librarians struggle with the questions of acquisition versus access: should "collections" or "connections" be the priority? Is a library defined by its holdings or by its capacity to provide access to materials, which might be housed, owned, and maintained elsewhere? Aside from this basic issue of resource allocation, there are obviously space and equipment implications, as spending might need to be diverted from book and periodical acquisitions toward CD-ROM readers, database servers, and access terminals—a difficult conceptual shift for many traditional faculty members to accept. Finally, there are the changing patterns of scholarship among our students, now well along on their "information highway" journeys. While many of them are quite sophisticated in using the technology to obtain information, they may be considerably less well prepared to sift, appraise, and reconstruct that information in ways that define the learning process. This suggests an intellectual challenge that universities will have to meet as the sheer volume of information available surely comes to exceed our ability to structure and assimilate it.

Lifelong Learning

It is, finally, the human dimension of education that is, and will continue to be, our greatest challenge and the most pervasive force for change facing universities. As we, particularly in Canada, move progressively from a resource-based economy and culture to a knowledge-based society, the role of higher education will become increasingly important. The phrase "lifelong learning" has gained a particular currency in recent years, and it is a reality that we can see in our burgeoning continuing education programs. In the professions, periodic upgrading of skills, techniques, and perspectives has become a necessity for effective and responsible practice. New professions themselves are evolving, especially in health care and social services, and these frequently require credentials that can only be obtained at colleges or universities.

Perhaps most striking, however, is the personal career mobility that seems an emerging characteristic of our evolving society. Predictions that most of our students' lifetimes will see several basic reorientations of their careers suggest both opportunities and responsibilities for universities. In many cases, we are responding to these as they arise, providing part-time, distance, and continuing study courses geared to retraining, upgrading, and personal development. The growing requirements of a changing work environment will see us expanding these areas of service in diploma and advanced degree programs, as well as in the far broader range of "interest courses," which will more firmly integrate universities into their communities. The university will increasingly become a part of individual lives as the potential constituency for personal development and self-cultivation grows and as these potential participants in higher education become aware of the resources available on our campuses.

Finally, as today's students look forward to a life characterized by the ever-increasing pace of external change, it is particularly important that their university experience has fostered the broad understanding, creativity, and resourcefulness that will be essential for their success in that life. This will be the greatest challenge as we face the years ahead.

RESISTANCE TO CHANGE

For precisely the reasons they have endured in our society for nearly a thousand years, universities are also quite resistant to change. If the certainty and rapidity of change noted above are characteristic of the external environment, universities themselves may face serious difficulties of adaptation. In Canada, the relative autonomy granted to individual institutions in determining their academic directions may seem an impediment to rapid and responsive change. While independence and self-determination are jealously guarded as institutional prerogatives, they can also be seen in some quarters as insulating universities from the immediate and pressing social realities. In government circles, particularly, "university autonomy" is often regarded as a well-worn defense mechanism against tempting intervention for purposes of "social engineering" toward a variety of outcomes: shaping the workforce in particular ways, fulfilling policy objectives in areas such as accessibility, and employing leverage to manipulate other sectors, such as health care and the professions. This is an area of genuine contention in every province in Canada, and is made more poignant by the wholly public system of Canadian higher education. Almost all colleges and universities are totally dependent on public policy and public funds, exercised at the provincial level.

While this situation has its most pronounced effect with regard to institutional autonomy, the lack of a parallel private group of colleges and universities eliminates much of the stimulus toward innovation and competition that is found in the United States. The interinstitutional pressure is much less, and the impetus toward creative change in response to an evolving environment of educational demands and possibilities is correspondingly reduced. As the incentive to compete among institutions is inhibited, so also is the potential for cooperation among universities or between the college and university sectors. The relative policy vacuum at the federal level and the different ways in which individual provinces have articulated interinstitutional relationships contribute to "insularize" both the institutions and the overall university sector. In some provinces (Alberta and British Columbia, for example), the patterns of settlement across large geographical areas were accommodated through a community college network that would quite closely feed into and articulate its programs with the small number of centralized universities. In Ontario, on the other hand, colleges and universities developed independently, each sector having a discrete and specific mission, with very little interaction. As we look toward a time of integrated "lifelong learning," this latter system seems ill-adapted to address the needs of an increasingly mobile and occupationally volatile student population.

Within the universities themselves, there are many factors that militate against a vigorous and energetic response to external change. The character of the professoriate, particularly in recent years, has become far more discipline-focused and less broadly collegial. Most students of university culture have observed that individual academics place their primary loyalty with their discipline or, at best, with their departmentalized unit, rather than with the university. They regard their true colleagues as those who share their professional scholarly interests and with whom they interact electronically and at conferences on the basis of discipline allegiance and common academic pursuits. The growth of interdisciplinary studies has done little to alleviate this compartmentalization, since those areas that coalesce to pursue particular research emphases or work from shared perspectives are generally close in their individual disciplinary identities.

Maintaining the university as a community therefore requires much attention in the face of many stresses and competitive interests. Making this all the more difficult is the growing redefinition of that community in terms of constituency or advocacy groups. In most Canadian universities, there has been a strong movement toward "democratization" of institutional operations—often directly encouraged by governments eager that "stakeholder consultation" become a part of all decision-making processes. This move toward empowerment of various groups is, most generally, fragmenting in its effect and cumbersome in its direct manifestations. The requirement to galvanize the support of all factions within the university—faculty, support staff, groundskeepers, and graduate and undergraduate students—makes change in the direction or structure of this institution an extremely difficult challenge. Since this in many instances is now a requirement for government support and facilitation, resistance to change is practically guaranteed as the avenue of least administrative resistance: a "risk aversion" factor characterizes this type of consensus building and inhibits institutional responsiveness.

A final impediment to vigorous change within institutions is the changing nature of the university presidency. Traditionally, the president has been seen as an internal leader and shaper of the institutional priorities and identity. As "chief colleague" as well as executive officer, the president has exerted leadership within the university community. Increasingly, the energies and the time of the president are invested in commitments outside the university. As has become typical in the United States, Canadian university leaders are spending an increasing number of days each month away from the campus, lobbying ministry officials and appearing before parliamentary committees, developing collaborative research and development ventures with corporate partners, and convincing alumni and friends to participate in building the future of the universities. In Canada, this has not been a tradition, and the cultivation of prospective donors is challenging new ground for many presidents.

While the demands of an increasingly external focus are being addressed, however, the internal leadership requirements of a vigorous collegium are very difficult to sustain. The stresses here may very well produce a new pattern of institutional management, drawing the president more away from active engagement with the internal academic affairs of the university and increasingly toward the larger public context in which the university and the higher education sector must become more visible and more proactive. In practice, university presidents may soon be recruited more for their entrepreneurial than their academic skills, with the institutions themselves adapting through more direct vice-presidential leadership in matters of policy and management. Such a diffusion of responsibilities may in itself present challenges to universities facing the need for change and evolution in addressing their academic mission.

THE INSTITUTIONAL RESPONSE: A PERSONAL PERSPECTIVE

A university presidency is the most interesting job in the world. At the time of my retirement from the University of Western Ontario in July 1994, I was the senior Canadian university president, having served 16 years in that capacity at 3 institutions. During that time, there were many challenges and many personal and professional rewards—which I remember with particular satisfaction. All through those years, I have especially relished the opportunity to know and to work with outstanding young people. Canadian university students are among the most enthusiastic and committed in the world, with a tremendous sense of dedication to the educational process and to the society they will serve as its most effective and productive citizens. Sharing the adventure of learning with these bright, eager young minds has been a constantly invigorating experience.

On a practical policy level, the most fulfilling part of my several presidencies has been the opportunity for advocacy of Canada's universities and of university education. It has been my commitment to build support within the broad community for the value and the values of higher education. First of all, the public must embrace the principle of education and what it means to society—but individuals must also be brought to realize the potential within themselves that can be tapped through their own participation in the educational experience. If the public values universities, this should be reflected in the policies and priorities of their elected leaders. Building political support for higher education has been a major effort and a major challenge for me and for all Canadian university presidents. Politicians and bureaucrats inherently resist overtures from universities seeking support, believing that other public institutions and services more immediately touch the lives of their voting constituents. While this supposition may have some substance in the short run, there is no doubt that the long-term contributions of universities have an absolutely determinant effect on the life of a society. Making this case in the halls of government is difficult and often frustrating. It is made the more so because most of those political leaders are themselves the beneficiaries of a university education and should have an appreciation of its value.

As a complement to efforts at engaging the government more fully in support of universities, much of my effort and attention over the past two decades has been directed toward more actively involving the private sector in underwriting university activities. This takes several forms, including the direct solicitation of financial support but also the interaction of creative partnership in research and development. Universities in Canada are the focus of cutting-edge research in bioscience and biotechnology, pharmaceuticals, and disease prevention techniques; of advances in electronics and telecommunications, the physical sciences, and chemistry; and in structural, geotechnical, and environmental engineering. These are areas with practical applications in business and industry, and we have forged links with the corporate world that make Canada a world leader. An increasing number of Canadian universities have developed research and industrial parks, in which companies can locate close to the resident expertise and facilities offered by the campus, with opportunities for interaction at a very close and immediate level. The University of Western Ontario has such a research park, and it has served as a unique vehicle for consolidating cooperation among governments at the municipal, provincial, and federal level, as well as for linking privately funded research institutes and the university in several tremendously exciting research ventures. This stimulus for cross-sectoral involvement, with the university at its center, is an extremely important development as we look toward the future. It provides a model for interaction that brings together various aspects of the community in a joint academic venture.

Building on government and private-sector involvement with the university has provided another opportunity for very satisfying advocacy on behalf of postsecondary education and my own universities in particular. Discovering new friends of the university and meeting the stalwart and committed patrons and alumni at each of the three institutions with which I have been associated has been a source of personal satisfaction throughout my career. I was reinvigorated and found my own commitments reaffirmed at each encounter with a dedicated friend of the university. These people are there, and they want to help. At the University of Western Ontario, we sought them out aggressively and with some success. In 1989, we began a fund-raising campaign with the formidable (for a Canadian university) target of a resonant $89 million. At the campaign's close five years later, the total funding achieved had exceeded $126 million. Aside from very hard work and a particularly talented and effective group of staff and volunteers, this success was due to our having convinced a very broad general public of the value of our university to their community. Governments, corporations, and private citizens heard our message and responded generously. Importantly, our students made the largest contribution ever secured by a Canadian university from its student body, and our staff and faculty participation levels were truly outstanding.

I believe that we have a message: that universities are important, that they are places where excellence can be pursued and realized, and that they are worthy of support. A fundamental challenge facing all of us as academic leaders is to communicate that message, within our campus and throughout society.

In all the universities I have served, it has been important for me to remain visible and accessible as president. Each week, I tried to schedule an unstructured afternoon when anyone in the university community could talk to me on a personal basis. I have called these sessions the "Pedersen Exchange" and have tried to locate them in a place perceived to be "neutral territory," usually the student center. There was only one rule: people would see me on an individual basis in complete confidentiality but must wait their turn on a first-come, first-heard basis. This has been a valuable means for me to keep in touch with the sense of our various university communities, and I can report that people in this situation are very open and forthcoming.

Other personal techniques I have used to foster communication within the university include frequent breakfasts at the president's house with randomly selected members of the administrative staff at all levels. This was valuable for me, as I obtained perspectives from across the campus, but it was also a means of building understanding and a sense of community among staff members with different kinds and levels of jobs by bringing them into contact with one another. It has also been my practice to host as many events of formal recognition as possible during the year at the president's home: long-service award presentations for staff, welcome to new faculty members as the academic year begins, receptions for major scholarship winners, an annual celebration for faculty who are fellows of the Royal Society of Canada, and special thank-you events for retiring academic and administrative staff and for those who involve themselves with specific university functions, such as convocations. These kept my links open and afforded me an opportunity to hear the concerns that individuals might be less willing to communicate in a structured or formal office setting.

Communication on the campus with groups and organizations presents an even more interesting task for today's university president. As I have mentioned, progressive gestures toward "empowerment" of constituency groups have given employee organizations a voice of increased potency and assumed legitimacy. It has always been a president's responsibility to build a base of support throughout the academic community, relying particularly on a collegial relationship with the faculty to articulate the scholarly mission of the university. In today's environment, however, the faculty association is likely to perceive itself as an adversary to the president in both the setting of academic policy and the more traditional areas of collision related to professorial compensation. Involvement of faculty in university governance has become a matter of current concern across Canada, as a recent study commissioned by the Canadian Association of University Professors, a confederation of institutional faculty associations, examined senate and board structures across the universities and concluded that faculty are insufficiently represented on both types of bodies. This press for inclusion in the various senate and board processes has a range of relevant applicability as diverse as the various institutions across Canada that would be affected by any general change in governance structures. Interestingly, in the province of Ontario, a recent government commission investigating "university accountability" has proposed an alternative prescription for the constitution of institutional governing boards that would realign them toward increased representation from outside the institutions, presumably to provide a more accurate reflection of the diverse external community within which they operate and to which they are ultimately responsible.

From this discussion, it might be assumed that a good deal is "in the wind" with regard to university governance issues across Canada. That may be true, and the sense of suspension while things work themselves out is not particularly healthful for ongoing decision-making processes within the universities. It is in this context that internal communication within institutions assumes particular importance. All constituencies and advocacy groups should feel that they are getting the true and complete story and that they have a role in shaping its next chapters. As I look at my own experience as a university president, I feel that a balance must be struck between personal accessibility and the established structural mechanisms designed to see proposed changes through their proper course of approval within the appropriate governance structures. At times, this balance is difficult to achieve.

In 1993, following several years of budgetary constraint and a variety of collegial mechanisms to affirm and enact the principle of differential allocation of resources within my university, a recommendation came forward to terminate programs in one of our primary academic units. This would entail closing one of 17 faculties—to be precise, a graduate school of journalism with national eminence and international standing. On behalf of the university, I advanced this recommendation to the academic community at large and, in a more detailed and specific way, to the senate committees responsible for academic planning and policy. The committee discussions were lengthy and wrenching, resulting finally in a recommendation to the university senate that the proposals for closure be supported in the context of institutional academic priorities. At a special session of the senate, impassioned discussion covered all sides of the issue, but a motion for closure was passed by a conclusive margin.

The senate as an academic forum must, however, see its decisions ratified by the university's board of governors, in which fiduciary responsibility for university affairs is ultimately invested. The board is charged with conducting the university's business in the context of a broad perception of the public interest. Here, the debate took on an entirely new configuration, as those within the journalistic community in Canada and abroad were marshaled to convince board members from within and outside the university that the "information age" requires educated journalists to shape the public judgment and that a diminution of journalism education in Canada would be irresponsible on every possible level. On the day of the vote, at an open and public board meeting, the room was filled with reporters and cameras and, at the end of a vigorous debate, the senate proposal to eliminate journalism programs was defeated by a single vote. At the University of Western Ontario, therefore, programs in journalism continue to be offered at one of Canada's premier graduate schools.

In some ways, this could be seen as a major leadership crisis. It was not. As president, I carried a recommendation, which I supported, through the established processes of an academic review and senate approval. In transmitting it to the board, I acted as spokesman of the academic community and as chair of the senate, presenting our arguments thoroughly and directly. The board of governors chose to set another course for the university, and I and my successors share a commitment to work with the board to assure the appropriateness and legitimacy of that course.

During the course of discussing and acting upon the proposal for closure of an academic unit, questions naturally arose as to the validity and appropriateness of the process. As president, I continually stressed the openness of decision making and the collegiality of the course of discussion. The initial proposal was put before the university in a public way for the broadest possible consideration; the formal recommendation to eliminate programs was carried through the senate committee structure, with every possible implication being considered. Presentation to the board was surrounded by media attention and fervent representations from within and outside the university. At every stage in the process, the widest possible expression of judgment was solicited and acknowledged.

As an institution, the University of Western Ontario did not succeed in cutting an academic program to define our institutional priorities. The structural checks and balances of our senate and board systems worked to counter an academic decision in a broader political realm. This may be read as external interference or the "sober second thoughts" that are a characteristic of the bicameral system of governance in Canadian universities. In neither case, however, does the decision at my university represent a "go slow" signal to presidents, since the circumstances were unique and the arguments legitimate and strong on both sides of this particular question.

Of more enduring importance is the issue of presidential authority in questions of essential university identity. It is very useful to define the role of a president in establishing the mission and vision of any particular institution: does the president formulate, articulate, or execute the design? Does the president build a consensus by consulting with the collegium, or does the leader define a mission for the institution in personal terms?

The answers to these questions vary by circumstance and institution. More than frequently, presidents are appointed to change the directions of particular universities, but these new leaders should be very careful not to reject the elements of a strong tradition upon which they could build to generate support among potentially valuable constituencies. These new presidents should also remember the hazards of navigation involved in changing the course of educational juggernauts: quick turn-arounds require a good deal of maneuvering room and a fair bit of time. Build these into the equation of your agenda for change.

Despite the cautionary notes of the previous discussion, I would not want to be seen to advocate any type of complacency or any embrace of the status quo. Since I began my teaching career nearly half a century ago, I have worked for change. Education is the profession at the vanguard of new developments in science and technology and in our most revealing perceptions of ourselves. It is our responsibility to communicate the discoveries in our individual disciplines and our larger sense of the changes in the world of learning to those students who entrust their intellectual enrichment to us.

LOOKING TOWARD THE FUTURE

Much of this chapter has been concerned with the perspectives of a long-serving university president on the current challenges confronting higher education in Canada and, quite specifically, looking toward the future. Predictions and recommendations are to be found throughout the previous sections, but their major points can be summarized by way of conclusion.

Over the course of the last several decades, Canadian universities have entered the ranks of institutions possessing legitimate claim to international stature. Maintaining this quality and further realizing our aspirations for educational excellence will be our greatest challenge. Fiscal constraint has already had severe impacts on our ability to recruit the most outstanding faculty and provide them with the facilities and resources necessary to achieve their full potential. Remaining competitive in the academic marketplace will not be easy for universities that are reducing their budgets and, in many cases, having to freeze or roll back salaries of both academic and administrative staff. Our human resources are our most valuable asset, as they are our future and the key to all we do as a scholarly community. It is here that the most devastating effects of continued financial stress will be felt.

Recruitment of the best people also includes competition for the best undergraduate and graduate students. While assembling a great faculty is the first step toward an outstanding university, the students hold the future promise and the reputation of any institution. Also, bright and eager students are the truest stimulant to the committed teacher and researcher: quality builds upon quality, and success breeds continued success. Our aspirations toward excellence, however, run somewhat counter to the prevailing political emphasis on the numerics of higher education. We must guard against attempts to arrive at university systems that are merely extensions of secondary school for a generation of students who will be further trained in basic rather than advanced intellectual activity. There is increasing pressure toward homogenization of postsecondary education in Canada, and the universities must resist this.

The fiscal environment of deficit reduction through spending control is, however, a reality at both the federal and provincial levels. Universities will be getting less, and they will need to devise strategies to confront the undoubtedly wrenching times ahead. On the positive side, this will involve increased attention to revenue generation from outside the university: fund-raising on a scale heretofore unknown in Canadian higher education will have to bring us much closer to the American model; cultivation of increased interaction with business and industry will be necessary to sustain our vital research efforts and bring new facilities and equipment into the university. External partnerships with the corporate world, with all levels of government, and with constituencies such as alumni, parents, and friends of higher education will be increasingly important to ensure the commitment to excellence of Canadian universities.

On a less positive note, the shrinking resources available to sustain our academic activities will require some very hard choices about the range and scope of those activities. Individual institutions will have to redefine their mission and priorities in light of a new fiscal environment. As I noted, drawing from my own experiences, this is not an easy or a harmonious process. It will require some reevaluation of the collegial processes by which serious institutional decisions are made and a reassessment of the roles taken by officers of the universities, their senates, and their boards in following through on a commitment to quality through selectivity. There is very little likelihood that any university will be able to continue for another decade in the precise configuration in which it exists today. These reshaping decisions, since they will be self-defining, must come from within the institutions. The choices themselves must rest within the individual academic communities that will be most immediately affected and that will be shaped by their results.

Universities in Canada, as in countries throughout the world, are among society's most resilient institutions. They have endured for nearly a millennium both because of their commitment to the residual values of the acquisition and transmittal of knowledge and because the very intellectual ferment within them is a force for change. No other type of community is better equipped to shape and articulate its future, and this is the challenge we face.

NOTE

1. At the time of this writing, the deregulation of international student fees was under discussion within the Ontario government. The current differentiation has created a situation in which the small number of international students coming to Ontario universities has actually decreased international fee revenues. University presidents are pressing for a deregulation that would allow fees to be differentially set across programs, particularly to encourage international graduate student enrollments.

REFERENCES

Department of Human Resource Development. 1994. *Improving social security in Canada* (The Green Paper). Discussion Paper, 5 October. Ottawa.

Department of the Secretary of State of Canada. 1992. *Profile of higher education in Canada.* 1991 edition. Ottawa.

FURTHER READING

American Academy of Arts and Sciences. 1993. The American research university. *Daedalus: Journal of the American Academy of Arts and Sciences* 122 (4).

Bercuson, D.; R. Bothwell; and J. L. Granatstein. 1984. *The great brain robbery: Canada's universities on the road to ruin.* Toronto: McClelland and Stewart.

Cabal, A. B. 1993. *The university as an institution today: Topics for reflection.* Paris: UNESCO Publishing.

Commission of Inquiry on Canadian University Education. 1991. *Final report.* Ottawa: Association of Universities and Colleges of Canada (AUCC).

George, P. J., and J. A. McAllister. 1994. *The expanding role of the state in Canadian universities: Can university autonomy and accountability be reconciled?* Discussion Series, Issue 3. Toronto: Council of Ontario Universities.

Harris, R. S. 1976. *A history of higher education in Canada, 1663–1960.* Toronto: University of Toronto Press.

Holmes, M. 1989. *The character of Canadian education: Some contemporary issues.* Toronto: Corporate–Higher Education Forum.

McKillop, A. B. 1994. *Matters of mind: The university in Ontario, 1791–1951.* A publication of the Ontario Historical Studies Series for the Government of Ontario. Toronto: University of Toronto Press.

Porter, J.; B. Blishen; J. R. Evans; B. L. Hansen; R. S. Harris; F. Ireland; P. Jewett; J. B. Macdonald; R. Ross; B. Trotter; and R. B. Willis (Subcommittee on Research and Planning, Committee of Presidents of Universities of Ontario). 1972. *Towards 2000: The future of post-secondary education in Ontario.* Toronto: McClelland and Stewart.

Shapiro, B. J., and H. T. Shapiro. 1994. *Higher education: Some problems and challenges in a changing world.* Discussion Series, Issue 4. Toronto: Council of Ontario Universities.

Stager, D. A. A. 1992. Financing universities in Canada. *Higher Education in Europe* 17 (1): 132–40.

CHAPTER 9

Mexico

Sylvia Ortega Salazar

Executive Summary. Although there has been tremendous change in Mexican higher education during the last 30 years, the current context for institutional reform and policy reorientation dates to the 1980s, when a drive for national economic "modernization" began. This new approach countered previous trends of direct public investment, protectionism, and high dependency on oil revenues; it stressed balancing the budget, liberalization of tariffs, and the development of a market economy. However, after a decade of reform, the gap between rich and poor has widened, and Mexico faces serious problems of marginalization, poverty, and unemployment.

Higher education, viewed as a training ground for the elite, has long been oriented to traditional fields of knowledge. Rapid expansion dates from the 1960s, and today, there are 794 public and private institutions, including universities, technological institutes, technological universities, and teacher training schools, with more than a million students. Approximately 15 percent of the age cohort attends higher education, compared with 3 percent in 1960. This represents a 15-fold increase in approximately 30 years, but the participation rate is still below that of other countries. The rapid expansion of the 1970s occurred in the context of strong political and union activism that gripped higher education. During the 1980s, the combination of shrinking public funding, the legacy of uncontrolled expansion, and the politicization of higher education during the previous decade led to a questioning of the quality and effectiveness of public higher education. Thus, the policies of the late 1980s emphasized reform, evaluation, and economic efficiency. New agencies and programs have been created to implement this agenda, notably CENEVAL (the

National Center for the Evaluation of Higher Education) and CIEES, an agency of the Ministry of Education and the National Association of Universities.

The author was elected rector of the Universidad Autónoma Metropolitana-Azcapotzalco (UAM) in 1989 and served for four years. Historically, rectors have had more influence outside the institution than internally, although this changed with the election of rectors chosen more for academic merit than for political influence, and with the participation of broader constituent groups in the selection process. Instituting controversial reforms at UAM, such as increasing student fees, establishing accountability measures for teaching staff, and basing salary raises on performance, required debate, discussion, and careful listening.

Mexico faces many continuing challenges: professionalizing the faculty so that more have graduate degrees, redressing the imbalance of educational services available in different regions, channeling more students into the science and technology fields necessary to national development, curriculum reform, and building capacity in graduate education. The Mexican government has developed a National Program for Educational Development, calling for better articulation among the various levels of education, as well as increasing access, especially through open learning and distance education; improving quality; faculty development; and refining organizational structures to improve institutional management.

• • • • • • • • • • •

During the last 30 years, Mexico has undergone a process of radical transformation in all aspects of social life. The educational system, specifically higher education, has not been immune. Indeed, as a highly sensitive microcosm, it has led, affected, and at times, resisted trends of change. Higher education actors have tended to play important and visible roles in the national and local political scenarios. Just as in other American countries, Mexican universities have had a prominent place in the social structure, while workers, faculty, students, and administrators have engaged, at times, in conflict within the university and with the local and national political establishment.

The contemporary context in which university reform and educational policy reorientation have taken place can be traced to the 1980s. Before that decade, Mexico's economic policy was centered on fostering internal development through direct public investment, protectionism, and a high dependency on oil revenues. Under this economic model, a relative social stability was gained through a highly centralized, corporativist, and authoritarian political structure.

By the early 1980s, world economic changes, as well as an increasing foreign debt accompanied by fiscal and commercial deficits, rendered the model untenable. Convinced that the limits of the economic policy were evident, the Mexican government adopted a new economic approach that stressed balancing the budget, opening the national economy through the liberalization of tariffs, and cementing a social agreement with workers and the business sector. In sum, the goal was to institute a market-driven economy that necessitated sacrifice but offered long-term viability.

An analysis of the first years of the implementation of the new economic strategy, known as "modernization," provides paradoxical outcomes. The actions taken not only failed to resolve the crisis, but led to a greater concentration of wealth in a narrower sector of the population and accounted for greater societal dissatisfaction, as well as for the breakdown of traditional political alliances. The question today is whether the country should continue its pursuit of a market-oriented economy or temper its economic development with more social considerations. As a matter of fact, while the country must face up to the unavoidable process of political and economic modernization, there remain the basic problems of marginalization, poverty, and unemployment, which after a decade of economic and state reform have worsened. That is the case with the traditionally exploited and forgotten groups such as poor farmers, indigenous groups, and urban medium- and low-income families.

In this context, Mexico is facing a true paradox: how to modernize in order to have greater participation in the new globalized world economy, and at the same time, how to solve the most acute problems typical of a developing economy: illiteracy, health issues, and social services for substantial sectors. Two recent events clearly illustrate the reality of such a dilemma: the integration of Mexico into the largest economic bloc in the world, and the indigenous uprising in Chiapas.

In this framework, it is possible to understand the challenges that the higher education system increasingly will be pressed to address. Not only must it enhance the quality and pertinence of its products, whether it be graduates or research, but it is also expected to become more productive in its interaction with the national society and its basic needs. Social and governmental expectations and demands toward higher education are extremely high. Indeed, the completion of a university degree was, until very recently, seen as an avenue to upward mobility. Currently, social perceptions still associate higher education with better standards of living and as an indispensable tool to compete for scarce jobs. A brief overview of the history of Mexican higher education may better explain the reasons why it is central to national development.

THE MEXICAN HIGHER EDUCATION SYSTEM IN PERSPECTIVE

During the colonial period, special educational establishments modeled after Spanish institutions were created to train the military, the clergy, and government bureaucrats. It was not until the latter part of the nineteenth century that positivist thought fostered the creation of a higher educational establishment oriented toward science and the professions. Under the dictatorship of Porfirio Díaz (1877–1910), the National University (UNAM), created in 1551, reinitiated its activities and began offering degrees in medicine, law, engineering, commerce, and the fine arts (the National University was closed in 1865 due to its conservative inclination; see Osborne 1976). The postrevolutionary state considered education a vital part of its social policy, as a means to achieve national identity, and as an instrument to foster development. Accordingly, the National University was granted autonomy in 1929 and became a model for the creation of universities in other states of the republic. More oriented toward the traditional fields of knowledge and essentially closed to the masses, the National University was regarded during the 1930s as a conservative establishment and as the trainer of an elite, incapable of providing the technical cadres needed to set in motion a program of internal development based on industrialization.

The National Polytechnic Institute (IPN), founded in 1937, was designed as the technical arm of a reformist government. Its mission was not only to engage in the construction of basic infrastructure by the state (highways, communications, oil, and energy), but also to offer opportunities to the children of rural and urban workers to achieve better standards of living. By the 1950s, the national system of higher education comprised not only the 2 large model institutions, UNAM and IPN, but a network of 10 state universities and an emerging sector of private institutions of higher learning. Moreover, the institutionalization of academic careers through the assignment of the first full-time faculty contracts in 1954 laid the basis for further development of the academic establishment.

UNCONTROLLED EXPANSION AND IMPROVISATION: THE MEXICAN UNIVERSITY, 1960–1985

At present, the Mexican higher education system includes 794 institutions[1] classified into four distinct categories: universities, technological institutes, technological universities, and teacher training schools (see Exhibit 9.1 and Figure 9.2). Classified by their main source of funding, institutions may be public or private. In the first case, they are subsidized by the federal government or by a combination of federal and state appropriations, while in the second, although they are granted recognition by the Ministry of Education, they are not eligible for direct governmental support.

634 institutions distributed in four subsystems

Universities
  • **Public**
  • **Private**

Technological Institutes
  • **Instituto Politecnico Nacional (IPN)**
  • **Regional Technological Institutes**

Teacher Training Schools
  • **Public**
  • **Private**

Technological Public Universities

160 Colleges, Military Academies and other kinds of institutions

Total: 794 institutions

MEXICAN INSTITUTIONS OF HIGHER EDUCATION (PODER EJECUTIVO FEDERAL 1996)

EXHIBIT 9.1

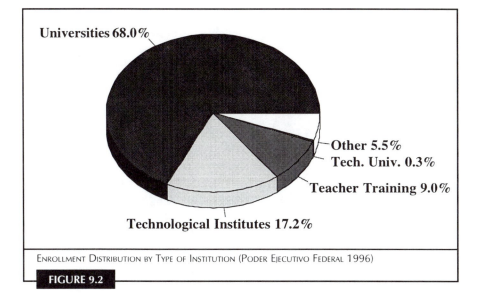

ENROLLMENT DISTRIBUTION BY TYPE OF INSTITUTION (PODER EJECUTIVO FEDERAL 1996)

FIGURE 9.2

The predominant organizational model until recently was the napoleonic university, in which teaching and research were more-or-less specialized functions, conducted by schools and institutes, respectively. It was not until the mid-1970s that departmentalized institutions started developing, thus reenergizing the professionalization of faculty, although in a context of a patent lack of personnel with graduate degrees.

The effort to develop faculty members and to design an academic career has been the subject of ongoing debate. Up to the mid-1980s, the predominant rationale tied academic contracts to labor rights, thus confounding the two arenas. Indeed, faculty recruitment, development, and performance were part of negotiation packages between authorities and unions. By the same token, student admission into higher learning institutions was limited only by the number of available spaces and not subject to any test of ability or knowledge.

The rapid expansion of the demand for higher education, as well as for other services such as housing and health, may be correlated with two phenomena: first a demographic transition resulting in a dramatic population growth and urban concentration, and secondly, a sustained economic cycle from 1958 to 1970 that was largely dependent on import substitution and industrial protectionism, although it was capable of stimulating internal market growth and consequently caused the expansion of the urban middle class.

As a result, enrollment increased at an uncontrolled pace for over 30 years, while faculty without appropriate academic credentials had to be recruited into an increasing number of institutions that were inadequately planned and funded. The pace of the process is documented in the following paragraphs; see also Table 9.3.

Enrollment

From 1960 to the early 1990s, the undergraduate student population has grown 15-fold, numbering close to 1,183,000 by 1994 (ANUIES 1995). A large proportion of this growth may be explained by female participation, a phenomenon especially visible after 1977. Over the next 15 years, women's enrollment grew by 256 percent, with the largest relative participation rates in fields such as engineering and technology, social sciences, and administration. By 1993, women accounted for close to 44 percent of total enrollment, in contrast to 16 percent in 1970.

In terms of access, it is worthwhile to note that in 1960, less than 3 percent of the national population in the 20- to 24-year-old age group attended institutions of higher learning, while by 1990, the number increased to 15 percent. Despite the obvious positive trend, access remains below that of other countries.

Higher Learning Establishments

The number of principal institutions, numbering 50 in 1960, grew to 372 in 1992;[2] of these, almost 50 percent had less than 500 students each. Private

TABLE 9.3

Basic Data of Selected Higher Education Institutions (Gil et al. 1994)

	1960	1970	1980	1992
Institutions	50	115	271	372
Undergraduate Enrollment	78,000	225,000	840,000	1,125,805
Higher Education/ Total National Enrollment	2.7%	5.8%	13.5%	15%
Faculty	10,749	25,000	79,000	113,238

universities constitute the fastest growing sector; their number has increased 10-fold. This rate of growth contrasts with a slower increase in the number of public institutions. It is also noteworthy that new types of higher learning establishments, focused on technological education, were founded during the 1980s in an attempt to increase capacity and to give opportunities to a more diversified social spectrum.

Faculty

As a consequence of the expansion of the system, new academic positions were created in a very short period of time. In 1960, there were 10,749 professors and by 1992, the figure was 113,238. This growth was especially intense from 1970 to 1985, when the rate was 12.92 newly recruited professors per business day. In most cases, new graduates and even personnel without a bachelor's degree were assigned teaching and research responsibilities.

Regionalization

In 1960, 67 percent of the national enrollment was concentrated in the Federal District (greater Mexico City), but by 1990 this percentage was reduced to only 30 percent. Despite that fact, the Federal District and only three states (Nuevo Leon, Jalisco, and Estado de Mexico) still accounted for 47.7 percent of the enrollment in 1993.

Educational Offerings

In 1960, there was little diversification of academic programs if we consider that almost 70 percent of all programs were in some type of engineering field. By 1993, there were 3,983 programs within 6 major study areas. It should be noted that in 1970, engineering and technology accounted for 31.5 percent of enrollments, while social sciences and administrative disciplines had grown to 40 percent. By 1990, the latter's numbers had grown to 50 percent. Graduate programs, for their part, have grown in almost every area, although current enrollment represents only 5 percent of the total.

FORCES FOR CHANGE

Clearly, the Mexican higher education system has been inextricably related to national politics and events. The 1970s witnessed not only the pressure created by the demand from students who had access to primary and secondary education in the previous decade and who were then demanding access to higher education, but also the political aftermath of the student revolt of 1968. The federal government's response was a more active public policy largely aimed at restoring its credibility and control over the middle income urban sectors.

In summary, efforts were made to expand the availability of educational services. It must be pointed out that this boom came under conditions in which many public universities were dealing with strong political and union activism, which relegated academic matters to a secondary priority. At the same time, emphasis was put on institutional planning as a mechanism to control the growth and governance of the institutions, as well as to coordinate the system as a whole.

Paradoxically, during the mid-1980s, as Figure 9.4 documents, public appropriations for higher education began to shrink, due to reductions in public expenditures, a key objective of economic and state reform. Institutions, more concerned with growth than with quality, began to suffer on account of the previous decade's rapid and uncontrolled expansion, and because of their inability to respond to the needs of the job market by preparing well-trained professionals. Higher education and universities were increasingly perceived as places of conflict and inefficiency. In turn, private institutions were seen as better than their public counterparts, thus explaining their expansion. Deteriorating salaries, the reduction in spending on the institutional infrastructure, and at the same time, the necessity of opening the doors to greater numbers of new students, all contributed to a deterioration in the quality of public institutions.

By the end of the 1980s, a shift in public policy was made in response to this situation. Modernization was made a major goal, based on improving education and an emphasis on evaluation rather than planning. This new approach has been utilized as a mechanism to assign public funds, to reform the curriculum and academic programs, to determine faculty productivity, and to link institutions to the business sector. Also, these new evaluation and budgeting mechanisms serve to strengthen public scrutiny of institutions and to make them accountable. The new strategy was actively applied beginning in 1989. It included, among other items, applying economic incentives to retain faculty members and to encourage their further preparation and development; using institutional and program evaluation as a basis for assigning resources within and among universities; and narrowing the scope of funding policies for

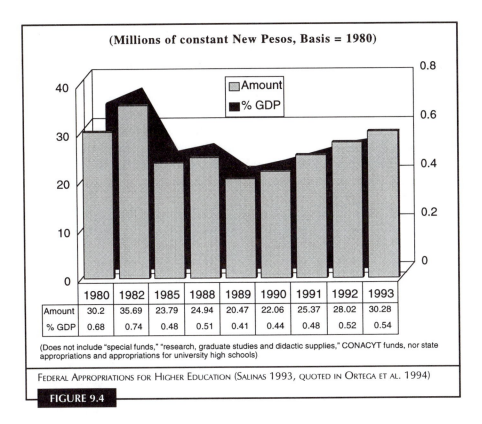

(Millions of constant New Pesos, Basis = 1980)

	1980	1982	1985	1988	1989	1990	1991	1992	1993
Amount	30.2	35.69	23.79	24.94	20.47	22.06	25.37	28.02	30.28
% GDP	0.68	0.74	0.48	0.51	0.41	0.44	0.48	0.52	0.54

(Does not include "special funds," "research, graduate studies and didactic supplies," CONACYT funds, nor state appropriations and appropriations for university high schools)

FEDERAL APPROPRIATIONS FOR HIGHER EDUCATION (SALINAS 1993, QUOTED IN ORTEGA ET AL. 1994)

FIGURE 9.4

graduate programs (through a national and international ranking of graduate programs of excellence) and for funded scientific research projects. The evaluation approach necessitated the creation of specialized bodies, such as CENEVAL (National Center for the Evaluation of Higher Education), an independent agency responsible for the design and application of standardized tests, and CIEES, an agency of the Ministry of Education and the National Association of Universities (ANUIES), which conducts institutional and academic program assessments through peer review.

The government's funding policy, traditionally a function of the size of enrollment, has been moving gradually in parallel fashion toward a new scheme focused on the quality of education, research, and infrastructure projects. One of the most visible funding mechanisms, FOMES (Funds for Educational Modernization), supports new programs and infrastructure on the basis of the submission of proposals subjected to review. Along the same lines, the federal government has been encouraging institutions to look for additional sources of revenues, derived from tuition and fees, external contracts, donations, and linkages with industry.

The varied responses of institutions to university reform can be explained by the heterogeneity of Mexican institutions. Each institution perceives, in its own way, that its autonomy could be threatened by modernization and changes in funding mechanisms. Some universities have moved from schemes grounded on politically based relationships among internal groups toward a new way of decision making grounded in academic considerations and internal demands. In all cases, managing change while keeping in mind the sensitivity of internal groups has created tensions in relationships among administrators, faculty members, employees, and students. This has required a special kind of leadership at all levels of the organizations in order to conduct institutional change.

THE MEXICAN BRAND OF UNIVERSITY LEADERSHIP

The process through which a university rector in a contemporary public institution is selected is not only a largely unknown and diverse process, but also an unexplored phenomenon. Contradictorily enough, the rector, as the highest authority in a university, typically will have almost unlimited influence within the community and will command a very significant amount of resources. Not surprisingly, the election of a rector is an event that mobilizes students, faculty, and administrators, as well as relevant sectors of non-university influence groups. Each public university has its own specific methods for electing a rector, but the elections at all institutions are dominated by a similar spirit, characterized by the participation of various internal groups such as faculty, students, and staff. Such is not the case at private universities, where generally the rector is selected by a governing board in a less inclusive process.

Of course, internal regulations determine the formal process. In general, at public institutions, such norms are decided within academic bodies where students, faculty, deans, and all other employees are represented in varying proportions. However, form and substance are far from each other. In fact, academic and programmatic platforms have tended to be less influential in the final decision than the political influence, charisma, and external ties of contestants.

There is a recent trend, and a very healthy one indeed, toward paying more attention to the academic merit, commitment, and service records of candidates in the election of the rector. A positive expression of maturity can be seen in several normative bodies that stress academic merit and past performance as basic criteria to select authorities.

This last trait has been a salient characteristic at the Universidad Autónoma Metropolitana (UAM), an institution established in 1974 with the explicit intention of innovating existing academic models. UAM was the first public university with a departmentalized structure. Currently it has an average enrollment of 43,000 students and approximately 3,000 faculty members. The institutional design required full-time faculty especially well suited to develop ambitious research agendas. Organized as a three-campus system, UAM's governance is the responsibility of collegiate bodies.

During its short existence, this university has consolidated its model, has excelled in its academic performance, and has become a national reference on account of its continuous dedication to planning, self-assessment, and budgeting. In all of those processes, academic bodies have a fundamental role.

Accordingly, the institution has devised precise rules to select its academic authorities. Department heads are selected from a set of three candidates who are nominated by the rector after hearing the opinions of the professors, students, and workers. The selected candidates are expected to publicly defend a working plan for their tenure. The final election is made by the academic division's internal council, in which student and faculty representatives have the majority of the votes. Division directors, who are expected to oversee department activities, are elected through a similar process. However, in the case of the division directors, the university council is the responsible body for the final designation. In contrast, the UAM campus and system rectors are selected in a more open contest. According to its bylaws, any member of the Mexican academic community is, in principle, eligible to stand for election. The university governance board, composed of distinguished faculty from within and outside the institution, decides who will head the institution for a four-year, nonrenewable term. The most obvious candidates for the position are typically the directors of the academic divisions, although high-ranking administrators are sometimes in contention.

The regulations at UAM have rendered extremely positive results as the selection of new leaders has increasingly become a participative and academically oriented process, albeit a highly complex and tense event. In 1989, I was selected as rector of UAM-Azcapotzalco, the largest campus in the system with about 16,000 students. To my surprise, it turned out that a woman had never before been elected to a rectoral position in a public university in Mexico's history, a fact that gave added visibility to the election.

The Challenges and the Opportunities: Establishing Leadership

As in any previous change, the one in which I participated aroused alignments around candidates. On this occasion, an explicit agreement among the contenders that the future of the institution was at stake made for an essentially respectful and clean contest of ideas and provided the opportunity for the participation of informed members of the community in large proportion. The only obstacle, but an important one, was the opposition of a small, isolated group of "radical" students that took it upon itself to "defend the interests of the majority." In the midst of unintelligible declarations, the group managed to put together a series of demands that ranged from cut-rate photocopies to the implementation of a different procedure to select the rector based on the direct vote of all members of the community, most conspicuously the student body, whom they regarded as the source of "democracy." Fortunately, the influence of the group among mainstream faculty and students proved to be negligible. The fact that contenders had agreed to participate under the established process, with passion but with respect, allowed for a legitimate selection. Nevertheless, the visible leaders of the student movement decided to engage in a hunger strike before the final decision was announced.

The incoming rector is sworn into office in a public ceremony that is well attended by the members of the community, educational authorities, and the media. This is the first public appearance of the rector and is planned carefully because it will convey an image of the leadership style of the administration. Preparing a ceremony with the menace of strikers intruding upon or boycotting what is essentially an academic event necessitated appealing to supporters and former contestants to unite around the institution.

This concern over a disruption of the ceremony turned out to be an opportunity to establish leadership based on the active participation of my colleagues and students. It forced me to begin my tenure by pursuing direct dialogue with groups of faculty and students and to present my ideas while remaining open to criticism and alternative proposals. My lack of experience in the face of the responsibilities of the new position was soon resolved through continuous dialogue and by a sincere willingness to accept counsel from my more experienced and older colleagues, on whom I depended to organize a dignified first public appearance. The inauguration ceremony was a major success, and the press coverage facilitated the communication of my leadership style, one based on the recognition of personal limitations but confident of the force of collective, responsible action; one that acknowledged institutional fragility but was certain that through dialogue and reason, academic projects can prosper and develop; one that conceived the rectorship as a place for service rather than as a platform for a political career.

Inspiration, Timing and Responsiveness: The Qualities of Successful University Leadership

I had the rare opportunity of heading my university during the years when reform was the predominant theme. It was a period that demanded judgment calls that were crucial to the definition of the content and pace of implementation of educational and policy measures. These were initiatives that shook long-time traditions and that affected unquestioned "rights." Some of the new measures included an increase of student fees, and wages and promotions for faculty based on merit rather than length of service. Other new policies included the introduction of differential earnings defined by productivity and quality of academic performance, and the subordination of budgetary and administrative decisions to academic considerations.

Even in an institution like UAM, founded to be a model of modernity and efficiency, daily practices and internal relations were permeated by the predominant university culture. Unionization had fostered untenable labor relations and permitted privileges that demanded the use of scarce resources to support a pathetically inefficient bureaucratic structure, to the detriment of academic needs. Although many faculty members had full-time positions, they had little stimulus to develop and even honor their basic obligations toward their students and colleagues. Despite its efforts, the university as a whole had not placed enough emphasis on its performance in terms of graduation rates and acceptance of alumni into the job market. Although planning, and to some degree, self-assessment, were not alien to departments and divisions, it was not clear what next steps needed to be taken based on their results; therefore, many well-identified problems remained basically unresolved.

UAM in those years was a very young institution (as it still is); however, it was rapidly becoming a national model. Both facts made it a university inclined to respond to the demands of the times. The reorientation of government policy directed toward higher learning institutions was, indeed, an opportunity for UAM to become more effective in accomplishing its founding principles and add momentum to its process of consolidation. The two basic instruments of policy, evaluation and assignment of resources according to results, were logical developments of the emphasis on planning and the basis of programmed substantive activities that were explicit components of our university culture from the beginning. Even with that important advantage, the transition was far from painless. Legitimate concerns over the neglect of values such as equity, commitment to the needs of the poor, and internal democracy, seemed unavoidably opposed to concepts such as academic merit, efficiency, and decision making based on academic considerations.

Debate and sensitive promotion of gradual change, grounded in large sectors of the community, were the means through which UAM cemented its transition. Serious and responsible self-studies that invited external evaluation, a decisive action stressing faculty development and the defense of high quality research, have proved to be the cornerstones of institutional development. Continuity in policy orientation and a major effort centered on accountability have given social legitimacy and political credibility to what is now an exemplary institution, fortunately not isolated from others that have enacted similar policy measures.

I had four years to represent my peers and to discuss with them the renewal of a shared academic project. I benefited from the opinions of those who opposed me and those who were in favor of me, and I learned to stay the course no matter what the consequences. I was fortunate enough to find out that one must build consensus based on values and convictions, even when it means losing popularity.

LOOKING TOWARD THE FUTURE

Maintaining and improving the transformation process that has begun is crucially important, not only for UAM-Azcapotzalco, but also for all public and private universities in Mexico. Universities have achieved some important accomplishments in recent years, such as the breaking of negative patterns and recognizing the importance of quality. Despite these outcomes, it must be said that structural and contextual characteristics that influenced public policy for higher education at the beginning of the 1990s still are present. As it has been pointed out, the Mexican higher education system continues today to deal with the consequences of an accelerated and, in several cases, unplanned expansion, which resulted in a low level of academic preparation and professionalization of the faculty body. This continues to be an important restriction in development efforts at universities and to the pursuit of goals such as the self-sustainability of Mexican science and technology.

Table 9.5 shows the degrees held by the professoriate teaching in undergraduate programs. It can be seen that the proportion of those holding advanced degrees is extremely low. Table 9.6 illustrates that only a small percentage of the total national faculty body has a full-time contract. It is important to mention that both institutions and umbrella organizations such as the Mexican Association of Universities and Higher Education Institutions (ANUIES) have developed aggressive and ambitious programs for faculty development aimed at resolving this problem.

Also, some imbalances such as the inequity in the level of educational services available in various regions and a distorted distribution of the enrollment concentration have not been solved and continue to be important items on the agenda. The fact is that despite the diversification and decentralization process that has been stressed recently, several states still have few options for their students, not only at the graduate level, but at the undergraduate, as well. Four states, as it has been mentioned, constitute almost half of the national enrollment. The rate of persons with a higher education degree is higher in those four states (22.75 percent of the 20–24 age population) than in the states with a lower economic development level such as Quintana Roo, Chiapas, and Oaxaca, in which the mean is 6.85 percent (Taborga 1995).

Students are increasingly choosing to study social sciences, as Table 9.7 and Figure 9.8 illustrate. This trend is to the detriment of important areas for

TABLE 9.5

Highest Academic Degree of Faculty Members Teaching in Undergraduate Programs, 1994 (ANUIES 1996)

	Public	%	Private	%	Total	%
Technical Level	1,170	1.7	318	1.04	1,488	1.52
Baccalaureate	46,815	69.5	21,911	72.11	68,726	70.31
Post-baccalaureate Specialization	6,200	9.2	1,656	5.45	7,856	8.03
Master's Degree	11,058	16.4	5,576	18.35	16,634	17.00
Doctorate	2,112	3.1	922	3.03	3,034	3.10
Total	67,355*	100.0	30,383**	100.00	97,738	100.00

*25,337 are not included because there are no data available regarding their credentials.
**215 are not included because there are no data available regarding their credentials.

TABLE 9.6

Undergraduate Faculty by Work Status, 1994 (ANUIES 1996)

Work Status	Public Institutions	%	Private Institutions	%	Total	%
Full Time	29,431	31.7	4,123	13.50	33,554	27.21
Part Time	7,591	8.2	2,276	7.43	9,867	8.00
Hourly Basis	55,670	60.1	24,199	89.08	79,869	64.70
Total	92,692	100.0	30,598	100.00	123,290	100.00

TABLE 9.7

Undergraduate Students in Universities and Technological Institutes: Percentage Distribution of Students by Study Area, 1970–94 (ANUIES 1975–91)

Area	1970	1980	1985	1990	1994
Agricultural and Cattle Raising	3.5	9.1	9.2	5.2	2.9
Natural and Exact Sciences	2.9	3.2	2.8	2.6	1.9
Health Sciences	18.6	21.5	13.1	10.3	9.6
Education and Humanities	2.9	2.7	3.0	3.1	3.0
Social and Administrative Sciences	40.6	37.2	43.8	47.1	50.0
Engineering and Technology	31.5	26.3	28.1	31.7	32.6
Total	100.0	100.0	100.0	100.0	100.0

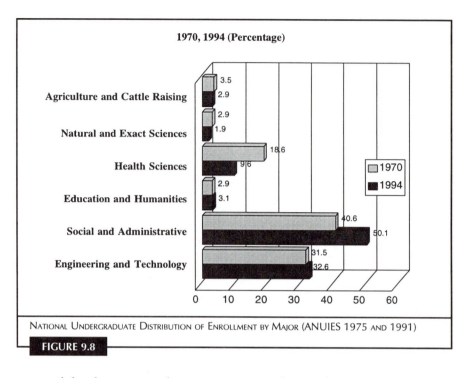

1970, 1994 (Percentage)

NATIONAL UNDERGRADUATE DISTRIBUTION OF ENROLLMENT BY MAJOR (ANUIES 1975 AND 1991)

FIGURE 9.8

national development, such as engineering and natural sciences, which have either leveled off or have seen reductions in their share of the total.

In order to build a core of highly qualified human resources to strengthen scientific research and technological development, graduate programs must receive first-priority attention. There are several indicators that would seem to support this emphasis. First, graduate students represent a small proportion of the total national higher education enrollment, and approximately 4 percent of the number of undergraduate students in the last 10 years. Second, the number of doctoral students is very small, only five percent of the total graduate enrollment. Third, institutions in only 18 of the 32 states and the Federal District offer some kind of doctoral program. Until these serious obstacles are solved, national development will be seriously limited.

In addition, and as a fundamental principle in any strengthening strategy, it must be mentioned that public financing continues to be relatively low. Figure 9.4 shows that despite a recovery in real terms in public appropriations for universities, the level of support has not exceeded the levels recorded at the beginning of the 1970s, neither in real terms nor as a proportion of the GDP. Finally, issues such as curriculum reform, institutional reorganization, and the need to play a greater role in national development through better articulation with the external environment, must be tackled with energy and creativity.

This will be crucial to face the coming millennium, in which increased interdependency among countries, accelerated scientific and technological advancement, and the importance of knowledge as a key factor in defining social and economic dynamics, will predominate. Considering that it has been demonstrated that knowledge is increasingly becoming a main competitive advantage, the development of human resources is particularly important within a context characterized by globalization, opening of economies, and creation of commercial blocs. In the new era in which communications and computers have changed the way business is conducted, world trade is becoming increasingly based on the international flow of products with high value added—applied knowledge—that is to say, technology, services, and information.

Mexico entered the global trend of international trade with its affiliation in GATT, and most recently, with the signing of free trade agreements with Canada and the United States, Chile, and Costa Rica. Other affiliations include the Group of Three and the OECD. These actions illustrate a trend toward a worldwide free flow of goods, services, capital, workforce, and information. Within this context, globalization includes not only such cross-border flows, but also a new, shared conceptualization of reality, which includes growing cultural and informational dimensions. More and more, the quality parameters for goods are based on international benchmarks. Many goods previously produced with the same characteristics to supply a big market are being replaced by goods especially designed for specific market segments that are more and more stratified. On the other hand, services associated with the sale of goods are increasingly important; in many cases, these services determine the preferences of the customers who, at least in theory, have the possibility to choose from a wide range of goods and services produced nationally and abroad. In the words of French sociologist Michael Crozier, the reign of the quantity is being supplanted by that of quality (Crozier 1992). In summary, the symbol of our times at the international level is competitiveness, which is based less and less upon reserves of natural resources or geographic location and more and more on trained human resources.

Obstacles to an Effective Agenda

In light of the phenomenon described, the federal Mexican government has recently issued general guidelines that will drive public policy on higher education for the period of 1996–2000. The so-called National Program for Educational Development reestablishes the need for a strengthened articulation between lower levels of education and the higher education sector, as well as calling for the following general actions:

- **An emphasis on increased access.** In light of demographic pressures, an expected increase in the number of students in primary and secondary schools, an increased participation rate in higher education, and the current imbalances in enrollment distribution by majors, it is necessary to expand and to refocus educational services and to stimulate the development of alternative educational models, such as open learning and distance learning education. The strategy delineated proposes the development of these two models, as well as the creation of new institutions and the planned growth of those already established. It also considers the importance of creating incentives for students to pursue disciplines related to science and technology.
- **A continuous quest for quality.** In order to support the improvement of quality, the proposal seeks to perfect assessment systems, create incentives for research, update curricular contents, expand and improve physical infrastructure, and improve funding for higher education through the use of competition-based special allocations such as FOMES and the National Researchers' System, a program established by the federal government to supplement the salaries of faculty members through a peer-reviewed competitive grants process intended to reward faculty research activity.
- **Faculty development.** As previously mentioned, this issue has a strategic impact for the future of the Mexican higher education system. Attending to it will strengthen the real possibilities of development for the institutions. The National Program for Educational Development seeks to improve the quality and professionalism of faculty and staff through innovative ways to establish, update, and strengthen incentive programs for academic productivity. This will allow that in the mid-term, the proportion of faculty members with a doctorate degree will increase, that their professionalization will be stimulated, and new ways for faculty development will be available to support institutional goals.
- **A renewed interest in relevance.** In order to attain more congruence among the universities, societal needs, and employers' requirements, the plan proposes that institutions develop a regional and local emphasis; make students' required social service more effective; redesign their organizational structures; and make major applied research an axis of a more useful and productive relationship between universities and business.
- **A refinement of organizational structures.** In order to address the management problems so apparent in such a highly heterogeneous system, the plan hopes to stimulate communication among institutions, pursue a better articulation between higher education and the

previous levels of education, and, at the institutional level, to work
toward more transparent, open, and efficient administrative and
financial systems that will make them more accountable. Also, increasing the level of additional income from nontraditional sources
will be emphasized. In short, the target of current policy is undoubtedly capacity building; that is, the construction of a strong system of
higher education, science, and technology, capable of supporting
national goals of modernization, increased productivity, and enhanced competitiveness. Capacity building demands a sustained financial effort commanded by explicit political will and actively led by
high-level national authorities. Along these lines, the highest priority
will continue to be the training of the next generation of scientists
and engineers. Indeed, only through the enlargement of a world-class
group of active researchers may the system be expected to become
self-sustainable.

National scholarship programs will continue to absorb a considerable amount
of resources. Nevertheless, it is indispensable that an important proportion of
public resources be assigned to the retention of professors and researchers
through a competitive compensation scheme. Recently promoted policy measures have had an enormous impact on the academic culture. The community
is now persuaded that peer evaluation and competition for research grants are
the mechanisms by which to identify high quality intellectual products. In
turn, the decisive government support of the National Researchers' System
has allowed for a fair, although perfectible, strategy to assign economic
compensation to active researchers. In addition to credibility, the challenge
that the national educational policy will need to address is adequate basic
wages for all faculty members. It is unreasonable to pretend that bonuses and
special compensations, important symbols of prestige and social recognition of
merit, can compensate for monthly earnings that are patently insufficient to
provide for basic family needs.

The enlargement of the pool of high-level academicians requires an institutional environment conducive to intense and lifelong dedication. In this
sense, public and private universities and research centers with demonstrated
excellence may be expected to evolve and multiply, provided that enforce-
ment of evaluation policies continues and that the flow of financial resources
continues to increase. However, the main challenges that universities and
centers will face are the development of their internal organizations, the
enhancement of their academic and scientific infrastructures, and the offering
of high-quality services. Capacity building also demands a more clear, predict-
able, and consensual set of norms and regulations for higher education. In
effect, without a legal framework that assigns specific roles to the different

social segments with vested interests in higher education and scientific production, continuity and political commitment may not be warranted.

In the near future, higher education will be increasingly questioned about its ability to relate to social needs and the technical demands of the market. This second emphasis is also part of the agenda, although in this instance, much remains to be understood and resolved. Paradoxically, at a time when competitive participation in the global economy largely depends upon technological innovation and scientific knowledge, the Mexican university, although more competent that in the past, has very few effective channels of communication with the employment and social sectors. The interface between knowledge and application remains an important area of concern.

CONCLUSIONS

Evidently, the reform of higher education is in its initial stages. The general orientation has been defined, but specific programmatic activities now need to be stressed and conducted in the midst of unprecedented social, economic, and political pressures. Leadership will certainly play a crucial role in the foreseeable interplay of social forces. Dialogue, sensitivity, and determination, although crucial components of effective leadership, will not be enough. Leaders will need to rise to expectations by being better prepared and by stressing creativity, expertise, and international sophistication. Indeed, Mexico is a part of our contemporary global world. It shares concerns and problems with other nations and it can also benefit from collaboration. It is impossible to expect to resolve our problems in isolation at a time when most endeavors are essentially collective enterprises of an international nature. Moreover, increasingly limited resources demand a proactive policy for cooperative programs in higher education at regional, national, and international levels.

NOTES

The author is grateful to Dr. Francisco Marmolejo for his help in preparing this chapter.

1. This data was obtained from the National Program for Educational Development 1995–2000, published by the Office of the President of Mexico (Poder Ejecutivo Federal 1996). However, there are discrepancies between the different sources of information such as the Ministry of Education and the National Association of Universities and Higher Education Institutions (ANUIES). Some researchers have established typologies based on the quality of the institutions and whether or not they conduct research, etc.; see Kent 1991 and Gil, et al. 1994.

2. The discrepancy between these numbers and those mentioned in the National Program for Educational Development is explained in note 1, above. It should also be noted that since 1993, "Normales" or teacher education institutions have been included in the official count of higher education institutions.

REFERENCES

ANUIES. 1975–1991. *Anuarios estadísticos 1974–1990*. México: Asociacíon Nacional de Universidades e Instituciones de Educacion Superior (ANUIES).

———. 1995. *La educación superior en México*. Temas de hoy en la educación superior. No. 1. México: Asociación Nacional de Universidades e Instituciones de Educación Superior (ANUIES).

———. 1996. *Anuario estadístico de licenciatura y posgrado 1995*. México: Asociación Nacional de Universidades e Instituciones de Educación Superior (ANUIES).

Crozier, M. 1992. *Estado moderno, estado modesto*. México: Fondo de Cultura Económica.

Gil, A. M., et al. 1994. *Los rasgos de la diversidad: un estudio sobre los académicos mexicanos*. México: UAM-Azcapotzalco.

Kent, R. 1991. Expansión y diferenciación del sistema de educación superior en México: 1960 a 1990. Paper presented at the Workshop of Experts on Mexican Higher Education Policies. México: UAM-Azcapotzalco.

Ortega, S., et al. 1994. Educación superior. In *Educación superior, ciencia y tecnología: rectos y propuestas*. México: Fundación Méxicana Cambio XXI Luis Donaldo Colosio.

Osborn, T. N. 1976. *Higher education in Mexico: History, growth and problems in a dichotomized industry*. El Paso: Texas University Press.

Poder Ejecutivo Federal. 1996. *Programa nacional de desarrollo educativo*. México: Presidencia de la República.

Taborga, H. 1995. *Análisis y opciones de la oferta educativa*. Temas de hoy en la educación superior series, No. 5. México: Asociación Nacional de Universidades e Instituciones de Educación Superior (ANUIES).

FURTHER READING

Kent, R. 1993. Higher education in Mexico: From unregulated expansion to evaluation. *Higher Education* 25 (1): 73–84.

———. 1993. What is changing in Mexican public universities in the face of recent policy initiatives for higher education? Paper presented at the Annual Meeting of the Association for the Study of Higher Education (ASHE).

Levy, D. C. 1980. *University and government in Mexico: Autonomy in an authoritarian system*. New York: Praeger.

———. 1986. *Higher education and the state in Latin America: Private challenges to public dominance*. Chicago: University of Chicago Press, chapter 4.

Lorey, D. E. 1992. Universities, public policy, and economic development in Latin America: The cases of Mexico and Venezuela. *Higher Education* 23 (1): 65–79.

Martinez, N. H. 1994. Myth and ceremony in financial decision making under stress: Case studies from Mexican universities. *Higher Education* 27 (3): 297–312.

McGinn, N., and S. Street. 1986. Educational decentralization: Weak state or strong state? *Comparative Education Review* 30 (3): 471–90.

Ornelas, C., and D. Post. 1992. Recent university reform in Mexico. *Comparative Education Review* 36 (3): 278–97.

CHAPTER 10

Australia

Brian G. Wilson

Executive Summary. In the last 20 years, higher education in Australia has been reshaped in major ways by government initiatives. Since 1974, it has been funded solely by the national government, replacing the previous combination of state and national funding. A series of important changes were launched in 1988, including the creation of a "unified national system" that funded universities under a single system, the reduction through institutional mergers of the number of institutions from 67 under the binary system to 35, and the planned growth for expansion in enrollments. Student numbers have increased by 40 percent in the last 7 years. A reduction in institutional budgets created a fund for redistribution for research. In 1991, a similar pool of funds was created to reward quality on the basis of the results of an institutional assessment. The author is skeptical that these changes promoted the desired effect of increasing diversity and options among institutions, or that economic efficiencies were achieved through the amalgamations. Although there are concerns about the methodology of the quality assessments, they have occasioned a massive reevaluation by universities of how they carry out their business and assess quality.

As the government became more activist, the higher education community needed more sophisticated and rapid responses, which they developed through an increasingly professionalized representative body, the Australian Vice-Chancellors Committee. At the institutional level, many universities have developed managerial structures, with devolution of responsibility and authority to deans, pro-vice-chancellors, and department heads that coexist with the traditional academic boards and elected committees. But these new changes are not easy to make. The author describes how, as a new vice-chancellor at the University of Queensland, he proceeded carefully to create a committee of representative persons, which after 18 months of deliberation, developed a mechanism to place financial responsibility on appointed rather than elected individuals. Their recommendation was approved by the academic board only by a narrow margin, with the provision that it be tested for five years. Other responses to the new environment include private fund-raising, intensified public relations and marketing, and intensified recruiting of international students.

• • • • • • • • • • •

Governments play an important role in Australian education, although this role varies significantly among the various educational sectors. While universities and technical colleges are almost entirely publicly established, coordinated, and financed, almost 30 percent of secondary school pupils are enrolled in private schools.

Constitutionally, in the six states and two territories, education is the responsibility of the individual state or territory government. However, because of its control over the major sources of revenue (in particular, retaining the sole right to levy income tax), the Australian government (or Commonwealth) has become increasingly involved in education. While this occurred initially at the university level, the government is now heavily involved in the support of education at all levels, in both public and private sectors.

THE EVOLUTION OF HIGHER EDUCATION IN AUSTRALIA

The first university in Australia, the University of Sydney, was inaugurated in 1850, 62 years after the arrival of the first British colonists. A powerful force for its establishment was, reputedly, to protect students from the perceived "baleful influence of the universities of Oxford and Cambridge"! Over the following 70 years, each of the other 5 states established, under an act of Parliament, a university in its capital city—a situation that was to remain unchanged until after World War II.

The Role of the Commonwealth

Although higher education had been almost exclusively a state responsibility before the Second World War, the Commonwealth government began to provide significant financial assistance in the 1940s to help cope with wartime needs and, later, the postwar increases in student numbers, which, in 1946, totaled 25,500 (Martin 1964, 12). This involvement continued until the late 1950s, largely through ad hoc arrangements—there was no formal acceptance by the Commonwealth of a long-term commitment to universities, with the exception of its own creation, the research-based Australian National University (ANU), established in Canberra in 1946.

The first major change in the balance of formal responsibilities between federal and state governments with regard to universities was initiated by Prime Minister Sir Robert Menzies who, in 1956, invited the chairman of the British University Grants Committee, Sir Keith Murray, to preside over a committee of inquiry into the future of Australian universities. This committee recommended new relationships between state and Commonwealth governments with regard to university support, including the appointment of an Australian University Grants Committee to advise the Commonwealth government, after consultation with the states, to ensure balanced development.

The Murray Report (Murray 1957) was largely accepted by the government. The Commonwealth agreed to share financial responsibility for universities with state governments on a matching grant system—dollar for dollar for capital expenditure, and $1 of federal funds for each $1.85 of state support for recurrent expenditure. The proposed Australian Universities Commission was, however, established as a statutory agency rather than a grants committee. This modification was presumably made to maintain greater government control, as the chair of such an agency would become a full-time member of the public service for the term of appointment; a grants committee, on the other hand, would normally be chaired by an external, part-time appointee.

This matching system of financial support for universities operated from the establishment of the commission until the mid-1970s. During this period, the Universities Commission operated a triennial system of planning and reporting. Every third year, the commission considered detailed submissions from each university and, after visits to campuses and consultations with state governments and other parties, recommended the levels of financial support to be given to each institution for capital and recurrent expenditure in each of the following three years. The commission also proposed appropriate levels of student enrollment and which major new academic developments, if any, should be approved for each institution. In effect, the commission acted as a broker between the universities and the state and federal governments; this mechanism encouraged increased involvement by the states in order to gain the benefits of additional matching funds from the Commonwealth.

The six original universities (Sydney, founded 1850; Melbourne, 1853; Adelaide, 1874; Tasmania, 1890; Queensland, 1910; and Western Australia, 1911) were augmented by only three others, apart from the ANU, through the

1940s and 1950s. By 1960 the student population had reached 53,000 (Martin 1964, 13). However, significant expansion of the system occurred through the 1960s and 1970s, with nine more universities being established by 1975. The first private university was not founded until 1987—there are now two, both small.

State governments were slower than the Commonwealth to establish special statutory coordinating agencies for higher education. Until the mid-1960s there had been little incentive for them to change their traditional administrative patterns. In most cases, they had to relate directly to only one or two universities. Other postsecondary institutions—teacher colleges, technological institutes, agricultural colleges, and technical colleges within the states— were under the direct control of relevant state departments.

But higher education institutions other than universities also grew rapidly after the Second World War. Existing institutions expanded quickly and many new teacher colleges and other specialist institutions were established. A second review of postsecondary education was initiated by the Universities Commission itself in 1963, reporting the following year (Martin 1964). Following the recommendations of the Martin Report, from the mid-1960s the Commonwealth government provided financial help to many of these non-university institutions and guided their development to form a separate "advanced education sector," parallel to the university sector. Called "colleges of advanced education" (CAEs), these institutions were funded through a mechanism similar to that used for universities. By 1972, there also existed a parallel recommending authority for CAEs, the Australian Commission on Advanced Education. The higher education structure thus formalized in Australia became known as the "binary system." The major distinction between the two components of the binary system was the research role of the universities, and its corollary, the training of postgraduate research students. Universities were funded at a somewhat higher level than colleges because of their research responsibilities.

Until the Second World War, the states had paid little regard to universities as places for research. Research was seen as the responsibility of the federal government and was carried out primarily by its agency, the Commonwealth Scientific and Industrial Research Organisation. Indeed, research within universities was largely an idiosyncratic activity.

Apart from its founding of the ANU as a research institution, the Commonwealth created the Australian Research Grants Committee in 1964, which provided funds through a competitive process to individual university researchers throughout the country. A National Health and Medical Research Council (NH&MRC) was later established to support medical and related research.

Consequently, by 1970, the Australian higher education system was similar to those of many other countries, with funding provided by a combination of government grants and fees paid by students. Research funds were implicit in university funding levels and were also accessible to individual researchers from external competitive sources. Research was not seen as a necessary component of the CAE sector, although individuals were not restricted from applying for external funding.

A Federal System of State Institutions

A second major change in funding mechanisms occurred in January 1974, when the matching system of financial support was discontinued. The Commonwealth, by agreement with the states, assumed full responsibility for providing all capital and recurrent funds to universities and colleges of advanced education. This led to the unusual situation, still current, where virtually all public higher education institutions remain under state influence, with state governments appointing about a third of the membership of their governing bodies—called senates or councils—even though they receive their public funding from the federal government. The advisory mechanisms—the two commissions—continued, however, as did the triennial funding mechanism. At the same time, the newly elected Labour government abolished tuition fees in a bid to broaden access to higher education.

As would be expected, increased federal involvement in the planning and funding of higher education has been associated with an enlarged governmental bureaucracy and increased centralized control. In 1977, the Universities Commission, the Advanced Education Commission, and the trades-oriented Technical and Further Education (TAFE) Commission were brought under a new structure—the Tertiary Education Commission, later renamed as the Commonwealth Tertiary Education Commission (CTEC). That commission reported, as before, to the Commonwealth minister for education.

As far as the universities were concerned, these structural changes had limited impact. Of greater significance to them was the commencement of a decade of virtually static enrollment. Only limited capital funds were made available. Operating budgets were adjusted annually to meet the costs of system-wide approved salary scale adjustments, inflationary increases in costs of materials, and costs of promotions—the "incremental creep" of the salaries of an aging staff. However, additional but unfunded responsibilities reduced budgets and morale throughout the period.

The CAE sector had continued to expand. In 1967, there were 40,000 students; in 1979, 160,000 (CTEC 1979, 7). The numbers in the two sectors were then essentially the same. With the right to offer degrees, first at the undergraduate level and then at postgraduate course level, the differences between the two sectors were diminishing. Coupled with the acquisition by colleges of research-trained staff during a period when there was little hiring by universities, the exclusion of colleges from access to research (and particularly, Commonwealth funding for research) increasingly developed tension between the sectors.

The Unified National System

In mid-1987, a new combined Department of Employment, Education and Training (DEET) was established at the federal level, and John Dawkins was appointed as minister. Much to the surprise of the tertiary education community, the Commonwealth announced two months later that the commission would be abolished and institutions would henceforward negotiate directly with the newly established department. This was the beginning of a third set of major changes to affect Australian higher education.

A variety of issues was raised for discussion purposes in a green paper (Dawkins 1987); subsequently, government policy for the higher education sector was announced in a white paper released by the minister the following July (Dawkins 1988). The policy was directed at making university education more relevant to societal needs and demands in the context of Australia's economic environment, which was changing from one with major dependence on the production and export of primary products to one more oriented to value-added industries. While changes in university management were encouraged, including reducing the size of governing bodies (some of which had more than 50 members) and giving greater authority to vice-chancellors, of much greater significance were the following elements.

First, the binary system, with its separate sectors for universities and CAEs, was to be abolished and replaced with a so-called "unified national system" (UNS), comprising institutions whose "educational profiles" would be negotiated annually with the Commonwealth department. Increased funding would be based on agreed increases in student numbers, taking into account the relative costs of the relevant degree programs.

A second element was the federal government's expressed commitment to having fewer and larger institutions, in the declared belief that this would increase student choice and credit transfer, provide better academic services and facilities, offer better career opportunities for staff, and achieve greater efficiencies.

This policy was achieved through amalgamations, with the 67 members of the binary system in 1987 being reduced to just 35 members of UNS. The exercise was facilitated through a combination of implied threats and incentives. Institutions with fewer than 2,000 equivalent full-time students (EFTS) would be excluded from the UNS and forced to seek annual budget appropriations. Institutions with more than 5,000 EFTS would be able to have "a broad teaching profile with some specialised research activity," while those with more than 8,000 EFTS would have "a relatively comprehensive involvement in teaching and with the resources to undertake research across a significant proportion of its profile" (Dawkins 1987, 34).

To promote amalgamations, financial incentives were available to institutions. The publication of the green paper had immediately given rise to a large number of smaller institutions seeking suitable university or college partners in order to pass the enrollment hurdles. The process had a certain resemblance to suitors seeking marriage partners offering the best "deal." The use of the term "implied threats" in the previous paragraph recognizes the inability of the federal government to legislate formal changes in the status and structure of state institutions. State governments, however, were remarkably compliant in introducing the necessary legislative changes.

Third, in order to increase the numbers of graduates, the government committed itself to funding a significant expansion of student numbers; this action was regarded as an essential response to changing economic conditions, and to achieving greater equity of access to higher education. Special emphasis was also to be given to promotion of increased enrollments in disciplinary areas considered by the government to be of high priority for economic growth. In part to pay for this expansion, contributions by students were reintroduced by a government of the same complexion that had eliminated fees 13 years earlier. Indeed, there was little evidence that the absence of fees had significantly changed the social and economic demography of enrolled students during the period.

Targets for expansion were set: from 475,000–495,000 in 1987 to 530,000–550,000 by 2001 in total enrollments, including higher degrees; and growth in graduations from about 88,000 in 1986 to over 100,000 by 2001 (Dawkins 1987, 11). Both targets were achieved in 1991—10 years ahead of schedule (DEET 1991, 15)! Students commencing postgraduate research programs increased from 4,000 to 7,000 in the same 4-year period (DEET 1991, 15).

Fourth, special efforts were to be directed to increasing the levels of research activity and output, with responsibility assigned to a renamed and restructured Australian Research Council (ARC) to undertake an enhanced role in allocation of research funds. To provide additional funds to the ARC for allocation to the enlarged system of universities, since the system now included colleges which had not been previously funded to do research, the Commonwealth increased its commitment of funds to the ARC and progressively reduced, over the following four years, the operating grants to the pre-1987 universities by five percent.

This "clawback" process, bitterly opposed by the universities, has been likened to "adding a second floor to one's house by dismantling the basement"! In addition, operating grants to all higher education institutions were permanently reduced by one percent, to provide a reserve fund to allow for development of new projects of "national priority." Allocation of research funds by the

ARC was to be determined on a merit basis following application by researchers in national competition for grants.

A fifth element was the planned rationalization of external studies programs, reducing the numbers of providers of distance education from 41 to 6 (later increased to 8), to be designated as Distance Education Centres.

A sixth element was the establishment of a National Board of Employment, Education and Training (NBEET), advisory to the minister. The board has four constituent councils, responsible for higher education, research, schools, and skills training, and it provides some of the advisory functions formerly held by the CTEC.

Perhaps the most far-reaching of these Dawkins initiatives, introduced over a short time scale, has been the unexpectedly successful outcome of pressure on smaller institutions to amalgamate with universities or other CAEs, in order to participate in the triennially funded unified national system. This has eliminated the formal distinction between institutions funded to undertake teaching and research—the universities—and the CAEs, initially set up with teaching mission. All but one are now called "universities."

The end result is that the number of publicly funded institutions has been reduced from 67 to 36 (one merger came apart in 1994), but no campus has been closed. In the amalgamation process, formal agreements were negotiated between representatives of the relevant universities or CAEs for endorsement by their governing bodies. These agreements have often involved the definition of a transition period during which administrative policies and procedures, developed separately by each institution, would be phased into a single set. Of particular importance were issues related to tenure and promotion, where university expectations of academic staff performance were usually quite different from those held in the CAE sector.

Admission of the consolidated body into the UNS required satisfaction of five basic conditions: one governing body, one chief executive officer, one educational profile, one funding allocation, and a single set of academic awards (degrees and diplomas).

Inevitably, satisfying these conditions has required reassignments of responsibilities of senior administrative staff, some of whom took advantage of early retirement, but there have been few, if any, redundancies in the system. Since all the merging institutions have been state instrumentalities, each amalgamation has required an act of Parliament to bring it into effect. In general, this process has taken place without significant problems or delays, since it had involved open discussion and, finally, agreement by the parties. The involvement of state governments in the discussions has been rather limited; state interests have been more oriented to ensuring a fair share of additional funding coming to the particular state.

The introduction of an "educational profile" to be agreed upon between the government and the university for funding purposes in an expanding system suggests a formal limitation of university autonomy in determining its future disciplinary growth; however, this has in practice had little real effect. Indeed, the removal of the Commonwealth Tertiary Education Commission as an intermediary recommending body to government has introduced certain freedoms to the system, with wholesale expansion of law and MBA programs whose approvals would have been unlikely in the past. Even limitations in growth in numbers of funded postgraduate research student places have been circumvented without penalty other than attracting the lower funding appropriate to undergraduate places. These "freedoms" do not necessarily contribute to a better public system.

A further requirement of government—that all institutions develop strategic plans, including missions and goals statements—has perhaps been more beneficial than anticipated when first introduced. Few institutions had given any structured thought to the development of 5- and 10-year plans, other than responding to the pressures of student interest and relating effectively to perceived needs of the communities they served. In particular, the requirement to develop a research management plan has assisted not only institutions with limited experience in research, but also those with well-established research programs.

Of the institutional mergers that have occurred, many seem on the surface to be little other than marriages of convenience for the merged institution to become large enough to gain access to the unified system and its triennial funding arrangements. Some new universities have constituent campuses lying scores, even hundreds, of kilometers apart, with little previous commonality of interest. Most amalgamations faced the difficulty of incorporating within one group two sets of academic staffs, appointed using different criteria, with different career expectations, with different academic cultures, and, industrially, represented by different unions. In some cases, entrance standards for students are quite disparate between the partner campuses for the same university degree outcome.

The professed government intent was to improve the diversity of learning experiences for a significantly larger body of students and to obtain economies in operation by increasing the scale size of the amalgamated institutions. As yet, no detailed studies as to the success in these expectations have been published. It is evident that the former CAE sector components are moving to achieve the perceived status of the "university," with increasing orientation to research activity and seeking additional research infrastructural support. The general interest in the "university" providing the norm of behavior may gradually reduce interest of academics in teaching at certificate and associate diploma level, rather than at the "real" degree level, reducing current options that relate more directly to practical training. Consequently, instead of increasing diversity, the amalgamation process may well reduce it.

While lawmakers may legislate the demise of a binary system, it would be naive to conclude that all institutions have, as a consequence, become equal. Amalgamations have created new kinds of institutions. In some cases major universities have merged with CAEs; in others, CAEs have merged with other CAEs; while some universities have remained intact. The larger, well-established universities can still be identified as a grouping which holds that the dispersal of limited research funds across a larger system is counterproductive to the nation's interest. At the same time, those universities that have had little research funding or experience seek a "level playing field." As the former CAEs gradually abandon the certificate (one-year) and associate diploma (two-year) courses, some of the technical colleges in the TAFE sector are developing new courses to take their place. This may lead to the development of a new binary system not unlike the one discarded only a few years ago.

With respect to economic gains, there is considerable skepticism about potential success. Where campuses are contiguous, there are clear economies possible in administration, provision of library and computing resources, and use of building facilities. But these are likely to be significant only where one of the combining institutions is small. After all, institutions are funded equally for teaching purposes on a per-student basis, taking into account faculty mix and the undergraduate/graduate proportions. This suggests, *a priori,* that there are no significant advantages of scale in amalgamation of developed systems. Where constituent campuses are widely separated, a condition more common than not, communication costs, particularly in person-hours through traveling, are likely to outweigh any marginal economies of scale.

While the distribution of tertiary institutions across the country was relatively unplanned and there have been some direct benefits in specific mergers, one suspects that a major element in the amalgamation policy has been to reduce the number of institutions from 67 to a much smaller number that could be more easily managed by a new government departmental structure with no direct experience of management of higher education.

International Students

Although there have been significant numbers of overseas students studying in Australia since the Second World War, following the introduction of the Colombo Plan and other aid initiatives, until the mid-1980s there were severe restrictions on acceptance of full-fee-paying students into a regime where university education was "free." With the reintroduction of payments by Australian students through the ingenious Higher Education Contribution Scheme (HECS)—wherein students have the option to pay the government a discounted up-front "contribution," standard for all faculties and all universities, or pay back through the income-tax system when they are employed after graduation—the restrictions on foreign fee-paying students have been progressively relaxed and universities have been encouraged by the government to market their courses overseas.

Over 45,000 such students were studying in Australia in 1995, compared to 1,019 in 1987, when data were first collected (DEET 1995, table 65). The great majority of such students come from Southeast Asia, but increasing numbers are coming from much further afield, including "year abroad" students from the United States. This activity has provided a significant source of extra-government funding for institutions, as well as developing a sizeable Australian "export industry" in education. It also ties in well with the increased governmental interest in identifying Australia with Asia.

Recruiting overseas students has become a major preoccupation of universities with representatives of virtually all institutions being present at major "education fairs" in Southeast Asia. Many institutions use the services of overseas agents to attract students, and some have cooperative campuses in overseas countries. The Australian Vice-Chancellors Committee (AVCC) set up a committee to assist in Australian educational aid provision in 1967; this committee became a company in the early 1980s, and at the time of relaxation of entry to fee-paying overseas students was titled the International Development Program of Australian Universities and Colleges (IDP).

IDP set up offices in overseas capitals from 1989 to provide generic material about Australian education, predominately higher education, and to provide a "one-stop shop" where would-be students could access information and enroll in institutions of their choice, even obtaining visas for entry to Australia. Although competitive with the education industry agents overseas, it has achieved effective working relationships in most cities and processes a significant proportion of all overseas entrants to Australian institutions. It now operates under the business name Education Australia.

The Quest for Quality Assurance

Quality is not a new concept in Australian universities; it has been a matter of concern since they were established. Interest in improving the quality of the university system has not been solely the province of governments. The Australian Vice-Chancellors Committee (AVCC) came into being 75 years ago to provide a forum for discussion of matters common to all institutions and has, from time to time, published reports on quality-related issues. These have included an inquiry into teaching practices published in 1965, a report on academic staff development published in 1981, and reviews of several honors courses by discipline across the university system throughout the 1980s. External accreditation of professional courses, such as medicine, dentistry, and engineering, have been standard for many years.

Pressures for more open accountability led the Commonwealth to set up a national inquiry into education and training in 1976 to examine and report on the means of evaluating the quality and efficiency of the system. Subsequently, CTEC initiated a series of national discipline reviews to examine the quality of teaching and research across the system as a whole. These reviews have included law, engineering, accounting, and teacher education in mathematics and science.

As a result of the "clawback" of funds from the universities established before 1987 to increase the level of funds available to the Australian Research Council for competition throughout the system, claims by vice-chancellors that the quality of the system had been eroded caught the sympathetic ear of the government minister then responsible for universities. In 1991, he convinced the government that a sum approximately equal to that extracted in previous years should be made available to the system to actively reward quality. He invited the Higher Education Council to consult the universities and other constituencies and advise him how this should be done.

The council, through a committee, carried out an extensive consultation process over a 12-month period, meeting with representatives of all universities in capital cities around the country, together with a wide variety of stakeholders—unions, politicians, employers and students—and inviting written submissions by public advertisement. The council's report, *Higher Education: Achieving Quality* (Higher Education Council 1992), recommended the creation of a Committee on Quality Assurance in Higher Education (CQAHE) to carry out the task of evaluating quality processes and outcomes, and provided guidelines on the appropriate approach. The minister accepted the recommendations and, after some months' delay caused by a general election, the committee was appointed by his successor in mid-1993.

The committee of nine included five members from universities, including a vice-chancellor as chair, two members with experience of industrial quality assurance practice, the deputy secretary of DEET, and the head of a state higher education office. The committee included in its membership a balance between the long-established universities, those created in the expansionist phase of the 1960s and 1970s, and those created by amalgamations in the former CAE sector; a balance in geographical representation and gender; and representation from government and industry.

Following guidelines from the minister, the committee invited submissions from the 36 institutions in the form of a portfolio of 20 pages plus appendixes setting out self-evaluations of their quality-assurance processes and the quality of their outputs in relation to their own strategic plans. Teams of five reviewers were proposed by the committee and approved by the minister. Each team included two committee members and three others from universities and industry who visited each university. The teams sought verification of ownership of policies throughout the institution and tested claims by interviewing administrators, policy makers, senior and junior academic staff, and students.

The first three years of reviews have now been completed, covering evaluation of the institutions across their responsibilities in research, teaching, and community service in 1993, and specifically in 1994 in the areas of teaching and learning, and in 1995 in research and community service.

The mechanism of self-evaluation subject to audit provides for relatively limited involvement of external examiners at modest cost compared to that of the infrastructure necessary to undertake disciplinary reviews across the spectrum of university offerings. It can provide effective assessment of strengths and ownership of quality-assurance processes within and across the university and has the further advantage of promoting realistic strategic planning. However, an assessment that covers broadly the strengths and weaknesses of an institution may provide little specific information about them.

Since a bonus of almost two percent of the system's operating grants was available for allocation in 1994 on the basis of the quality assessments, all universities agreed to participate in the program, despite considerable concern that a possible outcome could be a rank-ordering of institutions. This was seen as undesirable not only in principle but because of its likely impact on the recruitment of overseas and, to a lesser extent, domestic students. Indeed, the first report of the committee was subject to considerable criticism since media reports on the first round interpreted the committee's banding of institutions into six groups, based on evaluation of their documentation of quality-assurance procedures and of their quality outcomes, as a rank-ordering of the overall "quality" of the institutions. In addition, since funds allocated to institutions on the basis of the committee's recommendations were percentages of their operating grants, some media reports ranked lower-placed large institutions above higher-ranked smaller institutions.

Nevertheless, the self-interest of institutions in gaining both status and funds has created a massive reevaluation by universities of how they carry out their business and how they evaluate the quality of their courses and staff performance. Despite misgivings about the outcomes and about the methodology of evaluation of institutions, all institutions continued their participation through the second round.

By 1994, most institutions had made considerable effort to develop and document their quality-assurance processes effectively, reducing the significant disparity noticeable between universities in the previous year. With the more limited data available about the quality of learning outcomes—as compared with research outcomes that had been included in the previous round—the committee decided to band universities into only three groups.

In 1995, the committee evaluated institutions separately on the basis of their research management processes, their research outcomes, their improvement in research performance over the previous three years, and their community service planning and performance. Institutions were rated in each division by placement in two, three, or four bands.

The committee's individual assessments of institutional processes and outcomes have generally been well received. While there remain concerns about the methodology, which provides institutional rather than disciplinary evaluation tested on a one-day campus visit, and about the groupings of universities in what are inevitably seen as performance bands, there is general acceptance of the view that the scheme has led to significant internal institutional improvements in the overall approach to "quality." The committee is currently publishing a book providing examples of good practice reported by its teams over the first three years of the program.

Fears that the exercise would have a deleterious effect on individual university success in overseas recruiting seem to be unfulfilled. Indeed, 1995 enrollments of overseas students in Australia have increased by 17 percent over 1994 (DEET 1995, table 65)!

The Australian Vice-Chancellors Committee (AVCC)

At a system level, Australian universities have a major advantage in being able to present a united front to the federal government, which is the predominant funding source, rather than being subject to the political and economic influences of individual state governments. Apart from the funding imperative, the federal government also controls immigration policy, with its potential impact on appointment of overseas academics. (With New Zealand, we probably have the most open access to such staff, with most positions being advertised throughout the world.) The federal government also controls entry of overseas students and has a major impact on industrial legislation that affects unionized staff. It is also the major source of research funding for universities and provides a significant number of postgraduate scholarships and postdoctoral awards. Consequently, while there is now increasing involvement with state governments in relation to issues of economic development relevant to a range of government departments, the main preoccupation of universities remains with federal policies and initiatives.

Collectively, universities are members of the AVCC through the individual participation of their chief executive officers. The AVCC, organized in its present form in 1935, dates its origin to a conference of the Australian universities held in Sydney in 1920. While there had been previous meetings of university representatives, the 1920 conference was the first of a continuous series whose minutes have been preserved. It is, perhaps, characteristic of the university ethos that, whereas virtually any other organization—commercial, governmental, ethnic, artistic—would claim its origin from the earliest documented date, the AVCC dates its origin from the earliest set of minutes!

Membership grew from the 6 universities of the prewar days to the current 37—the 36 public universities plus 1 private institution. The agendas of the AVCC have become longer and more complex with the advancing years, but the hardy annuals of the nature of undergraduate curricula, matriculation standards, and timings of the AVCC "common weeks" or breaks within semesters, which were on the 1920 agenda, have lost little of their immediacy.

In its prewar days and early postwar period, the committee resembled an exclusive club. No woman graced its meetings until 1987, when the membership had reached 19. The committee related to government through mild lobbying interactions with the federal minister for education, who was rarely a member of the cabinet before 1987. It was all very well-mannered and not particularly effective in its attempts at modifying government policy. The controlling agency, CTEC, and its predecessors were by far the principal advisors of government.

The appointment of John Dawkins as minister of the combined portfolio of Employment, Education and Training led to a transformation both of higher education and the AVCC. The impact on the higher education system has been referred to above; the potential impact on the mode of operation of the AVCC was not immediately recognized—the then chairman saw no need to change his plans to take a well-deserved three-months leave overseas, leaving the author as acting chair.

The minister lost no time in proposing and effecting change, first dismissing the CTEC and then interacting with a number of selected senior university administrators—the "purple circle"—in major discussions about change to the system, developing the green-paper proposals. The action was accompanied by numerous press releases, which required a system response. In pre-Dawkins days, press releases from the AVCC were written by the vice-chancellors at their bimonthly meetings, often about events that had occurred several weeks before. This was now clearly inappropriate, and I had little trouble in convincing my colleagues that the time had come to vest in the chair, the deputy chair, and the secretary of the committee (whom we retitled executive director) authority to speak for the group without delay, with the expectation that individual vice-chancellors would refrain from publicly denouncing their statements!

I also pressed for the immediate appointment of an experienced press officer who might encapsulate our separate or collective wisdom into prose attractive to the media. A further senior administrative appointment of a deputy secretary was made to assist in developing policies. As a result of these initiatives, the AVCC became an effective lobbying group for the system as a whole. It has to be recognized that, on the government side, major initiatives in higher education were unusual and, with a new department with little experience in higher education affairs, there was perhaps less than total confidence in what might emerge from the rather dramatic initiatives of the minister.

When I assumed the chairmanship of the AVCC in 1989, relations with government had become relatively stable. Over the previous 15 months, I had established a good personal relationship with the minister. However, the higher education scene was itself changing as a result of the minister's initiatives to reduce the number of institutions directly responsible to his department. The advanced education sector was being disrupted by the amalgamation process. It was clear that it was necessary to move to a merger of the two representative bodies, the ACDP (Australian Council of Directors and Principals), which had represented the colleges of advanced education, and the AVCC. After a period of negotiations, the two peak organizations agreed to combine in an enlarged AVCC. My final meeting as chair of the AVCC, at the end of 1990, was attended by the directors and principals as observers, before their becoming full members of the enlarged group in the following year.

This marriage ended a period of public jousting between AVCC and ACDP as to which sector was more relevant to the development of Australian society, an activity that had relieved the government of the responsibility to defend many of its policies. With the combined sector representation, the new university system, acting through the AVCC, became a more effective and influential lobbying power.

FORCES FOR CHANGE

Although the university system in Australia has been through major changes in the past 8 years—amalgamations of institutions of different backgrounds and cultures; a 44 percent expansion of student numbers (DEET 1995, table 1), with a major focus on postgraduate students; reintroduction of payments by students through the HECS scheme; opening of access to full-fee-paying overseas students; emphasis on equity goals; improving credit transfer mechanisms; rationalization of distance education; federal unionization; external scrutiny of institutional quality; and improving links with industry—change remains on the agenda.

The forces for change, whether new or continuing, may be grouped under seven headings—demographic trends, accountability for quality, research needs, legislative changes, industrial developments, delivery systems, and funding issues.

Demographic Trends

A major characteristic of high school education in Australia has been the progressive increase in the proportions of students continuing for the full 12 years, from about 30 percent in 1970 to over 80 percent in the early 1990s, but the proportion is now declining (ABS 1994). The fraction of high school graduates wishing to continue into tertiary education has, however, remained relatively static, creating significant increases in the demand for higher education places. This growth was partially met prior to 1987 by expansion of the

CAE and TAFE sectors. However, unmet demand increased significantly through the 1980s and persists today even with the unprecedented growth in higher education places from 1988.

This unmet demand has peaked and is now declining significantly, in part due to a short-term dip in the school-leaver age group, and by the declining participation growth rate through Year 12. The improving employment situation in Australia since 1994 may also be a contributing factor. Consequently, the political pressure on government to provide additional university places has diminished. In 1994, the Commonwealth indicated its intention to restrict further growth to the TAFE sector. Universities that had become used to increasing numbers and almost commensurate additional funding are now faced with static or declining budgets in real terms.

Further, a historic imbalance in the allocation of funded student places relative to population across the Australian states has led to demands for reallocation of places to achieve equity of opportunity; this imbalance is currently being exacerbated by strong internal migration from the southern states of Victoria and South Australia to Queensland and Western Australia. The required number of additional places in Queensland, for example, is estimated at 10,000 by the end of the decade, a figure accepted by the government as realistic. Reallocation on such a scale would place many southern institutions in a difficult financial position. An alternative is to fund the required additional places, but the government is under pressure to reduce its own budget deficit. While it had been anticipated that the solution would probably be a compromise between reallocation and creation of additional places, the government has decided to fund the necessary places through reallocations of discretionary funds in the education budget, commencing in 1996. The funding has been provided by reducing the provision for allocation in the third round of quality reviews and by requiring accelerated HECS repayments by graduates. It is likely that funding for the quality program, if it is continued in 1996 and beyond, will be further reduced.

Accountability

As noted above, the federal government has established CQAHE to undertake reviews of universities on the basis of their quality-assurance processes and quality outcomes across the spectrum of institutional responsibilities in teaching, research, and community service. While participation in the review is voluntary, the committee has the responsibility to recommend bonus allocations to individual institutions of up to five percent of their annual government grant. This provides a powerful incentive for institutions to participate.

Although the program has come under criticism, the university system has been concerned to retain the additional dollars within the higher education sector, at a time when all government departments are under pressure to reduce expenditure. This led the Australian Vice-Chancellors Committee (AVCC) to lobby for continuation of the program for the third round, when other groups were suggesting there were higher priorities for the resources. The program was continued for the third round, although the final budgetary allocation for the disbursement was reduced from $80 million to $50 million just when the committee was meeting to review the teams' reports and to determine its recommendations.

The future of the scheme is now under consideration. There remains strong support from the university sector for its continuation in some form—not only because of a concern that the funding might be addressed away from the higher education sector, but in part because of the value to institutions in having available formal published advice from an external source to promote those necessary changes in their individual institutions that would otherwise be difficult to achieve. While it seems likely that a quality-assurance program will continue in some form, the decision has been deferred pending the outcome of the general election to be held in March 1996.

Research Needs

The removal of the binary division created expectations within the former CAE sector for a "leveling of the playing field" in provision of research infrastructure. In recent years, the ARC has had separate funding for acquisition of equipment, particularly in response to cooperative bids between institutions. On the general issue of research infrastructure, the Department of Employment, Education and Training sought the advice of the Boston Consulting Group on the needs of the system in 1992. Its report (Higher Education Council 1993, appendix C) documented the need for an immediate provision of $125 million—and the government provided $6 million in response! Nevertheless, there is recognition of significant need for equipment replacement and for provision of new equipment.

Apart from research infrastructure needs, there is a severe shortage of funding for competitive research schemes. Reflecting the increased numbers of research-oriented academic staff resulting from retirements of many staff appointed in an earlier, less research-conscious period, and the greater participation of the former CAE sector, success rates in the major schemes—the ARC and the NH&MRC competitions—have fallen below 30 percent. Such low success rates discourage many staff members from the time-consuming task of applying for grants, diminishing the enthusiasm for research regenerated by the major growth in universities over the past seven years.

Legislative Changes

A further complication, with as yet unforeseen outcomes, is the rapid move of states and the federal government to introduce legislation against age discrimination. As a result, universities may no longer introduce a compulsory retirement date for tenured academic staff and "permanent" general staff. While in one state, the legislation only affects contracts entered into after July 1994, it seems likely that the impact will become more general over the next few years. The introduction of similar legislation in other countries appears to have had limited impact on the actual retiring dates of staff; however, the rapid growth in numbers of research postgraduate students in Australia may lead to unrealized expectations of opportunities for academic positions, following earlier predictions of serious staff shortages. Inevitably, the impact of the legislation will force institutions to develop more sophisticated staff evaluation processes to ensure that significantly lessening performance in older staff can be properly identified. Since the legislation will require that any such developments apply also to younger staff, a by-product may be increasing standards for the award of tenure.

Industrial Relations

The separate establishments of federal unions covering academic and nonacademic staff throughout Australia have transformed the industrial relations scene. While federal awards in the academic sphere do not, at the time of writing, extend beyond negotiated or arbitrated salary scales, job descriptions related to levels of academic appointment, limitation in the percentage of noncontinuing junior positions, and disciplinary procedures leading to reprimand or dismissal, the areas of possible future contention are legion. On the general staff side, the main effort thus far has been devoted to rationalizing the huge variety of positions and scales that have developed over the history of higher education across the country into 10 salary classifications common to all institutions.

This process has been followed by the reassignment of staff into the new categories within each institution. The process has involved in-depth analysis of the responsibility level of each staff position. Inevitably, this has led to modifications of levels and potential salary horizons for some staff—although no staff salary has been reduced—with considerable anguish both about the outcomes and the time delay in reaching them. The process is as yet incomplete on many campuses because of the requirement to assess appeals.

The industrial situation has been made more complex because of the concurrent development of the federalization of unions and the amalgamation process. Academic staff expectations in the CAE sector, such as confirmation of appointment after a six-month probationary period and the carry over of annual leave provisions, for example, contrasted with the three- or five-year probationary periods and lack of formal leave provisions in the universities.

Even as these processes are bedding down, the federal government's interest in moving away from industrial bargaining over whole industries, such as metal-working, to "enterprise bargaining" with negotiations being at business or company level, has returned bargaining to the universities on a range of issues, but subject to ratification at the national level. These processes are only beginning and are likely to be fairly drawn out. Salary scale increases are dependent on productivity increases that are demonstrable to an industrial commission at a time when the system is reaching steady state in student numbers.

THE INSTITUTIONAL RESPONSE: CHALLENGES AND SUCCESSES

The Australian university system was modeled on English and Scottish systems of 100 years ago. Practical power was in the hands of (full) professors appointed to head up their departments for the length of their career, although the power of the registrar, in charge of the administration, was far from negligible. The university, then, comprised a set of fiefdoms based on disciplines, with a professorial board arbitrating on academic matters. The academic business of the university, including a significant role in the allocation of resources, was entrusted to committees of the professorial board.

The vice-chancellor, the chief executive officer of the university, is a relative newcomer on the Australian scene. The first six universities located in the state capitals had no full-time or paid vice-chancellor before 1920. Academically, the institution was a community of scholars, run by the senior scholars within the financial limits negotiated by councils and senates, the governing bodies of the universities, with the relevant state government.

At the University of Queensland, for example, the first vice-chancellor was appointed in 1938—28 years after its foundation—following his retirement from the directorship of the public school system. He served without remuneration for 22 years, retiring at 87 years of age! Consequently, the university was 50 years old, with over 8,000 students, before a modern-day vice-chancellor was first appointed. In the early 1970s, democracy took its toll on the concept of professorial heads of departments being approved for the length of their careers, with many universities moving to a system of elected heads serving for defined terms of three to five years, with the position being open to any full-time academic staff member. As a result, the positions became less attractive to professorial staff. In recent years, however, there has been a reversion to headships being held by elected or appointed senior staff following formal or informal advice from departmental staff.

Academic authority has remained with the professorial boards, usually redefined in the early 1980s as "academic boards," with considerable nonprofessorial and some student representation. Their financial authority, however, has become more limited with the rise of academic managerialism later in the decade, with devolution of responsibility and authority to deans, pro-vice-chancellors, and department heads, in manners not dissimilar to the North American tradition.

Reorganization of Administrative Structure

As discovered in this author's personal experience, a neophyte vice-chancellor entering the Australian academy in 1979 from a North American professional background was clearly in a learning situation. While universities throughout the world have depended on collegial committee structures to function effectively, total reliance on such structures to optimize the allocation of tens or hundreds of millions of dollars was a surprise. Elected committees worked each year with great diligence to allocate funds for teaching staff, technical and administrative staff, equipment, library, and so on, while departments heads labored to maximize the return from each of 10 or 12 resource committees. There was little opportunity to advance interdisciplinary interests or conjoint proposals—everything was a free good, if the case could be made successfully. On the other hand, even a successful department head could not transform hard-won academic salary dollars to purchase equipment or promote conference travel, or vice versa.

At a time of declining real resources, it was not difficult for me to see the advantages of a more flexible system of budgeting, where a dollar won was real convertible currency. Reallocation of resources to areas of developing strength could also be perceived to be potentially advantageous. I promoted the decentralization of funding with the responsibility for allocation to be placed on deans and department heads. It was clear that such individuals, who constituted a majority of the board, found the proposal attractive in principle. Nevertheless, the existing allocation mechanisms had been honed over decades and, with recent memories of disciplinary "barons," a move to delegate authority to individuals instead of elected committees could only be regarded with suspicion. North American experience, while relevant to this particular debate, was hardly persuasive; the concept was "undemocratic."

In these circumstances, with a clearly foreshortened honeymoon, I had only one resort (short of gambling all on appeal to the governing body)—the senate. In accordance with universal custom, therefore, I proposed to the senate the establishment of a committee to review the academic administration. Obviously, the membership of such a committee would be crucial to the outcome. The issue had been debated with considerable heat in both staff and student arenas, and considerable polarization of the community and identification of vested interests had occurred. Calls for nominations for election to a review committee could lead to polarized representation. On the other hand, filling such a review committee with the vice-chancellor's nominees could lead to a result that would have limited credibility in the internal community and consequently might prove unworkable.

The committee was, therefore, structured to comprise individuals who held the confidence of the community, having been elected by it for other academic purposes. It included the presidents of the academic board, academic staff association, and student union, as well as chairs of senior academic committees, and was itself chaired by the university librarian who was at that time also the state chair of the council for civil liberties. While I was consulted by the committee, I was not a member of it. The committee worked for 18 months and finally produced a mechanism that placed financial responsibility and authority on appointed rather than elected individuals, but supported by advisory councils. The report was adopted by the academic board by a margin of 5 out of 100 voting. Even this narrow support was probably dependent on a last-minute amendment introducing a caveat that the proposed new system be subject to a sunset clause after five years. The governing body—the senate— easily accepted the recommended structure by 26 votes to 1. After 5 years, the required review received 72 submissions, all but one of them supportive!

The adopted mechanism superimposed on the existing administrative structure for curriculum approval and student supervision by deans, a financial and personnel management structure by pro-vice-chancellors—the epitome of the committee camel! However, the camel has proven to be an effective animal and has even evoked some admiration and affection. Most Australian universities have subsequently adopted structures whereby appointed academic managers take responsibility for the allocation of resources to academic groups and departments. Institutes of technology and colleges of advanced education have usually had hierarchical management systems from their inception.

Revising the Tutorial System

A similar approach was taken contemporaneously to review the tutorial system in the university. In Australia, tutorial responsibilities have traditionally been assigned largely to tutors who have had limited career and salary expectations and whose workloads reduced their involvement in postgraduate research to modest part-time activity. With relatively few postgraduate scholarships available, research was a part-time activity for most other students. I proposed to the senate a committee comprising one senator and two members each from the administration, the academic board, and the academic staff association to review the existing system; I chaired the committee. After several months of discussion, the committee recommended a shift from the existing system to one of quarter-time and half-time teaching positions (teaching assistants and teaching fellows), whose teaching-related responsibilities would be limited to the 26 teaching weeks and with those positions available only to full-time research students. This provided modest but effective financial support to such students while also providing them with teaching experience. These proposals were accepted by the board and senate. The change was phased in over three years to limit departmental and personal dislocations; it has stimulated a major increase in full-time research student numbers across the university. The impact on the university's research output has been remarkable, but in this instance, other institutions have not followed our example.

Initiating Private Fund-Raising

Although there are some notable examples of private endowment in Australian universities, in general, universities have not often been regarded as potential recipients of philanthropy. In part, this state of affairs may have been influenced by the government's assuming full responsibility for the funding of higher educational institutions in 1974. In such circumstances, business and personal contributions through taxation would have been seen as substituting for direct donations. Private schools and many other charitable organizations have, on the other hand, had considerable success in gaining philanthropic support over the years, and the conspicuous lack of success of universities is worthy of remark.

I attempted to change this environment by the initiation of a foundation for support of research in the university. However, rather than setting it up so that the university would be both the recipient and the controller of the funding allocations, the foundation trust has a board of governors on which the university representation is limited to its chancellor and vice-chancellor, the other governors being significant citizens in their own right. These external governors are thus identified as the group making the final decisions on how private subscriptions and donations should be used, rather than "a group of long-haired academics"!

It would be a fitting end to the story to be able to claim significant success; however, the foundation was finally established in 1983 on the downside of a boom in mineral development in the state, so that the lead-off donation came in at only 20 percent of expectation, which set the pattern for others. Nevertheless, the scheme has, over the years, identified several hundred subscribers, many of whom have been prepared to support other fund-raising efforts by the university. It has also provided a welcome source of seed-funding for research by newly appointed staff.

The development of an annual appeal program from 1990 has similarly identified a large number of graduates—although only about three percent of the total—interested in supporting their alma mater on a regular basis. This support, together with the first evidence of high-level business and government support, enabled us to raise $5.5 million toward the restoration of one of Brisbane's magnificent heritage buildings—the Customs House—in 1994. While the building provides a first-class city location for the university, the fund-raising drive also represented an attempt to change the environment for funding for universities, by identifying the university with a significant public interest in heritage.

Managerial Leadership

The crucial element in university leadership is the ability to attract colleagues of recognized merit to assume positions of responsibility in the organization. First-rate academics who may make first-rate academic managers are not in huge supply, and often the rewards in administration do not compensate for the loss of the significant attractions within academe. The University of Queensland requires that even the most demanding of senior positions engage in continued participation in the research and teaching activities of the university; these are matters of formal contract. Nevertheless, the chemistry of effective administrative teams is catalyzed by the style and personality of the executive head.

Public Relations and Marketing

At the institutional level, universities have also become much more extensively involved in professional public relations and marketing activities. In 1988, the AVCC rescinded its voluntary code of restraint on competitive institutional advertising—a move which only just preceded the arrival of the much more competitive operating environment introduced by John Dawkins. At the same time, university information offices were evolving from a relatively limited function in the 1970s—perhaps publishing a campus newspaper and acting as a point of news media contact—to multifaceted public relations services often embracing a range of media liaison, publications, marketing, advertising, protocol, special events, and other communications activities.

This transition has been assisted by the AVCC, which commenced sponsorship of national conferences of institutional information officers in the 1970s. Momentum increased in the late 1980s, and these conferences have become highly successful developmental events for university public relations professionals and help keep the sector competitive with other national entities in the quest for public support.

Evidence of success emerged through market research conducted by the AVCC in 1989, which showed an unusually high level of respect for universities as public institutions, especially for their research activities—an image which, at that stage, had been fostered by a decade of sustained media promotion by several of the major universities (including my own), which recognized the natural news value of the outcomes of university research.

The value of being proactive in recruiting students and in garnering the emotional, political, and financial support of our graduates and the wider public is widely recognized in the Australian university system in the 1990s. Market research, corporate identity programs, and careful nurturing of corporate identity, together with strategic communication, are part of the contemporary way. Positive "brand image" and effective friend-raising activities are also seen as necessary preconditions for the growing aspirations in university fund-raising.

LOOKING TOWARD THE FUTURE

Delivery Systems

Although Australian universities developed with structures based on British institutions, they have been very different in important elements of their operation. In the first place, they have been receptive to part-time students, with most institutions since their inception providing classes to students in the evening. The University of Queensland has also offered its regular undergraduate courses in many disciplines by correspondence since 1911—the second university in the world to do so. For 50 years, it remained the sole provider in Australia; however, by 1987, distance education was being offered by 47 institutions (DEET 1987, 41). These developments reflect the great distances between cities in Australia and the fact that, even though the Australian population is relatively strongly urbanized, many people are not in a position to attend classes.

To provide greater efficiency, this number of distance education providers was reduced to eight in the Dawkins reforms, with the other institutions, discouraged by a 25 percent reduction in the grant per external student, largely leaving the field. Almost before such programs had been phased out, however, this provision was relaxed, since it became accepted that, if institutions could offer whatever courses they wished (with the exception of medicine), it was absurd to restrict *how* they should teach them.

At the same time as this process was unfolding, high levels of unmet demand for student places caused the federal government to endorse the concept of an Open Learning Institute (OLI) that would offer programs by public television, supported by other media. An increasing number of disciplines are being offered in the early morning and may be recorded. While courses are open to anyone, to gain credit students must register and pay the relevant fee, thereby obtaining access to written and other support material, and examinations. Credits may be transferred to any of the universities in the consortium of distance providers.

With the advent of the "global information superhighway," there is the potential for this Australian system, available throughout the country, to come into competition with courses offered by other countries, perhaps with distinguished presenters. While the advent of OLI and the various distance programs, largely conducted in print form, has had little, if any, impact on numbers seeking face-to-face instruction in universities, it is not obvious that this would remain the case if prestigious overseas universities offered their degree programs in competition. Consequently, this external "force for change" must be taken into consideration.

Funding

When the Commonwealth government assumed responsibility for the funding of universities in 1974, the grant accounted for over 80 percent of university income. The figure now is just over 50 percent. Universities have diversified their sources of research income, and they have gained access to fee payments from overseas students. The system has been fortunate in not having experienced dramatic falls in per-student support from government, as has occurred in many countries, particularly since universities have not been permitted to charge fees to Australian students (whose HECS contribution is paid directly to the government), a situation partially relaxed recently with respect to some classes of postgraduate students.

With little prospect of further increases in domestic student numbers in the near and intermediate future—indeed, numbers may fall—and the ever-present potential of reductions in governmental per-student funding as government budgeting tightens, the maintenance or improvement of universities will depend on increasing their funding levels from private sources. With the overseas student market highly competitive and subject to external political constraints, fund-raising and revenues from exploitation of intellectual property represent potential areas for development.

It is surprising that fund development within the university sector is relatively new to Australia, since philanthropy in general, and in the private school sector in particular, is well established. Over the past 20 years, the fact that the government was the sole paymaster was clearly an important negative influence. Companies and individuals paid their taxes, and their taxes contributed to the running of the universities. However, over the past 10 years, universities have started to put their house in order by improving relationships with their graduates, through improving their graduate rolls and regularly issuing magazines to establish better contact.

The oldest alumni organization in Australia dates back only to 1967 and was initiated by graduates rather than by the university. Setting up development offices for fund-raising purposes has often been criticized within institutions as money wasted or even as a rather unethical practice. Consequently, some years will pass before large scale fund-raising drives will become standard practice in Australian universities. However, in the past two years there have been two or three successful drives that raised several million dollars each.

The opportunity to raise funds through the licensing of patents or acquisition of venture capital for exploitation of discoveries has been rather limited in Australia. Although Australian scientists publish a disproportionately large number of the world's scientific papers, the subsequent development of scientific discoveries within Australia has been meagre. The modest development of a venture capital market was devastated by the 1987 stock market crash and is only now becoming reestablished. While most universities have an "arm's length" company seeking to utilize the intellectual and equipment resources of the institution, the level of profit produced thus far does little more than cover the costs of operation of the companies. Nevertheless, this is a source of real potential with increasing sophistication of researchers, managers, and external financial markets.

The Political Environment

Although the two main political parties have quite different philosophies towards participation in university studies—with Labour seeking greater equity of opportunity for all potential students, while the Liberal/National coalition supports a user-pays approach and, particularly, allowing Australian students unable to gain a quota place to pay full fees as do overseas students—there is unlikely to be significant differences in practice between them, in government.

Australian society has moved increasingly to a user-pays mode as governments attempt to reduce public expenditure, so that the large government-led expansion in higher education in the late 1980s and early 1990s is unlikely to recur. Additional expansion will likely come through increasing contributions from students, with public funding being capped and increasingly directed at first-time undergraduates, at students undertaking research degrees, and at students at the postgraduate level.

Continuing Commonwealth initiatives directed at mechanisms to bring university research and industry closer together to improve manufacturing and value-added industrial activity may be anticipated. However, there may be lessening governmental interest in directing the higher education system. For better or worse, universities are now regarded as contributors to the national weal rather than as mere providers of graduates for the professions and the maintenance of government bureaucracies.

> **Editor's Postscript.** Since the author completed this chapter, the situation for higher education in Australia changed considerably. In March 1996, after 13 years in power, the Labour Party lost the federal elections to a conservative coalition. The new government proposed a five percent cut for universities, phased in over three years, and the bill is expected to pass. This would mark the first cut in higher education funding in 15 years. Compounding the situation is the requirement that universities find the funds internally to finance a salary increase for faculty members, which is expected to be approximately 10 percent. The government has also called for higher tuition and differential

tuition rates according to academic program, and has set up a national inquiry on the future of Australian higher education. Institutions are preparing for significant reductions of faculty and staff in a period of great uncertainty (see Maslen 1996, A47).

REFERENCES

Australian Bureau of Statistics (ABS). 1994. *Schools, Australia 1994.* Catalogue No. 4221.0. Canberra: ABS.

Commonwealth Tertiary Education Commission (CTEC).1979. *Selected advanced education statistics.* Canberra: CTEC.

Dawkins, J. S. 1987. *Higher education: A policy discussion paper.* Canberra: Australian Government Publishing Service.

Dawkins, J. S. 1988. *Higher education: A policy statement.* Canberra: Australian Government Publishing Service.

Department of Education, Employment, and Training (DEET). 1987. *Selected higher education statistics.* Canberra: Australian Government Publishing Service.

————. 1991. *Selected higher education statistics.* Canberra: Australian Government Publishing Service.

————. 1995. *Selected higher education statistics.* Canberra: Australian Government Publishing Service.

Higher Education Council, National Board of Employment, Education and Training (NBEET). 1992. *Higher education: Achieving quality.* Canberra: Australian Government Publishing Service.

————. 1993. *Higher education research infrastructure.* Canberra: Australian Government Publishing Service.

Martin, L. 1964. *Tertiary education in Australia: The report of the Committee on the Future of Tertiary Education in Australia.* Canberra: Government Printer.

Maslen, G. 1996. An Australian university adjusts to deep budget cuts. *The Chronicle of Higher Education* October 4: A47–A49.

Murray, K. 1957. *Report of the Committee on Australian Universities.* Canberra: Government Printer.

FURTHER READING

Aitkin, D. A. 1994. *The universities of Australia.* London: Association of Commonwealth Universities.

Baldwin, P. 1991. *Higher education: Quality and diversity in the 1990's.* Canberra: Australian Government Publishing Service.

Committee for Quality Assurance in Higher Education. 1994. *Report on 1993 quality reviews.* Canberra: Australian Government Publishing Service.

————. 1995. *Report on 1994 quality reviews.* Canberra: Australian Government Publishing Service.

————. 1996. *Report on 1995 quality reviews.* Canberra: Australian Government Publishing Service.

Gamage, D. T. Recent reforms in Australian higher education with particular reference to institutional amalgamations. *Higher Education* 24 (1): 77–92.

Goedegebuure, L. C. J.; A. Lysons; and V. L. Meek. 1993. Diversity in Australian higher education? *Higher Education* 25 (4): 395–410.

Hughes C., and S. Cohler. 1992. Can performance management work in Australian universities? *Higher Education* 24 (1) 25–40.

Linke, R. D. 1995. Improving quality assurance in Australian higher education. *Higher Education Management* 7 (1): 49–62.

Mahony, D. 1990. The demise of the university in a nation of universities: Effects of current changes in higher education in Australia. *Higher Education* 19 (4): 455–72.

———. 1994. Counter images of Australia's movement to an undifferentiated higher education system: An analysis. *Higher Education* 28 (3): 301–24.

Marshall, N. 1995. Policy communities, issue networks and the formulation of Australian higher education policy. *Higher Education* 30 (3): 273–93.

Massaro, V. 1995. Quality measurement in Australia: An assessment of the holistic approach. *Higher Education Management* 7 (1): 81–100.

Smyth, J. Higher education policy reform in Australia. In *Reform and change in higher education: International perspectives*, edited by J. E. Mauch and P. L. W. Sabloff, 51–81. New York: Garland.

Taylor, M. G. 1991. New financial models: Australia. *Higher Education Management.* 3 (3): 246–56.

CHAPTER 11

The United Kingdom

Kenneth J. R. Edwards

Executive Summary. Higher education in the United Kingdom has undergone nothing short of a revolution within the last decade. Enrollments have expanded dramatically—by 53 percent between 1988–89 and 1993–94—representing a doubling in the participation rate of young people from approximately 15 percent to 30 percent. The government has played an aggressive role in regulation through funding mechanisms, aiming to exert greater control, demanding increased accountability through mandated assessments of research and teaching, while at the same time cutting funding on a per-student basis. With reduced government funding—now accounting for 70 percent of university budgets—institutions have turned to a number of activities to generate additional revenues.

Absent severe external pressure, a university is likely to change incrementally, through a slow-moving process of consensus building. In this scenario, the vice-chancellor is at the "center" rather than at the "top," with primary responsibility for building consensus and applying only subtle steering. Intense pressures, such as those experienced in the past few years in British higher education, have changed the role of leadership and the nature of the change process. The vice-chancellor links external constituents and the university, interpreting one to the other, balancing speed of decision making to respond to external demands with the internal cultural requirements for involvement and consultation. Devolution of power and decision making to faculties has proved to be a useful strategy at the author's university, providing a balance between centralized control, and decision making and problem solving in the units and faculties. This approach was fruitfully

applied to significant problems in the Faculty of Arts, where a committee from the faculty and the central administration was able to make
difficult decisions about reorganization and cuts.

Further expansion of higher education in the United Kingdom is
likely, but it raises important questions about the shape of universities
in the future—in terms of curriculum, funding, and the role of other
providers of education.

• • • • • • • • • • •

The United Kingdom has 92 universities.[1] There are also more than 70
colleges of higher education that do not have university status; many
of them award their own degrees for undergraduate courses and taught
master's degree courses. Otherwise, these colleges offer programs under the
supervision of universities, which then grant their degrees to the student who
complete the studies.

All these institutions of higher education are legally independent organizations. However, apart from the University of Buckingham, which can be
regarded as the only "private" university in the United Kingdom, they are all
heavily dependent on government funding. Therefore, their autonomy is
limited. Government funding accounts for 70 percent of the total income of
the higher education system (CVCP 1995). This funding includes provision of
tuition costs for virtually all British students who are undertaking a first degree
course. The total expenditure of government funds on higher education,
including that provided to support research, is approximately £9 billion per
annum, and there are now 1.4 million students of whom approximately 1
million are full time (CVCP 1995).

The significance of these facts is less in their absolute value than in the
changes that have taken place in the last few years. Table 11.1 demonstrates
the remarkable increase in students numbers in a five-year period. Because of
a decline in the size of the cohort leaving school at 18 or 19, the increase in
numbers has produced a doubling in the participation rate of young people in
higher education between 1989–89 and 1993–94. Toward the end of the
1980s, the government announced its plans to expand higher education to
reach a 33 percent participation rate by the year 2000.

Growth in the first years of that period was so rapid that a 30 percent
participation rate was reached in 1993, when the government decided to call
a halt to further expansion until 1998 at the earliest. However, the target of 33
percent remains, and it is anticipated that the growth will commence again

after 1998. At the same time that the government has promoted rapid growth of the higher education system, it has also assumed an increasingly regulatory stance through funding mechanisms. Its aim has been to exert greater control and at the same time to limit government expenditure. A considerable rise in government expenditure on higher education has accompanied the rise in student numbers, but has not matched it. (Over the period 1988–89 to 1993–94, the cost to the government rose by approximately 65 percent, and student numbers rose by the same amount.) While the cash increase almost precisely matches the increase in student numbers, such a comparison takes no account of the effect of inflation in eroding the real value of the funding. In fact, the real value of government support over that period, on a per-student basis, has declined by 26 percent (Department for Education 1995). Whether this is seen as an efficiency gain (the government's opinion) or as cost cutting (which is how the institutions see it) depends on the point of view.

Given this dramatic rise in spending on higher education, it is not surprising that there has also been a greater interest in scrutinizing how this money is used. Such scrutiny has extended beyond concerns of financial probity to processes of governance of the institutions and to assessment of the quality of academic activities.

TABLE 11.1

RECENT GROWTH IN HOME STUDENTS (DEPARTMENT FOR EDUCATION 1995)

	Full Time	Part Time	Total	Age Participation Index (under 21)
1988–89	563,000	377,000	940,000	15.1%
1993–94	930,000	511,000	1,441,000	29.7%
Growth	65%	35%	53%	

FORCES FOR CHANGE

This brief history indicates that change in British higher education has been considerable. Because it has also been very rapid, the speed of change has presented the greatest challenges to the management of higher education institutions. The major landmarks during the last 15 years are as follows:

- **1979.** The government of Margaret Thatcher was elected, with its commitment to reducing the size of the corporate state, reducing the level of public expenditure, and getting better value for the money provided by taxpayers.

- **1981.** Substantial cuts were made in the government funding provided for universities, with the cuts falling particularly heavily on institutions perceived to be of poorer quality.
- **1985.** A major review of the ways in which universities govern themselves suggested that a much stronger and more clearly focused internal management system was necessary in order to make the best possible use of limited resources.
- **1986.** The first research assessment exercise[2] was carried out on all subjects in all universities, giving each a rating on a four-point scale. At this stage, the assessment had no funding consequences.
- **1988.** The Education Reform Act transferred all polytechnics from the direct control of local government authorities into legally independent organizations funded directly by the national government.
- **1989.** The second research assessment exercise was carried out, leading to selective allocation to universities of the government funds provided for the support of research (previously, this allocation had been related directly to student numbers). Also, the government decided to encourage institutions to take more students by providing a high level of marginal funding per student.
- **1992.** The Further and Higher Education Act gave university status to the polytechnics and brought all the universities and the colleges of higher education within a single funding mechanism operated by separate Funding Councils in England, Scotland, and Wales.

  The third research assessment exercise was completed, and as a result, more than 90 percent of the general funding for university research was allocated according to the research ratings awarded (HEFCE 1994). In addition, a further increase in selective allocation of the total government funds for university research was achieved by transferring 20 percent of the funding that had previously come through the Funding Councils to other government agencies (particularly the Research Councils) for allocation to specific research projects. These changes increased differentials between universities in the level of government funding for research and reduced the amount of "free" money that any university had for research.
- **1993.** The government decided to halt, at least temporarily, the rapid growth in student numbers. The Funding Councils also initiated a series of assessments of teaching quality on a subject-by-subject basis. The nature of this assessment varied throughout the United Kingdom, but the Higher Education Funding Council for England (HEFCE) used a classification of "Excellent," "Satisfactory," and "Unsatisfactory." The English system was designed so that a finding of "Unsatisfactory" would lead to a demand by the Funding Council for immedi-

ate action on the part of the university concerned, with the threat that the funding for that activity would be removed unless the rating was improved within a year.

- **1995.** HEFCE announced a revision in the teaching quality assessment methodology; in the future, six separate aspects of teaching and learning will be assessed, each on a four-point scale.

This very intense period of change has been induced by specific government policies aimed at creating a better educated population that includes a higher proportion of university graduates. Expansion has involved an increase of government expenditures and an accompanying heightened concern to ensure value for money, but there has been more to it than that. Academics, in common with other professionals, have seen a marked rise in public skepticism regarding their motivation and objectivity in managing their own affairs. At the same time, there was a rising expectation that universities, and the activities that took place within them, should contribute more to the economic success of the nation and of local communities.

Financial pressures—in particular, those arising from the reduction in the funding per student—have forced universities to develop activities that create alternative sources of income. These activities include

- Recruitment of overseas students, who are required under government policy to pay fees that cover the full cost of their tuition
- Activities with industry and commerce that raise additional income, such as contract research and consultancy work
- Specialist courses at postgraduate level and for working people, which are paid for by students

The result of these profound changes has been an increased workload for university staff. At the same time, financial constraints, which have severely restricted pay increases, have had a detrimental effect on morale. Furthermore, these financial constraints have restricted the replacement and upgrading of equipment for teaching and research and the enhancement of student facilities such as library stocks, commensurate with the increase in the number of students.

It has to be said, however, that the pressures have had some beneficial effects. Hard decisions must be made about the justification of undertaking research unless it is of demonstrably high quality, and teaching has been more carefully scrutinized because of the initiation of teaching-quality assessments. Institutions have been forced to pay more attention to their overall strategic planning and to ensure that there are clearer definitions of programs.

THE INSTITUTIONAL RESPONSE

Managing Change

In considering how universities are able to organize themselves to respond to vigorous campaigns that arise externally, we must first consider evolutionary or internally generated change. It is a basic organizing principle of a university that it is an association of professional academics. Like many associations of professionals, the reason individuals belong to such an organization is a matter of convenience. The opportunity to practice as professional academics outside a university is severely limited. Membership in a university affords two principal benefits: first, it covers the costs of an academic's overhead (such as libraries, computer facilities, and student services), and second, the degree of specialization allowed enables the scholar to attract "customers" much more readily than could an individual practitioner. Thus, academics may regard the university as a necessary evil, and would not wish to receive much direction therefrom. There is an interesting tension between the desires of individual academics to pursue their subjects according to their own professional standards on the one hand and the concept of academic collegiality of the community of scholars on the other. In such circumstances, the role of the vice-chancellor is seen as one of providing the appropriate framework within which his academic colleagues can pursue their interests of teaching and research.

This confederation of loosely affiliated academics, known as a university, would preferably place the vice-chancellor at the "center" rather than at the "top." In other words, the process of change was traditionally one of attempting to arrive at a consensus within the university, with the vice-chancellor having a responsibility for achieving that consensus, possibly exercising some steering to do so. To be effective, such steering had to be subtle; in fact, anything that was seen as an obvious attempt to influence the direction of the university would probably be resisted by the academics as a matter of principle.

The Role of Leadership

In the context of increasing external pressure, the task of the vice-chancellor is to try to balance the need to ensure the university's survival (by being able to respond adequately to external pressure) with ensuring that the university is clearly able to develop policies in line with its fundamental mission. This requires a vice-chancellor to be much more proactive and to recognize the leadership responsibility of the position, helping the institution to interpret its purpose in the light of the changed world in which it now exists. The essence of this process of leadership is to help the university to recognize and present its fundamental aims, an activity that can be understood through the metaphor of focusing an image. The academic activities within a university can be regarded as an array of many points of light of varying brightness arranged in three-dimensional space. A lens will focus these points of light in a recognizable image. It will have a particular focal length that will determine which of the points of light can be brought into focus in a single image. Changing the focal length of the lens will change which points of light can be focused into a single image. Reducing the aperture through which the light passes will increase the depth of field—and thus bring more of the points of light into simultaneous focus—but at the cost of reducing the total amount of light transmitted. Unless all the light sources are bright, it will be very difficult to create an image in which they are all in focus.

Leadership can be seen as ensuring that the university makes decisions about the choice of lens and the size of the aperture to create an image which is appropriate for the institution, both internally and externally. But it may be impossible to satisfy both. If the external world has very little interest in the nature of the image, it is likely that the decision will be made that the image produced should maximize the range of light sources that are included. This inclusiveness may well be at the cost of generating an image that is in "soft" focus. However, pressures in the external world may make it necessary to adjust the system so that a very clear image is produced, although at the cost of excluding from the contribution to that image some of the sources of light. Indeed, the process may go further by removing the source of fuel from some of the activities so that the remainder can be better resourced and, therefore, generate more light and make a greater contribution to the image of the university as seen by the outside world. An alternative strategy would be to reposition some of the sources of light so that they, too, are in focus.

The Dilemma of Rapid Decision Making versus Participation

Changing the image of the university by changing the lens or adjusting the aperture does not affect the internal structure of the university. Changes that involve repositioning of the activities within the university, or indeed the elimination of some in order to strengthen others, are much more fundamental and difficult. To accomplish such structural changes rapidly in order to cope with changing external demands is a very difficult leadership task. To do this successfully depends upon the recognition of the responsibilities of key individuals at various levels within the university. In leisurely times, the relationships between these key individuals operate within a formal and often elaborate network of committees. But committees are slow to make decisions and the communication among these bodies will be determined by the speed at which meetings can be arranged. The committee system does have the benefit of ensuring the involvement of a large number of individuals, creating a culture of participation and thorough consideration. Indeed, one underlying assumption may be that consideration can be thorough only if it takes a long time. The committee system values maximizing the chance of making the right decision more than making it by any particular deadline.

But how can such a community survive in such a rapidly changing world that demands quick responses? This conflict has forced the university community to recognize that the scholars are but one of the stakeholders in a university. Students, employers who will recruit the graduates, and the government that represents society and provides the major source of funds are also stakeholders who have their own views of the university's role. When the pressures from external stakeholders or from students are intense, the university, that is to say the community of scholars, must satisfy these demands by ensuring that their activities have clear aims and objectives. The price of such responsiveness may be constraints on the freedom of individuals to pursue their individual academic paths.

The pressures of change pit involvement against speed in decision making. How can the community as a whole be involved, presumably through a slow committee system, when rapid responses to external pressures are often required? A management system in which detailed decisions are taken at the center cannot be *both* quick and collegial. Such a highly "managerial" centralized system can make decisions quickly, but it will not involve large numbers of the academic community. At the other extreme, a system that is highly "democratic" is bound to be slow. It is possible to create a system that combines the best of both worlds, however. A response to this dilemma is a system of interlocking decision-making networks that involve a manageable number of people at any given point. To accomplish this requires a devolution of decision making to component parts of the university. For some, devolution of budgetary control is used mainly to improve efficiency and responsiveness, but I would argue that its most important benefit is that it involves the people who will implement the decisions. To devolve decision making in a well-structured way is to create an acceptable system for the academic community to be involved in those discussions and decisions that are most immediate and important to them. However, the central administration of the university must also be involved in the major decisions. Therefore, the number of devolved units must be relatively small for the central team to be able to relate successfully to them all.

Creating Interlocking Networks of Decision Making

Effective networking is a key factor for such a decentralized system to work without sacrificing coherence and a sense of collegiality. A series of interlocking decision-making networks composed of teams of about a dozen persons has provided a useful structure for the University of Leicester. There, the major devolved units (budget centers) are based upon existing faculties. There are seven academic budget centers, and the academic services and the administrative services form two further budget centers. The heads of each of these units, together with the vice-chancellor and the 3 pro-vice-chancellors, form a team of 13. The budget managers form a team of heads of the units within their own faculty or budget center. In addition, other networks exist that cut across the budget centers for a variety of purposes. Devolved budgeting and devolved decision making does not have to mean a loss of central financial control or academic coherence. A sense of the whole can be achieved not only for the whole structurally—through interlocking networks—but also through the development of mission statements, strategic planning, and so on. The benefit and importance of creating such statements derives at least as much in the process that has created them as in the products themselves. Genuinely wide consultation through the system will create commitment to the aims and objectives and thus enhance the possibility of implementing them. The community must also recognize that the creation of strategic statements and plans provides a framework for the future development in a changing world, rather than unchangeable targets. They are guidelines for anticipating and preparing for change, as much as specific responses.

Creating devolved units does not mean that the central administration of the university is not involved in the development of strategies in the departments and faculties. It is also important to create a sense of shared responsibility between the units and central administration in the decision-making process.

In 1988, the University of Leicester had undergone a period of several years of financial cuts which involved, in particular, leaving a large number of academic posts unfilled as they became vacant. This was an opportunistic strategy to reduce expenditures in the face of financial problems. However, it had created a situation in the Faculty of Arts in which the approximately 80 members of the academic staff were distributed in 13 different departments, some of which contained only 2 or 3 academics. There were only two full professors in the whole faculty. Furthermore, it was known that the Universities Grants Committee (the funding agency at the time) was undertaking national subject reviews in classics and music, and it seemed likely that the university would be told to close those programs and thus lose funding for them. Not surprisingly, morale in the faculty at that time was very low.

I formed a small team consisting of myself, the senior pro-vice-chancellor, the dean of the faculty, and the staffing officer to consider options. We had extensive formal discussions with the Faculty Board and informal consultation with individuals. Our first task was to persuade the faculty that change was necessary and that it was crucially important that the faculty itself accept responsibility for devising solutions. Eventually, a sense of shared ownership was created between the faculty and the university's central management. A plan was created that was reluctantly accepted by the faculty, and of vital importance, it was also acceptable to the University Grants Committee, who allowed us to redeploy the available funding. The eventual solution involved the closure or amalgamation of several departments, with some staff taking early retirement and a few being transferred to other universities. This transformation was difficult, but it was also a springboard for future growth. The Faculty of Arts has since then acquired a number of new staff, including several professors, and is now vigorous and healthy.

The process arose out of a recognition that we could not leave the development of a solution entirely to the faculty, nor could we have tried to solve it entirely from the center. It was vital to persuade the faculty to accept the problem and ultimately the ownership of a solution. It was also crucial to the successful resolution of this problem for the faculty to have the support of the center in making difficult decisions that would inevitably disadvantage certain sections within the faculty, a support that also created a sense of confidence in university policy for future collaboration.

An essential requirement in managing change is to persuade those involved that adaptation to changed circumstances is necessary, not simply for the sake of change, or to be responsible to external pressures, but in order to maintain the basic intellectual and academic aims of the institution in teaching and research. Sometimes change requires achieving these basic aims differently, but at other times the aims themselves may need to be fundamentally reappraised. Under those circumstances, change may involve profound and qualitative transformation in which cherished practices and even cherished activities may have to be replaced.

In all circumstances, successful leadership requires persuasion. This takes time and effort and, if time is in short supply, the amount of effort must be compensatingly increased. Change that is too fast to allow for the persuasion of the affected individuals can destroy morale very quickly.

LOOKING TOWARD THE FUTURE

The combined effect of the rapid increase in the size of higher education and the attempts by government to develop a consistent and coherent policy for higher education has been very disruptive. While universities may be unclear about where they are heading and what to expect to be by the year 2000 and beyond, the government has also been uncertain about what kind of higher education system it wants and the country needs. Policy has all the appearances of having been made up on the hoof.

It is, therefore, some comfort that at the end of 1994 the Department of Education (the government department responsible for education in England) began conducting a review of the purposes, shape, and size of higher education for the beginning of the next century. It seems inevitable that by the year 2000 the size will increase beyond the official target of 33 percent of the traditional university age group. Until very recently, the United Kingdom had, by international standards, a very low proportion of young people remaining in full-time education beyond the statutory school-leaving age of 16. However, the situation has changed rapidly in recent years. In 1988–89, for example, only 39 percent of 17-year olds were full-time students, but by the year 1993–94, this proportion had risen to 61 percent (Department for Education News 1995). The rate is still rising, with every indication that it will lead to an increased demand for higher education. Furthermore, there is a growing awareness in business and industry of the need for the economy to have more university graduates. The Confederation of British Industries, for example, has suggested to government that 40 percent of young people in the relevant age group should participate in higher education, rather than the 33 percent government target (Confederation of British Industry 1994).

Further expansion does seem certain, therefore, but that prediction raises a number of questions about the shape of such a large higher education system. Should all the additional undergraduate students be taking conventional three-year courses, or should some of them be starting, at least initially, on two-year courses? Should some students be combining work experience with higher education and therefore undertaking part-time courses? What would be the effect of an increased number of undergraduates on the number of students wanting to pursue graduate courses? How would such an increase be combined with the research missions of universities, missions that vary enormously from one university to another in any case?

But the one overriding question is how an even larger system than the current one is to be funded. Government support has not matched the recent increase in the number of students, and further increases in student numbers will certainly not be matched by government funding. How, then, can the system maintain a high quality of education if it continues to expand without commensurate funding? At present, tuition is free for all British and European Union undergraduates on approved courses (which covers virtually all undergraduate programs). To ask students to pay for at least some part of these costs will raise a very controversial and emotional issue, but the possibility cannot be ignored. Many believe that it is undesirable for students to be forced to contribute to the cost of their education, but the alternative is indeed too awful to contemplate. For that alternative is expansion without any increased funding, which would inevitably cause a very serious and rapid decline in quality.

The Institution

But even the most optimistic funding scenario is limited to maintaining the income per student at its present level, which has severely decreased in the last few years. During this period, higher education institutions have been able to maintain, or indeed even increase, their total income by increasing the volume of student numbers. Such a strategy has ensured survival, but it has generated the need for a fundamental reappraisal of the institutional aims and objectives and of its processes. It has also created a major problem for a leader in generating willingness by a battle-weary staff to undertake such a reappraisal. In so doing, an institution must first reconsider its position. What are its strengths and weaknesses compared with other institutions? What are the potential market niches that it might hope to occupy? Should the institution aim to change its ratio of full-time to part-time students, or its proportion of graduate students? Should it concentrate on research efforts in certain areas and, if so, should this focus be on its basic research strengths or on areas that have a potential for industrial collaboration and support?

But if redefining the objectives of the institution is difficult, reorganization of its internal structures and procedures presents even greater problems. The processes by which an organization works tend to be so taken for granted that they become part of a comfortable routine. Any attempt to reengineer these processes is seen as a threat, especially in the core academic activities of teaching and research. Yet it is in the teaching and learning processes that change is not only necessary, but inevitable. The reduction in funding has put intolerable strains on traditional methods which, in any case, placed an undesirable emphasis on teaching and too little on learning. New technologies will also have a tremendous impact on the delivery of teaching and on learning experiences. The much-used term "computer-assisted learning" has a number of different meanings. At its simplest, it describes the availability of information—as in books—that can be brought up on a computer screen at a range of locations. A more complex view involves providing access to databases. More sophisticated still are interactive systems in which the students' understanding and learning can be tested. At any of these levels, the technology can be multimedia with pictures as well as text.

So far, most computerized learning is generated and based at individual campuses. Increasingly, however, such materials are accessible at a distance through high-speed cable links or even satellite links. Distance learning is now much more feasible, relying on a variety of electronic links in addition to the traditional radio or television broadcasts and study guides.

The next stage—which will have enormous significance for the university system—will make such methods of teaching and learning available at a distance and will be generated to a considerable extent outside any one specific university. The production of such educational software is likely to become big business. There is a huge market, not only for the well over one million students in higher education in this country, but also for vast numbers of students throughout the world, many of whom use English as the medium of instruction. Commercial operations will be important players in the market.

The revolution this will generate is unpredictable in detail, but it is clear that a major impact on universities will result from widespread availability of material generated outside the control of the specific teachers in a particular institution.

In fact, the availability of this educational software through cable and satellite links, facilitated by the relative cheapness of the necessary hardware, will create the possibilities of much more study at home. The question may then be asked, Why go to university at all if home study is likely to be much cheaper? Indeed, the Open University in the United Kingdom has already shown that there is a tremendous demand for home study. The government will jump at further development of home-based study since it will clearly be much less demanding on the public purse.

What, therefore, is the future of universities? Will there be universities by the year, say, 2020, in any form that we would currently recognize? While some body will be needed to validate the outcome of the study and to provide certification for the students to use for employment and future study, might this function be undertaken by a single national agency?

It may be argued that universities are necessary to carry out research. But in some countries, the bulk of the publicly funded research is carried out in institutes, which may only be loosely attached to the universities. There will be no reason why postgraduate and research students could not be accommodated in such institutes.

This doomsday scenario for the future of universities may seem frightening, but it does allow us to ask the question, If such a scenario does not actually happen, what will have prevented it? Why might it not happen? And to put this rather more specifically, what is it that universities do in addition to providing information and issuing certification that students have mastered a certain set of information?

A university education has a number of distinctive elements. A major one is, perhaps, intellectual training; that is, helping students use their minds more effectively through understanding ideas, mastering knowledge, and developing the ability to criticize theories and ideas. In his memoirs, Harold Macmillan describes the beginning of the course in "Greats" at Oxford, noting that the introductory lecture had concluded with the following statement:

> For some of you—who may become scholars or school teachers—what you will learn during this Greats course will be of direct relevance. For the bulk of you, however, who may go into the City or the professions or whatever, it will be of no direct use to you whatsoever, save that you will be in a better position to understand and determine when someone is talking absolute rot. (Macmillan 1966)

That statement captures a highly important part of a university education, which does require face-to-face contact between teachers and students.

Higher education also helps students develop skills for lifelong learning. Increasingly, education will not stop immediately after graduation, but will need to continue throughout life. Individuals will have to learn new skills or in some cases will have to be reeducated with new intellectual and conceptual frameworks for their jobs. Thus, the first degree provides critical help to students in developing the ability to go on learning throughout life. This, too, requires direct contact between teacher and student.

A third element in the educational process that is much discussed at the moment is the development of "core transferable skills." These include teamwork, communication skills, problem-solving skills, a reasonable knowledge of information technology and information systems, and some knowledge of a foreign language. To develop these skills requires interaction with teachers and with peers. It is hard to imagine, for example, how sitting in front of a computer screen on one's own could help to develop skills of teamwork, or how oral communication skills could be developed unless there is an individual with whom to communicate directly.

The fourth highly important consequence of being at university is what one might call social skills, the experience of working and living with others, and of having a better understanding of people from a wide variety of backgrounds.

For these reasons, I believe that there is still a great need for universities to exist as communities and not simply as institutions to channel information and to accredit an individual's acquisition of that information. But these truths are not necessarily evident to everyone. Universities will have to convince the larger society, which funds them through taxes, that there are very good reasons for students to spend time on a campus working with teachers and tutors and alongside other students, and that this experience benefits not only the individual but also the economy and the greater society.

The great challenge for universities in the future is to demonstrate that they can carry out these processes with effectiveness and efficiency, that they can provide excellent value for cost, and above all, that they can provide an environment so attractive to students that they will want to come to the universities in large numbers.

NOTES

1. The Committee of Vice-Chancellors and Principals of U.K. Universities has 103 members, however, because some of the major colleges of institutions such as the University of Wales and the University of London have independent membership.

2. The research assessment exercises are carried out by review with a separate panel for each of approximately 70 academic subjects.

REFERENCES

Committee of Vice-Chancellors and Principals (CVCP). 1995. *U.K. higher education statistics.* London: CVCP.

Confederation of British Industry. 1994. *Thinking ahead: Ensuring the expansion of higher education into the 21st century.* London: Confederation of British Industry.

Department for Education. 1995. *Annual report.* London: Department for Education.

Department for Education News. July 1995. London: Department for Education.

Higher Education Funding Council for England (HEFCE). October 1994. Circular 31/94.

Macmillan, H. The winds of change: 1914–1939. London: Macmillan, 1966.

FURTHER READING

Committee of Vice Chancellors and Principals. 1993. *Review of options for additional funding of higher education.* London: CVCP.

Fulton, O. 1991. Slouching towards a mass system: Society, government and institutions in the United Kingdom. *Higher Education* 21 (4) 589–606.

Green, M. 1995. Transforming British higher education: A view from across the Atlantic. *Higher Education* 29: 225–39.

Kogan, M. 1992. Models of governance and developments in the United Kingdom. *Higher Education in Europe* 17 (3): 46–58.

Middlehurst, R. 1993. *Leading academics.* Buckingham, England: Society for Research in Higher Education and the Open University Press.

Scott, P. 1995. University-state relations in Britain: Paradigm of autonomy. In *Reform and change in higher education: International perspectives,* edited by J. E. Mauch and P. L. W. Sabloff, 1–21. New York: Garland.

Trow, M. 1992. Thoughts on the White Paper of 1991. *Higher Education Quarterly* 46 (3): 213–26.

U.K. Department of Education and Science. 1991. White Paper. *Higher education: A new framework.* London: Department of Education and Science.

Watson, D. 1995. Quality assurance in British universities: Systems and outcomes. *Higher Education Management* 7 (1): 25–38.

Weil, S., ed. 1994. *Introducing change from the top in universities and colleges: Ten personal accounts.* London: Kogan Page.

Williams, G. 1992. An evaluation of new funding mechanisms in British higher education: Some micro-economic and institutional management issues. *Higher Education in Europe* 17 (1): 65–85.

CHAPTER 12

France

Suzy Halimi

Executive Summary. The upheavals and student unrest of 1968 began an era of change in French higher education—more profound and far-reaching changes than are generally recognized. A series of laws since 1988 have simplified this very complex system. Expansion has been dramatic; since 1984 all baccalaureate holders have the right to enter higher education. Enrollments in postsecondary institutions have grown by 50 percent since 1987, creating a situation of severe overcrowding. A differentiated system provides short- and longer-cycle courses, but instead of serving as different career tracks, students often wish to transfer to the longer university courses to obtain further credentials to broaden their employment possibilities.

French higher education remains highly centralized, with the government providing nearly 90 percent of institutional funding, degrees awarded nationally rather than by individual institutions, the development of new programs of study subject to Ministry approval and accreditation, and a voluntary system of accreditation directed by a national government agency, the Comité Nationale d'Evaluation. At the author's institution, Sorbonne III, the governance machinery is slow, composed of 3 councils which together form a 140-person General Assembly. A more flexible administrative arrangement has been launched on a pilot basis at a few institutions, with an external board that reduces the power of the three councils, but objections from students, professors, and trade unions have halted further expansion of the experiment. In another attempt to give more autonomy to institutions, the government instituted policy in which each university develops a four-year plan and negotiates a budget with the Ministry that will finance the plan. The result of an evaluation of the plan and negotiation yields funding for specific projects over a four-year period, funding that is granted in addition to the enrollment-based formula funding. Regional planning represents another effort to link institutions to their communities and regions.

The author describes the process of developing and negotiating the four-year "contract" with the government as an important opportunity for institutional leadership, for the development of consensus and a common vision of the institution, and for the president to pull together the work of the various groups before it is reviewed and approved by the Administrative Council. The president is also charged with the responsibility of negotiating the contract with the Ministry, assisted by experts as needed. Although the president does have opportunities to exercise leadership, academic culture, students, unions, and faculty members who are civil servants can exert a powerful influence, as the editor's postscript describes at the end of this chapter.

●　●　●　●　●　●　●　●　●　●　●

I n response to the period of student unrest of May 1968, the Law of Higher Education (*Loi d'Orientation de l'Enseignement Supérieur* or *Loi Edgar Faure*), was enacted that year to reorganize higher education in France. Its direction was affirmed and extended by the *Loi Savary* of 1984. More recently, the *Loi Jospin* (1989) brought further adjustments, aimed at simplification of the whole system and better clarity for its users and for the partners—both French and foreign—of institutions of higher education.

A description of the basic structure of French higher education gives an overview of its complexity and a hint at its potential difficulties. In spite of its reputation for a certain resistance to innovation, and a deep attachment to tradition, French higher education has undergone, and is currently undergoing, deep, far-reaching changes with remarkable resilience and adaptability. An important part of the process are the concerns of young people about higher education, their future, and issues affecting it. These concerns periodically lead students into the streets, sometimes for peaceful and festive marches, at other times for violent demonstrations. What conclusions can university presidents draw from this picture about their role in leading and managing change? What are the opportunities for and constraints on leadership?

THE BASIC STRUCTURE

French higher education is highly complex, in large part as a result of spontaneous growth and successive adjustments rather than a history of planned policy. As in most other European countries, it includes a university and a non-university sector, both of which differ in their origins, purposes, and admission requirements.

Higher Education Institutions

The Grandes Ecoles

The *Grandes Ecoles* go back to the end of the eighteenth century, created by the French Revolution and Napoleon to provide the country with highly qualified officials. The *Ecole Normale Supérieure, Polytechnique, Saint-Cyr,* and *L'Ecole Nationale d'Administration* (ENA) are famous institutions, hotbeds of genius, and highly selective. At the end of secondary school, after the baccalaureate, students take two years to prepare in special classes for the competitive entrance exams for the *Grandes Ecoles*—only a happy few are admitted. Less than 20 percent of all students who enter higher education in a given year attend the *Grandes Ecoles*. These schools have a highly professional character, training their graduates for such professions as teaching, engineering, the army, or to assume high positions in the government or in business.

The Universities

In 1968, the vast universities of the past were broken up into medium-sized institutions. There are now 87 universities, including those created more recently. By law, no selection of candidates is allowed. A political choice was made in France to provide equality of opportunities for everyone. The *Loi Savary* of 1984 gives all baccalaureate holders the right to enter higher education in the disciplines of their choice. Only medicine and paramedical fields are allowed to be selective, protected by a *numerus clausus*.

Students fees are very low. However, French students do not cost any less to educate than their counterparts in other countries where tuition fees are much higher. Rather, French taxpayers pay the bills. It was decided recently that 80 percent of the university-age cohort should obtain the baccalaureate and have the option of pursuing higher education. In 1993–94, 1.4 million students matriculated in the universities, and this figure is to reach—and exceed—2 million by the end of the century.

Courses

Short-Track and Long-Track Courses[1]

Short-track courses (two years) were created in the 1980s, mainly in the field of technology, to meet the need for high-skilled technicians. They are provided in three main ways:

- The *Sections de Techniciens Supérieurs* (STS), or Programs for Skilled Technicians, are located within the lycées of secondary education and lead to a diploma called *brevet de technicien supérieur* (BTS), skilled technician certificate, after two years.
- The *Instituts Universitaires de Technologie* (IUT), University Institutes of Technology, are located within universities—though they enjoy a large amount of autonomy. They train highly skilled specialists in specific fields, who obtain a *diplôme universitaire de technologie* (DUT), a university technical diploma.
- Some universities provide short, two-year courses leading to a similar diploma for higher level technicians.

All those short-track courses were directed to a public similar to that served by the German *Fachhochschulen*: young people with immediate professional concerns, unwilling or unable to undertake long studies. Training is more important than research in such curricula, which were created to respond to the needs of the local labor market. Offering a faster way to qualifications, they should serve to lower the pressure on universities by diverting a number of applicants to those professional channels.

The system is not, at the moment, working as was intended. Eagerly solicited by young people anxious to get a diploma as a safety net, the STSs and IUTs have become selective, the demand exceeding the number of places offered. So they take the best candidates, rejecting others for whom the universities then become the next-best solution, having been turned away by the short-course system!

There are other indications that the machine is not working properly. Because of the lack of economic security and the fear of unemployment, young people try to obtain academic qualifications at as high a level as possible. Once they have received their diploma, instead of looking for a job, they come back to the university where they ask for recognition of their prior studies and for the right to go on studying in order to achieve the highest possible academic level. A recent attempt to establish a clearer distinction between short and long courses, and to assert that moving from one to the other should remain exceptional, stirred deep discontent among the students of the IUTs, who were firmly determined to take advantage of the two systems of higher education.

Normally, long courses are provided by universities, in three successive cycles; the first two years lead to the *diplôme d'etudes universitaires générales* (DEUG), the general university studies degree. The second cycle covers the *licence* (Bac + 3) and the *maîtrise* (Bac + 4). For those who wish to go further, a choice has to be made at Bac + 5, either to seek a highly professional diploma, the DESS (*diplôme d'études supérieures spécialisées*, the specialized higher studies degree), leading to a job in a narrow specialized field, or to preparation for a doctorate. After the DEA (*diplôme d'études approfondies*), advanced studies degree, the doctoral thesis is normally completed within four or five years.

National and University Degrees

Apart from a few *Grandes Ecoles* that award their own degrees, certification is the privilege of universities and is granted on a national basis. When an institution sets up a course of studies to prepare for a particular degree, it seeks accreditation from the Ministry. The Ministry deploys teams of experts— academics chosen for their outstanding competence—to examine the project submitted by the university to ensure that it is congruent with national requirements and standards. Accreditation is granted for four years; another evaluation is conducted before accreditation is granted for another four years.

The accreditation process for new courses considers national distribution so as to meet the needs of students while avoiding unnecessary duplication. The degrees awarded are valid nationally. Because they are said to have the same value all over the country, mobility is possible. However, the expectation of equality may be a fiction, because universities are also known for their accomplishments, and students do their best to apply for admission to the institutions with reputations for high achievements in the disciplines in which they are interested. Should anyone dare to point out the differences and propose decentralization of degrees on a regional basis as a solution, they are sure to raise a tempest in the French academic world!

In spite of this deep devotion to national degrees, each university is free to set up its own university degrees (*diplômes d'université*), corresponding to its specific strengths and to some needs not covered by national certification. They have to be financed by the institution's own resources, however, because they enjoy no recognition—and no funding—from the government. Thus, they may be costly and reach a limited number of students, but they usually reflect some unique strengths of universities in the recruitment of their students, in the courses offered, and in meeting specific education needs.

University Management

Governance Structures

Universities are composed of a number of multidisciplinary faculties or departments. Each teaching and research unit (*unité de formation et de recherche* or UFR) is run by an elected council of representatives of the teaching and administrative staffs, students, and also people external to the institution. The latter are chosen for their academic accomplishments, or to represent external partners such as department members of local authorities, trade unions, or employers. The council elects the director of the UFR.

The university as a whole is administered by three councils: the Administrative Council, which is the executive organ that votes all decisions and the budget; the Scientific Council, which deals with everything connected with research; and the Council of Studies and of University Life (*Conseil des Etudes et de la Vie Universitaire*, CEVU), which examines all matters related to courses and student life. The latter two councils are merely consultative bodies.

When convened together into the General Assembly, the 3 councils—140 members all together—elect the rector of the university for 5 years. The rector is not eligible for reelection at the end of this term. This election process confers legitimacy on the rector, and some elections are indeed very tough. Directors of the *Grandes Ecoles*, by contrast, are appointed by the country's minister of higher education and research.

The general secretary leads the institution alongside the rector, also called "president." The general secretary is a senior official appointed by the Ministry of Higher Education and is mainly responsible for institutional administration, whereas the rector is responsible for general policy and decision making in an institution. Being the two headlights, the rector and the general secretary had better see eye to eye on the main issues and get on well together. In cases of conflict or even mere divergences of opinion, the rector may fire the general secretary and ask for the appointment of another one.

The whole machine of university management is heavy and slow, as the three councils have to be consulted on all events of university life, with constant risks of votes of defiance. Such is the price to be paid for the democratic working of the whole institution whose many constituents—represented in the three councils—can thus take part in the decision-making process.

From the democratic perspective, an experiment has been launched for a few years in some of the newly created universities around Paris. They have been granted a *derogatory* status, not quite in keeping with the Law of 1984: their rectors are called provisional administrators (*administrateurs provisoires*) because they are appointed by the Ministry instead of being elected by the members of the university. An Orientation Council, mainly composed of representatives of the world of business and local authorities, advises the leader and supports the president in policy and decision making. This creates greater efficiency but reduces the influence and prerogatives of the three traditional councils provided by the Law of 1984. Nevertheless, the universities that enjoy this special status seem satisfied. A report was issued early in 1995, called the *Rapport Laurent*, written by the head of one of those universities at Marne la Vallée. The report proposed that other institutions be permitted to adopt similar structures on a voluntary basis, but a violent reaction followed, by students, professors, and trade unions refusing a "two-speed system," and as a result, the government set the report aside to put an end to the agitation.

Financing

In France, higher education is considered a public service: tuition fees are very low to ensure access to higher education by needy students. This is a highly sensitive issue. Although public opinion and the rectors' conference are not hostile to a moderate rise in fees accompanied by financial assistance to help needy students, the slightest mention of such a possibility provokes deep emotion among the students.

Universities are supported by the government, which provides 89.5 percent of their funds. Funding is calculated according to the San Remo system, which uses a formula that estimates cost per student, according to the discipline (sciences, arts and humanities, law and economics) and level (first, second, or third cycle). On the surface, the formula seems fair enough, as all institutions are judged and financed according to the same criteria. But the system needs to be improved, and a working group has been set up to refine the criteria and especially to introduce qualitative next to quantitative parameters.

It is generally felt that state financing will not be able to go much further. The number of students is increasing steadily, but the state budget for higher education is said to be reaching its limit in the present period of economic difficulties. Per-student funding is among the lowest in the OECD countries. Universities are being asked to reduce their expenses and to look for other sources of financing, but the possibilities for this are limited. Tuition fees are low, and quite a number of students do not pay them—those who have scholarships, political refugees, and students who do not have sufficient resources. Continuing education may be another source of tuition income: universities are increasingly convinced that here lies one of their basic missions for the future, as education can no longer be acquired for life between the ages of 17 and 25.

Partnerships with corporate enterprises and the economic world may also bring in money, mainly through the transfer of technology and the delivery of patents. But this can affect only departments or universities with a scientific focus, and it always raises the problem that profit-making partners will want something in return for their financial help, perhaps a share in the management of the academic institution.

Last but not least, universities are trying to involve local authorities in their funding process, although strictly speaking, higher education is not within their purview. Because many local councils, regional, or municipal bodies have realized that a university on their territory is a political, economic, and cultural asset for them, they agree to listen to the rectors of those institutions and help them to finance special projects. For instance, the local authorities in Rhône-Alpes and Bordeaux-Aquitaine have built efficient strategies to help and cooperate with the local universities and generously support student mobility.

While such collaboration is very helpful and highly appreciated by those who benefit from it, others do not have the same luck. There are poorer and richer regions, and local authorities may be inclined or opposed to supporting higher education. In the search for extra funding, inequality is bound to reappear among universities, and we run the risk of creating a two-tier system.

To summarize this overview of the basic structure of higher education in France, we must emphasize its great complexity. Structures, courses of study, requirements for admission, management, financing—indeed, the entire land-scape—may be rather confusing for outside observers. Because it is also sometimes unclear to its users, since 1988 there has been a steady effort by public authorities to simplify the system. *La rénovation pédagogique* (pedagogi-cal renewal), promoted by the *Loi Jospin*, was a policy to achieve greater clarity, urging institutions to contribute to this simplification effort to better serve students and their families, employers, and our foreign partners concerned with student mobility and the recognition of degrees of students who study abroad.

RECENT TRENDS

The world of higher education in France is often considered to be averse to change, attached to its traditions and privileges, and reluctant to question its mode of operation. Such a reputation is no longer true, if it ever was! Since 1968, the French universities have given ample proof of their resilience, their openness, their adaptability, and their capacity for dialogue.

Contractual Policy

The contractual policy is one of the new trends French universities have adopted as an answer to their changing needs and a changing environment. It was launched in 1984 to organize development and planning in research. Four-year contracts were signed between each institution and the govern-ment. The approach proved so successful that it has been extended to the other activities of the university.

Each institution defines its *projet d'établissement* (plan). Priorities are estab-lished that correspond to its individual strengths and needs. A four-year program is drafted, and the means necessary to finance this program are evaluated. Finally, the plan is submitted to the Ministry for approval. In this first phase, the university becomes conscious of what it is and what it would like to become, of its weak and strong points, and develops a document that gives a snapshot of the whole institution and its plans for the future.

Next comes the dialogue with the government experts who analyze and discuss each current and future project or activity. The university leaders— the rector and his or her team—make their case for a particular activity that represents a must for the institution, for some project that lies close to their hearts. At the end of this period of negotiations, which may last several weeks and may be very tough, both parties develop and sign an agreement that sums up the main fields of development and binds them each to their part of the contract.

Thus, in addition to the San Remo funding formula based on purely objective and quantitative criteria, the contract finances specific projects of each institution using a qualitative approach. The monies are granted over a four-year period and so, for the first time, universities can plan ahead and organize themselves for a longer term, without having to renegotiate every year and risk being unable to implement their plans. Two years into the contract, a first evaluation is carried out to see if the program is proceeding according to schedule, and to make minor adjustments as necessary. When the four years are over, a thorough assessment takes place before a new contract is signed.

Because this new procedure seems to work for all parties involved, plans call for contracts negotiated in 1996 and beyond to cover—in one global, single contract—all the activities of the institution, including research, education, training, and international activities. Universities will thus be prompted to coordinate all their principal functions and to harmonize their various concerns; they will establish institutional priorities and develop a clear, coherent view of themselves and their future development. Their autonomy is preserved in this process, and the state becomes their partner by bringing financial support to their plans.

Regional Plans

Les schémas régionaux, regional plans, constitute the wider frame within which institutional development is to take place. Partnership is extended to local authorities and to regional councils in order to take the whole region into account in a plan of global growth of the university world. Université 2000 was a first attempt to situate higher education in its regional environment. Adopted in May 1991 by all parties concerned, the scheme was designed to answer the following four main objectives:

- To cope with increasing student enrollments and to improve conditions of university life
- To adapt higher education to the needs of the labor market by developing preprofessional curricula
- To insert higher education in the plans of regional development
- To adapt universities to their new European context and dimension

This policy was rooted in the need to create a closer partnership between the state and local authorities. Its major implications were a diversification of curricula, the creation of a number of IUTs (some 150 planned to be opened by 2000), and a better balance between regions, the north and the west parts of the country being strongly supported to compensate for their traditional underdevelopment. Three new universities were created for that purpose: *l'Université de l'Artois* (1992), *l'Université du Littoral* (1992), and *l'Université de la Rochelle* (1993). At the same time, some important provincial universities received substantial support to renovate their buildings and equipment. Finally, universities and other institutions of higher education were encouraged to join forces to form "European poles" of significant academic weight. Similar creations of new universities in Ile de France (Evry, Marne la Vallée, Cergy Pontoise, Versailles/Saint Quentin-en-Yvelines) were intended to lower the student pressure on the universities in Paris. In all these cases, an important financial contribution was accepted by the state and the regions, the latter joining the government on a purely voluntary basis.

The new policy aims to bring to the same table all those who are involved in the development of higher education for the next decades: the Ministry of Higher Education and Research, the regions in which the campuses are situated, the universities and their branch campuses, and the trade unions (including student unions).

The aim is to examine all aspects of higher education development in order to build a coherent whole. Many towns—even small ones—and many local potentates want to have a local university. Furthermore, students increasingly want the university at their door, which is justified, to a certain extent, by the quest for a better "quality of life." But there is also a general map to keep in mind. Duplication is unnecessary and usually costly. On the other hand, what is a university? Is it enough to place a faculty here and there, however closely linked to local needs, to have a university? Academics agree that education—to be valuable—must not be separated from research and that research of good quality cannot grow overnight in a brand new faculty. Money and a political will are not enough; the spread of new universities, local branches, and decentralized first-cycle programs have limits. The uncontrolled proliferation of fledgling universities may have disastrous effects both for those new institutions and for the old ones, which are bound to lose part of their funding to finance the new ones. The cake cannot be divided endlessly! Such were the conclusions of a recent symposium of the rectors' conference.

Regional plans drafted with the consent and active participation of all the partners involved—including the representatives of the labor market and employers—are new attempts to avoid incoherent, chaotic growth and to build schemes that take into account needs and possibilities, supply and demand, dreams and reality.

Quality Assessment

Quality assessment is the cornerstone of the whole edifice. Public financing demands visible returns for money invested; universities are expected to turn out the labor force needed by the country. Where money is short, it cannot be wasted, and sound government policy requires a satisfactory relationship between cost and quality. Finally, no contractual policy could be valid without regularly checking that the program has been well executed. Last but not least, the internationalization of higher education, with the mobility of academics and students it implies, can work only if our curricula and diplomas can be trusted for their high quality—as we would want our partners' to be trusted, of course.

To ensure this quality in the French system of higher education, a standing committee was set up in 1985, the *Comité National d'Evaluation* (CNE), the National Evaluation Committee. It is composed of 17 members appointed for a maximum of 4 years; 11 of them represent the university sector and are chosen from lists provided by the *Conseil National des Universités* (CNU), the National Council of Universities. In addition, two members each are proposed by the *Conseil d'Etat* (State Council), the *Conseil Economique et Social* (Economic and Social Council), and the *Cour des Comptes* (National Court of Audits). The whole body is responsible to the president of the republic and is independent from the Ministry of Higher Education and Research.

The aim of the evaluation is to draw a picture of each institution for all those with a stake in its quality: the institution itself, students and their families, employers, and the government. There is no direct connection between the report of the CNE and the funding of the institution. Nonetheless, harsh criticisms of the functioning or failures of a university will not go unnoticed, and the university will feel bound to improve what is going wrong within its walls—especially once it has been made public.

The procedure is pragmatic, starting with a written document prepared by the institution, which provides all possible information and statistical data. This evaluation is a voluntary process, enabling the university to learn more about itself. After the document has been examined by the experts of the CNE, the university is thrown open to peer reviewers, who are free to move around, interviewing members of the staff or students, checking the quality of the premises, and the like. After this process, the evaluation group drafts a report with its findings and conclusions. The rector of the university has a right to respond if he or she feels that any aspect of the institution has been misrepresented. Next, the report—including the rector's response—is made public.

Two types of investigations are carried out by the CNE: (1) overall evaluations of an institution; and (2) evaluations of a discipline, cutting across all the universities at which that subject is taught. Whichever approach is chosen, the indicators used by the experts to form and finalize their judgment are the same: the pass rate of students, the ratio of teachers to students, the average length of time required to obtain certification, the opportunities open to degree holders, research and its development, the achievements in the field of lifelong learning, the sources of financing, expenses per student, equipment and services, and the quality of life on the campus.

On the whole, the process is appreciated by the universities because it helps them to determine their priorities and to build their policy of development before signing the contract with the Ministry. Quality assessment is a helpful preliminary step before undertaking the contract process. It helps point out strengths and areas for improvement; many a rector has used the CNE report on his or her university to negotiate with the Ministry before signing the final document of the contract.

CHALLENGES FOR THE FUTURE

New Demands

If the basic structure of higher education in France has become complex, and if new trends are noticeable in facing traditional problems, it is because universities face new demands and new pressures to redefine their functions. The public knocking at their doors is no longer what it used to be, both from quantitative and qualitative points of view.

The Quantitative Dimension

It has become commonplace in France, as in most other European countries, to talk about the "massification" of higher education; this is certainly the main challenge for the future. An unprecedented growth of enrollments in all branches of higher education has occurred within a few years. Postsecondary enrollment now stands at nearly 2.1 million, up from 1.3 million in 1984. Between 1979 and 1989, university enrollment has increased by 19 percent; in the IUTs, enrollments rose by 31 percent; and *Section de Techniciens Supérieurs* (STS) by 188 percent. Also, enrollments in the preparatory classes for *Grandes Ecoles* rose by 43 percent, engineering schools by 46 percent, and commercial schools by 159 percent (Massit-Folléa and Epinette 1992, 35). Since 1987, overall postsecondary enrollments have risen by 50 percent (due also, in part, to the prolongation of students' studies), and as the numbers of students who pass the *baccalauréat* exam continues to rise, the pressure mounts.

Enrollment of new students continued to rise, by 2.4 percent between 1991 and 1992, and by 6.5 percent the following year. The increase was particularly sharp in arts and the humanities (up 12 percent)—the usual refuge for young people with no special vocation. In 1987, 33 percent of the age group passed the baccalaureate examination, and by 1994 that percentage had risen to 58 percent. Political leaders declared a goal of 80 percent. Already the student population exceeds the number of farmers and artisans, which means that they represent a pressure group not to be underrated!

This growing population is no longer as socially or culturally homogeneous as it used to be. Though children from the middle and upper classes still represent a majority of students, children from families of more modest means constitute an increasing proportion. As there is no selection, young people with a solid background and real abilities have the opportunity to embark upon a course of long studies and mix with others who are not really prepared for those studies but for whose families the university remains the symbol of social success and status. Very quickly, some 30 percent of the first-year students realize that they have not made the right choice. They drop out after a few months or, if they do not, they face great difficulties in keeping their heads above water. Thus, universities are developing new strategies to help them with tutors and tutorials.

Another trend visible in the last few years is for students to prolong their studies, thus further compounding the problem of student numbers. Whether it is due to a desire to get a better education or out of fear of unemployment in the present context of economic crisis—and it is probably often both—more and more students wish to attend long-track courses and get as advanced a qualification as possible. In 1992, 57 percent of the students entering the university proclaimed their intention to go as far as Bac + 5; in 1993, the percentage had risen to 62 percent. As we have seen before, many of those who start on a short, two-year course at an IUT get their degree first and then turn to the university and ask for recognition of prior study in order to go on studying for another few years.

The Qualitative Approach

Meanwhile, another sort of public is knocking at the door of universities in quest of what might be called "a second chance." It is an adult population made up of four categories of people identified by OECD (Organization for Economic Cooperation and Development) as follows:

- People who embark on "late or deferred studies," individuals who never got a degree when they were young and need one later on in life. Some may have professional experience and ask for recognition of that experience to get access to higher education—which was made possible by a law in 1985, reactivated in 1994.
- People who have never studied at the university but who need a short period of intensive training for special purposes (such as languages or computers). They need new skills for their jobs.

- People who have their diplomas but who come back to the university to improve their knowledge or to update it to advance in their careers.
- A growing number of retired people who wish to keep in touch with the world of learning and general culture. New institutions have been devised for this new public, *universités inter-âges* or *universités du temps libre* (intergenerational universities or universities of free time), which can also be included in the services offered by universities. The first one was founded in 1973, in Toulouse, by Professor Vellas. The experiment has proved so successful that there are now 70 of them in France. Their success is the best proof that the missions of the universities are changing and that higher education is adapting quickly to new demands.

Obviously, these new demands require new answers. Professors have to reconsider their methods of teaching and rethink their approach to their job. They do this with remarkable goodwill and efficiency.

New Answers

The massification of first-cycle courses can only be dealt with by a diversification of programs and the creation of new courses of study. Given the number of job opportunities in each field, it is pointless to admit large numbers of students into courses that may lead them to a degree—with no job at the end. Universities have realized this for quite a few years and have made real efforts to diversify their academic programs in connection with the needs of the labor market.

This concern with preparation for the world of work, which used to be limited to certain professions such as medicine, dentistry, and nursing, is now spreading to other fields. This is the origin of a number of new courses and new diplomas whose very names are highly symptomatic of the change: LEA (*langues étrangères appliquées*, applied foreign languages), MST (*maîtrise de sciences et techniques*, masters of science and technology), MIAGE (*maîtrise d'informatique appliquée à la gestion*, masters in applied information and management), and the last born, the IUP (*instituts universitaires professionalisés*, professional university institutes). These are some of the responses to recent trends.

All these programs of study are geared to professionals; they cater to small numbers of students—duly selected—who are brought into contact with firms that offer job prospects. Professionals are invited to join the teaching staffs and sit on juries at the final exams. Here we find a deep, far-reaching revolution in the academic world, where the mere mention of the world of money used to be a taboo and where association with professionals, business, or marketing was an abomination. Of course, the evolution is not yet complete; there are still a few die-hards who are fighting a losing battle against this trend in the name of pure, general culture. Yet, while recognizing that the trend cannot be reversed, it must not be forgotten that the basic vocation of the university is to be "universal," as implied by its etymology, and that professionalization, however necessary, should be kept within limits.

There is no such reservation about the new technologies to be used in modern pedagogy: audiovisual methods, radio, television, and computers become efficient tools to cope with the ever-increasing number of students. Their advantages are obvious: students can work at their own rhythm, even stay at home with slides and tape recorders. For people who keep their jobs while going back to the university, technology provides a good opportunity to reconcile work and study.

Distance learning is one of the other possible solutions. More and more universities have set up their own service and, at the central level, the *Centre National d'Enseignement à Distance* (CNED, National Center for Distance Learning), which is 50 years old, meets the needs of some 350,000 students including 280,000 adults. In the *23 Centres de Télé-Enseignement Universitaire* (CTEU, university centers for distance learning), there were 14,000 students in 1977 and their number had reached 32,000 in 1989. As this trend is not limited to France, such institutions are joining forces all over Europe and have founded the European Association of Distance Teaching Universities (EADTU).

The advantages of distance learning are well known, but the limits and drawbacks must be kept in mind, too: the necessary equipment is very costly, highly technical, and not easy to handle by all users. As far as possible, contacts must be preserved between teacher and student. Efficient self-service cannot—should not—obliterate the fundamental relationship between professors and their classes. With this said, no institution of higher education can dare ignore the new technologies, as performance in this new field of knowledge has become a sign of excellence.

Internationalization is another challenge—and certainly not the least one—for the universities of tomorrow must be fully aware that no research and no education of any value can be limited to the national level. Borders are falling down in Europe to give way to one common market; the Schengen agreement has made the free circulation of people a reality. But higher education goes even beyond the European Community. Through bilateral or multilateral agreements, universities all over the world are part of networks to promote the mobility of their students, their teaching and research staff, and even their administrative staff. This is becoming part and parcel of their daily life, and they are all trying to define and implement a proper policy for international relationships.

As we have noted, beginning in 1996, the contract signed by universities with the Ministry of Higher Education and Research will include a section on international affairs. Provided universities can plan their development in this field, outline priorities, and demonstrate that their policy is coherent with the rest of their activities and their mission, they will be funded for it. It is even suggested that the Ministry for Foreign Affairs may join in this contract in a deliberate attempt to join all forces around the same objectives instead of acting separately, in a disorderly—and more costly—manner. This is new: universities and different ministries have to learn to know each other and to work together efficiently. The dialogue is open, and where there is a will, there is a way!

This policy of international development and the mobility it aims to achieve has a corollary: linguistic pluralism, another challenge for tomorrow. Latin was the *lingua franca* in the Middle Ages, but those days are over and the national languages that represent the cultural wealth of our modern world are also barriers to exchanges and mobility. To work toward one common language such as Esperanto has proved a failure, because each language is a vehicle for a whole culture and has the flavor of the country in which it was born. Recent efforts aim rather at promoting wider training in foreign languages. The European community encouraged this trend with its Lingua Program. Recently in France, the Minister of Education, François Bayrou, stated in his *New Contract for Schools* that the teaching of foreign languages should be started in primary schools, continued and enhanced at higher levels. Here is the will to answer a modern problem. Will there be ways and means to make the project a reality? We hope so.

THE LEADERSHIP CHALLENGE

This brief survey of higher education in France has sought to show both the great complexity of a system inherited from centuries of adjustments, and the deliberate effort to simplify and increase its visibility for all its users and partners. We have also tried to demonstrate that, in spite of a reputation of traditionalism and hostility to novelty, higher education is undergoing unprecedented changes with remarkable resilience and adaptability. These qualities are certainly necessary at a time when the environment, the public, and the missions of higher education are changing rapidly, demanding new mentalities, new methods, and new responses to meet the challenges of tomorrow.

Given the overall picture—the structures of higher education, the challenges, and new trends for the future—what conclusions can rectors or presidents draw as to their role in leading and managing the university? What are the opportunities offered and what are the constraints on leadership?

Personal experience may prompt an answer, although there are some basic features that hold for all institutions.

The institution of the "contract" is certainly a chance for policy making. It is now the responsibility of the president to define the main goals for the future of his or her university, for which the conclusions of the evaluation committee can be used, pointing out both the strengths and weakness of the institutions. Formulating the contract provides an opportunity for involving as many members of the staff and students as possible in reflection, for defining together the identity and goals of the university, for building together a project that becomes the common vision.

I personally found it particularly rewarding to set up working groups on the important issues, groups open to all who thought they had something to say on the subject, including academics, students, members of the administrative staff, and even partners from the outside. Once each group has drafted its proposals, it is the responsibility of the president to gather all the threads and to write the final document, which will reviewed and voted on first by the Administrative Council of the university before it is discussed with the experts of the Ministry for evaluation and funding. Under such circumstances, it may be said that the leader—the president—is supported by the whole community. Being shared by colleagues, these views derive strength and authority from wide discussion and consultation of all parties concerned.

The dialogue with the Ministry is also the prerogative of the president, though it is safer, on each technical point, to be accompanied by the local expert who will bring in the necessary explanations and specific answers. The negotiation of the contract is an important highlight in leadership, for it is the responsibility of the president to demonstrate the validity of the views expressed, the coherence of the whole scheme, and to plead for the items which lie closest to his or her heart—in order to obtain accreditation, recognition, and (of course) funding from the Ministry. Once agreement has been reached and the final document has been drafted, the contract that binds the two partners is signed by the president and by the minister of higher education and research (or the minister's representative). Then the dream of the leader, shared by the university, has come true, and together they must see to its due implementation. Here, again, the rector alone will be held responsible for proper execution of all the schemes and plans written in the contract.

This is certainly the best opportunity offered for leadership, as the whole policy of the institution must then, logically, revolve around the contract. Research, training, continuing education, international relationships, cultural projects, and the management of human resources must all come in for their share in building the overall picture outlined in the contract; and here lies, for the leader, the best opportunity to manage change in his or her university. The president's role is not just to implement government policies, but to strike a line of development for the institution and find the means to reach its goals.

Does this mean that all is for the best in the best of all possible worlds? Certainly not. The most dynamic leader will, sooner or later, come up against various constraints and difficulties. First, there is no real tradition of fund-raising in France—not yet, at least—and lack of money certainly remains the main obstacle to be overcome. The government grant is still the main source of finances, and however eloquent the president is in negotiating the contract, ambitions and dreams have to be kept within limits, and some hoped-for projects have to be dropped for lack of funding.

Young people usually support change and are likely to respond favorably to new plans for their future—as long as they do not impinge on their own conceptions of higher education! They are entitled to have representatives on the three councils of the universities, but student participation in elections is very low. Consequently, those who are elected represent a small minority of the student population; a vocal, active minority that tries to put pressure on the "establishment," from the university president to the minister. As they contribute to the election of the president, they may act as umpires in contested elections, exact promises from the candidates, and then constitute a pressure group. In any case, students are not to be underrated in the political game, especially on such weighty occasions as the definition of new action or a vote on the budget.

Turning to other members of the university, the teaching and academic staff, other limits appear in the leader's power to manage change. Departments and faculties may behave as "states within the state," in a fierce attempt to preserve their autonomy. This is mainly true of some disciplines, such as law and medicine, which have always enjoyed a certain amount of autonomy and intend to keep it. To involve all departments in a global project is not always easy; building consensus and a feeling of belonging is a hard task, hence the necessity to develop all means of information communication to reduce those centrifugal forces.

Add to this the fact of the status of teachers in France as civil servants. This makes any teacher, any administrative employee, untouchable as soon as they have become *fonctionnaires*. It deprives the leader both of any way of sanctioning bad performance or rewarding genuine service rendered to the institution. This difficulty is being partly remedied by a system of bonuses distributed on qualitative criteria, but this is just starting and unions are striving to define the rules and parameters for the granting of such bonuses.

Finally, academic culture and tradition must also be taken into account. In France as in other countries, institutions of higher education consider their basic mission to be the generation and diffusion of new knowledge on a universal basis. To provide students with a general culture aimed at enlarging their views, developing their critical spirit, and promoting their individual progress: such is the traditional inheritance of the century-old Sorbonne. Service to society and answering the needs of the labor market comes far behind and is gaining ground only at a slow pace. This reminds leaders that they cannot move too fast or too far in that direction without endangering traditional values. And from that point of view, the business sector pays the university back in its own coin, holding a vague mistrust of students and academics as troublemakers. The memory of 1968 still rankles in a number of minds. The president who is so minded, who wants to build bridges between the university and the outside world, has to convince both parties that times have changed, that town and gown are meant to work hand in hand.

To face all those challenges, the president has to be supported by the university community and must find colleagues ready to accept administrative duties on top of their research and teaching. Here lies, in France at least, a last obstacle along the way, for the load of teaching duties has been increased so drastically over the last decades that there are fewer and fewer academics who accept such additional tasks. This poses serious problems at a time when universities are developing new missions, new activities, and new partnerships and are pushing the common project forward. Such is certainly a problem presidents—supported by ministry action—will have to solve to manage change and build the universities of tomorrow.

CONCLUSION

To conclude, let us remember that French universities are negotiating an important turn in their history: their structures and their missions are changing and developing. New demands are put upon them by the students who enroll in increasing numbers; by adults asking for "a second chance"; by society at large requiring a better balance and between training and the labor market, between cost and quality or efficiency; and by the internationalization of research and education. The president is at the helm of the ship, sailing toward the future. Managing change is a stimulating challenge; the best assets to manage change and weather the storms are resolution, conviction, and the ability to build consensus and support.

Editor's Postscript. Professor Halimi completed this chapter shortly before the general strike in France of November and December 1995. Joining union members in their protests against government cutbacks on social spending, tens of thousands of students took to the streets in French cities to demand more funds for overcrowded universities and to protest any reallocation of resources among universities. The Ministry had proposed $40 million per year in each of the subsequent four years to improve conditions in the most underfunded universities. The

Conference of University Presidents issued a statement calling for $75 million to be devoted immediately, and that 1,100 new faculty posts and 1,200 new administrative and technical positions be created in 1996. They also called for a $400 million capital investment in repairs and correcting deferred maintenance (Amelan 1995). Education Minister François Bayrou's plan to shift resources to the universities most in need of additional resources and teaching posts would have been funded through some reductions in budgets of other universities. As Halimi notes, any attempt to differentiate among universities or to challenge the notion that all French universities are equal "is sure to raise a tempest!"

French higher education is once again at a very difficult moment in history, with a policy of open access and nominal tuition that has not been matched by commensurate government funding since the expansion triggered by the *Loi Savary* of 1984 was initiated. The result is a volatile political situation and piecemeal strategies to correct the situation. According to one critic, "higher education is a political hot potato which no politician will touch because the main issues have never been resolved" (Ekeland 1995).

NOTE

1. The U.S. equivalent of this term is "programs of study."

REFERENCES

Amelan, R. 1995. Half of France's universities go on strike over funds. *Chronicle of Higher Education* December 8: A38.

Ekeland, I. 1995. Policy? What policy? *Times Higher Education Supplement* November 28: 16.

Massit-Folléa, F., and F. Epinette. 1992. *L'Europe des universités: L'enseignment supérieure en mutation.* Paris: Documentation Française.

FURTHER READING

French and European Sources

Actes de la conférence sur l'accès à l'enseignment supérieur en Europe. 1992. Parma: Università degli Studi de Parma.

Ministry of Higher Education and Research. 1994. *Les enseignments supérieures en France, 1993–4.* Paris: Ministry of Higher Education and Research.

Ministry of National Education and Culture. 1992. *General organization of higher education in France.* Paris: Ministry of National Education and Culture Directory of Higher Learning.

Universités: Les chances de l'ouverture. 1991. Report to the President of the Republic by the National Committee on Evaluation. Paris: Documentation Française.

Universités: La recherche des équilibres. 1993. (Report to the President of the Republic by the National Committee on Evaluation.) Paris: Documentation Française.

Books and Journals in English

Bloch, D. 1996. The French university system: assessment and outlook. In *Goals and purposes of higher education in the 21st century*, edited by A. Burger, 133–45. London: Jessica Kingsley.

Bordage, B. 1992. Continuing education in France: A dichotomous system. *Higher Education Management* 4 (1): 71–79.

Kennedy, S. 1995. Liberté, egalité, fraternité....et lisibilité: The French university system strives for transparence. *International Educator* Fall: 30–40.

Musselin, C. 1992. Steering higher education in France: 1981–1991. *Higher Education in Europe* 17 (3): 59–77.

Neave, G. Inspiration of the muse or management of the art? Issues in training for academic posts and teaching in France. In *Goals and purposes of higher education in the 21st century*, edited by A. Burgen, 146–54. London: Jessica Kingsley.

Ribier, R. 1994. Legal construction of higher education structures: The French case. *Higher Education in Europe* 19 (4): 76–78.

Trends, issues, and new laws in higher education: France. 1994. *Higher Education in Europe* 19 (1): 44–46.

Vincens, J. 1995. Graduates and the labour market in France. *European Journal of Education* 30 (2): 133–56.

CHAPTER 13

The Czech Republic

Josef Jarab

Executive Summary. The Velvet Revolution of 1989 attests to the power of students to bring about change. As major actors in the larger political revolution, they proclaimed the illegitimacy of the old *nomenklatura* in university leadership positions and demanded freely elected rectors and deans. While there was a great deal that required change in Czech higher education, the quality of instruction at primary and secondary schools had remained high, and there was much unofficial and underground instruction that kept free inquiry alive. The Communist regime, however, did great damage to the humanities and social sciences, as well as to the governance of higher education. Research suffered with the separation of research institutes from universities, and promotion in the academic world was more a question of political loyalty than academic accomplishment. In the rush to redesign Czech higher education in the wake of Communism, reform was hardly a systematic or sophisticated process. Higher education enrollments grew from approximately 15 percent of the age cohort in 1989–90 to 18.6 percent in 1994–95, representing an increase in the number of students of 14 percent. The number of universities has grown, as has the number of faculties. Yet, limited capacity permits only half the number of young people seeking access to higher education to enroll.

A great deal has been accomplished since 1989, including computerization, the development of new programs in new fields, the reduction of excessive classroom hours of instruction, and the internationalization of teaching and research. Significant obstacles remain, however, of a legal, economic, psychological, and political nature.

Underfunding is a significant problem, and economic survival has been an all-consuming focus for higher education leaders. Government funding policy has been the main instrument for reform, yet the absence of a more coherent policy (with four new ministers in five years) has hampered effectiveness of the reform process. This absence has given license to political factions and stalled further reforms. Government officials, pressed for additional sources of income, are pushing for students and their families to contribute to their education; the author sees this move as ill-prepared and premature, considering the general social situation in the country.

For long-term renewal, Czech higher education will depend on producing its own doctoral students, which poses a difficult challenge in light of the inadequacies of salaries and equipment. Focusing on quality and creating centers of excellence will be essential strategies, yet government funding has not as yet recognized this as a priority. At the institutional level, much change is possible (within the constraints of funding and the absence of coherent policies.) The author has faith in the ability of motivated teachers, scholars, and students to improve higher education in ways that government decrees cannot. Even where there is resistance to changing courses and pedagogy, there are also enthusiastic champions of excellence who will push others to change. Staying in close touch with the academic enterprise through teaching and research is an important way for rectors to think creatively about the university they are leading. Palacky University has demonstrated a considerable capacity to change—adding three new faculties, doubling the number of students enrolled in five years, adding a program for senior citizens, and developing links to the town of Olomouc. International links are crucial to the revitalization process, bringing the opportunity for self-assessment using external standards, new networks, ideas, and colleagues.

• • • • • • • • • • •

A few days after the dismantling of the Berlin Wall had become an item of the global news, two Dutch reporters from *De Tijd* magazine, on their way from Prague to Cracow, stopped in Olomouc to inquire about the life expectancy of the Iron Curtain in the region. Although we had hoped for nothing else in the last two decades but its fall, and a number of people had worked hard and in whatever way imaginable to bring the required changes about, my answer to the journalists concerning the chances of a turnover was rather skeptical. At that moment, I could see neither the working class nor the students as motivated enough to provide the needed impetus for the collapse of the regime, or even for a profound change to happen. The workers, in a general state of material poverty, were still relatively well provided for in their basic needs, and the young people in school seemed politically apathetic and quite indifferent to larger issues.

Then November 17, 1989, arrived, and I felt embarrassed and happy for having been so wrong in my judgment, especially as far as our students were concerned. I am convinced now that it was no mere coincidence that the Velvet Revolution started as a demonstration to commemorate the fiftieth anniversary of the closing down of Czech institutions of higher learning by the Nazi occupiers. The readiness to rebel must have been reinvigorated by the memory of the dramatic and painful national history of the past half-century; and as for the brutal reaction of the Communist authorities and their police forces, not only did it fail to stop the chanting and singing masses of students in the streets of Prague, it indeed became the immediate trigger for the revolutionary events that followed and spread quickly all over Czechoslovakia. It was an unexpected pleasure, but also an illuminating lesson, to work with the student leaders on the strike committee at Palacky University; and it was a dramatic experience to help constitute the Olomouc chapter of the Civic Forum, the spontaneous movement that effectively united all rebellious anti-government factions and individuals in the country during those days and nights after the 17th of November. Having repeatedly addressed, with words of support, encouragement, and hope, the thousands of students who kept gathering in the university sports arena, and even larger crowds of Olomouc citizens in the town square, I was suddenly catapulted into the position of revolutionary spokesman and negotiator with the university administration, the municipal government, and the representatives of the Soviet occupation troops in town. And it was certainly in the wake of the spirit of general enthusiasm which ensued from the recapture of liberty that I accepted the student candidacy for the position of rector. It was, above all, the driving force of the students that made the old administrators resign and that persuaded the academic community of the urgent necessity to create a self-governmental body (namely, the senate) that would, with 50 percent student representation, choose new academic leaders. So, on 21 December, I happened to become the first freely elected head of university in Czechoslovakia in decades. Within a few months, practically all institutions of higher education replaced the old nomenklatura in the positions of academic representatives by individuals who were freely elected. About a year later, after new legislature had been introduced, most of the "revolutionary" rectors and deans were reelected to their posts for a period of three years, which can only be repeated twice.

THE LEGACY OF COMMUNISM

What was the state of higher education and what set of objectives and tasks had been inherited in 1989? In sweeping statements to the media and at various gatherings, politicians presented both highly pessimistic and highly optimistic views, depending on whether they concentrated on the past or the future. But it soon became clear that neither extreme would offer a very productive basis for constructive thought aimed at true changes in the system of higher education and within the institutions themselves. For better or for worse, there are no new beginnings possible in Central Europe without continuity, and realists had to take this historical fact into account if they wanted to succeed in their endeavors.

Despite the moral, spiritual, intellectual, and material devastation of the educational system, despite its growing professional inadequacy, it should also be remembered that even under the totalitarian regime, teaching and learning did not cease to exist in Czech schools. The intended Communist brainwashing notwithstanding, the level of primary and secondary education, above all in the field of natural sciences, was still comparable with countries in the freer world, and so was the quality of the entire network of vocational high schools. Due to the effort of a number of good and courageous teachers, meaningful and effective instruction took place within the semi-official "gray zone" of the system, and knowledge was gained also in families and in various unofficial and even underground educational activities. After all, education has been historically valued by most Czechs as an important social good, and in times of lacking national and cultural independence, which have occurred quite frequently over the last four centuries, acquisition of knowledge and skills could even possess a quality of resistance to the domineering authorities. It is no wonder, then, that through our dramatic history a productive tradition developed in the nation of learning and teaching "between the lines."

It was higher education, above all at the university level and in the area of humanities and social sciences, that suffered most from the stifling constraints of ideology. With the regained academic freedom, it was relatively easy to remove from the schools the obligatory and dogmatic ideology of Marxism-Leninism that governed curriculum and institutional philosophy, and, along with the transformation of the political regime, to replace the autocratic central governance of the educational system with more democratic principles and some administrative autonomy. As early as the spring of 1990, a new Act of Higher Education was passed in the federal Parliament to give legal support to the structural changes.

What was not always readily understood was the more enduring and internalized aftermath of the totalitarian indoctrination, which affected the forms and contents of education, as well as the methods of teaching and learning. The goal of the Communist ideology was not just to spread the dogmas as the only "scientific" truth, but to prevent the very cultivation of critical thinking. Because of the inefficient bureaucracy and the rather lukewarm attitude of people toward the system, the authorities could never fully succeed; yet, society was afflicted with lasting harm.

To achieve their objectives, it was crucial for the authorities to control and manipulate information. Therefore, university and departmental libraries were poorly supplied, especially with Western books and periodicals. Learning of foreign languages was not encouraged, except for Russian, which was obligatory for pupils from age 10 to 18, and contacts with academic partners from abroad were discouraged, if not literally banned. Officially censored and approved textbooks were the main source of knowledge. The overloaded curricula, frequently with little substance, and heavy class schedules averaging 30 to 36 hours per week, were uninspiring and, indeed, hardly allowed the students to take any time for independent study.

Official, Soviet-inspired educational policy kept teaching at the institutions of higher education separate from research, which became the domain of the Academy of Sciences. Consequently, the research university as an institution practically disappeared, and after 1981, even doctoral studies were reduced and degraded to a mere formality, as an academic title could be obtained without sitting for specific examinations and without writing and defending a dissertation. Promotion in the academic world was much more a matter of degree of political loyalty than of professional merit, and as years passed, it became quite evident that university teachers who were not members of the Communist party were a dying species. After the occupation of Czechoslovakia by the Warsaw Pact military forces in 1968, even entrance exams for students turned into a lottery in which the candidates' academic performance might turn out to be the least decisive factor in the acceptance or refusal for enrollment.

THE "REFORM" PROCESS

It would be too daring to use the term reform if we wanted to describe the changes in higher education as they occurred after November 1989. There was no blueprint, no plan or scenario worked out by anyone. And yet ideas for improvements, emendations, innovations, and transformations started rushing in from all quarters, inspired and driven by the desire to liberalize universities from the burdens of the past, to reinstitute academic freedom, to increase the quality of studies but, above all, to enlarge and enrich the chances of providing access to higher education for those who, for various reasons, were unable to study under the old regime.

The very fact of the overwhelming and immediate interest in our country from abroad after the fall of the Iron Curtain was of great moral relevance, even before it could manifest itself in specific and concrete offers of assistance, exchange, or cooperation. Only much later did I realize, during a trip to Canada and the United States in February 1990 (when I had the honor to accompany, as one of the four newly elected rectors, our newly elected president, Vaclav Havel, on his state visit), that we might have sounded rather naive to our hosts, experienced university administrators, when voicing our enthusiastic expectations of facile and fast solutions to all the problems of our higher education. Our reality, indeed, proved to be much more complex and difficult.

In the fall of 1991, a team of expert examiners from the Organization for Economic Cooperation and Development (OECD) tried to assess the current situation in Czechoslovak higher education. The following spring, six recommendations were presented for consideration to the two national governments in Prague and Bratislava. Although a broad discussion of specific suggestions followed, which in itself contributed greatly to the general awareness of the issues, no conspicuous implementation of the ideas in official educational policy followed. Yet the guiding principles of the recommendations—calling for a more diversified system of higher education, an increase of resources devoted to it, and an enhanced role assigned to higher education in the overall reform process—have never disappeared from the agenda of negotiations of university representatives with government officials.

One of the OECD recommendations concerned the participation rate. In 1989–1990, not more than 15 percent of the 18-year-old age group were enrolled in institutions of higher education in Czechoslovakia, which was very low if compared with Western European countries and the United States. Even more importantly, this situation was providing an opportunity to only half of the high school graduates who wanted to continue their studies. The OECD proposition was to double the percentage by the year 2000, to be achieved mainly through an increased number of students of humanities, law, and social sciences (partly at the expense of engineering and agriculture, two fields overemphasized by the old regime). Also proposed was an introduction of bachelor degree programs both at traditional and newly founded, mostly regional, institutions of higher learning, and at vocational or professional institutes that were to be experimentally installed after the model of the German *Fachhochschulen* or the "alternative higher education" system in the Netherlands (OECD 1992, 10; see also Institute for Human Sciences 1992, and Center for Higher Education Studies 1992).

THE CURRENT SITUATION

What are the conditions like at present? By 1994–95, the proportion of the age group enrolled in higher education went up to 18.6 percent, the total number of students grew by 14 percent (currently 129,716), and one-quarter of those enrolled are involved in newly introduced bachelor studies, which are usually planned for three years, in contrast to the four or five years needed for a master's degree. Also, the ratio of teachers to students has changed over the 5 years, from 1 : 9.7 to the current 1 : 10.3; the total number of institutions of higher education grew from 17 to 23, and the number of faculties, which are to a great extent structurally and even legally independent parts of universities and other educational institutions, was increased from 72 to 106, thus, above all, filling in gaps in education for business and management, banking and finances, public administration, health administration, legal professions, media, and the social sciences (Ministry of Education 1995). While in 1989, there were in the Czech Republic only three classical universities—in Prague, Olomouc, and Brno, founded in 1348, 1573, and 1919, respectively—since 1991 seven more came into existence in Plzen, Ceskc, Budejovice, Ustí nad Labem, Ostrava, Opava, Pardubice, and Hrádec Králové. The total number of institutions of higher education in the country also includes technical universities; professional schools of chemical engineering, economics, and agriculture; and academies of performing arts and fine arts, as well as artistic crafts. Furthermore, four military and police academies operate in the Czech Republic. And as for the experiment with 20 or more vocational/professional institutes, which are currently trying to achieve accreditation, it has not yet been officially accounted for, but the schools themselves have demonstrated strong ambition and patent vitality. Despite the increased number and variety of schools, however, the statistics still show that only half of the young people who would want to study after graduating from high school can do so.

The questions to be asked, of course, include whether the country really needs—and whether, in the times of costly economic transition, it can afford—twice as many students at institutions of higher learning; whether the market will be able to employ all the graduates that schools would produce; and whether there are enough qualified teachers to guarantee the necessary quality of education. The demographic data also warn us that by the year 2005, the number of 18 year olds will drop dramatically in the Czech Republic (60,000 fewer than in 1992). Thus, there should be an increase in the proportion of the age group enrolled, even if the number of enrolled students remains unchanged, which it will not. After a more thorough examination of the whole system of education in the country, it becomes obvious that though the encouragement of the OECD experts to increase the participation rate appeared, at first sight, quite valid and legitimate, their picture of the national state of education may have been too dismal, especially if the educational level of graduates from grammar schools and vocational schools were considered, and compared with the standards of some graduates from Western colleges.

Obviously, qualified decisions concerning the whole system of higher education in the country will have to be made soon to secure institutional diversity, sufficient quantity, and good quality. If such decisions are not taken by government or regional administrations, the market itself will force institutions to think of themselves within a larger context and to work toward a more realistic distribution of roles. So far, new universities and institutions of higher education, which continue to come into being rather spontaneously, have mostly only provided opportunities for a greater number of students. They have not, however, contributed much to the creation of a more competitive environment, and perhaps hardly could do so in the first stage of their existence. Under the current circumstances, then, an atmosphere of healthy competition is still badly lacking in the realm of Czech higher education.

We have yet to appreciate that true competition improves quality, and to accept the fact that how good an institution of higher education is depends largely, if not totally, on the quality of its faculty. After the revolution, the task of faculty renewal appeared to be of crucial importance and, because of many political, moral, and economic implications, it has also proved to be a tough one. As the old Labor Code remained in force and the new Act of Higher Education proved to be quite an inadequate tool for developing hiring and firing policies, the attempts of postrevolutionary university administration to cleanse the institutions of intellectually impotent, immoral, if not outright criminal individuals turned quite often into legal nightmares.

Still, at most traditional institutions, during the first couple of years, up to 25 percent of teachers and researchers were replaced. The primary criteria for faculty evaluation were professional expertise, scholarly erudition, and simple human decency. New faculty members were recruited from those who did not "qualify" under the Communist regime; quite a few of the teachers who had been fired after the Prague Spring of 1968 were ready to come back, though not every one of those who did had much to contribute. Some experts returned from exile for temporary or even permanent stays, and dozens of foreign teachers accepted jobs at our schools. Institutions in Prague, especially, could also exploit the opportunity of choosing from researchers who were leaving the Academy of Sciences, which was forced, through economic measures, gradually to reduce its staff by one-half. However, general lack of mobility, which was one of the features and goals of the totalitarian regime and is still reflected in the current housing situation, continues to be a considerable practical hindrance in the renewal and rejuvenation of academic staff. Institutions outside the capital will also have to deal more efficiently with the aftermath of what used to be identified, and is being referred to, even today, as the mental phenomenon of "Pragocentrism."

By the end of 1992, it must have been clear that, for some time, institutions of higher education would have to rely on current faculty; that any dramatic staff development could come only from our own doctoral programs; and that this process would stretch over years. The imperative, therefore, becomes to create conditions that talented young people would find attractive enough to enable them to resist the temptations of jobs outside the academy, which offer incomparably higher salaries. Such conditions would have to include not just more generous wages or scholarships, but also more adequate laboratory equipment, better information resources, and opportunities for cooperation in international projects. Indeed, it seems to be high time that our priorities be turned from quantity to quality in our system of higher education. Undoubtedly, the creation of a few centers of excellence at our best universities, with the capacity for high quality postgraduate training, would be an important step in the right direction, a very important and rewarding endowment for the future. So far, regretfully, hardly any heed has been paid to this particular issue in official projects and budgets, as if the government did not realize that we have been missing a vital source of energy and potential to accomplish the transformation of our universities and other institutions of higher education.

TAKING STOCK

Having been involved in the business of transformation of higher education for nearly six years, I find it legitimate to ask whether and to what extent have we succeeded, and what have been the obstacles preventing us from further accomplishments—or, how justified is the occasional criticism voiced by politicians that the academic world contributed less than expected to the political, economic, and social reforms in the country.

My general sentiment is that a lot has changed for the better in higher education in the years after November 1989, and some of those who do not share the view were either too optimistic or never welcomed any changes to begin with. When we, with a few colleagues, recently tried to enumerate some of the improvements and achievements at Palacky University, we were surprised at the length and richness of the list; I am convinced that similar inventories could be produced at other institutions, although the contents might differ from school to school.

Among the positive items I would expect on most lists are the following: the dramatic computerization of teaching, learning, research, and administration; the replacement of the corrupted entrance examination practice with an objective and more professional system; the creation of a very wide scope of study programs available for the students to choose from (including new or newly conceived fields and subjects, such as specialized social sciences, management, business, journalism, free-market economics, civic education, environmental studies, European and American studies, religions, ethnic studies, etc.); the reduction of courses and obligatory class hours per week and semester to a more reasonable and efficient level; the advancement of foreign language capacity in the academic community, above all, among students; the spreading phenomenon of internationalization of many teaching and research projects and the subsequent exchange of teachers, students, and information with institutions in Europe and on other continents; the incipient cooperation with regional and state government, with business, and with industry; and the introduction and establishment of regular (and formerly, quite rare) summer schools, seminars, and colloquia, often with international participation. All these achievements, and a few more, can be attributed to the initiative of active, inventive, imaginative, and dynamic individuals and teams who were ready and able to exploit the opportunities presented by the newly acquired autonomy of the higher education institutions after the revolution.

At the same time, a whole catalogue of common grievances and complaints could be drawn up, in which administrators and members of the academic community would list reasons that prevent institutions from accomplishing a more efficient transformation. These include obstacles of a legislative, economic, psychological, and political nature.

Rectors, by law solely responsible for administering their schools, complain of the unreasonable and unrealistic distribution of checks and balances in institutional self-government, a situation that not only undermines the integrity of the institution but hampers more effective action, including the implementation of reform measures. Deans of faculties have been irritated by an amendment to the Act of Higher Education of 1993 that changed all open-ended work contracts of teachers and researchers at institutions of higher education into short-term contracts and, furthermore, introduced for each position competitions judged by commissions nominated by the minister of education. These legal actions were perceived as interference with academic autonomy, as something ineffective and therefore futile, and, above all, as an ill-timed tool for staff renewal because it came a couple of years too late; in fact, only after the changes that could be made had already been completed. Academic representatives and bursars are dissatisfied with the level of finances provided by the state budget. For most of the institutions of higher education, government funding represents up to 90 percent of their annual resources—funds which prove to be, however, hardly sufficient for operations and provide almost nothing for development. New building investments are very limited, although nearly all universities lack adequate libraries and laboratories. There is also a serious shortage of residence halls for the growing number of students. Although faculty salaries are rising slightly, a number of promising teachers desert schools for more lucrative jobs.

It may be true that higher education could have played a more important role in the political and economic reforms in the country, but it is far from fair and correct to assess its performance in this respect as a failure. It is saddening that in the present atmosphere, which I sometimes refer to as a mental "gold rush" fever, it appears that we need to remind society, or some of its members, that the revolutionary events of November 1989 began in the academy and were initiated by students who won the earliest support from actors and singers from national and local theatre groups. It is regrettable that in the past five years, time and energy that could have been used more constructively had to be devoted to struggling for financial resources that could secure little more than survival. (The Czech Republic devotes less than one percent of its gross national product to higher education. Data provided by the Ministry of Education indicates that in 1991, the percentage of GNP devoted to higher education was 0.64 percent; in 1992, 0.67 percent; in 1993, 0.73 percent; and in 1994, 0.82 percent.) Although it is generally recognized that public spending has to be closely watched by the government in the times of economic reforms and recovery, higher education believes that education has not been given the priority it deserves.

Pragmatic officials are increasingly introducing the argument—rather unfamiliar, if not alien, in Czech society—that education is more a private investment in one's career than a common good. The massification of higher education may, indeed, result in the unavoidable and logical development that students and others besides the government contribute to the financing of higher education. But at present, with still a relatively limited percentage of young people getting the opportunity to study, and the rather low salaries of most university graduates, this notion seems untimely. Education and educated people were vital even for national survival throughout our history. In fact, it was our capacity to activate the existing educational capital, stored in society over the decades and centuries, that was responsible for the success of the recent postrevolutionary political and economic reforms. Not only did enterprising individuals manifest their capability to adapt creatively to new conditions and opportunities, but also schools—as institutions—reacted readily and flexibly to new requirements following the revolutionary changes.

For hundreds of teachers and other professionals who suddenly found themselves useless and unemployable after 1989, universities immediately started various requalification programs. Primary school and high school teachers of Russian and of Communist civic education, along with others who had no more use for the educational "pure socialist output"—as the Polish economist and former minister Leszek Balcerowicz wittily and aptly referred to the ideological and, therefore, under the new conditions, unusable, portion of learning acquired in the totalitarian school system—all embraced the opportunity to regain some marketable skills (Institute for Human Sciences 1995, 49). Without delay, institutions of higher education, frequently with assistance from abroad, opened training centers in which missing and needed know-how was offered, above all in fields where no experts had been trained under the Communist regime (for instance, the Center for Economic Research and Graduate Education at Charles University, Prague). Later, full courses were introduced to respond to the needs of the new situation and the budding market, be it foreign language instruction, consultation on computer usage and managerial skills, or promotion of legal awareness. Within one or two years, whole new schools asked for accreditation to be allowed to launch programs that would fill gaps in the educational system. All these activities certainly have been beneficial for the climate of reforms.

Understandably, mistakes have been made in the hectic pursuit of the new objectives. In the rather unmanageable series of attempts to found new institutions of higher education, local and even personal interests, and over-ambitious plans, sometimes interfered with the true potential of those involved and even with the real needs. So far, however, there has been insufficient assistance from the political bodies in the country during the process of transformation, not just of individual educational institutions but, more importantly, of the whole system of higher education.

Government funding policy has been the main—if not the only—instrument for reform. This might not be harmful if the presence of a mastermind were felt in individual moves. But academics interested in true reforms can hardly be convinced of an overarching strategy when four new ministers have taken office successively within a period of five years. It was certainly unwise to ignore the first recommendation of the OECD examiners who, more than three years ago, suggested that an independent, high-level group be formed to become "an instrument for setting overall policy, long-term strategy and priorities in higher education" (Institute for Human Sciences 1992, 4). The team was right to assume that neither the ministry, with its regular staff, nor the educational institutions by themselves could be expected to accomplish such a task. And, mostly for very practical and organizational reasons, less than expected was delivered by the Council of Higher Education, consisting of representatives delegated by university senates, by the Research Institute for Higher Education associated with the ministry, and even by the Czech Rectors Conference that I myself take part in.

In the absence of a clear strategy, particularism of interests rules the scene. Two years ago, political factionalism prevented a proposal from even getting to the Parliament for an amendment that would have addressed some important gaps in the hastily drafted revolutionary Act of Higher Education of 1990. Since then, a draft of a new bill is being prepared and discussed, which at best promises to be a result of hardly compatible compromises. The government position allows no legally recognized partners, such as the Czech Rectors Conference or another expert body, to participate in formulating an educational policy which, therefore, would be entirely up to the ministerial officials. (In the current act, at least the Council of Higher Education is guaranteed the position of an obligatory consultant to the ministry on important policy decisions, such as budgetary criteria and principles.)

Two new proposals regarding economic and financial policies are expected to be introduced after the bill passes through Parliament; first, to make private institutions of higher education a legal possibility so that "the monopoly of the state schools will be challenged," as the government and a part of the media maintain; and second, to introduce payment of tuition by students that would cover 5 to 20 percent of the real cost of studies. The introduction of tuition would be accompanied, however, by a 10 percent reduction of the state contribution to the institution. The money collected from the students would not, therefore, enhance the economic independence of the schools, which in itself would be a worthy thing to happen. What remains of the positive argumentation for the fees is the expected increase in students' motivation to study and to become more interested in the quality of classes and curricula; the ensuing risk, however, is the introduction of thinking in terms of "service," "community," and "bills," which seems rather crude in the subtle world of education.

I am convinced that to introduce tuition would be a very important political and cultural decision for which we do not appear to be ready, especially in light of the unsatisfactory network of social support, scholarships, and loans. The danger is real that the introduction of tuition may cause undesirable preselection of students on social grounds. The traditional view of education in the Czech lands, similar to most European countries, also speaks against the fees. The pragmatic market mentality is spreading, however, and I understand that educational institutions cannot avoid it altogether, though it is not the same as complying with the business spirit entirely. I believe strongly that the responsibility of educational institutions, and above all of universities, reaches far beyond the immediate requirements of the market. And good schools should not only be able to respond to the immediate needs of society but also to help shape them. The mission of higher education is to train experts and professionals and to transfer knowledge that is currently available. But universities should also preserve and cultivate knowledge that, though it may not appear useful at the moment, provides a reservoir for new ideas that we might look for when seeking solutions to problems not only of today but of tomorrow and days to come.[1] The ultimate aim to pursue, then, should not be flexibility of institutions but rather an ability of their graduates to be flexible.

I place my trust in departments and educational institutions of high intellectual quality, sites of genuine inquiry where scholars and students are deeply involved in the process of probing, testing, discovering, and learning. From my own experience, I know that in such places teaching and research are complementary activities, and furthermore that they exhibit a capacity for self-guidance and self-improvement that can hardly be provoked through official resolutions and decrees. Resistance to changing the contents of the courses and teaching methods—which seems to be a serious problem at most institutions of higher education—can and will be challenged by those who seek academic excellence and whose need for continuous questioning and improvement of curriculum and whose engagement in interdisciplinary approaches will push others to change. There are signs that the call of university administrators to give priority to postgraduate or doctoral programs through special governmental funding may be heeded. I am certain that these programs will nurture a new generation of researchers and university teachers and will serve as hotbeds for ideas that will contribute to a positive transformation of the world of learning.

PERSONAL REFLECTIONS

As noted earlier, during the first, revolutionary, elections I was voted into the rector's office with the overwhelming support of the students. I have never stopped relying on them since and have to confess that, although there certainly exists within the student body a conservative faction resistant to reform, I have generally found more sympathy with innovations in their community than in the academic senate, where students occupy one-third of the seats but often fail to attend meetings, or among my colleagues, who are always more prepared to explain why anything new would not work than give it at least a try.

I have never given up teaching since I took the position of chief administrator of Palacky University. The one or two courses that I teach are vital to me in several respects: they force me to remain in touch with my field, which is American literature and American studies; they keep me in contact with students and colleagues in the department; they provide me the opportunity to try new formats and modes of instruction; and they provoke me into rethinking and restructuring the curricula. In moments of distress as an administrator, I do find in the lecture hall some reaffirmation of the purpose of an academic institution. Although it is sometimes said that we should switch to a system of a purely managerial university administration, I still believe the advantages of such a change would not make up for the loss we would experience if rectors and deans gave up research and teaching. This view is founded on an awareness of a long institutional history—and my university stems from 1573. That is, that the nature of its enduring mission can change over time, but it can hardly be replaced by objectives that would be entirely and incomparably different.

Olomouc is a town of some 100,000 inhabitants, and until 1990 it unwillingly "hosted" more than 20,000 Soviet troops; my meeting with the commander of the occupational forces 2 months after the revolution was one of the most dramatic hours in my life. Today, the foreign soldiers are gone and the university's pedagogical faculty is housed in their former military headquarters. Our growing university has added three new faculties to its former four (medicine, philosophy, natural sciences, and teacher training). The theological faculty, which secured the uninterrupted continuity of the institution from the sixteenth century up to 1950, when it was closed by the Communist regime, was incorporated again into the university; from the Teacher Training College, an independent faculty of physical culture split and started its own life; and in the most challenging act, we opened the first faculty of law in post-totalitarian Europe. Palacky University has doubled the number of students enrolled in the recent 5 years to its current 10,000 and has acquired further space that had been formerly used by our own military and by the Communist Party. The totalitarian authorities tried hard to keep the historical capital of Moravia and the ancient university town as provincial as possible, and after the revolution the university took it as a challenge to fight and alter the reality and mentality of small-mindedness and, difficult as it has been, the effort has produced some results. As newly elected rector, I also decided to run for a seat on the city council, and having been elected, I worked there toward a goal of bringing "gown" and "town" in Olomouc not only closer together but joining forces in the challenge to provincial and parochial ideas wherever they appeared. A weekly information paper and a university radio broadcasting program tried to make people feel part of a new endeavor, part of a transformation process. At Palacky, a number of courses have been offered to the public, including quite a comprehensive educational program for senior citizens, called the Third Age University. In 1991, I personally started a series of public talks with distinguished guests, among whom have been our leading politicians, scholars, writers, and artists. These talks have developed into an educational institute of its own, having attracted, in the 30 evenings, an audience of some 10,000 attendees and having been broadcast on national radio.

However paradoxical it may seem, it has been even easier to enhance the reputation and prestige of Palacky University beyond the city limits, and even internationally, than in Olomouc itself. For this town and this institution, therefore, as for many other places and schools in this country, it has been of immense academic, practical, but also psychological importance to introduce and establish international contacts. People who have participated in exchange programs with institutions from abroad or have become part of professional international networks have found many rewards in their new activities, and we launched quite a number of those immediately after 1990. It was a very special pleasure to be able to involve in some of the earliest international programs personal friends from Western Europe and the United States, which was true of an honors course program from Nebraska that we organized at our institution, lectures by visitors from abroad on subjects that were taboo up to 1989, arrangements for used books to be collected in Austria, Germany, Switzerland, the United Kingdom, and America and transported to Olomouc. But I dare say that for the initial period of opening to the freer world after the collapse of the totalitarian regime, the single most important thing was the opportunity for many people to experience a realistic self-assessment to gain or regain, in confrontation with the external world, their lost or undermined self-confidence. After this happened and after the first stage of assistance from, and linkages with, foreign countries had been established, we had a sound basis for true international exchange and cooperation that meets common interests and provides mutual benefit.

Internationalization of education is a task we will have to, and want to, seriously work on in the years to come for practical, political, and cultural reasons. Names of projects and organizations, such as TEMPUS, COST, HESP, Civil Education Project, Peace Corps, Fulbright Commission, Masaryk Scholarships, British Council, Open Society Fund, Central European University, and others, will be recognized or remembered as important building blocks of international academic activities. From my own participation in meetings of the Association of European Universities, where the new rectors from Eastern and Central European countries were welcomed as colleagues and where we learned a lot of practical wisdom from our more experienced counterparts, and from my involvement in a project involving U.S. and European academic leaders called Transatlantic Dialogue, I have arrived at an understanding that our problems in education and higher education, along with other more general issues, may, in fact, be of a global nature. I find this observation more encouraging than depressing, for dealing with such problems will logically call for common, truly international action and will bring us all closer together.

Editor's Postscript. The 1996 Hannah Arendt Prize was awarded to Palacky University for its accomplishments in transformation in the post-Communist era. The institution was recognized for its restructuring of the undergraduate curriculum, for its integration with the community, and for its Romany Education Project, which sponsors research and education programs concerning the Czech Republic's largest minority, the Gypsies. The Hannah Arendt Prize, sponsored by the Vienna-based Institute for Human Sciences, in conjunction with the Koerber Foundation of Hamburg, Germany, is awarded for "outstanding, self-initiated reform efforts in higher education and research in the formerly communist countries of Eastern Europe."

NOTE

1. In December 1995, the Governmental Bill for Higher Education discussed here reached the Parliament but was refused even before its first reading, and was returned for "rewriting." The reasons for the refusal concerned most of the issues mentioned in my analysis. It is unlikely that anything will happen in legislation pertinent to Czech higher education before Parliamentary elections in June 1996. It is more realistic to expect that a third attempt to prepare and pass a new Act of Higher Education will begin only after a new government is installed as a result of the elections.

REFERENCES

Centre for Higher Education Studies. 1992. *Higher education in the Czech Republic 1992–1993: Assessment of the implementation of the recommendations by the OECD examiners from March 1992.* Prague: Centre for Higher Education Studies.

Institute for Human Sciences. 1992. *Report on research and assistance programs pertinent to transformation of the national higher education and research systems of Central Europe.* Vienna: Institute for Human Sciences.

———. 1995. Western paradigms and Eastern agenda: A reassessment. TERC Report 8. Vienna: Institute for Human Sciences.

Ministry of Education. 1995. Unpublished data. Prague: Czech Ministry of Education, Centrum pro studium vysokeho skolstvi.

Organization for Economic Cooperation and Development (OECD). 1992. *Review of higher education in the Czech and Slovak Federal Republic: Examiners' report and questions.* Draft DEELSA/ED/WE (92) 5 (restricted). Paris: OECD Directorate for Education, Employment, Labour, and Social Affairs.

FURTHER READING

Campbell, C. G., and R. Dahrendorf, eds. 1994. *Changes in Central Europe: Challenges and perspectives for higher education and research.* TERC Report 6. Vienna: Institute for Human Sciences.

Centre for Higher Education Studies. 1993. *Higher education in the Czech Republic.* Prague: Centre for Higher Education Studies.

European Journal of Education. 1993. 28 (4).

———. 1994. 29 (1).

Gore, L., and J. Krapfl, eds. 1994. *Reflections: The journal of the 1992 Czechoslovakia honors semester.* Boise, Idaho: The National Collegiate Honors Council.

Harach, L.; J. Kotasek; J. Koucky; and J. Hendrichova. 1992. *Higher education in the Czech and Slovak Federal Republic: Report to the OECD.* Prague and Bratislava.

Hayward, J. C. F. 1993. The art of survival. Paper presented at Czech/Slovak/U.K. Administrators Conference, 13–15 October, Prague. Also presented to same conference, 12–14 September 1994, Olomouc.

Institute for Human Sciences. 1994. *Issues in transition 1994: The reform of higher education and research systems in Central Europe.* TERC Report 7. Vienna: Institute for Human Sciences.

Jarab, J. 1993. Higher education and research in the Czech Republic. *Higher Education Management* 5 (3): 309–16.

Kirk, M., and A. Rhodes, eds. 1994. *Continental responsibility: European and international support for higher education and research in Central Europe.* Vienna: Institute for Human Sciences.

Koucky, J., and J. Hendrichova. 1993. *Higher education and research in the Czech Republic: Major changes since 1989.* TERC Report 3. Vienna: Institute for Human Sciences.

Obnova ideje univerzity. 1993. Prague: Univerzita Karlova.

CHAPTER 14

South Africa

Brian De Lacy Figaji

Executive Summary. The newly elected democratic government in South Africa faces the monumental task of redressing the profound inequities created by the apartheid system, the systematically and legally entrenched racial segregation in effect since 1948. The maldistribution of resources is apparent in every aspect of society, with Whites making up nearly 13 percent of the population and earning 39 percent of the total personal income, and with 54 percent of the White age cohort participating in tertiary education, compared with 9 percent for Coloureds and 6 percent for Africans.

The shape and structure of a new higher education system has been the subject of intense study and debate, with the National Commission on Higher Education (NCHE) playing a major role in issuing recommendations to the government. The work of the commission has been grounded in the Reconstruction and Development Program, the overarching strategic framework proposed by the government and generally accepted by society.

Institutions and their stakeholders are also driving the change process, conscious of the moral obligation to bring about equity and the economic imperative to create an educated and skilled workforce of the majority population. The major issues to be addressed are expanding access for Blacks (in South African terminology, Black includes the African, Coloured, and Asian populations), more equitable distribution of funding among the historically White institutions (HWIs) and historically Black institutions (HBIs), and greater efficiency in the use of resources. The HBIs are significantly disadvantaged by the poor academic preparation of their students, the fact that they cannot afford to pay tuition, and the government funding formula currently in effect. In addition, technikons and universities need to provide a closer match between their educational programs and national and regional needs. The balance between institutional autonomy and accountability to the larger society—a society with urgent economic and social needs—will be major considerations in any national reform effort.

The author describes his experiences at Peninsula Technikon in the context of rapid change and contentious environment. Increasing the numbers of African students and faculty was a priority of the institution's leadership, and Pentech was successful in this, in spite of subtle resistance. "Transformation"—shedding the past created by apartheid—was the subject of campuswide discussion and negotiation with students in a "stakeholders and transformation forum," but since the legal authority for the institution resides in the chief executive office and the council (the board of directors), the transformation forum is an advisory group, formulating recommendations to the decision-making bodies. Leadership in such turbulent times requires firmness as well as a willingness to consult staff and students.

• • • • • • • • • • •

The changes in South Africa have been so dramatic within the last five years that it is essential to provide a national backdrop against which higher education can be viewed. Since 1948, the National Party governments systematically entrenched racial segregation in South Africa by enforcing legislation that ensured separation in every facet of society. The result was that each of the four major racial groups (African, "Coloured," Asian, and White) had separate residential areas, separate educational institutions, separate beaches, separate entertainment facilities, separate entrances to public places, and separate political systems. The culmination of apartheid was the establishment of independent homelands and self-governing territories for the different ethnic groups among the South African population.

South Africa's race laws and past human rights violations resulted in an increasing degree of international isolation. Given its sophisticated economy, a well-developed technological infrastructure, a relatively skilled workforce, and an advanced financial system, the international sanctions and internal turmoil slowed down economic growth from about 5.5 percent in the 1960s to 1.2 percent in the 1980s. Fortunately, there has been some recovery in the investment rates since 1994.

Income distribution in South Africa is very unequal and heavily biased toward Whites, who make up 12.8 percent of the population and earn 58.8 percent of the total personal income. In 1993, the average per capita income for Africans was R2,717 per annum, while the corresponding figure for Whites was R32,076.

South Africa's reintroduction into the international economy has increased the pressure for the removal of any form of tariff protection, which, in turn, is forcing South African companies to be more competitive. Greater international competitiveness requires more highly skilled production workers and managers. All this is happening at a time when labor is free to organize itself and the power struggle between unions and management has not had sufficient time to find its own equilibrium.

The democratic elections held in 1994, the first time that every citizen, regardless of race or gender, was afforded an opportunity to vote, resulted in the abolition of all laws based on race, gender, or ethnicity. The new government has had not only to establish a democratic culture, but also to abolish established governing structures in the homelands, self-governing territories, and the tricameral, racially based parliamentary system.

The new interim constitution established nine provinces, each with a provincial legislature and a premier. Central government retained control over defense, police, finance, justice, foreign affairs, and land affairs, while formulating national policy on health, education, housing, welfare, and sport. Universities and technikons are the responsibility of the national ministry, while all other education sectors and institutions are the responsibility of the provinces. The national ministry formulates policy on issues such as service conditions, salaries, and teacher-pupil ratios.

The Government of National Unity (GNU) had to put in place mechanisms such as the Truth and Reconciliation Commission to explore the atrocities of apartheid and help heal the wounds of the past. It has entrenched constitutionalism by establishing the Constitutional Court; ensured that human rights abuses are never again tolerated by creating a permanent Human Rights Commission and promulgating a bill of rights; and given the media a degree of independence by vesting power in the newly established Independent Broadcasting Authority. Parallel and as part of the establishment of all these new mechanisms, the old racially separate structures were dismantled and either disbanded or integrated into the new structures.

In education, the integration process was particularly extensive in that 15 separate education departments had to be brought under a single national ministry and 9 provincial ministries. The inherited system for which the new education ministries have responsibility consists of a school sector made up of public, private, and special schools; about 150 technical colleges preparing skilled people for specific occupations including trades training; about 112 colleges of education concerned solely with the preservice and in-service training of teachers; 15 technikons providing tertiary level, career-oriented education with an emphasis on the promotion and practice of technology; and 21 universities offering fundamental education and training while also preparing students for a variety of high-level professions. Except for the technikons, which were established in 1987, all the other institutional types have a long history with steady but small growth rates. (The enrollments in each sector are outlined below in Table 14.1)

TABLE 14.1		
ENROLLMENTS IN EDUCATION IN 1995 (NCHE 1996)		
Sector	Enrollment	Percent of Total Enrollment
Public Schools	11,614,857	93.21
Private Schools	171,692	1.38
Special Schools	45,517	0.37
Subtotal	**11,832,066**	**94.96**
Technical Colleges	65,477	0.53
Colleges of Education	78,190	0.63
Technikons	147,391	1.18
Universities	337,573	2.71
Total	**12,460,697**	**100.01**

The 32 nursing colleges and 73 nursing schools are currently the responsibility of the Department of Health, while the 12 agricultural colleges fall under the jurisdiction of the Department of Agriculture.

South African pupils ideally spend 12 years at school (Sub. A to Standard 10), with progress from one year to the next based on their performance in an end-of-year examination that is governed largely by the school. However, at the end of year 12, pupils write an externally set, marked, and moderated examination in order to obtain a senior certificate (or equivalent). To a large extent, tertiary education institutions base their admission criteria on each candidate's performance in this examination. A pass in the senior certificate examination is the minimum requirement for admission to a college of education, a technikon, or a diploma program at a university.

The provision of education in South Africa has faced and continues to face the following major criticisms:

- It was designed to serve primarily the needs of the White population; this is borne out by the 54 percent participation rate in tertiary education for Whites within the age cohort of 20–24 years (comparable figure for the United Kingdom is 45 percent), compared with 9 percent for Coloureds and 6 percent for Africans (NCHE 1996, 37).

- It is largely unplanned and is based on institutional autonomy that severely limits influence, direction, or steering by the state.
- It is uncoordinated, in that no provision is made for articulation from one sector to another with credit transfer.
- It is largely inefficient and not responsive enough to the social and economic demands of the country.

Concerned educators, academic unions, student organizations, and the liberation movements have had many meetings, conferences, and debates on the ills of the education system and the type of transformation needed. Even the previous government proposed a renewal of education. These debates and proposals are summed up in the following major reports: *Education Renewal Strategy* (DNE 1992), outlining the government's proposals for change; *The Framework Report* (NEPI 1993), a major work done under the auspices of the National Education Co-ordinating Committee (NECC); *A National Training Strategy Initiative* (National Training Board 1994), a document coordinated by the Department of Labour with significant stakeholder participation; and *Policy Framework for Education and Training* (ANC 1995), a report produced by the African National Congress's Education Department. Much of the actual implementation strategies have been developed during the country's transition period by the Centre for Educational Policy Development (CEPD).

The minister of education in the Government of National Unity has, in his white paper on education, made it abundantly clear that education provision at all levels will have to adhere to the principles of equity, redress, access for disadvantaged groups, greater student mobility, quality, cost-effectiveness, democracy, and accountability. A consequence of applying these principles has been the implementation of a national pupil-teacher ratio for all schools, which must be achieved over the next five years so that a national per-student cost will form the basis for the financial allocations for the school sector. These principles have also generated the appointment of the National Commission on Higher Education (NCHE) by government proclamation in February 1995, and the possible establishment of a Further Education Commission.

The NCHE has been given specific terms of reference that incorporate the principles outlined in the white paper. Clearly, the government is trying in the most consultative way to implement strategies that will move toward greater equity and access.

FORCES FOR CHANGE

All the historically Black institutions (HBIs)—and some of the historically White institutions (HWIs)—were sites of struggle against the previous apartheid regime. The strategies employed during this period demonstrated the power of collective action; students and faculty continue to use this power to ensure their participation in the process toward the transformation of both the education system and the individual higher education institutions. Within South Africa, there are probably three major forces for change, although each may be interpreting the necessary changes differently in terms of both the desired speed and the extent of the change. These forces are

- The government, which needs to demonstrate that things are different, particularly for those previously disadvantaged
- The institutions, which feel a moral obligation to bring about greater equity, although there is a great difference in the interpretation of this among institutions
- The stakeholders, and in particular students, who want greater access and more relevant programs

The overarching strategic framework proposed by the government and generally accepted by society is the Reconstruction and Development Program (RDP). This program makes people central to all development, aiming to redress the past social and economic inequities based on race and gender, and endeavoring to promote reconciliation in this divided society. While government resources and international aid are being channeled to the RDP, it is accepted that its real implementation will come from economic growth and job creation. This points to human resource development as the most critical factor contributing to the success of the RDP, which requires the active cooperation of the higher education sector.

CENTRAL ISSUES FACING HIGHER EDUCATION

It may be more appropriate to discuss the issues facing higher education in South Africa using the terminology used locally. The essence of the issues are probably the same for higher education in the rest of the world.

Access

There is a realization in South Africa, as is the case in the rest of the world, that a tertiary education qualification enhances an individual's chances of finding a job and ensures a higher level of income. The fact that nearly all of the top positions in commerce and industry are held by Whites in South Africa and that they have a 54 percent participation rate in higher education has clearly signaled to the Black (African, Coloured, and Asian) population that a higher education qualification made the Whites successful, and hence they must now demand higher participation rates in order to become meaningful players in the economy and improve their standard of living. Given that the African participation rate in 1991–92 was a mere 6 percent, and given that

Africans make up just over 70 percent of the population, the expansion required to accommodate this demand is quite significant.

In the last five years, in response to the clamor for access from disadvantaged students, many of the enlightened institutions, particularly the HBIs, admitted more students than their physical plants could accommodate. But, because of the subject choice at high schools or the lack of adequate teaching, many of those entering higher education could only enter programs in the arts or humanities, and the institutions were less able to provide space in the more costly fields of the natural sciences and technology. During this period, even the technikons experienced a higher enrollment in the fields of business studies, public administration, and education, as opposed to the science and technology fields of study. The expansion in student numbers was not accompanied by the necessary government funding, and as a consequence, institutions had to absorb the extra burden while critics were questioning the quality of education these institutions were providing. This situation demonstrates a classic conflict between issues of access and quality when the funding levels remain constant or decline.

While for students the major issue was access, for the more concerned educators and the government the broader issue was appropriate access; that is, access to programs that could contribute to improving the economy, such as science, engineering, and business studies; access for rural students; access for women; and access for the children of the poor. The quest for access has brought into question the current criteria for admission to higher education and the ways in which the existing institutions could improve efficiency to enable them to deal with more students using the existing resources. Both questions are being dealt with by the NCHE.

On the positive side, the demand for access has resulted in the creation of a large number of private colleges; they now enroll about 200,000 students. These colleges and their students currently receive no financial support from the state. The existence of these institutions raises the question of how to incorporate private higher education institutions into a funding model without tax dollars going toward corporate profits.

Finance

With the 1995–96 expenditure on education being about 9 percent of GDP and higher education spending about 1.1 percent of GDP, the feeling in some government circles is that because this is higher than the comparable value in the United States, we cannot allow this expenditure ratio to increase. However, only between 60 and 70 percent of the higher education budget comes from government funding, thus placing higher education in South Africa in the category of "low dependence on government funding," according to the World Bank classification of dependency levels on government funding. An argument can therefore be made, and is being made, for greater government argument can therefore be made, and is being made, for greater government spending on higher education in order to address the issues of access, equity, and redress.

The fact that it is accepted in South Africa that students contribute to the cost of their higher education helps institutions to balance their budgets. However, the level of tuition fees has gone beyond the financial capacity of many households. During 1995, the Ministry of Education, in response to a proposal from the NCHE, established a national student loan scheme for needy students in order to facilitate access to higher education for academically able students. This scheme helped to reduce the bad-debt situation at the HBIs.

Tuition fees are set by institutions in order to help balance the budget, while taking cognizance of the economic profile of their students. These fees range from about R3,000 ($705) to R12,000 ($2,825) per annum, depending on the institution and the field of study. The HWIs are able to set fairly high fees because their students are generally more affluent and the institutions have the financial resources to support the relatively few students who struggle to pay. At the HBIs, on the other hand, the students are poor and they struggle to pay even the lower fees. Because the institutions are more sympathetic, sometimes unwisely so, they experience a large bad-debt situation. Government funding is based on student enrollments during the academic year two years prior to the current year, through a formula that takes 50 percent of the students actually registered during that year, plus 50 percent of the students who achieved passing grades.

In summary, the HBIs attract the academically less-able students because of tougher admission criteria elsewhere, so these institutions are required either to spend more money on academic support or to accept large failure rates, which means a reduction in state subsidy. The academically disadvantaged students are invariably poor and therefore unlikely to be able to pay their tuition fees, which results in a bad debt for the institution. This situation of gross inequality is in need of correction, and the very survival of some HBIs will be the major force behind changing the government funding formula, supporting a student financial aid scheme, and promoting the notion of a national standard tuition fee according to study field.

Relevance

The mismatch between national needs and the endeavors of higher education is perhaps most starkly demonstrated by the fact that the first successful heart transplant was done in Cape Town and we continue to have an excellent international reputation in this field of medicine—but at the same time, we are unable to deal with a tuberculosis epidemic in the region. This may also

Similarly, the Ministry of Trade and Industry is committed to the removal of tariff protection and the promotion of exports, requiring that local products, produced by a more skilled workforce, meet international standards in order to compete globally. The Department of Agriculture now has to respond to the needs of the small farmers rather than to large farmers who were traditionally tied into powerful cooperatives, and this requires a fresh look at the training and support given to farmers.

There is, therefore, a strong force for change coming from the new government because it has to deliver services to the previously disadvantaged—who also happen to be the majority of the population—and because it has to ensure sustained economic growth and development. Higher education must respond to these needs for more highly skilled professionals. Without the full participation of Blacks, these economic goals cannot be achieved.

Technikons enjoy a very close relationship with their industry partners, who serve on liaison committees that are established for each program. Curriculum revision is done in consultation with the relevant industry; industry and professional bodies participate in accreditation visits, and most technikon students are required to work in industry for a specific period, which provides an internship experience that greatly enhances a student's employment opportunities. This relationship has resulted in high employment rates for technikon students and a call for universities to become more responsive to the needs of industry. The white papers on education and the RDP regularly refer to partnerships in developing a new education and training system.

Finally, the push for more mathematics and science in school and greater access to science and technology programs in higher education has become part of the call for more relevant education programs, because students with these specific skills are able to find jobs quite easily, and this is the area of need that has been identified by the government and business.

Modernization

The need for higher education to move rapidly toward modernization stems from a number of factors. First is the necessity to become part of the global academic community through electronic communication, which will reduce the historic isolation. Second, new technologies provide an opportunity for reaching more learners and making learning more effective. Third, students must be able to function in an environment that will increasingly be using computers and computer-controlled processes. Fourth is the need for technological innovations that will assist industry to become more competitive in the global market.

Some higher education institutions are already well advanced along the path towards modernization in terms of their computing facilities and the global electronic networks they are able to access. For effective modernization, every higher education institution should ensure that each student is computer literate and that all researchers have access to the global networks. But modern communication technology could also provide an opportunity for more learners to be reached, for learning materials to be used more effectively, and for more flexible learning opportunities. However, we must at the same time ensure that the basic infrastructure such as electricity and appropriate learning spaces exist in the rural areas. This type of expansion must be carefully planned so that the disadvantaged benefit.

As we become reintegrated into the international community of scholars, we will experience an increasing demand from foreign academics to teach in South Africa and from students who would want to study here. Already many applications are being received from people in other countries in Africa. While this would be valuable for South African higher education, it has to be viewed against the background of Black academics who could not improve their qualifications because of the struggle, and who will be sidelined by this influx of well-qualified faculty, along with the fact that the demand for student places in higher education far exceeds the supply. The practice in some countries of regarding foreign students as a source of income for institutions will meet with considerable opposition from local students. While it is important that we modernize and become part of the international community by enriching our teaching and learning with the presence of foreign academics and learners, it cannot be done at the expense of the national imperatives of equity, redress, and access.

Autonomy, Accountability, and Quality

As we move toward greater democracy, the tensions between autonomy, accountability, and quality become more apparent. While these topics are being fiercely debated, there is a general acknowledgment that academic freedom is an essential cornerstone of higher education and that institutions need a degree of autonomy. The concern is to find the correct balance between institutional autonomy and the institution's accountability to the state and its stakeholders and their coexistence in the interest of the broader society.

In its very simple form, we could take autonomy to mean "the power to govern without outside controls," while accountability means "the requirement to demonstrate responsible actions to one or more constituency" (NCHE 1996, 78). Currently, higher education institutions enjoy a very high level of autonomy with limited steering from government in the way institutions are funded; for example, through more money for students in science and technology as opposed to arts and humanities. It could be argued that if the state demands greater access for the historically disadvantaged, it is in a sense dictating who should be taught; and if the state directs education to respond to the economic needs of the country, it is in a sense dictating what should be taught. In essence, then, conflict will be created by the way in which the state intends to "direct" higher education. It is heartening to know that the minister of education has called for a new relationship, not expressed in terms of autonomy, but rather in terms of close collaboration, so that higher education becomes an agent of change, fully engaged with the state in fulfilling national objectives.

Measuring and enhancing quality implies evaluating products and services against set standards with a view to improvement, renewal, and progress. It would be a legitimate demand from the state that some form of quality measure be instituted so that it is able to justify the expenditure of taxpayers' money. It should also be the responsibility of higher education to ensure the maintenance of minimum standards and to promote the ideals of excellence. While some quality measures are applied to a part of the higher education sector, the challenge is to subject the whole sector to regular quality assessments and to provide incentives for improvement.

Broad Transformation Fora

The most significant force for change from the student body has come from the South African Students Congress (SASCO) calling for the formation of broad transformation fora at higher education institutions. It is envisaged that a forum consists of all stakeholders, both internal and external to the institution, and that its task is to oversee the transition towards greater democracy, participation, and openness at the institutions. The student proposal is that these fora will have final decision-making authority on a wide range of matters. This proposal has met with very different responses on the various campuses, ranging from the establishment of a forum with the decision-making powers as envisioned on the one side, to no institutional response at all at the other extreme. On April 16, 1995, however, the minister of education endorsed the idea and encouraged all universities and technikons to form broad transformation committees.

While this proposal has some merit in attempting to introduce more democratic practices at institutions, it could create a situation where the statutory power of the council (the governing board) and the vice-chancellor is taken over by a body of people who have no accountability to anyone for their actions. It also implies a disregard for due process and the rule of the law. The success of this proposal, to date, has been that the governing boards of higher education institutions have, in many cases, been changed to include a wider range of stakeholder interests.

LEADERSHIP IN INSTITUTIONAL CHANGE

There can be no doubt that higher education institutions need the total attention of their leaders if they are to respond to the many forces for change. Unfortunately, many leaders in education are being faced with the demands of participation on national bodies related to higher education—dealing with the energy-sapping issues of student protests, trying to adapt to and understand the fast-changing external environment, and at the same time also dealing with the changed attitude and demands of the internal constituencies who are fired up by their new rights and the general clamor for participation, democracy, and transparency.

Since institutions are affected in different ways by the forces of change, the institutional leadership manifests different approaches, ranging from giving the institution a new direction, to developing campus harmony and building institutional coherence, to spreading the responsibility and authority to lead among more of the senior members rather than keeping it as the preserve of the CEO.

A few years ago, the selection of a new vice-chancellor was the responsibility of a small committee appointed by the governing board, with responsibility to short-list and interview candidates. The final decision was made by the governing board. Today, the process is far more protracted and participatory. Applicants are interviewed by a large panel made up of board members, students, workers, faculty, administrators, and union representatives. In some cases, the interviews are held in public or they are televised to a wider audience. Some processes require applicants to address a public meeting and answer questions. After all of this, the committee presents its candidate to the governing board, which either ratifies the recommendation or sends it back for a new process if it has legitimate reasons for not ratifying the candidate's appointment.

In South Africa, it is not just about leadership, it is about leadership in a fast-changing and sometimes hostile environment; the tasks of leading are all-consuming. Many leaders find themselves in a very different situation today compared with the task they accepted when they were originally appointed, and the adaptation has been too great and too traumatic for some to handle.

THE INSTITUTIONAL RESPONSE: CHALLENGES AND SUCCESSES

In order to fully appreciate the comments that follow, it is important to describe the context and environment in which our institution is located. Established as an institution for higher education with a career orientation, in order to serve the Coloured population group of the country, the Peninsula Technikon is located about 30 kilometers outside of Cape Town in the Western Cape. The province of the Western Cape has a majority Coloured population, and it is the only province where the Coloured people are represented in significant numbers. The institution, like the University of the Western Cape, was created under the apartheid regime for a particular race group.

In the April 1994 general elections, seven of the nine provinces were convincingly won by the ANC; one province, KwaZulu/Natal, was won by the Inkatha Freedom Party (IFP), and the Western Cape was the only province won by the National Party. Political parties and social scientists have since spent much time speculating why the Coloured people, who experienced extreme oppression at the hands of the National Party and who were often leading the struggle for liberation, voted for it.

Since the inauguration of the Government of National Unity, there has been a growing feeling among Coloured people that they are being marginalized and that they have no respected leader who can articulate their needs and aspirations. This unhappiness has caused people to, firstly, retreat, then to openly distance themselves from the ANC, and now even to start speaking out against their perceived exclusion from the benefits of change, such as affirmative action practices by government and companies who are trying to win the favor of the government.

Given the political tensions in our region, our responses to the changes in our country have had mixed reception. What follows are some of the key responses and their effect on the institution and the community we serve.

Increasing the Numbers of African Students and Faculty

In the early 1980s, the institution decided to admit students of all races because it was the correct thing to do, although it was against the law at the time. We did this by simply inundating the departmental bureaucracy with applications for admissions from students who were not Coloured. This clogged the system, and because we were on a semester program at the time and students had to register for each semester, the rejection letter would arrive toward the end of the semester, when it was too late.

Although we had small numbers of African students in the beginning, this policy soon introduced a crisis in our language policy. In programs where the medium of instruction was Afrikaans, the African students, who often could not speak Afrikaans, were at a distinct disadvantage. We changed the language policy to one of English instruction, and this has been a source of unhappiness among some in the wider Coloured community and some of our faculty.

Today our student population is 50 percent African, 49 percent Coloured, and 1 percent White, which generates a feeling in the Coloured community, based entirely on their perception, that African students are given preference and that "their" children (the Coloured pupils) are once again being ignored. At the institution, we believe that our student population should reflect the demographics of our province, but this can only be brought about in a way that is not interpreted as racist or exclusionary.

In the interests of having the benefit of a diverse staff composition and appropriate role models for our students, attempts were made to ensure a greater degree of African participation as faculty members. Currently our staffing is about 65 percent Coloured, 30 percent White, and 5 percent African. This plan, while not openly opposed (because I believe now that staff felt it would have been politically incorrect to oppose the plan at the time), was subtly resisted in some areas and supported in a limited number of disciplines.

With the advantage of hindsight, it would be fair to say that the institutional leadership assumed that all the faculty were equally committed to the principles of equity and redress, and it failed to recognize people's fears of what this could mean for their own job security. There was insufficient dialogue on the need for this change and the exact interpretation of the extent of the change. The approach was too "top down," and it allowed for speculation about the future and the reasons for change.

Financial Issues

Frugal budgeting, good financial planning, and aggressive debt collection placed us in a favorable financial position, which enabled us to weather a few financial crises. However, over time, this has increased staff dissatisfaction with their workload and the inability to update equipment. The institution responded by having a more open budgeting process in which students and staff participate. The method for the allocation of resources between the academic and support activities is also reviewed annually with a focus on academic endeavors as our primary function. Much of the budget control has also been devolved to the dean and department level.

In order to avoid the crisis that usually occurs around tuition fee increases, we chose to negotiate tuition fee increases with our students. This has the advantage of providing greater institutional stability, but it also presents considerable problems. First, it is extremely time consuming. Second, such negotiations are held with a student leadership that is at the end of its term of office; if the leadership changes dramatically, the negotiated settlement may be rejected by the new group of leaders. We believe that this situation needs time to develop as an institutional practice and tradition, and that as the process of student participation matures, the contestation will decrease dramatically. In 1995, the students displayed a great level of maturity in both their demands and the way in which they negotiated.

In anticipation of the need to exclude students who have outstanding debt from the previous academic year, we established a financial exclusions committee. This committee consists of administrative staff, students, and faculty. The committee hears appeals from students who want to register but still have an outstanding account from the previous year. If the student is academically able, then the committee will arrange for the student to register; if not, the student is refused reregistration. This has worked well so far, because the criteria are well known and many students are actually helped. The final safety net for us is that a student does not graduate until his or her debts are settled in full.

Increasing Access

We have adopted a very flexible approach in that we have kept our criteria as low as possible and then selected students with the best chance for success based on a variety of criteria unique to each discipline and ranging from a portfolio of work, essay writing, and a particular rating scale. Even though we have tried to adhere to a closing date for applications, our student leaders regularly negotiate admission for students who have failed to apply in time. Generally, we will consider these appeals from rural students or other underrepresented groups.

In 1990, we anticipated the return of a large number of exiles as a result of amnesty arrangements. With the financial help of a foreign government, we introduced an access program that would cater to students who met the mature age exemption requirement, but who had an incomplete high school education. This program guaranteed admission to the mainstream programs for those students who satisfied certain pass requirements. When this plan was first discussed, it met with a considerable degree of resistance because the faculty felt they did not know what the standard of the access program would be, and automatic admission limited their right to select their students. Once this hurdle was overcome by involving the faculty fully, the program proved extremely successful. We hope that it will help to form the basis of a new type of further education college in the Western Cape.

Transformation

The debate about transformation started on our campus some years ago with participation by students, staff, and the senior managers, such as the vice-chancellor and deputies. Although initially an informal, ad hoc discussion, many fairly critical issues were raised and resulted in changes to curricula, procedures, and policy directions. At that time (and still today), we held firmly that a transformation forum could not assume the legal authority of the chief executive office or the board, both of whom have statutory responsibilities. Hence, recommendations from the transformation forum must be fed to the bodies who have the decision-making responsibility.

In order for this argument to be accepted, we had to demonstrate that this process would be effective, and this we did in three significant areas. In one instance, the forum suggested a change to the rules that excluded students from taking the final examination if they did not perform satisfactorily during the year. The rules were changed to provide for continuous evaluation, in terms of which the end-of-year examination was no longer the most significant contributor to the final mark. Another example of the process at work concerned admissions to the teacher education program. It was felt that the admission criteria set for the teacher education program excluded African applicants because business subjects were not taught at African schools. The curriculum for the teacher education program was changed so that the course could accommodate students who did not have previous exposure to business-related subjects at school. A third example concerned the governance structure. There was a need for greater student participation in the institutional governance structures, particularly at the highest level. Over a protracted period, the act governing the Technikon was changed to accommodate a general act for all technikons and a new legislative framework that allowed for participation of students and staff on the boards of technikons.

These actions have enabled us to ensure that the transformation forum does not regard itself as a decision-making body, and even though we have now formalized the forum, there is an agreement (albeit an uneasy one) that it will be called a "stakeholders and transformation forum," rather than a transformation forum. This, we believe, correctly reflects what the gathering really is, but the students would like to retain the name that has national significance, namely, a transformation forum.

Strengthening Science and Technology

In response to the country's need for more people to be skilled in the areas of science, engineering, and business, our most recent action has been to make this one of our strategic objectives. This implies increasing our enrollment in these study fields and focusing as much of our resources as possible in this direction, without unduly disadvantaging the other disciplines. While this objective has met with general acceptance, the matter is still being discussed quite extensively among faculty members. This initiative was developed by the vice-chancellor articulating it as part of his vision for the institution, together with the promotion of excellence in all academic departments and providing sufficient flexibility in the definition of science and technology for the strategic planning committee to suggest a more inclusive definition. This strategy has come at a time when it would be difficult to oppose such a focus, since science and technology are being promoted nationally, and science and technology enrollments at our institutions have dropped from 56 to 47 percent.

Strategic Planning

Together with all of the above, a key strategy over the last few years has been to put in place a strategic planning process that has enabled us to produce a statement of institutional vision, mission, and values. We set broad institutional objectives annually and ask operating units to focus on contributing toward the realization of these objectives. Our process currently includes reformulating or fine-tuning the objectives and tying this process into the budgeting process. The intention is that the budget setting must be targeted at achieving the objectives. We have had the support of a program sponsored by the American Council on Education that helped to get greater participation of our stakeholders in this process. With a sustained effort at planning, we will achieve a better focus for our activities and greater constructive engagement of our stakeholders.

Leading Change

My predecessor, Franklin Sonn, currently South African ambassador to the United States, and I (then vice-rector) believed very strongly that we should provide an environment and the learning opportunities that would help restore the self-respect of our students and lift us out of the second-class status which the authorities had planned for us. Against many obstacles, we insisted on a campus plan that would provide for the academic, social, and cultural needs of the students, and buildings that would make the whole Technikon community proud. This philosophy has been so successfully communicated to staff and students that we have a campus free of any graffiti.

Our statement of values is referred to at every possible opportunity that the rector has when addressing students, staff, or service workers. Of particular importance is the value of mutual respect among staff, among students, and between the two groups. Perhaps our greatest asset is our young, enthusiastic, and committed staff, who work hard and make every effort to ensure that students are successful academically. Every institution needs firm and fair leadership that is prepared to consult staff and students and work hard to improve quality and realize a vision.

LOOKING TOWARD THE FUTURE

The report by the National Commission (NCHE) will no doubt have a profound effect on higher education. Just how great an effect will depend on the reception the proposals meet with during the consultation phase and the political will on the part of the minister of education and his department to implement the recommendations. What is clear, however, is that higher education is going to have to do more with fewer or the same resources. It will have to provide for more students, while at the same time respond more creatively to the needs of the economy. This will require the effective and appropriate use of technology—an area that will require extensive investigation, research, and learning from others if we are going to achieve success with the minimum amount of waste through errors.

With respect to the higher education sector, it appears that single-discipline colleges (such as teacher education colleges and colleges of nursing) will be brought into the higher education sector by amalgamation in colleges. This means that colleges will be required to become part of a technikon or a university and will cease to exist as independent entities. At the moment, technikons and universities are still regarded as institutions with separate missions and together make up a differentiated higher education sector. It is possible that in the future, we may only have universities, and technikons may become technical universities.

Because higher education's greatest asset is its people, any forward-looking scenario must include the people directly involved in higher education. In South Africa, we are moving from a situation of decision making by a small group to consultation, from management to collaboration, and from central control to decentralized cooperative governance. These changes require more time, greater patience, and a clear understanding of the responsibilities of persons and groups at the various levels within the organization. We need to plan the transition from one phase to the other, prepare the people for this change, and build sufficient trust among people so that the process can be sustained through the difficult periods. Too often we believe that people who articulate democratic concepts actually act democratically toward their subordinates. At our institution, we assumed that because we fought for democracy, the internal application of democratic principle would come naturally; it does not. It requires training, discussions, and involvement in institutional processes in order to develop acceptable practices. We agree with the principles, but underestimate what implementation requires of us. This is probably the biggest challenge for each individual within higher education in South Africa, and in particular for those in leadership positions. A quotation by an unknown author summarizes this well:

> Coming together is the beginning
> Keeping together is progress
> Working together is success.

REFERENCES

African National Congress (ANC). 1995. *Policy framework for education and training.* Swaziland: Manzini.

Department of National Education (DNE). 1992. *Education renewal strategy.* Pretoria: DNE.

National Commission on Higher Education (NCHE). 1996. *A framework for a transformed higher education system.* Pretoria: NCHE.

National Education Policy Investigation (NEPI). 1993. *The framework report.* Cape Town: Oxford Press.

National Training Board (NTB). 1994. *A national training strategy initiative.* Pretoria: NTB.

FURTHER READING

Consultative Business Movement (CBM). 1994. *Building a winning nation.* Johannesburg: Raven Press.

National Education Policy Investigation (NEPI). 1992. *Governance and administration.* Cape Town: Oxford Press.

———. 1992. *Human resource development.* Cape Town: Oxford Press.

CHAPTER 15

Japan

Tadao Ishikawa

Executive Summary. Since the Meiji Restoration some 130 years ago, Japanese higher education has served the nation's drive for modernization. Since World War II, there has been dramatic expansion of postsecondary enrollment, which now stands at 60 percent of high school graduates. Thirty percent attend universities. Another significant postwar change has been the emphasis on higher education serving a democratic nation and the growth of private higher education, which now enrolls 77 percent of all students. Today, Japan faces the major challenge of creating a flexible higher education system that is geared more toward stimulating lifelong learning and students' abilities to think independently and creatively than to the acquisition of knowledge. Japanese higher education must also be more responsive to the needs of society, producing graduates with more practical skills. Institutional reputation can no longer be a substitute for educational results. To accomplish this will require a loosening of control by the Ministry of Education in order to provide institutions with greater freedom to determine their missions, their goals, and standards of excellence that derive from their unique institutional identity. Greater institutional differentiation will improve the quality of research and teaching, as will more flexible institutional structures and more interdisciplinary endeavors. The author describes how Keio University, a private institution, was able to create two new faculties in response to the changing needs of society. Through a process of participation, negotiation, and persuasion, sufficient support was gathered to launch these new initiatives. The author asserts that, in spite of the obstacles to change presented by Ministry regulations and the resistance one would expect in a large and successful university, it is possible to exercise leadership and promote innovation.

• • • • • • • • • • • •

I n Japan, "higher education" generally refers to graduate schools, colleges and universities, junior colleges, colleges of technology, and postsecondary courses of special training colleges. According to 1994 statistics from the Ministry of Education (Ministry of Education 1995a), the proportion of those 18 years of age who continued on from high school into higher education exceeded 62 percent: 4-year universities and colleges, 30.1 percent; junior colleges, 13.2 percent; technical colleges, 0.6 percent; and postsecondary courses of special training colleges, 18.5 percent. This chapter focuses on four-year universities and colleges and graduate schools, which are the main components of higher education.

To understand the current situation in Japanese higher education, it is useful to begin with a brief history. Japanese education has been influenced by national goals since 1868, when the Meiji Restoration ended nearly 300 years of feudal rule and brought to power men committed to the modernization of Japan. The goal of the Meiji Restoration was, essentially, to modernize Japan and to build it into an independent, strong, and prosperous nation through the introduction of Western civilization. The slogan "rich country, strong military" epitomized these objectives. The leaders of this period felt that the pace of modernization would be accelerated by raising the educational level of the Japanese people. In short, they viewed education as a prerequisite to modernization.

In 1872, the government began to implement a compulsory education system. At first, emphasis was placed on the parents' moral responsibility for their children's education. Compulsory education was legalized in 1886, and in 1900 the government mandated four years of schooling. Officials next took steps to insure that this system was put into place throughout the nation. In 1886, about the same time as the modern governmental structure was established, Tokyo Imperial University, the first imperial national university, was also founded. Through these steps, the basis of an educational system was organized from compulsory basic education to higher education.

Imperial national universities were conceived as institutions that aimed for the highest level of academic research, technical training, and education necessary for the development of the nation. Because of this focus, they were given preferential treatment by the government. During the 50 years of the system's existence, 7 universities were established in major urban centers. After the war, they became regular national universities. They are still strongly influenced by their prewar preeminence.

The government expected that the national universities, including the imperial national universities, would train students who would serve as the leaders of a modern nation. This goal resulted in a considerable investment in these universities. Private universities and colleges, such as Keio University, existed alongside the national universities and also produced qualified graduates. From the perspective of national educational policy, however, the national universities were primary. By 1943, there were 19 national universities. The 28 private universities only slightly outnumbered the nationals (Ministry of Education 1943).

After World War II, two major transformations occurred. First, there was a dramatic expansion of higher education. Second, amidst this expansion, the role of private universities grew in importance. There were 144 public universities by 1993, including national universities and colleges, and 390 private universities and colleges (Ministry of Education 1994). Today, there are 565 four-year colleges and universities (Ministry of Education 1995a, 1). This is clearly a significant increase from 1943. Also, fully 77 percent[1] of Japanese students in higher education (four-year colleges and universities, graduate schools, and junior colleges) now attend private schools, while only 23 percent are enrolled in public higher institutions. These figures leave no doubt about the contributions and significance of private school graduates to the country. The growth of private higher education is one important indicator of its success in Japan.

Three reasons can be cited for this expansion of Japanese higher education after the Second World War. First, postwar Japan removed "strong military" from the national goal established by the Meiji leaders and summarized by the slogan "rich country, strong military." Instead, the nation concentrated on achieving a richly democratic society. As a result, Japan changed dramatically after the war. The level of economic activity is a prime example. The Japanese economy is now 15.6 percent of the world's gross national product (Economic Planning Agency 1993, 4), representing astonishing growth since the prewar era. If economic activity increased to this extent, then other facets of Japanese society should have experienced similar growth. In fact, this expansion stimulated demand for university graduates. As a result, more people were encouraged to pursue higher education, and the number of institutions grew accordingly.

The second reason for the expansion of higher education in postwar Japan was the growth of democracy. Social equality became more important. Before the war, approximately two to three percent of the college-age cohort pursued higher education, largely from the upper class. The current participation rate is approximately 30 percent, indicating that higher education is now accessible to a wide cross-section of citizens. Social pressure also became a factor in promoting higher education participation; if my neighbor's child is going to a university, so will my child. Parents came to believe in the importance of academic credentials as a key to good jobs and the good life. The combination of the desire for social equality and the belief in academic credentials served to increase the demand for higher education.

The third factor contributing to the growth of higher education in postwar Japan was increasing affluence. Higher income levels made university education more affordable for parents.

FORCES FOR CHANGE

Higher education in Japan is now a system that is open to all citizens. Some maintain that the 565 currently operating institutions are sufficient. However, there is no precise way to measure how many higher education graduates the nation requires. My own sense is that the current number of institutions is appropriate to meet the needs of Japan's level of economic activity and social growth for the present and for the near future. However, the current high level of participation—30 percent of the age cohort—raises issues of quality. These issues will become increasingly important as we seek to improve the quality of research and teaching.

There are many pressures for change. The pace of this change is accelerating and its complexity is increasing. At the same time, the future is becoming increasingly opaque. Society, in turn, is becoming more complex and less stable. These characteristics of the present and future—complexity, flux, and opaqueness—are not passing phenomena. Current trends suggest that change and instability characterize the present and will characterize the future. Scientific and technological progress, industrial developments, and advances in information have brought about significant transformations and will continue to drive change.

For example, the Soviet Union has collapsed and the Cold War has ended. If we inquire into the causes for the collapse of the Soviet system, we find that its structure was not able to match scientific and technological progress, industrialization, or the growth in information. That the Soviet system could not accommodate these changes and thus disintegrated shows that the pressure of these changes can be truly decisive.

While not all scientific and technological progress is positive (we have only to look at our current environmental problems), a return to old ways or earlier lifestyles is not an option. Only further scientific and technological advances can address the costs and negative effects of progress. Thus, the factors that have created a complex, changing, and opaque society will continue to impact our future. To survive and meet the challenges of an increasingly complex and difficult world, the quality of Japanese higher education will have to improve.

In addition to improving its overall quality, Japanese higher education will have to pay more attention to the abilities and skills of its graduates. In Japanese society, the prestige of a degree from a selective university has become more important than the student's actual ability or competence. The value of such credentials has allowed some universities to neglect improvements in educational quality. The question, however, will no longer be "What university did you attend?" but "What have you learned, and what abilities have you acquired?" Thus, the value added by a university education will become the central issue. With increased competition for students because of a declining pool of 18-year olds, institutions will be held more accountable for their results and will no longer be able to avoid facing difficult questions about the quality of the education they provide. An institution's survival will depend on its capacity to provide a high quality education.

A third force influencing change concerns fundamental questions about the purposes of higher education. After the Second World War, the national emphasis was on the development of "a richly democratic society" rather than on a strong military. While the goals of education have changed, modernization has been a continuous strategy. Indeed, the key word of Japanese history from the Meiji Restoration until today has been "modernization." Using other nations as models was an important method to achieve this goal. An efficient approach was to adapt the thoughts and experiences of those in other nations that seemed appropriate to the Japanese situation. Thus, modernization meant that education in Japan entailed the acquisition of broad knowledge. We refer to this as a "knowledge-acquisition" type of education. Japan has historically placed very strong emphasis on this educational style, which aims at uniform teaching of knowledge that can be acquired by the average Japanese person, rather than emphasizing an individual's creativity or unique ability.

Now, however, Japan finds itself in a mature period of modernization, at least in material respects. There are only a small number of countries today that serve as models for emulation. Japan has entered a stage in which its course must be self-development. Learning from others remains important, but such knowledge alone is no longer enough. We have entered an era in which we must explore our own future. This necessitates a change in our education. We must draw out students' individuality, foster greater creativity, and strengthen the power of thinking. A profound change from a knowledge-acquisition type of education has become essential.

Institutional structures were designed to serve the knowledge-acquisition type of education. For example, institutional facilities centered around large classrooms. Now, however, facilities and equipment must be changed for the new education objectives. In addition, the teacher-student ratio must be changed to one in which the education of small numbers is possible. We must adopt new teaching methodologies in which students do independent research and pursue innovative ideas. They must report, receive feedback, and discuss ideas. I believe that the universities which move in this direction and change all relevant conditions, beginning with the curriculum, will improve. Those schools that do not are likely to fail. To effect this change, time and resources are necessary. However, after 10 or 15 years, the result will be a distinguished, innovative university, in contrast to a school that does things the old way.

A fourth force for change is the improved international position of Japan. International exchanges are prospering and with them come the influence of external scholarship and culture. Japanese universities and colleges play key roles in this international exchange. However, if the research and educational quality is low, the university's faculties and graduates will be unable to make a meaningful contribution. Thus, to facilitate and support scholarly exchange and the education of visiting students, we must think about improving the quality of our universities.

Fifth, there is the issue of a declining population of 18-year olds. In 1992, the peak year for that age group, they numbered 2,050,000. This number is expected to sharply decrease in the future. By the year 2005, the estimated cohort group will be 1,360,000. At one point, it was thought that this would be the lowest year for the 18-year-old cohort group. However, recent statistics estimate that by 2010, the number will be 1,210,000 (Ministry of Education 1995a). Thus, the number of 18-year olds may decline to approximately one-half of its high point in the prosperous years of the early 1990s. This estimated decline presents a danger not only to the universities, but to Japan itself. How can we stop this and foster a population increase? This is definitely a middle- and long-term issue that must be addressed by the government and the universities.

As the annual 18-year-old cohort steadily decreases, a slight increase in the percent of the population pursuing higher education will not conspicuously help to alleviate the decrease in total college enrollment. Today's universities may find themselves unable to fill their student capacity. Whether it is a national or private university, its future existence may be at stake. Some schools may just disappear. If this is to be avoided, then both private and national universities need to improve their quality and make their schools more attractive to prospective students. They must expand beyond the 18-year-old cohort to include nontraditional students such as working people, women returning to school, and visiting students from foreign countries. Some may think that women are underrepresented in Japanese higher education. In 1995, however, there were 1,300,000 women who went on to junior colleges and universities out of a total student enrollment of 3,100,000. This is an impressive 41.5 percent. Of these 1,300,000 women, 450,000 were registered in junior colleges.[2] These data suggest that it may be possible to increase the number of women attending four-year universities. At present, however, it is difficult to forecast whether there will be a broad increase in the number of women seeking higher education in the future.

Currently, the majority of Japanese college students fall into the 18- to 23-year-old age bracket; however, as universities endeavor to make education more appealing, the age composition will also change. Universities tend to be cavalier about these issues, but the environment of today's universities will not allow this. For these reasons, I wish to emphasize the issues that must be dealt with now in university research, education, and management.

THE UNIVERSITY RESPONSE

How should institutions respond to these challenges? While I think there are several ways to proceed, I have not been able to come up with a clever solution. There are many approaches. Some schools have begun flexible testing policies that recognize unusual student talent, others have renovated their facilities to create a comfortable environment. However, it will be very difficult to overcome the serious problems facing institutions by these devices alone. Superficial alternative strategies are only temporary and will not have an enduring effect. It is essential that universities stress improved research and education. The most important thing for an academic institution to pursue is its own mission. If we take this as a premise, then there are several possibilities worth exploring.

First, we must change the usual way of thinking in regard to our nation's universities. For instance, most people would define a university as a place where research and education occur, reflecting in their definition the prewar university system in which the university signified the highest pinnacle of learning. While I believe that this definition is correct, I also perceive a bias in the traditional view that a university must strictly maintain equal emphasis on research and teaching.

Because there were only a few universities in the past, it was possible to characterize them with a single definition. Now we see a popularization of higher education in which 30 percent of the annual eligible age cohort participates. There may be some students who wish to become researchers, some who have ability and aspire to be leaders in various social capacities, and some who go to university without a great desire to study. In addition, there are students and parents who think that the purpose of higher education is to create independent thinkers and good citizens. For them, difficult studies to prepare for a career as a scholar are not necessary. Students vary considerably in their interests and abilities, as do universities. Some universities may emphasize research, others stress teaching. Some are very large, others small. Because Japanese universities are so diverse, it is impossible to view them from only one perspective. Some Japanese universities, like some in the United States, continue to emphasize research. These schools support improvements in the future of Japan's academic standards, and through the development of fruitful research and learning, they fulfill their role in contributing to the future of Japan. Thus, these universities are important in our country. However, not every student wants to or should go into research. For some students and parents, quality teaching may be the highest priority. Our educational system has a need for all types of institutions—some with a research focus, some with a teaching focus, and some that equally balance the two.

The most important thing is for each university to specify its special character. That is, one institution may aim to provide a good education rather than train future scholars. Another institution may define its mission in a specific field. Another may be aimed at students who wish to receive an academic education in a given field. It will become important to identify an institution's particular strengths and to make these characteristics attractive to prospective students. This will enable students to choose an institution based upon personal goals. The quality of a university will be measured according to how adequately it meets its specified goals. Accordingly, we will also need to alter the standards by which we judge schools. Traditional standards have deemed research institutions as "good" and those that are not oriented toward research as "bad." From now on, even if a school has a reputation as a research university, it will not be of high quality unless the actual activities of the school meet its stated goals. Similarly, a non-research-oriented school can be good if it provides a high-quality education.

If universities develop specific missions and goals, then it is important that they be able to maintain independence over such decisions as the content of the curriculum. To date, the Ministry of Education has specified university standards by setting the conditions for a university charter. The Ministry of Education must approve the establishment of new universities, the creation of faculties, programs, and other changes. The Ministry of Education judges applications according to university chartering standards and approves only those applications that meet the standards. These established standards regulate a wide range of details, from the university's organization to the geographical size of the campus. To begin a new faculty, the largest organizational structure within a Japanese university, specific courses must be taught. Because of this ministerial control, it has never been possible to establish institutions with unique characteristics. The field of economics provides a useful example. There has been a tendency for all economics faculties throughout the nation to resemble one another.

Recently, however, the University Council (which serves as an advisory committee to the Ministry), on which I have served as president for many years, recommended a broad deregulation of these standards. The Ministry of Education approved and enacted these recommendations. This will free up the curriculum and encourage independent decisions by the universities. From now on, institutions will be able to create their own special educational programs; they will then promote their unique features and attract students. However, this freedom entails responsibility and will require continuous review and correction of educational and research performance. In this sense, the burden of responsibility to achieve quality educational goals will now become more severe.

My second point concerns graduate schools. As society continues to become more complex, in flux, and opaque, it is increasingly important to foster the development of highly talented individuals. Due to the postwar criteria for the development of Japanese graduate schools, they have not assumed the level of importance of undergraduate departments. For the most part, graduate schools have served to develop researchers. As their graduate education progresses, however, students gradually move away from the contemporary needs of society. In other words, graduate students shut themselves away in research institutes and become so absorbed in their own research interests that they separate themselves from the practical world. Holders of graduate degrees too often seem ill-suited to the demands of the workforce. Furthermore, Japanese employers seem to have long thought that students with only undergraduate degrees were sufficient; these individuals could become members of the firm's workforce through training tailored to the company's needs. Employers recognize, however, that this way of hiring new employees is no longer suitable. This presents an opportunity for graduate schools to prepare graduate students who will be successful in the modern workplace. The need for this, while already evident in the natural sciences, will also emerge gradually for students in humanities and the social sciences. The graduate school curriculum will have to become more responsive to the requirements of the employers. To this end, the curriculum must focus on the development of applied knowledge and the teaching of specialized skills necessary in the workplace. Current Ministry of Education regulations allow only between 10 and 20 students per year to participate in each of the courses in a graduate program. If this regulation is maintained, then professors will also need to teach undergraduate programs to support the graduate courses. A preferable solution would be to increase the permissible number of graduate students. For a given master's program in a university, 200 or 250 master's students per year are feasible. At the doctoral level, the number of students would not need to be changed, as most would become researchers.

With Japan's international status improving, more foreigners come here to study. While most of these are graduate students, an increasing number of scholars also visit our graduate schools. Unless our graduate schools are improved, Japan will not adequately fulfill the international role such exchange obliges.

Third, I have previously stated that some universities and colleges may face bankruptcy in the future due to the decline in young students. One way to respond simultaneously to the problem of excess capacity and the new needs of a rapidly changing modern society is to encourage lifelong learning and adapt the curriculum to this learning process. I believe an era of lifetime learning is approaching. We must develop a system in which study at higher educational institutions is always possible. Given the pace of today's scientific progress, yesterday's knowledge will soon be outdated. People will wish to return to their studies. Some will return to their former employers with renewed knowledge and skills, and others may feel they will be more productive in other areas; consequently, the number of people changing their workplace will likely increase. Thus, the lifetime employment system that many Japanese are used to may also change. Because lifetime learning will assume such a vital role in Japan, higher education institutions should position themselves to be centers for this activity. In this respect, they must become more open to, and more strongly linked with, Japanese society.

A fourth issue concerns finances. Public universities and colleges, including the national universities, may have less anxiety about finances because they are funded by taxes. For them, the question may be whether their appropriation is more or less than expected. But even total reliance on public funding will no longer provide adequate resources. New academic fields and subdivisions of specific sciences are emerging, and interdisciplinary research is growing steadily. Funding from national or local government is insufficient for improving research, teaching, facilities, and equipment. In the past decade, especially, this funding has clearly become inadequate.

This is a problem for private institutions as well as for public universities. Seventy-seven percent of all university and junior college students in Japan attend private institutions. The quality of the education provided to these students influences the fate of Japan as a nation. Government subsidies to private schools are completely inadequate for these national expectations. The government must pay equal attention to funding private institutions. At the same time, all educational institutions need to make serious efforts to consolidate their financial base. For example, the government could change the tax system to facilitate contributions. Schools, in turn, could more actively seek donations from alumni and corporations. Tuition could be set at more financially realistic levels. There are, in fact, many options for improving the finances of private institutions.

Another issue Japanese institutions need to focus on is international ex-change, particularly in regard to receiving foreign students and improving research conditions in universities. The number of foreign students has sharply increased in the past 10 years, but recently, this figure has leveled off. Despite vigorous efforts by various levels of national, regional, and local governments and schools, many problems remain. In the area of research, universities face several issues concerning meaningful international academic contributions. These include improving the quality of research, reforming conservative research structures, improving facilities and equipment for research and resi-dence, and finding ways to increase research budgets.

CHALLENGES AND SUCCESSES

Japan's challenge is to explore new approaches to research and teaching, and to reflect on how these approaches should be administered to satisfy the new demands I have discussed. We need to change the way we think about the faculty structure—the most fundamental organizational structure within a Japanese university. Since the Meiji era, the faculties of our institutions have been structured and centered on research and teaching according to specific disciplines, around which students and professors are grouped. While this structure is not totally a thing of the past, times are changing. Academic progress has, in large measure, been tied to disciplinary specialization, and a faculty with separate departments will continue to be important. However, the time has passed when the world could be comprehended solely from the vantage point of single disciplines. For example, the study of economic issues can no longer be accomplished only from an economic perspective. Political, sociocultural, scientific, technological, and information issues are all embed-ded in economic issues. Accordingly, faculties can no longer be structured with a single academic focus.

What kind of structures are appropriate? One approach would organize the university around issues that require solutions in the coming years, such as environmental and information issues. Such interdisciplinary inquiry will help identify the intellectual skills that individuals must develop to address these issues. In other words, we would need to create faculties that integrate theories and techniques of many disciplines to respond to the needs of a new era. Such a faculty would link various disciplines in a horizontal manner. It would foster the development of students who can consider an issue from various view-points, identify rich conceptual issues, conduct analysis, make judgments, and possess strong problem-solving abilities. The questions we would need to consider to provide these results include the selection of fields to be brought together and the form of their cooperation. Two fields provide suitable examples. First, there is the field of "policy," which has multidimensional elements requiring proposals, options, and decisions. The second example focuses on the interrelation between humanity and its natural and societal environments. Within an academic environment having an information infrastructure, students will need to develop abilities to process both natural and artificial (software) languages. These abilities would include competence in foreign languages, word processing skills, and advanced information processing techniques. So, we need to move from the lecture-centered, single-direction form of instruction to one that is based on dialogue between students and teachers. In this form, students become able to develop themselves, their creative skills are brought out, and an interactive form of education becomes the goal.

THE LEADERSHIP DIMENSION: REFLECTIONS ON PERSONAL EXPERIENCE

In Japanese colleges and universities, it is often said that presidents cannot exercise leadership, even if they wish to do so, because of the many restrictions that exist. In private schools with traditions and prestige, the faculty senate and the board of directors have considerable power. In the national universities, in addition to the faculty senate, the Ministry of Education exercises budgetary control. In spite of these powerful agents and the restrictions they impose, I believe that a president can achieve a great deal. A president must have a vision of societal progress and an ability to speak about the future of the institution. She or he must also possess a certain charm and an ability to persuade others. These qualities and skills enable a president to develop consensus, despite the limitations I have mentioned.

In 1990, Keio University established two new faculties in the Shonan-Fujisawa campus: the Policy Management Faculty and the Environmental Information Faculty. My reflections will center on the leadership role of the president and the creation of these faculties. Keio is an old, large university with tradition and a history of success. In this context, it is not easy to establish new faculty. Existing faculties are naturally interested in maintaining and developing their own research agenda. They react negatively to the emergence of a new faculty, fearing infringement upon what is perceived to be vested rights and a decline in budget allocations.

The main reason to establish these new faculties was to respond to the needs of the future. At the same time, I also hoped the new faculties would provide a strong competitive challenge to the traditional faculties, which were resistant to change because of past success and a tendency to be conservative. I also sought to encourage internal change in the existing faculties.

Traditionally, strong leadership by the president of a Japanese university is not appreciated. Instead, our universities seem to be characterized by a climate of avoiding competition and stressing harmony. In such a climate, a strong leader risks disturbing existing harmony and provoking chaos. So, I spent much time reflecting on how my leadership should be exercised to establish the new faculties. An undertaking this significant would never be completed without strong leadership—yet aggressive leadership could generate opposition both inside and outside the academy which would, in the end, only increase the probability of failure. I decided that the crucial point was to establish consensus, and I then devoted considerable effort to achieving it. That process found me negotiating many differing points of view to obtain agreement. On campus, I had to deal with deans, research center directors, department faculty, and, at times, students and their parents. Off campus, I had to consult with various groups, including council members, members of the university's board of directors, and university alumni.

I took every appropriate opportunity to raise questions and explain the issues in simple terms to generate support for the new faculties. I would pose these questions: If we were to make predictions about the future development and change in Japanese society, what kinds of individuals with what kinds of abilities will be needed? What kind of education will foster these abilities in people? What should Keio University's role be in all this? My position gradually gained considerable support, and I obtained consent from most of those from whom it was needed. At that point, I thought three to four years would then be needed to establish these faculties. We still had to conceptualize each faculty, develop the curriculum, organize faculty and staff, and receive approval from the Ministry of Education. A special committee was formed in 1986 with the goal of establishing the new faculties by 1990.

Procedurally, I did not become the head of this committee, but instead entrusted this task to a university vice president who knew how I wished the special committee to operate. For the committee itself, I selected professors from each faculty who understood the concept of the new faculties and would positively contribute their intelligence and wisdom. Next, I fully entrusted the committee with responsibility for development of specific, concrete plans. My role was to provide leadership in forming consensus, propose the basic concepts of the new faculties, and organize a committee capable of implementing this conception. After that, the committee and its staff composed a draft report. In 1990, right on schedule, the faculties were opened in accordance with the draft proposal.

Of course, developing the new faculties took far more effort than I have described. Financing the project was, for example, a major issue. I was able to exercise a leadership role in this area because of my dual roles as president and chair of the board of directors of Keio University, which, by university regulations, are concurrently held positions. Raising funds for the project could have had a negative impact on the research and educational activities of our existing faculties. Fortunately, the financial challenges of the project were mostly resolved by the sale of university real estate near Tokyo. Additional funding came by way of donations from alumni and various firms.

As president, I succeeded in the difficult task of creating the new faculties through the manner of participation I have described. I continue to believe that the new faculties should not simply be satisfied with responding to Japan's domestic human resource needs or with favorable evaluations within our country. They must be equal to international standards and internationally open in every respect. This includes educational goals, curriculum, teaching methods, quality of the faculty, level of research, facilities, equipment, and information resources. Implementing such goals in an existing faculty can take considerable time, and these efforts are now in the experimental stage. Nevertheless, I think it was important to have taken bold steps to improve the research and educational potential of Keio University. Through these efforts we hope to enhance our future value as an educational institution.

These were the convictions by which I served as president of Keio University. The founding of the two interdisciplinary new faculties has already been well received. The faculty of policy management, for example, has already inspired a few other private universities to follow us in creating similar new institutions. These early indications help me remain hopeful that Japanese universities will be able to renew themselves in response to the challenges of the future.

CONCLUSION

Since the Meiji period, the development of a system of higher education has been effective in raising the level of knowledge of the Japanese people. The Meiji leaders were responsible for starting Japan on its path of modernization. By fostering economic development, their successors helped to create the flourishing Japan of today. To achieve this goal, effective elementary, secondary, and higher-education institutions were developed. Today, however, it is our turn. We must now reflect on the future of higher education in Japan from the point of view that we are both Japanese and modern members of the world community.

In order to develop individual initiative, the old methods and ways of thinking are outdated and inappropriate. We must continue searching for new educational ideas and methods appropriate to the complexity, flux, and opaqueness of our times. As we try to discern which concepts must be changed and which should be maintained, we must also be developing thoughtful plans that foster individuality and possess inherent creative power. It is within this difficult tension that creative educational leadership must be found. This issue is not limited simply to the field of higher education. From elementary school to college, all those who are concerned with education and research must recognize the need for a fundamental transformation and then join together their wisdom, intellect, and creative power.

NOTES

1. Calculated from the figures of the Ministry of Education (Ministry of Education, 1995c).

2. Calculated from the figures of the Ministry of Education (Ministry of Education 1995b).

REFERENCES

Economic Planning Agency. 1993. *White paper on world economy (Sekai Keizai Hakusho Heisei 5-nenban)*. Tokyo: Ministry of Finance Printing Office.

Ministry of Education. 1943. *The 71st annual report of the Ministry of Education (Monbusho dai 71 Nenpo: Showa 18-nendo)*. Tokyo: Ministry of Education.

———. 1994. *1993 Basic statistics for Japanese schools: Higher education institutions (Heisei 5-nendo Gakko Kihonchosa Hokokusho: Kotokyoiku Kikan hen)*. Tokyo: Ministry of Finance Printing Office.

———. 1995a. Statistics prepared by the Ministry of Education for OECD Japan study group for higher education policy review. Tokyo: Ministry of Education, October.

———. 1995b. *Interim report on 1995 basic statistics for Japanese schools (Heisei 7-nendo Gakko Kihonchosa Sokuho)*. Tokyo: Ministry of Education.

———. 1995c. *1994 Basic statistics for Japanese schools: Higher education institutions (Heisei 6-nendo Gakko Kihonchosa Hokokusho: Kotokyoiku Kikan hen)*. Tokyo: Ministry of Finance Printing Office, 1995.

FURTHER READING

Amano, I. 1990. *Education and examination in modern Japan*. Tokyo: Tokyo University Press.

Arimoto, A., and E. de Weert. 1993. Higher education policy in Japan. In *Higher education policy: An international comparative perspective*, edited by L. Geodegebuure, et al. Oxford: Pergamon.

Beauchamp, E. R., ed. 1990. *Windows on Japanese higher education*. Westport, CT: Greenwood Press.

Ebuchi, K. 1993. Recent trends of academic mobility and policy in Japan. *Higher Education Policy* 6 (3): 19–21.

Fujimura-Fanselow, K. In press. Japan. In *Asian higher education: An international handbook and reference guide*, edited by G. A. Postiglione and G. C. L. Mak. Westport, CT: Greenwood Press.

Nakayama, N. 1989. Independence and choice: Western impacts on Japanese higher education. In *From Dependence to Autonomy*, edited by P. Altbach et al. Amsterdam: Kluwer Academic.

Teichler, U. 1996. Higher education in Japan. In *Goals and purposes of higher education in the 21st century*, edited by A. Burgen, 192–209. London: Jessica Kingsley.

Yamamoto, S. 1993. Research and development versus traditionalism at Japanese universities. *Higher Education Policy* 6 (2): 47–50.

CHAPTER 16

China

Bai Tongshuo

Editor's Introduction. With a population of 1.2 billion people, an annual birthrate of 20 million, and an estimated 1.3 billion by the next century, China's demands on the education system are considerable. Growth in higher education has been remarkable, with an enrollment increase of 39 percent since 1990 (Parkins 1995, 9). There are two types of higher education institutions in China: 1,053 "regular" institutions enrolling 2.18 million students and adult higher education institutions.[1] The former group includes both comprehensive universities, ethnic minority institutions, short-cycle vocational universities, and specialized institutions focusing on engineering, agriculture, forestry, medicine, teacher training, language, economics and finance, political science and law, physical culture, and art. Approximately 36 of the regular universities are under the direction of, and receive the bulk of their funding from, the State Education Commission; another 325 are affiliated with other central ministries and agencies, and roughly 700 are related to provincial and local governments. There are also 2,251 adult higher education institutions, with 1.56 million students in 1990 (Teng 1995), including workers' colleges, peasants' universities, management training colleges, educational colleges, and correspondence and TV institutions. (Min in press). The participation rate is very low, in spite of recent expansions, with 3 percent participation rate in regular higher education by 18- to 22-year olds in 1993 (Min in press). It is estimated that participation rates will reach seven percent by the year 2000.

Recent Reforms. Following the Cultural Revolution, the Communist Party developed new policies for internal development and opening

China to the rest of the world. Higher education was affirmed as an important contributor to modernization, and in 1985, the party's Central Committee adopted a series of principles that provided a basis for significant reform. The purpose of the reforms were to change "excessive government control," provide more autonomy to institutions, strengthen ties to the productive sector and other social organizations, and to enhance higher education's contribution to social and economic development (Hayhoe 1989, 40). These reforms gave institutions greater control over the curriculum (which had been tightly controlled by the Ministry), the flexibility to set admissions policies in concert with state plans, to charge tuition and to accept students sponsored by industry, and to participate in the job placement of students after graduation, which had also been a task of the government. At the 1994 National Conference on Education, Premier Li Peng reaffirmed China's commitment to deepening the reforms, opening to the outside world, and concentrating on economic development (Li 1994, 2). In his remarks, he cited the need to implement nine years of compulsory education, accelerate development of vocational and adult education, concentrate on the quality of teaching and learning, promote international exchanges and cooperation, and move to a system whereby most students choose their own jobs "under the guidance of state policies" (Li 1994, 14). Another important area of reform has been the curriculum. Overspecialization and a high degree of centralization characterized Chinese higher education prior to the 1990s. In the early 1980s, there were 1,419 specializations for undergraduates; now there are 12 major fields, with 832 specialties within them (Min in press).

Recently, tuition has been instituted, with a wide variety among institutions. By 1993, the average tuition ranged from 200 yuan ($23) to 400 yuan ($46). In 1994, many prestigious universities were charging 1,000 yuan to first-year students. Institutions are now setting up their own scholarship programs, redistributing about 40 percent of their tuition fees as scholarships (Wu and Hayhoe 1995). Private institutions are now explicitly supported, with 10 private higher education institutions in 1989 (7 in the formal sector, 3 in the adult sector). Public universities are expected to earn income from nongovernmental sources, including businesses owned by the institution and contracts with enterprises.

Project 211. This government initiative, created in 1992, is designed to promote excellence by identifying 100 key universities. "[The] goal is, at the beginning of the next century, to have a considerable number of higher education institutions, academic programs, and major subjects reach a relatively high level in the world in the areas of education quality, research, and management" (Communist Party Central Committee and the State Council 1993, 9; cited by Cheng and Zhou 1995). In addition to identifying 100 key institutions, Project 211 will also identify 800 key academic programs, many of which are expected to be located in the 100 institutions (Cheng and Zhou 1995). Institutions are in the process of working out the quality indicators that will be the measures for inclusion among the Project 211 institutions. This initiative is expected to attract investment in institutions from businesses and local governments who want to be associated with a nationally and internationally recognized university. Cheng and Zhou note that Project 211 has caused institutions to focus on issues of quality and to develop plans aimed at enhancing their excellence. Because additional governmental funding may be forthcoming to the institutions selected, the gap between the "haves" and the "have nots" may increase (Hauptman 1994, 4).

Future Challenges. In addition to the continuing reforms of moving toward a market economy, increasing access, and modernizing the curriculum, China is also confronting a system that is very expensive and inefficient. Student/faculty ratios average 7:1, with lower ratios of 3:1 or 2:1 at some institutions.

Jiaotong University. Hayhoe (1989, 67) cites Jiaotong University, a prestigious polytechnic university under the State Education Commission, as an institution that underwent significant reforms in the 1980s and which "managed to hold the national spotlight more compellingly than any other higher institution." Jiaotong pursued reform on several fronts: the reform of management, streamlining faculty and staff, pioneering a contract system for teachers, and a salary reform linking pay to workload. An important part of the reform was the curricular changes effected between 1978 and 1980 that reduced the number of specializations from 27 to 12. This important initiative provided much greater flexibility in the curriculum. Departments replaced specializations as the organizational units. The university also expanded the number of departments, including social sciences and literature and arts. The departments were given full responsibility for teaching plans, in contrast with the old system of the academic affairs office deciding on teaching plans and presenting them to departments. Hayhoe concludes that "the picture that emerges of Jiaotong University . . . is one of considerable vitality. Both a greater breadth of programs and a more flexible organization of teaching and research hold promise for a scholarly environment in which knowledge is advanced in an open, creative way" (Hayhoe 1989, 69).

• • • • • • • • • • • •

T
he drive for modernization of higher education in China was initiated approximately 100 years ago. Shanghai Jiaotong University, which was founded in 1896, is one of the oldest academic institutions in China. In the half-century prior to the founding of the People's Republic of China in 1949, the higher education system of China was basically the same as that of the United States and Western countries. After 1949, nationwide economic development was initiated and the resulting urgent need for human resources spurred rapid growth in higher education. The Chinese government initiated a sweeping reform and reorganization of the higher education system. The educational philosophy of the Soviet Union permeated China and had an overwhelming influence on the Chinese system. Institutions could only be established and operated by the government; tuition and housing were free. The government assigned students to jobs in different locations upon their graduation.

Institutions were specialized in their mission, focusing on a single area such as engineering, liberal arts, agriculture, medicine, or teacher training. Studies were organized by narrowly defined occupational classification and linked to specific industries, such as petroleum, textiles, railway transportation, diplomacy, or theatre. Students took five to six years to finish their studies, depending on the requirements of their departments; they could obtain certificates, but not academic degrees. Recently, this situation has begun to change, though the change is modest.

The eruption of the Cultural Revolution in 1966, which lasted for 10 years, did great damage to politics, the economy, and to traditional cultures. The effect on higher education was no less destructive. Education at all levels was almost completely ruined by the 10-year chaotic political upheaval. In the 1970s, the Chinese government initiated a series of policy efforts to promote recovery from the mistakes of the Cultural Revolution. Since then, the development of culture and economy has occurred at full speed, as has the development of higher education. Growth in Chinese higher education has been significant: The number of students in higher education in 1949 was 117,000; 856,000 in 1978; and 2,799,000 in 1994. The number of graduate students was 629 in 1949; 11,000 in 1978; and 128,000 in 1994. (These figures exclude Taiwan, Hong Kong, and Macau.) Even more important than this growth in numbers since 1978 is a sweeping reform of educational philosophy and the higher education system.

Two important forces drove the development of higher education: demands of the growing economy and the well-known Chinese tradition of respecting teachers and honoring knowledge. In China, educated people with professional skills are always respected, whatever their economic status. Every family aspires to provide the younger generation with advanced educational opportunities, not for economic gain but rather for the family's honor and prestige. Therefore, in a country with 1.2 billion people, the huge demand for higher education has accelerated its development.

The economic pressures driving the development of higher education have resulted from the shift from a planned economy to a market-oriented economy. Businesses are independent organizations rather than subordinate to the government, making their own decisions on whom they hire. With this open market for college graduates, institutions need to prepare their students to compete for jobs after graduation. This provides a strong incentive for high school graduates to attend universities with good reputations. Thus, the competition among prestigious educational institutions to attract good students has become a powerful driving force in the reform of the higher education system.

Reforming education in China requires the support of society and the state. Since China is a developing country with the largest population in the world, more government support is needed. The budget for higher education is, however, severely limited. Lowering the high illiteracy rate of young people and enforcing the nine-year compulsory education all over the country is an urgent priority requiring considerable resources. Thus, higher education institutions compete for limited government funding, striving to develop their reputations in order to increase this level of support. Since funding is tied to enrollments, those institutions that attract more students will receive more funding. Similarly, capital investments depend on a development plan approved by the government. Further increasing this competition is the decision of the Chinese government to select 100 universities that will be targeted for investment so that they can become the best in the country or in the world within the next decade.[2] In this process, an institution applies to the government to be a candidate in the competition. Academic experts are selected by the government to evaluate each university's excellence in teaching and research. This plan has been so well received that every school wants to be part of it and to become a center of excellence. Shanghai Jiaotong University has passed the thorough examinations and is on the government's list of candidates. It is determined to be one of the top universities in the world.

CHANGES IN THE HIGHER EDUCATION SYSTEM

While higher education has undergone significant reform since 1978, it is still not at the level it should be. The reform effort is multidimensional and includes the following elements: redesigning the higher education system, improving management, attending to students' development, updating course content, and improving teaching skills.

It is important to note at the outset that the stereotype that higher education institutions can only be established by the government is no longer valid. Non-governmental institutions and the private sector can play a role establishing new higher education institutions, as can organizations in other countries that cooperate with their Chinese counterparts. For example, Shanda University, a new university in Pudong, Shanghai, was established by the retired faculty from Shanghai Jiaotong University, and it is already a popular institution.

There are three types of organizations that can establish higher education institutions: the State Education Committee, the national industrial sector, and local governments. For a long time, each organization set up universities and other educational institutions acting independently of one another. Now, these three organizations cooperate. In 1987, the Ministry of Electrical Power and the State Education Committee established the College of Electric Power Engineering in Shanghai Jiaotong University to train more talented students in this field. In 1994, the Shanghai City Government and the State Education Committee reached an agreement to provide financial support for the growth of Shanghai Jiaotong University. Widespread support in Shanghai helped this university to grow and to strengthen its teaching and research. This collaboration will enable Shanghai Jiaotong University to train needed manpower for the city's industries and hi-tech research needs and will create closer working relationships between many different academic programs of the university and the surrounding community. Similar examples of collaboration with overseas organizations can be cited. The European Economic Community and the Shanghai City Government established the China-Europe International Business School in Pudong. This kind of collaboration promoted efficient use of resources by decreasing duplicative and wasteful expenditures. Some departments in these schools have benefited from such collaboration—becoming more responsive to the needs and demands of society. Sometimes collaboration impels the institution to improve its internal organization, broadening the fields of study and promoting more interdisciplinary courses.

REFORMING THE MANAGEMENT SYSTEM OF HIGHER EDUCATION

The reform of institutional management was one of the first tasks undertaken in the early stage of higher education reform. Prior to reform, the management of higher education in China was extremely centralized and institutions had little latitude in decision making. The establishment of academic departments, decisions about basic facilities, core courses, criteria for admissions, job arrangements for students upon graduation, faculty promotion, the issues of recruiting students and faculty, and designing teaching plans and syllabi, were all under the direct control of government authorities. This centralized management prevented institutions from actively participating in decision making that would help them adapt to the needs of a changing society. Such unresponsiveness made it difficult for society to support them. Consequently, this system became a formidable obstacle to institutional growth. However, the transfer of power from the government to institutions is not easy. Institutions need to be granted equal power and autonomy, and all of this must be done without causing managerial chaos. The reform of institutional management has several goals:

- To develop policy through rational and democratic procedures
- To improve operations so that they are efficient, flexible, quick, and accurate
- To develop clear and orderly rules of management
- To improve community services
- To develop fair and equitable systems of personnel management

To accomplish these goals, higher education institutions have undergone many changes—setting up management structures, systems, and standards concerning teaching, research, finance, and personnel. New programs and functions have been established; others have been strengthened. These changes have been instituted to create greater responsiveness to a fast-changing society, creating more ties with external groups and an increased level of activity in developing business ventures under the aegis of the institution.

Because faculty members are the central figures in instruction and research, reforming policies concerning personnel management is essential. Recent reform has dealt with employment, evaluation, promotion, payment, housing, medical care, and retirement, seeking to reverse the old policy of treating all faculty members equally, regardless of their performance. Thus, reform will create a new system in which people will be rewarded on the basis of merit. This reform, however, has still not produced the desired results. Three major problems persist: First, faculty salaries are still not attractive. Second, because most higher education faculty members are recruited directly after obtaining their master's or Ph.D. degrees, they lack practical experience in business or other kinds of organizations. Third, since teachers are responsible for conducting both teaching and research, it is very difficult to assign the appropriate weight to each activity and to develop an overall performance rating. It is not easy to fairly assess both tasks in terms of quality and quantity.

China has taken on the difficult tasks of developing educational legislation and establishing an evaluation system that will be monitored by external bodies, including academic and professional societies. The new system is expected to be supervised by the legal system, government authorities (the provincial and state education committees), and the public. Regular inspections are carried out and the results are published.

ACADEMIC REFORM

Higher education reform seeks to accomplish two major goals. One is to achieve better integration of teaching and research and to strengthen collaboration between educational institutions and the society. A second is to offer more diverse programs of study within a given institution.

Enhancing Research and Collaboration with External Partners

Prior to the reform, China's higher education institutions seldom emphasized research. Yet research is essential to the academic excellence of faculty, helping to update and improve curriculum and teaching methodology, both of which are essential to effective learning. Faculty members who do not conduct research cannot be excellent teachers. Faculty must also encourage their students to do research, thus enhancing their skills in scientific analysis and increasing their interest in academic experiments. Thus, this reform has to create more opportunities for college professors to conduct advanced research and to have opportunities to update their skills and intensify their awareness of developments in their field.

These innovations will also increase the sources of revenue for those institutions that can compete for research contracts with business enterprises and the government. These contracts represent a major source of university financing in China today. Many institutions have already enhanced their research activity and have become the centers of education and research. Shanghai Jiaotong University has earned 100,000,000 yuan (about $12,000,000) financial support for contract research in 1994, an amount far greater than the funds allocated by the government through its formula funding based on enrollments.

Before the 1980s, China did not have a full-scale higher education system for graduate students. There was little demand for master's and Ph.D. degrees. Little advanced research was undertaken. Recently, the government and industry have cooperated in research. The government has set up a number of research centers and laboratories; industry has provided research support.

Creating a More Flexible Curriculum

The second feature in the reform of the education system is to offer more varied courses of study, thus providing more choice to students, and to promote interdisciplinary programs. Interdisciplinary programs will expand students' knowledge, spark innovation, and promote breakthroughs in scientific research. Recently, many institutions have abandoned their conventional curricula and replaced them with interdisciplinary courses. Some have even renamed their institution to reflect their broadened mission: Beijing Steel College is now Beijing University of Science and Technology, Huadong Chemistry College was renamed Huadong Polytechnic University, and Shanghai Mechanical College is now known as Huadong Engineering University. Many technology institutes have set up new colleges in such fields as technical studies and social sciences.

For several decades before the reform, Shanghai Jiaotong University added only two majors: mechanical and electrical engineering. After the reform, it expanded its academic scope. It has added majors in architecture and chemical engineering and has improved the quality of technological fields such as computer science, communications, electronics, and marine sciences. We also established a college of management, a college of science and engineering, and a college of social studies. The college of management includes the following departments: industry management, hotel management, international trade, international finance, accounting, real estate management, and manpower source management. The college of science and engineering covers applied chemistry, applied physics, biology, and mechanics. The college of social studies includes English, philosophy, the law of economics, culture, and art. University enrollments have grown from 5,800 in 1985 to 13,000 a decade later, and they are still growing.

Also, separate, smaller institutions are merging into single universities. For example, Chengdu Technology University, with majors in science and technology, is merging with Sichuan University, with programs in social studies and science. In southwest Shanghai, Shanghai Jiaotong University and seven other institutes have decided to cooperate with one another. Mergers promote efficiency, combining various courses and expanding the scale of the institution. They have been cost-effective and have won praise from the government, which must approve the merger. It is certainly difficult, however, to combine institutions with different cultures, backgrounds, and administrative systems. To address these issues, university administrators are cooperating to share resources and thus to maximize them.

University-Owned Enterprises

Another new development is the founding and operation of enterprises by higher education institutions. While this was rather controversial in the beginning, it is now approved and supported by the government and is gradually receiving positive feedback from the general public. Opponents claimed that such enterprises would have a negative influence on teaching and research. In fact, it has been proven that if they are operated properly, these ventures generate sizable income for the schools without negative effects. There are two additional advantages of academic institutions starting a business. First, these industries provide an opportunity to transfer theoretical technology into industrial products. Many inventors do not have confidence in existing businesses because they do not apply technology efficiently to the development of commercial products. Enterprises developed by higher education institutions eliminate conflicts between educational institutions and industry concerning profits, since the business is owned by the university. Second, it builds a bridge for the faculty members to be connected with society and to increase their awareness of the market-oriented economy. Industries associated with academic institutions are not always established by Chinese universities alone; they can also be initiated through cooperation with foreign investors. Some companies have already been listed in the stock market. The South Ocean company, founded by Shanghai Jiaotong University, is now on the stock market; the chairman of its board is president of that university.

THE EDUCATION OF STUDENTS

A major area of higher education reform deals with students, whose education must include the following: acquisition of knowledge, development of morality, and maintenance of physical health. In addition to emphasizing students' academic achievement, higher education must also stress students' behavior and physical condition. Therefore, we reward good students, nurture those students who need to catch up with remedial work, and fail students who perform poorly.

The issue of assigning students to jobs upon graduation is also central to the reform process. Students who receive free education are supposed to be assigned to a job by the government, which they are obliged to take. A major drawback to this system is that students are not motivated to learn. As a result, the unit to which students are assigned to work has no motivation to attract and value successful students as employees. Similarly, the effect on institutions is that they are not motivated to improve educational programs for talented students.

In the early 1980s, institutional leaders began to take steps to solve these disheartening problems. Shanghai Jiaotong University and Tsinghua University were the first two universities to make changes to address the question of job placement. Both graduates and the employers were granted the right to make their own choices on employment decisions. At the same time, some students had to pay the costs of tuition and housing. Also, the government has set up all kinds of tuition waivers, scholarships, loans, and special awards for different types of students. Students with good academic performance are awarded scholarships even if they do not demonstrate financial need; other students with financial need, but lesser academic performance, receive student loans. Special awards are given to graduating students willing to accept assigned jobs. This plan has been adopted by most higher education institutions in China.

Another important drive for reform concerns training provided by employers for newly hired college and university graduates. It stems from the seemingly paradoxical need to ensure that graduates have high quality skills but that they require fewer instructional hours provided by employer-sponsored training programs. The labor market demands that graduates have broad knowledge and the capacity to undertake different kinds of work, but employ-ers also wish to save time and money on training so that trainees can start working within a short time. To address this issues, different courses of study have been created. Practical application and basic knowledge are emphasized in programs of two to three years for students whose careers do not require broad knowledge or advanced research skills. Professional preparation that requires four years of study or more should include wider theoretical under-standing and a certain level of research skills.

Students are admitted to these different programs according to their achievements and potential and according to admission requirements estab-lished by the institution. Gifted students are encouraged to broaden their knowledge base. Armed with a wider theoretical foundation, these students spend less time studying practical skills, but because of their superior academic abilities, they are more likely to be able to adapt to their jobs and to apply their knowledge in practical working situations. These students are also more likely to take on high-tech or management positions for which this broad prepara-tion is well suited.

Shanghai Jiaotong University is a prestigious institution with highly tal-ented students. Because our students are so academically strong, it is impor-tant for the university to offer a diverse and high quality curriculum. At Shanghai Jiaotong University, for example, there used to be three majors in the field of instrument engineering and science: precision instruments, the instruments of biology and medicine, and the technology of detection. Those three majors have been merged to become a single department, providing three directions for advanced students to choose. This more flexible arrange-ment allows students to study in all three areas and to change their major if they wish. We also encourage our students in the department of science to take economics and management courses. Students in mechanical engineer-ing are required to take the courses in electronics. This new approach is now accepted as beneficial to both graduates and employers. Students proficient in multiple disciplines are especially welcome in industry.

In the past, we ignored the education of humanities for students in science and technologies. We assumed they would receive sufficient preparation in these fields in high school. But, upon reflection, we found that appreciation of the arts should continue to be stressed as students mature. The basic art classes in high school should not be the last opportunity for students to learn about art; we need to continue to provide art courses for science students in universities, enabling them to appreciate history and magnificent works of art. It is especially important to provide such opportunities to our more talented students, since they are likely to assume high-level technical or managerial positions in the future. Expanded cultural appreciation and studies in art and literature help science and technology students to expand their creativity and imagination. A well-educated person must not only have good professional skills but should also play a role in creating and appreciating culture. Many institutions have actively developed more art and culture courses for science majors.

Another goal in educating students is to foster their individual personalities. The government is taking this point more and more seriously. During the past decades, uniformity was stressed and the individual development of students was ignored. While students educated under this standardized system gained knowledge in their professional fields, they did not develop personal character, other skills and interests, nor did they make use of their own special talents. No wonder we had less opportunity to nurture the most talented students.

Our goal is to educate students who can adapt to a fast-changing world. This will enable them to have maximum professional competence and at the same time fully achieve their personal goals. We believe that each student is unique. If we make good use of their individual talents, we can produce more competent professionals. It is a pity that their special talents are so often inhibited before students have the chance to develop them.

Chinese educators are now paying more attention to developing students' creativity and their ability to conduct research in different fields. In the past, we stressed the importance of acquiring knowledge and of producing students who could learn facts. In order to encourage our students to think creatively and to develop research skills, we must rely less on filling them with knowledge and instead devote more time to enhancing students' research ability. This presents a challenge because it is more costly to provide opportunities for research than to teach theory. Different approaches are being taken to address this problem. In some cases, we are redesigning experimental courses to concentrate on research design, setting up laboratories, conducting data analysis, and processing information. We also encourage our students to get involved in research with faculty members. Their early involvement and contact will improve their research skills.

In recent years, we have started to reform our admission procedures for entrance to higher education. In the past, the test scores were the main criterion in determining students' admissions. However, test scores do not always reveal a student's true ability, and once they began their studies, students' academic performance often revealed significant variation from their test scores. Now, high school graduates who demonstrate greater creativity or manual ability will have a greater chance of admission. In college, we are shifting the conventional evaluation paradigm from overall performance to individual course performance. Credit-awarding procedures were also modified.

UPDATING CURRICULUM AND IMPROVING TEACHING

The curriculum is another crucial issue in Chinese higher education. To catch up with the rapid development of technology, society, and the economy, updating the higher education curriculum is vital. For example, computer technology has a remarkable impact on our curriculum. New computer technology has been widely adopted in most fields for word processing, graphics, data processing, and testing.

Faculty members are encouraged to develop their own teaching styles, and they can incorporate their research findings in their teaching. Close contact and cooperation with industry will help them obtain valuable advice and information to update their courses. Recently, instructional methods and technologies have received a great deal of attention. We have been using video, audio, projectors, slides, and films for years. As hardware becomes less expensive, we are likely to adopt the computer as a new medium for education. Computer-assisted instruction (CAI) is now of great interest.

Recently, many higher education institutions in China have started a credit system. Compared with the similar systems in Western institutions, the credit-awarding system in China is less flexible and provides fewer choices for students. A more flexible system would require offering more courses and at different times, which would be more expensive. Another problem with the credit system is that students are not mature enough to make choices on their own. Shanghai Jiaotong University has gradually increased its flexibility and options for students by teaching students according to their aptitudes. Through consultation with the instructors, who make teaching plans based on students' interests and strengths, students can learn efficiently according to their needs. This practice has successfully addressed the problem of inflexibility in instruction.

I believe that the most important task in reforming Chinese higher education is to motivate students to learn independently. Teachers should reduce the time devoted to lecturing and increase the time spent with students to help them answer questions, solve problems, and think independently. However, in the long run, this approach has its risks. It may widen the gap between the good students and the weaker ones, since the latter group is more dependent on receiving information from their teachers.

CONCLUSION

China has gone through fundamental and extensive education reforms in the past 19 years. The quality of education has been improved through a series of reforms in our educational system, teaching methods, and curriculum. The reform of higher education has also greatly contributed to the modernization of China.

NOTES

1. Postiglione cites 1,074 institutions in Chapter 3. These discrepancies are attributable to different data sources.

2. Editor's note: This competition, known as Project 211, is summarized in the editor's introduction to this chapter.

REFERENCES

Cheng, X. D., and Zhou, Chuan. 1995. Global impact of China's higher education "Project 211." *Asian-Pacific Exchange (Electronic) Journal* 2 (1). Published by the University of Hawaii-Kapiolani Community College.

Hauptman. A. 1994. Finance and governance issues in Chinese higher education. Unpublished paper.

Hayhoe, R. 1989. *China's universities and the open door.* Armonk, NY and London: M.E. Sharpe.

Li Peng. 1994. *Report at the National Conference on Education* (November 3). Department of Foreign Affairs of the State Education Commission of the People's Republic of China.

Min, Weifang. In press. Higher education in China. In *Asian higher education: An international handbook and reference guide,* edited by G. A. Postiglione and G. C. L. Mak. Westport CT: Greenwood Press.

Parkins, G. 1995. China sets out reform guide. *Times Higher Education Supplement* November 3.

Teng, Teng. 1995. China, People's Republic of. In *The international encyclopedia of national systems of education,* 2nd edition, edited by T. N. Postlewaite. Oxford, New York, and Tokyo: Elsevier Science.

Wu, Huiping, and R. Hayhoe. 1995. Fee paying public universities and private institutions. *China News Analysis* 1534 (May 1).

FURTHER READING

Hayhoe, R., and Wenhui Zhong. 1993. Chinese universities and Chinese science: A new visibility in the world community. *Higher Education Policy* 6 (2): 37–41.

Hertling, H. 1995. The costs of autonomy at China's universities. *The Chronicle of Higher Education* February 10: A40.

Keming, H. 1995. Chinese higher education: 21st century challenges. *International Higher Education* 2 (Fall): 14–15.

Min, Weifang. 1991. Higher education finance in China: Current constraints and strategies for the 1990s. *Higher Education* 21 (2): 151–62.

Seeberg, V. 1993. Access to higher education: Targeted recruitment reform under economic development plans in the People's Republic of China. *Higher Education* 25 (2): 169–88.

Shouxin, L., and M. Bray. 1992. Attempting a capitalist form of financing in a socialist system: Student loans in the People's Republic of China. *Higher Education* 23 (4): 375–88.

Wang,Yongquan. 1992. China, People's Republic of. In *The Encyclopedia of Higher Education,* vol. 1, edited by B. R. Clark and G. R. Neave. Oxford: Pergamon Press.

World Bank. 1986. *China: Management and finance of higher education.* Washington, DC: World Bank.

Yiping, H. 1993. Higher education in China: Problems and current reform. *Higher Education Policy* 6 (4): 20–24.

CONCLUSION

Madeleine F. Green

B ecause the chapters of Part Three were authored by current and former
institutional heads, they recount history from a particular vantage
point. Government policies and external pressures are not abstractions
for these writers; they are very real and concrete determinants of how many
students will show up at the institution's door at the beginning of a given
academic year, what level of resources will be available to conduct the business
of the institution, and to varying extents depending on the country, how that
business will be conducted.

In Chapter 1, we elaborated a major premise of this volume: that higher
education institutions are profoundly shaped by their societies and by the
moment in history in which they find themselves. French higher education
bears the imprint of the high degree of centralization of French society;
apartheid created the architecture for South African universities and
technikons; Communist principles governed the structure and the contents of
higher education in Eastern and Central Europe; Africa's economic decline
and political instability have weakened higher education to the point of near
collapse in some countries; and the drive for expansion has reshaped higher
education throughout the world.

But these pressures and influences do not tell the whole story, nor do they
explain entirely the fate of individual institutions. Students have varied
expectations and abilities, and they have exerted a profound influence at
various moments in history on the fate of their institutions. The core functions
of colleges and universities—teaching and research—continue to be carried
out largely by faculty members steeped in their disciplines and socialized by
their graduate training to preserve and perpetuate the traditions of scholarly

inquiry. They do not exercise their professions in a vacuum, and it is as members (and employees) of institutions that they are confronted by such realities as more students, angry students, government mandated reviews, and the diminishing size of their paychecks. It is at the institutional level—on the ground—that external forces are received, interpreted, and translated into action; where decisions are made that will affect what happens in the class-rooms, in laboratories, the library, and around the campus. Institutional traditions, structures, policies, and personalities create a distinctive profile and trajectory for each college or university.

It is here, at this intersection of external forces and the daily business of higher education, that institutional leadership comes into play. With varying degrees of explicitness, the chapter authors described the possibilities for them, as leaders, to steer their institutions—sometimes taking the institutions in new directions, and other times keeping them on course in stormy seas. Many authors gave great emphasis to the national scene and historical trends and less to telling the stories of their institution's responses or their personal experience. As we noted in Chapter 2, institutional heads have different views of their own mandate and capacity to act as change agents, depending on the structure and traditions of their national systems. To write about one's own experiences can be difficult and sometimes awkward. But however the authors view their own roles, each sees his or her institution as distinctive, and demonstrates the conviction that its future can be shaped by the members of the institutional community. The authors describe the quiet, unglamorous processes of building consensus, and of working through existing governance structures to change those structures themselves, to modify the curriculum, to create new programs, or to close or consolidate others. Building collective energy to counter the built-in homeostasis of academic institutions is a slow and laborious task.

Perhaps the most striking similarity in the descriptions of how change takes place at the institutional level is the recognition that no one—and least of all leaders—can "go it alone" in the change process. Committees and consulta-tive processes abound in the descriptions, and although the authors acknowl-edge the slowness and frustration that accompany consultation and shared governance, they also recognize that they are, for better or for worse, the hallmarks of higher education, distinguishing colleges and universities from most other kinds of organizations. Johnstone suggests that the real problem for leaders in the change process is not a lack of vision, but the management skills and the courage to implement and institutionalize needed changes that may run counter to the faculty's self-interest. Edwards raises the question of whether institutions can be collegial and consultative and at the same time be flexible and responsive to the external environment in a timely way. In the United States, there is a growing feeling among some legislators and corporate leaders who sit on college and university boards that if higher education institutions were run more like businesses—that is, without tenure or the slow-moving committees of shared governance—they would be more effective and efficient. The authors, all insiders to higher education, voice no such opinions, in spite of the frustrations they encounter. While they recognize their obligations to promote institutional effectiveness, efficiency, and responsiveness to external demands, they also see the need to do this *with* faculty, staff and students, not *in spite of* them. They describe their role as building a shared vision and enabling their institution to manage collectively the forces bearing down on it.

These chapters underscore that academic institutions around the world have a shared academic culture, derived from their fundamental missions, that shapes the change process "on the ground." One of the defining characteristics of that culture is resilience. Universities are survivors. While political unrest can close institutions, and repressive regimes intimidate, imprison, and murder students and faculty, universities have a remarkable capacity to reemerge, weakened to be sure, but with the possibility for revival and renewal. Similarly, even severe and prolonged underfunding, as is seen in Africa, has not prevented dedicated and ingenious individuals from continuing to teach and conduct research, even under the most adverse conditions. The ability of institutions to flourish is tested in less dramatic ways in most countries, by government regulation, diminished funding, and by the growing expectation that higher education can continuously serve more students with fewer resources.

And, as we have noted, there is a high correlation between institutional autonomy and the need for institutional leadership. If democracy continues to take hold throughout the world, we can expect less ideological control and less direct government control of matters related to teaching, research, and learning. The pressures for accountability will not abate, and if institutions can demonstrate vigorous self-regulation, they may keep some of the government regulators at bay. Competition among institutions, although it clearly has its unhealthy side, is testing institutional ingenuity and assertiveness. As institutions are forced to become entrepreneurial and more active seekers of nongovernmental revenue, there will be a greater need for leaders to serve as ambassadors to their communities, forging links with the business sector, and fostering a greater involvement of their institutions with partners outside of higher education. These trends suggest that in the future, the role of institutional leaders will become more rather than less important, and more rather than less difficult.

The evidence from the authors is overwhelming that higher education has undergone profound transformation worldwide in the twentieth century in general and in the last 30 years in particular. Conventional wisdom holds that the pace of change is accelerating each day; we can hardly keep up with the advances in technology and the increase in the rate of production of knowledge. To a great extent, higher education is, like all other social and human institutions, a product of forces far larger than itself and can only carve out its future in the context of these forces. The challenge that faces higher education, however, is the extent to which it will be only a product of those powerful forces, swept along by the giant waves of social, economic, political, and scientific change, or whether it will shape its own future, standing up and riding those waves. That is the universal challenge to higher education institutions in every part of the world.

INDEX

by James Minkin

Madeleine F. Green is vice president for international initiatives, and director, Center for Leadership Development, American Council on Education (ACE). She also has directed the ACE Fellows Program and served as a member of the board of trustees of Wilson College in Chambersburg, Pennsylvania. She holds a B.A. from Harvard University and a Ph.D. from Columbia University, both in French literature. Dr. Green's recent publications on leadership development and management include *Investing in Higher Education: A Handbook of Leadership Development, The American College President: A 1993 Edition,* and *Leaders for a New Era: Strategies for Higher Education.*